Praise for this book's previous edition, *Mastering Business in Korea: A Practical Guide*

"For a foreigner, learning about Korean social and business ways can take a lifetime. Certainly after three decades here I am still discovering what I did and didn't know and relearning what I misunderstood in the past. But even the smallest effort pays a dividend, and with this excellent book the reader has a chance to tap into the insight of a Korean businessman who has spent a whole career relating to foreign managers, as well as of a Western consultant who has integrated himself into Korean society almost as much as it is possible for an outsider.

"We, the guests in this country, will never be insiders, and so should always recognize that the business relationship is not going to be equally balanced. But a lot of our frustrations will be eased if we understand some of the reasons, motivation, and cultural and historical background behind behavior that otherwise seems unfathomable.

"I recommend this book not only for the newcomer to Korea but also for long-term expat residents who may think they know it all already. As they will discover, modesty is not just a virtue, it can be a very useful state of mind."

Alan Timblick, OBE
Head of Seoul Global Center

"The authors have written a superb book that is a "must read" for any foreigner doing business with Koreans or working amidst Korean colleagues. The book is full of insightful recommendations on a broad range of topics as well as practical, common sense tips useful for all expatriates. Moreover, the book's insightful advice is underscored with a deep and nuanced understanding of modern Korean culture that is as invaluable as it is rare. Quite simply, this is an authoritative book that demystifies Korea and offers comprehensive advice to anyone interested in living in the country, working with or for Korean managers, or doing business with Korean counterparts."

Robert Fallon
Former Chairman of the Board of Korea Exchange Bank

" *I*t's all here! This is a superb effort to help expat executives deal with the tremendous complexities of Korean business. Lots of examples and practical advice grounded in the experience of the authors and their corporate colleagues. This book will save you years on the learning curve if you really take it to heart."

Jack Lewis
Assistant Dean of the Marshall School of Business at the University of Southern California

DOING BUSINESS
IN KOREA
An Expanded Guide

First published in 2007 by Seoul Selection as *Mastering Business in Korea: A Practical Guide*

105-2 Sagan-dong, Jongno-gu, Seoul, Korea
Phone (82-2) 734-9567 Fax (82-2) 734-9562
http://www.seoulselection.com
email: publisher@seoulselection.com

ISBN 978-89-91913-68-4 13320

Printed in the Republic of Korea

DOING An Expanded Guide
BUSINESS
IN KOREA

Table of Contents

PART IV.

MAKING IT IN THE KOREAN MARKET

PART V.

REFERENCES

FOREWORD TO THIS BOOK'S PRIOR EDITION, *MASTERING BUSINESS IN KOREA*

*B*efore I came to live in Korea five years ago, I had traveled quite frequently to Japan and visited other countries in the East, but never stopped in Korea. I met several people who had traveled and done business there, but only one who had lived there. I sought their opinions. I received conflicting views with lots of anecdotes and examples of negative or peculiar symptoms, but many without explanations.

There was no book like this one that I knew of to help guide or advise me, so I had to find out for myself. The only regret that I have about this book is that it wasn't available when I needed it! Why should you need it? The reason is that it is not Japan or China. Korea is unique and shares only few similarities. Also, it is easy to misunderstand, to get wrong first impressions and to get off to a bad start. In five years, I have seen many people spend time in Korea. Many have succeeded personally and professionally; several have failed, some getting no further than the negotiation stage. All the failures or unhappy people blame the Koreans, never themselves.

As I read this book, I was able to identify with so many of the comments and conclusions. Of course, one person's experiences are never exactly the same as others', but I found this analysis to be very well thought through, well expressed, accurate and fascinating. Yet it is not a book of theory and history. It is essentially a very practical guide full of useful data, information, explanation and tips.

From the brief history, which is an essential piece of background to help understand what follows, through to the example at the end, the whole book is valuable. It helps an understanding of behavior in various situations, the culture, the regionalism, and Korea's feelings for its neighbors. Korea is still a nationalistic and highly homogeneous society, heavily influenced by Confucianism, where rules and laws are often subordinate to "humanity considerations."

This book provides specific advice for people coming to work for a Korean firm, a joint venture, a multinational or a smaller foreign-owned company. There is also an explanation of the history and role of the "chaebols" and the close relationship between government and industry.

Negotiating in Korea is difficult, and it is essential to understand the perspective of the Korean negotiator who works according to a very different set of rules than most others. Also, one must realize that the signing of a contract is only the beginning of negotiation. But if you understand the background to this apparent lack of business ethics and integrity, then you know how to prepare for negotiations.

In the author's view, there is so much opportunity in Korea if you can get it right. The country offers well-educated, highly skilled people with an amazingly strong work ethic and corporate loyalty. This is a business climate where the "can do" attitude is prevalent and things get done much faster than elsewhere. There are some inefficiencies and old management practices that need to change and are slowly changing. Examples are the frequent shuffling of management from post to post, which creates generalists who rely on an autocratic top-down hierarchy where the boss is not questioned. It also avoids accountability and impedes cross-departmental cooperation. Promotion based on age is also slowly giving way to promotion based on merit.

As I mentioned above, this book imparts a lot of knowledge but is also a very practical guide. It includes the author's "11 Commandments for Doing Business in Korea," a practical guide to work rules, hiring and firing, salary and benefit structures, the "7 Myths of Korean Sales" and an introduction to the Korean legal system. It even has a list of useful blogs and a guide to table manners as well as business etiquette.

Personal relationships are very important in Korea, and the reader will understand these between the boss and subordinate, between peers, and between old school friends. There are tips on how to approach personal relationships in business as a foreigner. You will also understand that form and process are often as important as content. If you get this part right, life will be much easier—but if you get it wrong you won't get much natural cooperation, whatever your skills or level.

Like so many other things in Korea, the approach to effective sales and marketing requires a good understanding of the culture. Public relations and a strong corporate image are more important than advertising, and it is important to understand who is influencing the buying decisions.

Public opinion has a disproportionate influence in Korea, especially on the decisions of public officials. On more than one occasion while we were negotiating the GM Daewoo deal, I found descriptions of some very confidential and sensitive matters appearing anonymously in the media. This was a way for the Korean negotiators to judge how a particular development in the negotiations might go down with the public. The reaction strongly influenced their next steps.

There is an interesting contradiction in Korea that is well explored. On the one hand is the negative opinion frequently expressed of foreign countries and companies. Don't expect Koreans to think about or treat foreign companies in the same way as they expect their companies to be treated. It's okay for Hyundai or Samsung to get special incentives in foreign countries, but the reverse is generally frowned on by the general populace. Koreans working for purely foreign enterprises can sometimes be made to feel unpatriotic. On the other hand, there is a genuine friendliness, welcome and openness toward individual foreigners and a penchant for foreign goods, fashion, music, films and so on. But Korea is full of such apparent contradictions, which is why it is such a fascinating place to get to know.

Korea is also still changing fast. This book recognizes that. For this very reason, however, the book may well become more of a history book in another generation. The younger people do think differently, even though they are heavily influenced by their history and their culture. Who knows where they will be in 30 years?

Right now this book is highly topical, relevant and a very welcome addition. I would advise the reader to read carefully, be sensitive to what you learn, and to take your time when first arriving in Korea. Keep your eyes open, your ears open and your mind open. And finally, remember that it is the foreigner who is the guest in someone else's home.

January, 2007

Nick Reilly
Former President, GM Asia Pacific
Current CEO, GM Europe

ACKNOWLEDGEMENTS

*I*n many ways, this book is a community effort. Several leaders in the Korean business environment—both foreign and local—have generously donated their time to this effort. During the course of preparing material for this book, the author was vindicated in his belief that many in the international business community are almost as eager to see others succeed as they hope to do so themselves in Korea. In addition, there have been others who, though not involved in Korean business per se, have contributed to getting this book off the ground.

To avoid any possible controversy, the author thanks these people in alphabetical order:

Dr. Ahn Young-Ok of DuPont Korea, who was formerly the First Chief Technology Officer at Samsung Group at the corporate level, for offering his perspective based on his experience as a Korean executive working in joint ventures,

Mr. Peter Bartholomew, Managing Director/COO of **Industrial Research & Consulting Ltd.** and Korea business veteran of more than 40 years, for giving practical advice on negotiating contracts with Korean companies and contributing greatly to the "Korea's Shortage of Analytical and Evaluation Skills" section,

Mr. Edwin Betz, former officer of **Samsung Fire & Marine**, for conceiving of the need for the first edition of this book and for offering his insight on expatriate executives working in Korean corporations,

Mr. Steve Bowen of **Edelman**, for sharing his insight on advertising and public relations,

Mr. Brendon Carr, Foreign Legal Consultant (Washington State Bar; not admitted in Korea) of **Hwang Mok Pak**, for providing his insight on the legal and practical pitfalls of extending credit in Korea,

Mr. Joe Day, President of **Market Entry Services Ltd.**, for organizing excellent monthly business seminars with the British Chamber of Commerce from which our chapters on human resources and legal affairs drew some of their material,

Joseph J. Dallao, Vice President of Business Development, Asia Pacific at **L-3 Communications LSG**, for reviewing and providing guidance on "Korea's Defense Industry,"

Edward Eun of **Watson Wyatt**, for offering his insight on pension program trends,

Mr. Robert Fallon, former Chairman of **Korea Exchange Bank** and adjunct professor at **Columbia University**, for offering his insight on managing a Korean organization as well as working with Korean labor unions,

Mr. Sean Hayes, lead attorney of the **International Practice Group of Joowon Attorneys at Law**, for providing a final review of the legal chapter,

Mr. Charles Lankester, President, North Asia, for **Edelman**, for updating current Korean consumer trends and attitudes,

Dr. Lew Young-ick, Chair Professor of Korean Studies at the **Yonsei University** Graduate School of International Studies, for reviewing and making necessary corrections in the chapter on relevant Korean history,

Mr. Niall Morrissey, an officer of **Macquarie**, for offering his insight into managing Korean employees and working with Korean business partners,

Mr. Laxmi Nakarmi, Managing Partner of **Saturn Communications**, for offering his insights based on 20 years reporting Korean political economy and business as a foreign correspondent,

Mr. Brian O'Brien, former EVP of **Samsung Fire & Marine**, for sharing his experiences serving as an expatriate executive in Korea and in general,

Mr. Timothy O'Brien, an American attorney with **Kim & Chang**, for sharing his insight on the foundations and history of the Korean legal system and how that history affects current practices,

Mr. Bill Park, an executive at a foreign financial services company in Korea, for offering his insight on managing Korean employees, as well as working as a Korean-American executive,

Mr. Nick Reilly, now Executive Vice President of GM but President of **GM Daewoo** when the first version of this book was being written, for giving his insight on managing Korean managers, as well as working with Korean labor unions,

Mr. Stephen Schueler, prior Managing Director of **Procter & Gamble Korea**, for providing his views that were included in the chapters on marketing and distribution,

Mr. Seo Young-Soo, VP Sales for Asia-Pacific for **Otto Künnecke** and formerly with **IBM Korea** and **Datacard**, for sharing his experience and advice as a Korean executive working for multinational corporations,

Mr. Stefan Spreu, prior Senior Vice President of **Leschaco Korea**, for providing his insight on managing Korean employees as an expatriate executive,

Mr. Christopher Teras, attorney at law at the **International Practice Group of Joowon Attorneys at Law**, for his review of the legal chapter,

Mr. Keri Theophilus, a former officer of the joint venture with **BP plc Samsung Petrochemical**, for offering his insight on managing successful joint-venture relationships,

Mr. Peter Walshaw of the **Hyatt Hotels**, for sharing his experience based on over 17 years of general management in Korea,

Ms. Linda Yang of **Japan Tobacco International Korea**, for offering her insight on international human resource management and compensation, and

Anonymous, Korean senior manager at a Korean financial services company, who offered his insight on foreigners working in a Korean corporation.

Last but not least, I must mention my copy editor, Irene Park, for her thorough review and editing of this manuscript; and of course, Yeri, my Korean wife, who has helped and put up with me all these years, including with this latest project, as just one more event in our long marriage.

If I have overlooked anyone else who supported this effort, I sincerely apologize.

INTRODUCTION

S ince the earlier edition of this book, *Mastering Business in Korea*, came out, Dynamic (or shall we say "Volatile"?) Korea has moved forward. During that time, I have learned something about book distribution and marketing—particularly online—as well. For that reason, I have renamed the second edition of *Mastering Business in Korea* to *Doing Business in Korea* to make this book more easily searchable on the Internet, since search commands are more likely to use the word "doing" than "mastering." Also, I am a bit more humble with the book title, since obviously no one can master a subject as complex as Korean business by reading a single book. And as one may recognize by the cover, my by-line is "tomcoyner@gmail.com." In other words, I'm trying to catch up with modern marketing.

This book is written—and now significantly updated and expanded—with the expatriate business professional in mind. *Mastering Business in Korea* was the first such book written in collaboration by a Korean and a Westerner, both of whom have built their careers in international business between Asia and the West. I was responsible for updating and expanding this book, but Mr. Song-Hyon Jang, co-author of *Mastering Business in Korea*, reviewed and made important updates to this book's manuscript.

Well-meaning and experienced foreign businesspeople routinely make serious errors that ultimately impede their success in the world's twelfth strongest economy. But while Korea is reputed to be a tough place to do business, much of that reputation is unfair. While doing good Korean business is not easy, it can be much easier than what many foreign businesspeople make it out to be. This book is based on numerous interviews with both seasoned expatriate executives and highly experienced Korean managers and directors. The reader will discover both subjective and objective observations. As such, it reflects the international business community in Korea, and not simply the perspectives of strictly Koreans and Americans.

South Korea is in a state of flux. Given these modern times, and particularly given the global recession at the time of this book's writing, one may say that about many countries. But Korea is probably changing more than most, and it certainly has come much further than most countries in the past half-century. In 2010, it will be the first country to host the G20 summit, symbolizing global recognition that South Korea is no longer a developing country.

Already South Korea has proven itself capable of being a global business leader. As recently as 2006, the number of Korean products that had achieved the largest global market share in their respective markets numbered only 86. But by 2007, 127 Korean products had done so. Today, Korean memory chips account for 49.1 percent of the international market, while Korea produces 80.5 percent of the huge LNG (liquid natural gas) ocean carriers. Among the devices in your home and office that employ thin-film LCDs (liquid crystal displays), there is a good chance that at least the LCD component came from Korea, as the nation produces 38.5 percent of the world's LCDs. Environmental quality has also become a major Korean concern, and Korea now produces 43 percent of the world's fresh water treatment facilities.

From virtual to actual dictatorships and on to being one of the strongest democracies in Asia, the Republic of Korea has a political track record that is in direct competition with its literal rise to riches from the ashes of a devastating war. In the process, the Korean people have been promoted from recipients of foreign aid to donors. They even have their own organization, KOICA, similar to the U.S. Peace Corps, and have sent more Korean volunteers abroad than U.S. Peace Corps Volunteers ever served in Korea.

With wealth comes a deep political struggle from being the government's people to having a government of the people. Today there are stronger human and civil rights within South Korea than in any time of Korea's multi-millennium history. Coming part and parcel with democratic development, various interest groups and NGOs add a new dynamism to both the public and private sector arenas.

Not so long ago, Koreans looked enviously at what others achieved with advanced technologies. Today, Korea not only emulates but even advances beyond the most advanced nations in cutting-edge application of the latest technologies—most notably in the practical integration of broadband networks into daily home and business life.

Korean consumers are no longer satisfied with cheap products; they demand—and get—quality. They are also more vocal about products and services in the context of their rights as citizens of this republic. Stockholder and consumer rights are coming to the forefront. For example, product liability is no longer a subject studied as a feature of overseas, advanced economies. Such issues and concerns are now part of daily Korean life.

Through the rapid economic growth of the recent past, and now through the steady progress of a mature economy, Korea holds its own as an OECD nation. Mercantile protectionism is not yet fully an issue of the past, but the Korean markets have opened considerably. Korea recognizes that its long-term growth is dependent upon being an active member of a globalized economy. At the time of this book's writing, Korea had completed its first Free Trade Agreement (FTA) with Chile and had signed other FTAs with the U.S. and the EU that had yet to be ratified.

Despite such international dealings, Koreans have often—and sometimes rightly—been described as being "frogs in a deep well." And yet some 10 million South Koreans travel abroad for pleasure per year. On a per capita basis, that means more South Koreans are getting out and exploring the world than their typically wealthier neighbors, the Japanese.

Internally, Korea has one of the strongest physical infrastructures in the world and continues to improve it. The recent KTX bullet train has, within a year of its opening, changed the consumer patterns of the nation. Hospitals and department stores in regional hubs are now in direct competition with the best that Seoul has to offer. The ubiquitous access to broadband networks—both wired and wireless—makes South Korea a test bed for many multinational companies to explore what will be the future in markets elsewhere.

Given South Korea's amazing modern history and how much the nation continues to dynamically grow, even Korean marketing analysts are struggling to keep pace with their nation. Their task of forecasting future trends is growing increasingly harder. The task is even more so for foreign managers and executives who accept expatriate positions to work in Korean firms or foreign multinational organizations with branches in Korea.

In the end, it matters not if one be a Korean or a non-Korean. Once one has grabbed the Korean tiger by its tail, it can be an amazing adventure simply hanging on. But for those who wish to ride the tiger, this book's author has written this book from a combined century's managerial experience—from both a Korean and an American perspective. There are other, excellent books on the market dealing with narrower perspectives on doing business in Korea. However, there has not been a general survey book on this subject for twenty years.

In closing, this book stands on the shoulders of those Korean and foreign businesspeople whose knowledge and expertise have been shared in the creation of this book. Of particular note is Mr. Song-Hyon Jang's 1988 work *The Key to Successful Business in Korea*, on which the earlier version of this book's structure was based, and a good quarter of the material of which has been replicated, updated and incorporated into this book.

While no single volume will provide the business reader with all the answers, the author endeavors to provide practical, streetwise knowledge one cannot readily find on the Internet and from other public information sources. Together with other aids in understanding Korean business, the author wishes the reader the best of success in doing business in Korea.

© YONHAP PHOTO

PART I.
GETTING TO KNOW THE KOREANS

1. WHAT AN EXPAT MANAGER REALLY NEEDS TO KNOW ABOUT KOREAN HISTORY

Most introductory books on Korea provide an extensive section covering the entirety of Korean history, a period of some 4,000 years. This book is different. As a business professional, one need not be conversant on historical trivia as much as just knowing the important basics that Koreans will eventually expect even a foreigner to know at a minimum. Perhaps even more importantly, one should have some insight on the impact of the legacies of Korean history in the workplace.

© ILLUST TANK INTERNATIONAL INC.

First, there is the mythology of "5,000 years of Korean history." This is more of a legacy of the Korean government's self-promotion campaign of the 1970s than what happened in 3,000 B.C. Many Koreans, however, have swallowed it unquestioningly. In all fairness, there is some scant evidence of people inhabiting the Korean Peninsula as far back as 30,000 years ago, including ancient Chinese records referring to the tribes dwelling in what is now known as Korea; there are also surviving relics and large, table-shaped dolmen rocks that form the outer chambers of coffins similar to those found in Ireland and elsewhere. But what is not found is compelling evidence of a civilization with a written legacy going back to 3,000 B.C. There are not even large-scale, 5,000-year-old remains such as Stonehenge in Britain or Newgrange in Ireland. The point is that the British, Irish and others do not claim a historical legacy rivaling the Egyptians, while many Koreans do. It's probably not a good idea for one to debate this matter with Korean colleagues, but consider this as a point of reference.

Eventually one will hear of Dangun, the mythological founder of Korea who, according to tradition, founded the nation in 2,333 B.C. This event is celebrated each year with a national holiday on October 3. Though the system is no longer commonly used, the nation traditionally numbers its calendar years from that year. Dangun supposedly was born from a beautiful woman who had transformed herself from a bear. His father, Hwanung, was no less than the son of the King of Heaven.

Things become more credible at about 300 B.C. with the substantial evidence of the so-called Ancient (Go) Joseon Dynasty, which was probably more like a collection of tribes along the Chinese border. That ended when the Chinese Han troops conquered what is now known as the Ancient Joseon kingdom in 108 B.C. The Chinese maintained some level of control over much of the peninsula for the next 400 years.

ORIGINS OF PRESENT-DAY REGIONALISM—THREE KINGDOMS (57 B.C.—A.D. 668)

Some of the perennial headaches of present-day Korea can be traced to the prides and prejudices held by many Koreans based on where they are from, and how they can distrust others from competing regions. This regionalism is a serious challenge for the present national government. It has a way of tearing the nation apart in politics and business, while sometimes being a touchstone for corruption based on commonality of region. Much of this can be traced back 2,000 years.

Calling Korean political institutions before 2,000 years ago "kingdoms" or "dynasties" can be misleading, since Korea was ruled primarily by warring tribal chieftains. Over time, however, the chiefdoms developed into three kingdoms that roughly made up what are now Gyeongsang-do (then Shilla), Jeolla-do (Baekje), and North Korea (Goguryeo). The middle provinces of Gyeonggi-do that presently surround Seoul—Gangwon-do on the east coast and Chungcheong-do in the middle of South Korea—saw the boundaries of the Three Kingdoms extend and retreat over their terrain almost constantly. Consequently, the populations of these buffer regions tend to be relatively neutral in the context of present-day regionalism.

WITH A LITTLE HELP FROM A "FRIEND"—UNIFIED SHILLA (688—936)

While Goguryeo dominated the northern half of the country, Shilla in the southeast quarter of the peninsula was quicker to absorb and adopt Chinese civilization in the arts, administration and military knowledge. Baekje was relatively self-absorbed in being a Buddhist kingdom, spending disproportionate resources evangelizing Buddhism at home and to Japan. The result was that during the first half of the seventh century, Shilla was able to conquer its two neighbors. Through alliances with China, Shilla conquered Baekje, and later destroyed Goguryeo. Establishing the Unified Shilla dynasty in 668, the new kingdom then had to drive the Chinese out in order to unify the peninsula. After 60 years of contention, the Chinese eventually recognized in A.D. 735 the borders from the Taedong River to the Bay of Wonsan. This mixed relationship of dependency on and resistance to China would be repeated regularly right up until the Korean War of the 20th century—and the current standoff between North Korea and the rest of the world. As would also be the case in the future, Koreans gave minor credit to the role of China in their military history.

While Korean civilization bloomed during this period, corruption among the royal oligarchy grew steadily, resulting in violent and constant political intrigue, ultimately at the expense of the common people. This in turn led to peasant revolts, until one rebel was finally able to unify his authority in 936 and hold off challenges from rival tribal groups until all recognized a new dynasty, Goryeo (from which the modern name "Korea" derives), in 994.

PIRATES, MONGOLS AND CULTURE—GORYEO (936—1392)

During this period, Korea's generally unhappy experience with the Japanese took a turn for the worse. While Japanese pirates had long been a sporadic problem, the pirates now took things inland, requiring the army to repel them—but often only after severe damage was done. Even worse were the Mongols during the last 150 years of the dynasty. Repeatedly the Mongols invaded the country, leaving destruction in their wake. Ultimately, Korea faced the humiliation of being subjugated. It is probably from about this period of time that one can identify the origins of Korea's well-known xenophobia as being based on traumatic abuse by foreigners.

It was also near the end of this period that the ongoing conflict between Korea's Buddhists and Confucians intensified. Calls for reform by the Confucians became louder, while resistance by the corrupt Buddhist priests and the ruling oligarchy stiffened. Only in modern times have the two groups come to a truce.

Still, not everything was bad news. Goryeo potters devised a remarkable celadon glaze that made them the envy of their neighbors. Two hundred years before Johannes Gutenberg, texts were being printed with movable type. Also, the world's oldest and most comprehensive Buddhist scripture blocks were carved—twice, actually, after the first set was destroyed during warfare—totaling 81,258 wooden blocks. These blocks can still be seen at the Hae-in Temple in the mountains near Daegu.

GOING CONFUCIAN, FEUDAL, AND XENOPHOBIC—YI DYNASTY (1392—1910)

A general who was recklessly dispatched to take on China's armies by the man who would become the last king of Goryeo founded the Yi, or Joseon, Dynasty. Recognizing the folly, Yi Seong-Gye turned on the court in Gaeseong. The new king, recognizing the power of China, asked the Ming court for a new name for the country. The Chinese chose the traditional name Joseon. Three years later, the new king moved the capital to Hanyang (modern Seoul). From this time the conservative branch of Confucianism, neo-Confucianism, took hold and became the dominant sociopolitical force and influence.

Neo-Confucianism works off a catechism of queries and discussions from which all practical wisdom is thought to derive. Given this narrow intellectual construct in a relatively small nation, in time the Koreans became—and remain—even more Confucian than the Chinese.

The next generation of royalty brought forth Korea's greatest king, Sejong, who is credited with instigating the richest period of musical, philosophical, scientific and technical innovations of the dynasty—not least of which was the development of *hangeul*, the alphabet still in use today for the vernacular language. Prior to then, all written communication was done in Chinese. Actually, *hangeul* did not widely take hold until the arrival of Western missionaries at the end of the 19th century, when they translated the Bible into vernacular Korean using the script. The Bible served as a *hangeul* reader, among other things. Prior to then, the educated looked down upon *hangeul* as many look upon Esperanto today. The common snide comment by the literati of the times was that mastering *hangeul* was so simple that "even women could learn it."

As fortune would have it, just when Korea seemed to be really getting things stabilized, the Japanese military ruler Hideyoshi was scheming how to rid himself of an excess of Christian samurai in Kyushu now that he had reunified Japan. The answer was obvious. Perhaps the Japanese could take on China via Korea, and possibly be victorious. If not, Hideyoshi would have rid himself of potentially dangerous excess samurai and soldiers. In 1592, he invaded Korea. Two weeks later Seoul fell.

The brightest light for the Koreans during this conflict, called the Imjin War, was Admiral Yi Sun-Shin, who developed the world's first ironclad "turtle ships." Admiral Yi is lionized to this day for his skill and courage in sinking the Japanese armada, which included supply and troop ships. Tragically, he died in battle. In the view of many Korean historians, Admiral Yi purposely exposed himself to enemy fire rather than face jealous court intrigue that included plans for his fatal downfall. Once again, Korea was hobbled by bad government.

In the meantime, the destruction was seemingly complete. The Japanese spared few cultural buildings and monuments from destruction or defacement. Thousands of civilians were slaughtered, their farmlands spoiled. Once again, the Koreans called on the Chinese to help them drive out an enemy. With the Chinese army, the Koreans were able to drive out the Japanese—only to have the Chinese of two competing armies invade the peninsula in 1627 and 1636. After another humiliating capitulation of Seoul, the Koreans developed a policy of avoiding foreign entanglements. This attitude and policy in time gave Korea its reputation as the "Hermit Kingdom."

Much more than the pirates' plunder during Goryeo, the experience left a huge legacy of bitterness toward the Japanese. At the same time, while once again giving short shrift in the history books to the Chinese driving out the Japanese, the Koreans were victimized in the end by their allies. To this day, Koreans are often skeptical of the "good" intentions of their allies—especially those who send troops into their land.

A SLOW AND INVOLUNTARY OPENING TO THE WEST

The Koreans gradually became aware of the West via reports from China, which had Jesuit missionaries and other Europeans in its capital. The Dutch unwittingly came into contact with the Korean court when the ship Hollandra in 1626 came ashore for fresh water, only to have three of its sailors captured by the natives. More famous was the Sparwehr (Sparrow Hawk), crashing on the shores of a Korean island in 1653. A famous account written by Hendrik Hamel survives and has been translated into English.

Eventually, clandestine Catholic missionaries began arriving from China. For almost 150 years a gruesome, repeated pattern took place of foreign priests converting local populations only to be tortured and executed with their converts. Early Korean Christianity has more than its share of martyrs. Whatever the attraction to Christianity may have been, many Koreans were looking for some kind of spiritual alternative to the misery of a feudal economy dominated by an ultra-conservative form of Confucianism.

By the mid-19th century, Korea had reached its political, economic and spiritual nadir. Social order was on the brink of collapse, and government institutions were no longer effective. Into this void, the newly internationalized Japanese spotted an opportunity to create a buffer state between themselves and the Western powers. As much as the Koreans feared and detested the Japanese, the Japanese offered what appeared to be an Asian alternative to being colonized by a Western power. In any case, the Korean government was militarily too weak to resist signing an amity pact with Japan in 1876. Advances by French and American warships demanding that Korea open itself to trade had marked the prior decade. Given this chaotic environment, it made sense to some Korean leaders to get close to the Japanese.

Soon after, Japanese merchants and residents poured into Korea. Within a few years, many aspects of government and the military appeared as Meiji Japan copies. Japanese interests exploited the resources and taxed the people. This in turn led to a xenophobic peasant revolt, the Donghak Rebellion, in 1894. The Korean court again called on China to send in troops to help crush the revolt. The arrival of Chinese troops triggered the Sino-Japanese War. Following the resulting 1895 Japanese victory, Korea came under virtual Japanese control. Yet within these circumstances, a modern, if frustrated, nationalist movement was formed.

With Russia at its northeast border and Japan dominating its economy, the Korean court made a desperate move to counter Japanese control by improving relations with the Russians. The Japanese retaliated by invading the Seoul palace and murdering Queen Min. The king escaped to the Russian legation and formed a pro-Russian court as the population rose up against the Japanese. But this was short-lived, and anti-foreign antagonism reached such a point that the Russians felt it proper to move Russian troops into Manchuria. The Japanese countered by landing troops at Incheon. This pitched the two dominant powers into the Russo-Japanese War, resulting, in

1905, in a Japanese victory. With that, Korea's Yi Dynasty ended, and at the Treaty of Portsmouth, brokered by Teddy Roosevelt (for which he received a Nobel Peace Prize), the international powers laid the foundations for Japan to formally colonize Korea five years later.

THE ROOTS OF KOREAN ANIMOSITY TOWARD JAPAN—COLONIAL PERIOD (1910-1945)

Some years ago, an Irishman once mused about the Koreans being so uptight about 35 years of colonial history when the Irish do not harbor such intense feelings toward the English after 700 years of colonization. Perhaps the reason for this difference in emotion is that the Irish were able to liberate themselves as a result of World War I, while the Koreans had to wait to be liberated by others at the end of World War II.

Within the memory of many of today's senior citizens, the shame of the systematic national and cultural destruction perpetrated by the Japanese can be recounted. Photographs of Seoul and Pyongyang taken during that time often look as if they were taken in Japan. The Japanese language was forced on all segments of society, including public schools. Farmlands were routinely confiscated due to the previous, obscure land registration system. All of Korea's natural resources were up for plunder by Japanese interests. Most architectural monuments to Korean culture were destroyed, and 368 large and small Shinto shrines were established in Korea, including two major shrines on Namsan in Seoul. Finally, the colonial powers forced the ultimate dishonor onto a Confucian society: the adoption of Japanese names by all Koreans. The Koreans were very much on the same path forced upon the Okinawans.

Being essentially Confucian, the Koreans have a strong sense of rank among older and younger brothers. Many Koreans revere China as the elder brother who can be unfair at times, but who can be depended upon on occasion to help his sibling Korea in times of severe need. Japan, on the other hand, the recipient of Buddhism and other advanced culture during the Three Kingdoms and Yi Dynasty periods, is the younger brother. Japan is therefore regarded as an insolent and ungrateful sibling who quite improperly tries to dominate its older brothers.

On March 1, 1919, the Japanese were startled by nationwide protests that focused on a Declaration of Independence read publicly in Seoul's Pagoda Park. The Japanese panicked and fired indiscriminately into the 1,500 protests of some two million demonstrators nationwide. The resulting carnage was traumatic: 7,000 killed and 15,000 wounded, with destruction by fire of some 700 homes, 47 churches and two schools.

Though the movement failed, it crystallized Korean nationalism, and both Koreas today celebrate March 1 (Sam-il) as a national holiday. Today, one can find the Sam-il included in various naming conventions in Korean culture, society and business.

History by itself arguably comprises just half of the overall explanation. Much of the animus toward Japan is due to its refusal to specifically acknowledge—as opposed to generally apologize for—its offenses toward its neighbors as the Germans did, and to truly move on to a new chapter in its national identity. The recurring textbook fracases, the interminable "comfort women" complaints, the offensive "unofficial" visits to the Yasukuni Shrine, and so forth are thumbs in the eyes of Japan's neighbors, including both Koreas.

FREEDOM AND HORROR—A NATION DIVIDED (1945—1953)

Korea was liberated by the U.S. as part of the defeat of Japan in August 1945. After three weeks of celebration, the Koreans realized that the nation was divided between the Soviet Union and the U.S. along the 38th Parallel. Though both occupying forces looked upon the division as a temporary measure, they were at odds as to what kind of unified political nation state would be Korea's future.

The first three years of this period were marked by chaos. It often seemed that the occupiers had ended up with the wrong halves of the country. Pyongyang was the stronghold of Korean Christianity; it was often called the "Jerusalem of the Orient." In contrast, Seoul was the hotbed of rivalries between the right and the left, including the Korean Communist Party, with leftist organizations dotting the southern half of the country. As a result, there were demonstrations and riots ruthlessly put down on both sides of the 38th Parallel. In August 1948, the Republic of Korea (ROK) was formed in the south. A month later, the Democratic Republic of Korea (DPRK) was formed in the north.

The U.S. military often saw itself as a brake preventing the ROK from marching northward. Accordingly, it kept the ROK's military limited to a national police force, devoid of any tanks or planes. In contrast, the Russians worked with the DPRK in developing an invasion force. With Stalin's encouragement and Mao's reluctant support, the DPRK's Kim Il-Sung launched a surprise attack on the ROK on June 25, 1950. In a few days Seoul fell, and soon thereafter the North Korean forces swept as far as Daegu. With UN support from 15 nations, U.S. General Douglas MacArthur landed in Incheon and cut the DPRK's overextended invasion into halves. This led to a route taking the UN forces almost up to China's border, in spite of China's warnings.

The People's Republic of China had only consolidated its power in 1949. Fearing MacArthur's worst intentions, the Chinese invaded with human waves, forcing the UN's mechanized army into a slow and disastrous retreat through mountainous North Korea. What had begun as a Korean civil war was now primarily a slugfest between the Americans and the Chinese. The communists once again captured Seoul but were driven back in March 1951 to approximately the 38th Parallel, where both forces slugged it out during two years of armistice negotiations. Again, the statistics, this time from war, were traumatic: 3.7 million refugees, 2.4 to 3 million casualties, 300,000 orphans and 100,000 widows.

It is worth noting that the Chinese alone lost 500,000 soldiers and yet, from what foreign observers can detect, there is not a single monument to their sacrifices, and only scant mention in North Korea. Rather, according to Pyongyang's official mythology, the U.S. backed a South Korean invasion of North Korea only to be driven out by an army inspired by Kim Il-Sung, with only minor assistance from China. In the South, one can find various monuments to the fallen UN troops, and there is widespread, albeit fading, appreciation for those foreigners who gave their lives for the Republic.

The ROK's stubborn first president, Syngman Rhee, a lifelong patriot who had devoted his life to the independence of Korea, retained power during the 1950s. In time, his administration became unpopular, forever increasing corruption by his cohorts. Finally, he had to leave the country with his Austrian wife in the face of the April 19, 1960 student revolution—but only after 180 students had died in street battles with the police.

THE POLITICAL AND ECONOMIC MIRACLE—MODERN SOUTH KOREA (1960—PRESENT)

Syngman Rhee led the First Republic. The Second Republic turned out to be only a footnote in history, as it lasted only nine months, overthrown by a military coup in May 1961 headed by Major General Park Chung-Hee. He later was officially elected and inaugurated in December 1963 to establish the Third Republic.

Park Chung-Hee's rule was dynamic and remains controversial to this day.

During the 1960s the two Koreas were very much at war, with ongoing terrorist activities by the North ranging from kidnappings and attacks on passenger buses to a daring attack on the presidential Blue House. As a result, President Park declared martial law and effectively ran the nation as a fascist state, with severe curtailment of civil rights.

At the same time, President Park essentially kickstarted the South Korean nation and its economy into gear by aggressively promoting a positive national self-image and a confidence in self-reliance through the New Village Movement (*Sae Maeul Undong*). Working closely with business, he oversaw the planning and successful execution of five-year economic development plans with heavy government support for the largest business conglomerates' exporting activities. In the process, per capita income soared from US$80 to US$2,000. Yet this was politically his undoing. In effect, Park created a substantial middle class that became increasingly demanding for political rights similar to those enjoyed in other market-oriented nations. It may be said that Park Chung-Hee was tactically brilliant in moving his country forward but lacked a strategic vision of how the nation might evolve into the next paradigm.

Whatever his actual thinking, it was clear that President Park was unable or unwilling to relinquish power. The 1970s witnessed surges in the economy, with growing demands by students and church leaders for true democracy. Finally, in October 1979, his own Korean Central Intelligence Agency director assassinated President Park during an argument over the future of the nation.

After chaos and confusion, an Army general, Chun Doo Hwan, emerged as the new strongman of the Fourth Republic. While his term of power was marked by major personal corruption, he made one major step in advancing the Korean political process by agreeing to limit his presidency to a single eight-year term, which was followed by relatively free national elections. The black mark on his term was the Gwangju Democratic Movement of 1980, when dozens and possibly as many as 200 pro-democracy demonstrators were killed. Many Koreans quite unfairly charge that the U.S. Government either directly or tacitly supported the suppression of this uprising. In fact, the U.S. representatives were confused and upset as events swirled beyond their control—and have since been even more frustrated as this event has proven to be a primary catalyst in the growth of anti-Americanism in Korea.

Chun's successor Roh Tae Woo, also a former army general, reigned for what is now the standard term of office, five years. He is credited with bringing back civilian control of the government and opening the doors to a modern democratic state. At the following truly democratic elections in 1992, a civilian politician, Kim Young-Sam, was elected from the same conservative party as Roh. A member of the political opposition, Kim Dae-Jung, followed President Kim. "DJ" is remembered for skillfully guiding the nation through the so-called IMF Crisis and for launching the controversial "Sunshine Policy" peace initiative toward North Korea that culminated in his being awarded the 2000 Nobel Peace Prize. But perhaps of equal significance, Kim Dae-Jung's election was the first time in Korean history that power had peacefully shifted from one power base to another.

In 2002, Roh Moo-Hyun, a self-educated labor lawyer, was elected. In 2004, he was impeached and found guilty of misdemeanors, though these were not deemed severe enough to warrant removal from power. In effect, the Koreans implemented a system of checks and balances incorporating the legislative, judicial and executive branches of government. During his final years, President Roh found himself at odds with the mainstream populace, who generally respected his integrity but realized he was incapable of adequately managing the complex issues facing a head of state. Meanwhile, as the ranks of government grew, many university graduates found themselves facing daunting odds in gaining their first jobs. At the same time, continuance of the "Sunshine Policy" came under increasing criticism as being unduly one-sided in favor of North Korea.

In 2007, former Seoul Mayor, national legislator and Hyundai Construction CEO Lee Myung-Bak was elected as the next President by a comfortable electorate margin. His election was largely seen as a repudiation by many voters of the immediately preceding two presidents' policies and a desire by many Koreans to return to a more economy-focused, conservative form of government in the face of increased international competition—particularly from China and developing nations, and to a lesser degree from Japan. In other words, the political pendulum swung back to the right from the left, completing its cycle by fully democratic means.

President Lee's broad-based electoral mandate was largely scuttled during his first half-year in office when the so-called "anti-mad cow disease" wave broke out in Seoul. From May 2008 through early July, downtown Seoul was frequently paralyzed by candle-lit mass demonstrations. Ostensibly, the demonstrations were over public health safety following President Lee's quick reopening of the Korean market to U.S. imports, without adequate consultation with the opposition party. The demonstrations were also fueled by wild rumors and speculation over the Internet and SMS messaging, initially starting with high school students. In time, many others, particularly those in their 20s and 30s, joined these demonstrations to criticize the government and the elite of society for widening the gulf between rich and poor, as well as weakening the basement floor of the middle class. While there were superficial aspects of anti-Americanism in these spontaneous events, the primary drivers were based in domestic opposition to the re-established conservative political forces.

Since then, the conservative forces, along with President Lee, slowly regained some of their lost public support—particularly in the face of North Korean missile and nuclear threats following the closing of access to the cross-border Geumgang-san mountain resort upon the shooting death of a female South Korean tourist. At the same time, economic strain from the 2008-2009 global recession caused greater tensions between South Korea's upper and lower classes.

UNDERSTANDING THE KOREA-U.S. ALLIANCE—MYTHS AND REALITIES

Even if the reader is not an American, some understanding of the more common myths and realities of this particularly complicated relationship can be insightful in dealing with Koreans. Here are a handful of myths for consideration.

Myth: Anti-Americanism is a significant force within the Korean political and social environment.

Reality: While there is a core of die-hard anti-American Koreans who have adopted this ideology for whatever reason, almost all participants in anti-American demonstrations are not anti-American. Rather, they tend to be anti-ruling class. (At the same time, Koreans are acutely sensitive to any sign that their government is kowtowing to the U.S. on any given issue, but seem to be less so when it makes a concession to most other countries.)

Attacking the foreign partner of the elite while still pressing home the same issues is infinitely safer than butting heads with the elite itself. During the years of the prior authoritarian governments, taking on the Republic of Korea's government was risky business. Also, during most of the republic's history, the government has been ruled by the conservatives, who are generally perceived to represent the interests of the rich. Given the upper class's business ties with America, the South Korean government has often been accused of being the Americans' government. So demonstrating against America can be a convenient foil, due to America's extremely close relationship with the Korean establishment.

Myth: America is responsible for the division of Korea.

Reality: In a sense, this myth is true, since had the U.S. not rushed to South Korea's defense during the Korean War, the country would have been unified. But from a broader view, this is a myth. For example, the liberation of Korea from Japan was an accident.

The role of the American forces had no direct significance other than in forcing the Japanese government and its military to globally surrender. For 35 years, Korea had not politically existed, having been absorbed into Japan as a colony in 1910. During the closing days of World War II, American senior commanders reportedly had to look at an atlas to determine Korea's location. The Soviet Union, belatedly and cynically leveraging the principles of the Cairo Declaration, declared war on Japan a few days after the atomic bomb was dropped on Hiroshima, rushing troops into Manchuria and later northern Korea. Hoping for nationwide free elections, the U.S. agreed with the Soviets on a temporary division of the peninsula. After repeated U.S. efforts to reach agreement with the U.S.S.R. on a formula for pan-Korea elections and unification, the elections were held in the South, but never in the North.

Note that in all but its formal name, the Democratic People's Republic of Korea was up and running prior to the formal surrender of Japan on Aug. 15, 1948.

Myth: The American government and, by extension, the U.S. Army control the government and military of the Republic of Korea.

Reality: Except for the three-year period of the U.S. military occupation following World War II, the Republic of Korea has maintained independence, often bordering on defiance, from the U.S.

During the Korean War, the autonomy of the ROK government and its Army from the UN Command and the U.S. government was obvious when then President Syngman Rhee released POWs rather than forcing their repatriation to the communists, as the UN had agreed to do at Panmunjeom. Earlier, in September 1950, the ROK Army's chief of staff, Lieutenant

General Chung Il-Kwon, told President Rhee that he thought he needed the approval of UN Forces to send his troops north of the 38th Parallel. The ROK general was curtly told by Rhee that, as Korean Army chief of staff, he should obey the Korean president. "I gave General MacArthur authority over the Korean Army temporarily," Rhee said. "If I want to take it back, I can take it back today."

Myth: The American government and its military have had at least tacit, if not complicit, involvement in political coups.

Reality: In all cases, the Americans have been given too much credit for possible involvement in Korean internal affairs.

For example, prior to Park Chung-Hee's bloodless takeover of Korea in May 16, 1961, the U.S. military did not take reports of an impending coup seriously. The ROK Army chief of staff had assured American generals that the situation could be handled. When the rebellion did occur, the Americans were caught off guard as to how to address the uprising. Unfortunately, because Koreans had the incorrect mindset that the U.S. was responsible for protecting Korea not just from external forces but also in internal matters, they took America's inaction as evidence that the U.S. was supporting the rebellion. To further complicate matters, some Korean academics have looked back on Park's coup and, feeling that Koreans couldn't have carried out the coup alone, concluded it must have been managed by the Americans. This pattern has been frequently replicated throughout the South's history.

In the subsequent "creeping coup" by Chun Doo Hwan in 1979-80, the American military was again left feeling that their trust in their Korean counterparts had been violated. The Korean military had violated the strict procedures of the Combined Forces Command (CFC). U.S. General John Wickham was reportedly irate that Chun Doo Hwan and Roh Tae Woo had moved troops from Roh's vital front line Ninth Division into Seoul on Dec. 12, 1979, outside of proper process, in flagrant violation of CFC procedures.

Trust is strategically important between the two armies, since it is the glue that holds together consolidated control in the defense of a nation. In other words, the Americans have felt a crisis of confidence about their ability to defend Korea from external attack whenever ROK military commanders have taken unilateral and unexpected actions for political reasons.

Some Koreans have rationalized these military actions, such as those during the coups, as "domestic matters." The Americans have acknowledged that reality, but as one former CFC commander observed,

"Either you have operational control or you don't."

Nonetheless, the American side has always understood that operational control for the mission of defense against attack from the North does not give the Americans the right to interfere in Korean internal affairs.

Myth: The U.S. Army has ultimate authority over Korean units assigned to the CFC.

Reality: Since 1978, the CFC has been accountable to a joint military committee that gets its authority from both U.S. and South Korean national command authorities.

The Korean units assigned to the CFC are designated by the Korean side and can be withdrawn by South Korea at any time simply by notification. The CFC commander cannot refuse such notification; all he can do is point out the impact it may have on the performance of his mission.

These points have not been well understood by most Koreans or most Americans. Nor have they been well explained. When U.S. officials stated their position publicly in 1980, they were stymied by martial law and censorship from Korea. Subsequently there was little effort to set the record straight because of the priority accorded to stability.

In other words, despite a military technological gap, the relationship between the two sides has been much more equal than is publicly imagined. But to be fair, as of today, the U.S. maintains a four-star general command CFC and two-star generals—C3 (operations and training, the primary war-fighting team) and C5 (plans, policy and strategy)—to head up the most important staff sections, with a Korean four-star deputy and one-star Korean deputies, respectively, to offset them on the Korean side.

But most Korean officers seem quite comfortable with the current arrangement where U.S. forces are stationed in Korea, realizing as they do that their hierarchical system and relatively rigid training simply do not equip them to react swiftly and flexibly to events and situations as the CFC would have to in case of hostilities. Hence the persistent opposition to wartime operational control transfer by 2012 from so many retired Korean generals and officers, as well as from other conservative groups, despite Korea's efforts to push the U.S. out.

However, we should note that the U.S. Army continuously maintains the lead in cutting-edge military technology, sophisticated command and control procedures, and air power—and, thanks to Iraq and Afghanistan, comes here "battle-hardened." All of which makes the perception of the South Korean

Army operating under the U.S. Army very much a reality, despite legal technicalities. But, as noted above, come 2012 much of this will change.

At times one may wonder if some politicians have found it advantageous to allow the public to remain ignorant of the evolving complexities of the relationship. It could be advantageous for Korean politicians to tacitly give the impression to the public that they have less power than they actually do. After all, being "under the thumb of Big Brother" gives Korean politicians a plausible rationale for suggesting that they have no choice but to do what may be unpopular.

Of course, this potential misleading of the public carries with it the liability of Koreans understandably jumping to the wrong conclusions during populist movements—such as last year's anti-mad cow demonstrations.

Myth: The U.S. government at least tacitly backed the South Korean military's suppression of the 1980 Gwangju uprising.

Reality: Many Koreans assume that the U.S. had excellent intelligence about what was happening in their country. Actually, the Americans have proven to be remarkably uninformed time and again. In the case of Gwangju, the American government had little accurate knowledge of what was happening, other than a general awareness that there was significant civil unrest in that regional capital.

In fact, it took over a day for the U.S. government and its military to understand that violence had broken out on Gwangju's streets on the morning of Sunday, May 18. Meanwhile, the U.S. Peace Corps at the time had ordered its volunteers out of Gwangju. But some of the male volunteers refused to leave, and on several occasions were seen physically shielding demonstrators from army troops with their bodies.

Back in Seoul, things were made even murkier for the U.S. government by the Korean government's news blackout. It did not understand until Monday, May 19, what had happened over the weekend or why there should be reports of 100,000 people in the streets. In other words, it took over a day for the U.S. government and its military to understand that violence had broken out on Gwangju's streets on the morning of May 18. Contrary to many people's perceptions, the Korean units from the CFC had been withdrawn earlier than the Gwangju events—not suddenly, just before the government's response to the Gwangju civil unrest.

In other words, Korean units had already been withdrawn in response to the ongoing demonstrations in Seoul some time prior to the Gwangju incident. Here again, the Korean public, lacking knowledge of the relationship between the CFC and the Korean military, assumed that U.S. officials supported Korean Army operations in Gwangju.

Myth: South Korea is forced by the U.S. government to accept the stationing of U.S. forces on the peninsula.

Reality: The presence of U.S. Forces Korea is entirely at the pleasure of the Korean government. As demonstrated in the case of the Philippines in 1992, and more recently in Kyrgyzstan (though this demand was later rescinded), it only takes a request by the host country's national government to send the U.S. military packing.

So where does this place the Korea-U.S. relationship? No alliance can guarantee there will be no problems between friendly countries, but a good alliance can provide a means of solving problems and dealing with common threats. More than many people realize, the two countries stand together as equals, and the U.S. recognizes and encourages the increasingly significant, multi-dimensional role Korea plays on the peninsula, in the region, and in the world.

The leadership of both countries would do well to better explain the benefits both sides derive from the present relationship, as well as the benefits that will accrue to both from continued, close cooperation.

* * *

As we look back upon modern Korean history, South Korea's political development has been every bit as impressive as its economic growth. Within the span of a single century, the Koreans have moved from a backward, "feudal" state to a modern, market-oriented liberal democracy. As one may expect with this kind of phenomenal development, there are still some rough edges that need to be smoothed out—but the Koreans are a practical people, and better things are yet to come.

2. KOREAN HEARTS AND MINDS— TRADITIONAL YET CHANGING

*T*o attempt to describe the mentality of any group of people in a single book—much less a single chapter—is at best a daunting task. But since the purpose of this book is to provide a practical guide, the author will try to cover some of the major points in the following pages. Ultimately, it will have to be up to the reader to do additional research and, more importantly, to get out and learn from experience and interaction with Korean employees, business partners and friends.

Currently, the two most recommended books to newly arrived foreigners are the Royal Asiatic Society—Korea Branch's classic *Korean Patterns*, by Paul S. Crane (1967), and *The Koreans: Who They Are, What They Want, Where Their Future Lies*, by Michael Breen (1998). Both books have gone through reprinting due to their being in constant demand. The earlier book, though 40 years old, is still relevant and useful. The fact that it can still be invaluable after the passage of so many years betrays the strong, traditional nature of the Koreans. At the same time, it is essential to look at a modern text such as Breen's, given the many changes in the Korean psyche resulting from and mirroring this rapidly developing society. For those not inclined to read straight prose, the comic book *Korea Unmasked—In Search of the Country, the Society and the People*, by Won-bok Rhie (2002), provides an entertaining yet insightful overview of the Koreans.

THE CONFUCIAN TRADITION CONTINUES

Whether one looks to Korean academics or experienced executives to get a handle on the Korean mentality, the essential starting point is an understanding of the basics of Confucianism. Though of Chinese origin, this practical philosophy has taken deeper root in Korea than in any other nation. Unlike China, which comprises a number of ethnic groups and languages over a vast territory, Korea is a compact nation with a homogeneous society. As a result, national institutions and cultural traditions have held a more consistent grip on this smaller country and have integrated Confucianism further than was the case in China. Today, if one looks beneath the façade of a Korean, be it a South Korean capitalist or a North Korean communist, a Confucian is almost always revealed.

Foreign businesspeople are often exasperated by Korean behavior and wonder if the whole society is ruled by emotion. Yet if one appreciates a Confucian sense of priorities, a different kind of rationale—if not logic—appears. The civilized Korean considers the highest virtue to be *injeong*, or "humanity," in the context of society, family and self. This sense of loyalty, compassion and responsibility outweighs simple rules and regulations if the circumstances dictate otherwise. Perhaps this is one of the reasons the entire society often seems to be "illegal." Foreigners are routinely flabbergasted at the inconsistent enforcement of laws. Part of this may come down to the need to wink at the law given the competitive nature of a society where everyone else ignores the regulations. Koreans are often motivated by what they consider a higher standard than simply the law or some other logical consideration.

Another important perspective deriving from Confucianism is *hyo*, or "filial piety." Most Korean social units strive for harmony, usually with a strong top-down authoritarian structure. Within this context, *hyo* is considered proper and the norm. There is near-absolute obedience upwards and a strong sense of responsibility downwards. The almost stereotypical ideal of the Korean boss is that of a tough so-and-so with a heart of gold, whose minions do whatever he commands. Of course, the reality is usually less than that, but traditionally that has been the model. Consequently, when juniors snap to at the elder's whims, whatever they are, they are in effect training themselves and thereby earning the right to rule, as well as the ability to assume what are often very heavy obligations when their time comes.

The codes and rules of Confucianism detail loyalties, obligations and responsibilities between ruler and subject, parent and child, husband and wife, young and old, and one friend and another. It is important to note that there is never a truly co-equal relationship in the Western sense; rather, there is a balance of power, if you will, between privilege and obligation in all relations. Even between friends, someone is always older, and that person is often expected to take on the dominant role. So what is "fair" in Korea is rarely "even Steven" by Western standards. But it is possible for Koreans to have a fair exchange of duties and obligations in a vertical relationship, in the sense that each person has both benefits and obligations that come with his or her position in society.

Given all these types of Confucian relationships, one may generalize that the ruling factor is age, whether it overtly presents itself or covertly controls social structures. Those familiar with the Japanese concept of *sempai-kohai* will quickly recognize that the Koreans also have a mirroring set of values in *seonbae-hubae*—meaning something between "senior-junior" and "master-disciple." As a practical model, one may consider this the overriding principle, particularly between two people of the same gender.

Matters can become complicated within most Korean companies should a younger manager need to supervise an older employee, regardless of sex. As Korean companies move more to merit-based promotions and away from seniority systems, this Confucian mentality often forces the early retirement of senior managers as a means of preventing the discord caused by a younger employee managing one or more older staff members. (The author will discuss the dynamic repercussions of this issue later on in the book.)

So foreigners should not be taken aback at how often their Korean counterparts try to determine and even bluntly ask their age at a first encounter, since seniority is essential in properly establishing a relationship.

FAMILY AND SPECIAL RELATIONS

As one can see, relationships are often defined and weighted differently than those found in Western societies. The key factor is to determine how close two individuals may be from common social factors—including those that might be dismissed by a Westerner as simply coincidental. For example, extended family relationships via blood and marriage, though gradually shrinking in span as the nation modernizes, are still very important and can weigh heavily on the individual Korean's behavior.

Many modern Koreans hold a special regard for loyalties and obligations defined by having a common hometown—especially if the hometown is a village or town rather than a large city. Often Koreans will play or respond to the "alumni card," most strongly if the two individuals graduated from the same high school in roughly the same six-year period. But regardless of age difference, finding commonality with someone who has simply graduated from the same grade school, university or any other such program or institution can strongly influence decisions and behaviors.

DIFFERENTIATION OF THE SEXES

Most Westerners expect and witness a major separation—and often discrimination—between the sexes. While men may dominate in society, the real rulers of Korean society are the women—traditionally at home, while often running the small family businesses.

While everyone traditionally bowed first to the eldest male in the home, the real power has normally been the mother of the husband, who managed the affairs of everyone in the home, followed by the wife, who was second in command, with direct responsibilities for the welfare and education of the children as well as investing the family income.

It is often the case today as in the past that the difference between two similar male wage earners' incomes is due to the business acumen or investment luck of the wife. Should all parents-in-law be deceased or living apart, the husband assumes the de facto authority of his mother. In this case, his wife carries on controlling the home—which even includes management of the husband's discretionary spending.

As strong as the superficial and real advantages of men over women may be, the even stronger controlling factor is age. Even in the business world, an older woman can hold sway over younger men—which may be one of the reasons why Korean companies have traditionally urged women to retire when they become pregnant. Things remain simple with an older male manager supervising a younger female employee. Today's young men, however, are generally at ease when reporting to female supervisors—provided the female supervisor is older or, at the very least, has more years of relevant company experience.

Nonetheless, a 2009 OECD working paper stated that Korea's male workers received 38 percent more than Korean female workers, a discrepancy that was the highest among the eighteen OECD countries surveyed. The average gender-based wage gap based on the 2008 data was 18 percent. Japan came second among the eighteen members at 33 percent, followed by Germany, a distant third at 23 percent. The same paper cited the OECD family database. Among all thirty OECD members with data available, Korea had the fourth highest gender-based wage difference. Meanwhile, according to the ROK Labor Ministry, in 2007 Korean men on average received a monthly wage of 3.039 million won (US$2,377), which was 59 percent higher than the 1.908 million won (US$1,492) average for women.

While the gender wage gap in Korea is often attributed to a deep-rooted sense of male superiority, there are other contributing factors. "Like many other countries, more women in Korea are working part-time or in places with poorer working conditions compared to men," said a Labor Ministry official, who wished to remain anonymous. Men have also been known to work for longer terms.

However, the male superiority factor in workplace success has been subsiding quickly, the official added. Note that in May 2007, the country's female workforce hit the 10 million mark. Women are also increasingly being promoted to middle management. According to the Labor Ministry's 2006 survey of some 540 companies with more than 1,000 employees, women represented 10.2 percent of all managerial positions (manager or higher) with authority in personnel management and decision-making. In 1997, women in managerial positions at 586 companies of the country's top 50 groups numbered just 729 out of 110,000 total managers, or a mere 0.7 percent. In other words, there had been more than a tenfold increase in the percentage of women managers over the prior nine years.

Some examples of change:

- In March 2007, the Korea Exchange Bank's personnel announcement in March surprised many of its staff. Out of 114 officials promoted to the position of manager, thirty-eight, or 40.4 percent, were women. Compared with 2005, when the KEB figure stood at 18 percent, the proportion of females promoted to the manager level more than doubled. It was an uncommon phenomenon in the generally conservative financial community.

- In 2002, there were just three women among all 369 mangers at SK Corp. But the figure increased to 20 out of 382 in 2007. Due to the nature of the petrochemical industry, there were fewer women willing to work for the company. Therefore, the fact that there was such an increase at a point in time when it had been just nine years since the first women college graduates joined the company was significant.

While there are now more than 10 million women workers, low-level workers have little influence on organizations, no matter how many the employees may number. On the other hand, an increasing number of women today hold middle manager positions, demonstrating that the so-called "glass ceiling" is being broken. It is only a matter of time before more women hold high-ranking positions.

However, the largest presumed weakness of Korean women is business leadership. According to a 2006 survey of 200 women scientists and researchers by the Korea Women's Development Institute, respondents answered that, in actual practice, male workers tend to be superior to their counterparts in leadership. Many Korean women themselves admit that leadership is not their forte.

A common explanation is that many Korean companies still maintain a male-dominated workplace culture, including elements such as after-work entertainment. Yet some observers point out that masculine charisma is not what leadership is all about. With changing organizational environments, leadership needs are likely to be more diverse. An interesting example was suggested by a female team leader at Amore Pacific, who said, "I praise men and women subordinates differently because they are different. For women, I praise them repeatedly, while praising men specifically based on facts." She added, "This is from the point of view of a woman's sensitivity and another form of leadership."

Today, more people are watching to see whether the growing numbers of female middle managers will achieve promotion to the executive level by demonstrating their capabilities and leadership. Not totally unrelated is the fact that the above-cited OECD paper also positioned Korea at the bottom of the OECD countries in terms of fertility rate. According to the 2008 OECD factbook, Korea's fertility rate, which is the number of children a woman has in her lifetime, was 1.08. Japan followed at 1.26.

EDUCATION AND EMPLOYMENT

There has been rightful concern about Korea's unemployment in the face of the recent global recession. But this current set of traumas has a way of hiding a bigger picture that transcends both good and bad economic times.

As many labor economists point out, in advanced economies, unemployment statistics are understated, since they only reflect workers who are actively but unsuccessfully looking for jobs. In all nations, there are also the "discouraged" workers who have given up looking for work, usually representing about 5 percent of the population in advanced economies. So if a nation claims a 6 percent unemployment rate, the real unemployment rate is closer to 11 percent.

To make matters even more confusing, where is the line that separates those who are categorized as being unemployed from those who are employed? If one tutors for a couple of hours a week or works Friday evenings at a convenience store, is one unemployed? Probably. But let's say one normally works Friday afternoons through Sunday evenings in a convenience store. Is one now considered employed? By the reckoning of many governments, one is no longer part of the unemployment statistics.

While attending business school in 1987, this author was the lone American assigned to work with Korean students on a microeconomics class project focusing on South Korea. Since he had at the time just left a career in human resources, he was given labor-related portions of the study. What he discovered came as no surprise: there was a serious imbalance between education outputs and labor inputs. In other words, the Korean population as a whole was overeducated in terms of academic qualifications relative to job requirements. As a result, many college graduates who could not bring themselves to swallow their dignity and do blue-collar labor were unemployed. So it followed that there was labor shortage in many factories.

But let's put the above into today's context. In 1990, about 30 percent of South Korean high school graduates went on to complete secondary education at two- and four-year colleges. Since there is a low dropout rate in Korean schools, conservatively speaking, at least a quarter of the population had some kind of college education back then.

Now consider this: today almost 100 percent of young Koreans finish high school, and a whopping 84 percent go on to secondary education. That means eight out of ten young Koreans have at least a college degree, not to mention that South Korea has the world's highest per capita rate of Ph.D holders.

Looking at employment by industrial sectors, let's compare 1990 and today. In 1990, roughly 47 percent of workers were in services, 28 percent in manufacturing, 18 percent in agriculture and 7 percent in construction. In 2008, roughly 68 percent were in services, 17 percent in manufacturing, 7 percent in agriculture, and 7 percent in construction.

While looking at percentages alone can be misleading, we can still surmise that the imbalance between education output and labor demand has been growing. While the number of workers in the service sector has nearly doubled, that of secondary school graduates' has grown by two and two-thirds. And, of course, many service jobs include work that requires wearing a name badge and asking banal questions such as "Would you like fries with that?"

One of the disturbing results of all of this is something that started in Japan and has been observed in Korea in recent years, namely the NEET (Not in Education, Employment or Training) generation. At least until a year ago and before the current recession, more than 1.3 million young Koreans were not employed or in formal education or training. Many were hanging out at home, "studying" on their own for some kind of qualification or barely working part-time. As a result, only about 63 percent of South Koreans in their twenties were economically active at the time.

The number of NEETs has climbed steadily from 330,000 in 2004 to 391,000 in 2006 and 399,000 in 2008, before surpassing the 400,000 mark in 2009 with a total of 430,000. Taking into consideration the fact that the number of Koreans aged 15 to 34 has actually declined by more than 7 percent—from 15.3 million to 14.1 million—since 2004, the overall percentage of NEETs has increased.

Furthermore, Korea, the world's most Confucian society, is facing generational competition as never before. As in other countries, many younger Koreans born after the Baby Boomer demographic tidal wave resent the relatively fewer opportunities left in the wake. As a result, many more recent university graduates compete for fewer suitable jobs. At the same time, as with other advanced countries, Korea's mature economy means that business organizations are becoming increasingly pyramidal in shape. Consequently, company men, as they approach the age of fifty, often find themselves prematurely retired and out on the streets, as there is little capacity for many Korean companies to accommodate older and more expensive workers. Naturally, this forced retirement issue has been exacerbated by these current economic difficulties.

All of this is brought home to this author when he meets human resource professionals, and especially when he introduces the idea of a private coaching or mentoring service led by recently retired executives of multinational companies as a means of upgrading "rising star" junior managers. On more than a few occasions, the first reaction has been quite negative when the HR manager is a younger person. The young manager often misunderstands the concept as yet another ploy by aging Baby Boomers to deny employment opportunities to younger Koreans. Upon reiteration of the concept, the young Korean inevitably comes to understand that the program is meant to enhance the job skills of younger employees and not to deny employment opportunities. But on more than one occasion, the author has been taken aback by this strongly defensive generational attitude held by younger Korean employees.

In other words, there is a growing generational friction caused by skyrocketing educational levels among Korea's young that are being matched by employment opportunities for the older generations.

TRUST

Finally, the matter of trust needs to be taken into account. While trust is a cornerstone for virtually every society, Koreans often take it further than most. From a Westerner's perspective, the degree to which Koreans trust each other—only to be taken advantage of by the less scrupulous—can be amazing. Trust, however, is simply the water that flows through a Confucian society's channels. To block trust often causes a rupture of relations that can even cascade into further disharmony beyond the immediate control of the skeptical party. Given this ripple effect, Koreans will often voluntarily expose themselves—if reluctantly—by trusting someone so as not to create discord.

The trust factor in relationships translates into a phenomenon quickly recognized by even the most oblivious foreigner—there are no secrets in Korean society. That, at least, is what normally seems to be the case. But given the above, the cause for the lack of secrecy is self-evident.

If a Korean has a relationship with another Korean, then the factors noted above come into play. Should the first party recognize that the second party is withholding information for whatever reason, the first party is likely to become agitated about the second party not trusting the first party with the secret. And so a "secret" eventually becomes part of public information in Korea's tight-knit society. Consequently, rumors tend to be more prevalent—and accurate—in Korea than in most economically developed societies.

This really became clear to the author during the IMF Crisis about a decade ago. His distributor was forced to reduce the head count. The Korean company's management was conscientious about ensuing morale problems —particularly how the rank and file regarded its executives. Having good relations with middle managers, the author heard some critical but not necessarily accurate opinions on the senior management's priorities. Over dinner, the author passed on what he had heard to the company president. The president was naturally anxious to know specifically who had made the comments. As an American, the author refused to violate the confidence of the middle managers. This really piqued the president, who considered the American's sense of ethical principles to be a violation of their cultivated personal relationship. Even after the author pointed out that had he broken his promise by revealing the managers' names, the president would have good reason not to trust him with future secrets, the president never quite forgave the American for keeping the employees' names secret.

JANMEORI

The term *janmeori* in many ways defies translation into English, but once the foreigner gets the hang of the concept, much of Korean society snaps into focus.

Literally, the word means "small mind." While it has a similar connotation to the pejorative English expression "small-minded," it has a broader and yet more specific meaning. So to simply think of someone having *janmeori* as meaning he or she is "small-minded" is just asking for trouble. The concept is much more complicated and can have multiple meanings and uses—both positive and negative.

Any adult who has lived in Korean society for more than a few months will readily recognize the *janmeori* aspect of this culture. That is, most Koreans are constantly and daily working the angles, pushing the envelope in small, quiet measures so as to gain some kind of incremental advantage—without paying attention to the larger consequences of the cumulative effects of their behavior.

Living in as competitive a society as they do, Koreans truly excel at *janmeori*. It can often be a way of not only getting ahead but also keeping up with the pack. The obvious downside is that these creative and industrious individual behaviors often sabotage the group's overall vitality. This concentration on the *janmeori* level may explain in part why Koreans are not generally well regarded for strategic or long-term planning. On the other hand, *janmeori*'s positive aspects include the justifiable reputation of Koreans as world-class tacticians, capable of leveraging special opportunities and/or psychologically wearing down their opponents—often with little or no preparation.

Discussing this aspect of Korean culture with some mature Korean friends, we surmised that while this kind of behavior is common in most cultures, it is unusually strong in Korea. Our best guess as to why this is so involves going not so far back in time to when Korean life was confined to small villages and the neighborhoods of larger towns and cities.

Back then, there was little mobility in Korean life. Everyone knew everyone else in their immediate environment, and people rarely ventured away; that is to say, there was marginal horizontal mobility. At the same time, by living within a strict Confucian culture, everyone knew his or her place in society; there was also very little vertical mobility.

In other words, Koreans have learned to live within narrow social constraints. Naturally, most people are not satisfied with social limitations, particularly if they see others about them trying—and succeeding—at beating the system whenever possible. Since so many people are engaged in this kind of activity, most people are capable of getting away with various dodges, with only a few unlucky individuals getting caught and punished. Furthermore, many people rationalize that if they don't exercise a bit of *janmeori* here and there, they may end up at a major disadvantage.

Janmeori is not only found in the lower levels of society. One might argue that the mentality can even be found in the highest and most sophisticated levels of Korean thinking. For example, it has been opined that the ultimate downfall of Park Chung-Hee was, in a sense, due to *janmeori*.

The late dictator was masterful at goading and cajoling South Korea forward to attain his short- and medium-term goals. At the same time, he lacked a practical, long-term political vision that could accommodate South Korea's economic and intellectual development. As a result, for the greater welfare of the nation, his early demise in office—by natural cause or otherwise—was a foregone conclusion.

Janmeori also seems to be at work in North Korea's highest levels. The Pyongyang ruling oligarchy has been absolutely brilliant at going it alone, playing friends and adversaries against each other, while confounding the rest of the world from a remarkably weak position. At the same time, it is painfully obvious that the North lacks a genuine long-term survival strategy other than to continue practicing *janmeori* statecraft until some unforeseen miracle happens.

Looking back at matters closer to home, many Korean and expatriate managers alike are often exasperated by *janmeori* behavior among their staff. One Korean physician I know runs a major health center with 300 employees just outside of Seoul. When she was made managing director, she found the nurses and the doctors were often competing against each other on the *janmeori* level. She resolved to put a stop to it.

First, she made it clear through a series of announcements and one-on-one conversations that she would not tolerate *janmeori* interfering with the overall mission of the center. Second, she noted who was paying attention and who was ignoring her admonitions. And third, she created an inner circle of doctors and nurses who got the message, excluding those who refused to give up *janmeori* behavior. In time, the entire center got the message. While *janmeori* still exists there, it has been greatly reduced.

So, Koreans have a word for it. And they have ways of dealing with it. Though difficult, an accurate understanding of the word can give the foreign manager a better focus on this aspect of Korea.

MILITARY

Almost all men between 20 to 30 years of age are subject to compulsory military service. The service obligation ranges between 24 and 28 months, depending on the military branch involved (to be reduced to 18 months beginning in 2016). Women between the ages of 18 and 26 years are eligible for voluntary military service, including the infantry, but they are excluded from the artillery, armor, anti-air, and chaplaincy corps.

For most Korean men, this often traumatic rite of passage from adolescence into adulthood provides life-long friendships with others of the same military unit, as well as a sense of responsibility. To outsiders, this type of relationship is often the hardest to detect, but nonetheless can be an extremely important factor in business as well as in society in general.

NATIONALISM

Koreans on both sides of the demilitarized zone (DMZ) are among the most nationalist people on earth. In a positive sense, this love of country is a collective desire to improve the society and stand tall in the community of nations. In a less positive sense, nationalism may be an ongoing recovery exercise aimed at firmly establishing a national culture and identity that was nearly wiped out during the Japanese colonial period between 1910 and 1945.

America may have put an end (albeit unintentionally) to Japanese domination of the country with the 1945 surrender by Tokyo, but America is more widely regarded today as being party to the division of the two Koreas, being the key factor that stopped the nation's destruction by its neighbor. Given the tragic history of the country's repeated humiliations at the hands of the Chinese, Mongols and Japanese, the invited foreign presence of the U.S. Army is increasingly attacked by younger Koreans as yet another example of a foreign power attempting to subjugate and control Korea, as well as prolong its division.

Today's schoolteachers, who were born after the Korean War, sometimes feel compelled to instill in their students a form of nationalism that is often labeled by foreigners as being "xenophobic"—and by older Koreans as being "leftist." In truth, these labels often cloud understanding. Most

Koreans are normally friendly to foreigners on a personal level. Even self-described "leftists" rarely think beyond the confines of the Korean Peninsula, and most fantasies about communism have been dispelled by recent disclosures about North Korea. However, note that there does seem to be more than a mere fringe that looks with favor on its northern brethren. There also remains among academics and middle-aged college graduates (of the so-called "386 generation") a dream of a unified, socialist nation.

In 2006, the U.S. jolted both Korea's left and right by announcing plans to lessen its presence in Korea. After so many years of ignoring fringe protests against its Korean presence, the Pentagon had thrown matters off kilter by its virtually unilateral decision to deploy many of its Korea-based forces elsewhere. Today, South Korea has agreed to take on greater defense responsibilities, including assuming wartime control of all military forces from 2012. At the same time, the U.S. has consistently reaffirmed that it has not diminished its commitment to the defense of the Republic of Korea.

Regardless of current politics, it is highly prudent for foreign business professionals to be aware of nationalist sensitivities. Particularly when dealing with younger to early middle-aged employees and business partners, one should use tact when the topics of nationalism, reunification, North Korea, and Korean-style socialism arise.

In 2003, the Asia-Pacific Center for Security Studies in Honolulu held a conference on the impact of 2002 South Korean presidential elections. The conference report included an attempt to identify how anti-Americanism masks four different phenomena in Korea. The following is from that paper:

> The first background type of general and unfocused anti-Americanism inclines Koreans to see what is valuable in their way of life under constant pressure from a dominant American-led Western culture. This sense of East-West polarity with clear racial overtones and consequent cultural victimization mentality predisposes Koreans to sympathize with whoever opposes America in a dispute, regardless of the issue at hand.
>
> The second coming-of-age type of sharper and more acute anti-Americanism is a reaction against perceived discrimination, a demand for parity and equality between Korea and the United States. It is rooted in a perception that the United States does not appreciate the progress the ROK has made and still wishes to treat Korea as an inferior client state. It is more policy sensitive than other types

of anti-American sentiments.

The third type of hope and disappointment anti-Americanism stems from perceived inconsistencies between American ideals and American practices as related to the image of America in Korean eyes. Whenever very high (and often unrealistic) expectations of the United States were not met, the disappointment felt by Koreans whose faith in America was shattered gave birth to anti-Americanism. This is a cumulative sentiment, which can be triggered by controversial policies or the behavior of U.S. representatives in Korea.

Finally, there is a breed of anti-American sentiment resulting from the South Korean public's growing sense of solidarity with North Korea. When America is seen as taking a hard line toward North Korea, Washington's actions are viewed with suspicion through the lenses of all other types of anti-Americanism. This form of anti-Americanism, related to the ROK's intensifying sense of common identity with North Korea, poses the greatest potential challenge to the U.S.-ROK security alliance. It is likely to increase over time. The closer the North and South grow together, the more likely the South will display an anti-American sentiment from a sense of solidarity with the North. Although anti-Americanism does not pose a grave threat to U.S. interests at present, clearly, as time passes by, it will no longer be viable for the United States to think it can be friends with one half of Korea while remaining a mortal enemy with the other half, because of growing Korean national consciousness.

In any event, the foreign business professional must be keenly aware of how very nation-centrically Koreans in general think and operate—and how thin-skinned they may be about any real or perceived slights against Korea. Controversial calls in an international sporting event or some perceived slight at the UN can throw the nation into a temporary tizzy. On the other hand, any positive recognition of Korea or Koreans from the international level down to the personal level is met with unabashed appreciation.

To give a minor example of how easily strong nationalist passions may run, consider the following incident. A couple of years ago, a European executive ran his business unit to great success during his tenure in Korea. He was known as being a tough yet fair hands-on manager. Through his adroit management, the company significantly expanded its market share in Korea. As a result, the head office promoted him to a larger position elsewhere in Asia. About a year after his transfer, the Korean operations hosted an all-Asia management meeting. All visiting managers to this conference were required to send in a questionnaire regarding health and food concerns. To the shock of the Korean staff, this former Korean manager admitted that he really did not like kimchi—or pickled cabbage,

Korea's national dish. As a matter of national honor, the Korean staff went out of their way to include kimchi into every possible course prepared for that particular manager during his return visit to Korea. The good news in this story was that the Koreans were able to make their point, and the former manager was able to leave Korea once more to successfully resume his career elsewhere—devoid of kimchi.

FOREIGN POPULATIONS

The non-Korean population in South Korea continues to grow in number and percentages. According to an August 2009 story in the Korea Times, as of that year there were roughly 1.1 million foreigners in South Korea, or 2.2 percent of the population—a 24 percent increase over the prior year. A large percentage of foreigners are ethnic Koreans from countries such as China, Japan, and North America. Of the non-ethnic Korean foreigners, Chinese immigrants accounted for 56.5 percent. Next came the Filipinos and Vietnamese, at 21.2 percent each—large numbers of whom are women married to farmers. Finally, the Americans came in at 5.4 percent, with all other nationalities making up smaller numbers.

ARE KOREANS REALLY THE IRISH OF THE ORIENT?

The stereotype that the Koreans are the Irish of the Orient has been around for at least half a century, and some may argue much longer than that. The author of this book first heard this statement in the mid-1970s, but did not become convinced until he became active in the Irish social community of Tokyo in the 1990s and later headed up the Irish Association of Korea during the first five years of the new millennium. This assumption was further buttressed by comments from an Irish long-time executive in Seoul. While this kind of statement may seem fraught with the peril of misunderstanding, please consider the following about what the Irish and Koreans generally seem to have in common:

1. Among the most religious populations in their respective parts of the world, with a comparatively high rate of regular churchgoers.

2. Very family-oriented, taking sides along clan lines quite readily.

3. Extended families gather frequently, regardless of members' ages, to share togetherness, often taking turns entertaining each other by singing songs.

4. Compared to their neighbors, they wear their hearts on their sleeves.

5. Quick to fight and quick to forgive.

6. Famous (or infamous) for their drinking habits.

7. Less regarded for planning and better known for forming successful—if chaotic—teams at the last minute.

8. Have a healthy disregard for authority but will at least superficially show and demand honor and respect as tradition dictates.

9. Often ask strangers about their hometowns due to regional stereotyping.

10. Quick to laugh and quick to cry—as well as to break out into song and verse.

11. Known and respected beyond their borders for their music and ability to entertain beyond language barriers.

12. The nation is divided as a result of foreign power intervention.

13. Well regarded for their sense of humor and playing of pranks, while having little use for the person who cannot laugh at him- or herself.

14. Nations were colonized by island neighbors and forced to speak the language of their oppressors.

15. Traumatized by the colonial experience, with additional decades required to psychologically recover—as a result, they have the collective behavior of being a bit edgy, nervous and inhibited at times compared to their neighbors.

16. In recent times, their respective diasporas have somewhat reversed for the first time due to the nation's rapidly developing economy.

As suggested at the beginning of this chapter, the foreign business professional needs to ultimately explore the culture for him- or herself. Obvious though it may be, the executives interviewed for this book repeatedly stressed the need for expatriate managers to keep an open mind about the cultural differences. This is often easier said than done in the context of workplace pressures. Maintaining that mindset, however, is a real necessity when dealing with this very different culture. A good book to keep on hand, given its clarity and conciseness, is Paul S. Crane's *Korean Patterns*, which can be ordered from the Korea Branch of the Royal Asiatic Society. Though originally published in 1967, this small book has stayed in print, as it is a perennial reference guide to the Korean mind and behavioral patterns.

3. KOREA'S CHANGING ANALYTICAL AND EVALUATION SKILLS

*T*he South Korean economy, largely driven by extremely bright and hardworking entrepreneurs and supported by national economic planning, has climbed out of post-war poverty to OECD member status. While many of the thought systems belonging to Korean business professionals have served them extraordinarily well during the last half of the 20th century, the 21st century is challenging Korean companies with the advent of so-called developing countries offering competitive products and services at significantly lower prices.

As such, Korean companies are being forced to move their offerings upscale to where the overall value proposition needs to be marketed at prices greater than the sum of the parts. Buyer-perceived value requires Korean sales and marketing professionals to think in terms that go beyond features, functions and price. To sell the overall benefits of Korean products and services, a new mindset now needs to be developed.

Today, the lack of adequate awareness of this competition shift is evidenced by the drop in Korean export market shares in advanced economic markets. Furthermore, to date, few Korean companies have been able to move from the earlier authoritarian mindset stressing the "one best answer" approach to problem-solving. However, the Korean education system stresses rote memorization as the only practical path for academic achievement. In contrast, Western education introduces critical and creative thinking to young students and then reinforces this approach to problem-solving later on in their academic careers. Following their graduation, Western business management expects this approach to problem-solving to be further developed and implemented by their employees.

Of special concern is the fact that most Korean managers and executives are inadequately aware of critical thinking and how their competitors are effectively implementing this kind thinking, both abroad and, increasingly, at home. Contrary to the unfair stereotype held by many non-Koreans, and even Koreans themselves, creative thinking does exist within Korea, but it is often systemically repressed within large organizations. Only a few senior executives may expect the intellectual freedom to apply critical thinking in these largely top-down, strictly managed organizations. Yet to be internationally competitive in this new century, Korean managers at all levels need to adopt critical and creative thinking without undue fear of reprisal from senior management. The good news is that in some of Korea's more progressive and multinational corporations, this problem is being rectified, albeit perhaps not as quickly as younger managers may wish.

To make the transition from Korea's current status to where it needs to go, intensive training in business professional skills may be in order. For example, training should first be conducted at senior management levels, and later at middle and junior managerial levels, to ensure that the new thinking is properly understood and accepted, especially as young university graduates bridge over into business. Ultimately this form of training would be included as part of new employee training programs. In any case, senior executive management will need to consistently support and endorse this kind of thinking and related training as part of the overall solution for Korea to regain much of its recently flagging competitiveness.

REVIEW OF RECENT BUSINESS HISTORY

It is important to remember that the "Miracle on the Han River" was no fluke. Korea's rise from poverty was created by business geniuses in executive management and by entrepreneurs. The author must acknowledge how Korean thinking patterns and management practices have worked extraordinarily well during the last half of the 20th century. Korea's remarkable climb from poverty is undeniable proof that the current, prevalent forms of thinking and management have brilliantly succeeded—at least until recently.

THE CURRENT DROP IN KOREAN COMPETITIVENESS

Having stated the above, the author must note that the current situation is still looking a bit grim. Korean exports have slid in U.S. market share in each of the past three years, with electric goods and electronics slipping from 9.25 percent to 5.37 percent, according to the Korea International Trade Association (KITA). Blame for this slippage is attributed to the loss of Korean products' price competitiveness against goods made in developing countries such as China, India, Brazil, and Vietnam.

In spite of Korea's efforts to be a hub of Asia, as of March 2010 Seoul was ranked just 28th in the world on the Global Financial Centers Index (GFCI) released by the City of London Corp. At the same time, China had three cities ranked substantially higher—specifically, Shenzhen at 9, Shanghai at 11, and

Beijing at 15, not to mention Hong Kong at 3 and Singapore at 4.

Today, the top four financial centers in the world—in descending order, London, New York, Hong Kong, and Singapore—have had little change in their standings over the years. Meanwhile, Tokyo has climbed up to fifth, and Taipei to 21st. In any event, Korea's government-sponsored international slogan campaigns, which lack serious financial reforms, seem to have been a failure.

Search for "international competition" on Korean newspaper websites and one can find additional examples of Korea's drop in international competitiveness. But the point here is that within an international context, the Korean mindset sometimes appears to be potentially responsible for this drop in relative international competitiveness. More than ever, international commerce, particularly at the advanced levels, requires detailed planning based on critical thinking and imagination. Contrary to the emotional need to get things done as quickly as possible, even in Korea there are no shortcuts to good planning and execution.

Employees at all levels must appreciate that their jobs are at risk, if for no other reason than the increased levels of international competiveness. A more competitive awareness needs to become more widespread within more Korean companies—and not just in the presidents' offices and international departments.

During the past five to ten years, just as world class competitors have entered the Korean market and Korea companies have been seeing the need to compete more effectively on the global scale, ideology has taken priority at the national government level, which has led to confused and sometimes contradictory government planning. With the recent inauguration of Lee Myung-Bak, however, many hope Korea may be back on a practical business footing. Obviously, international commerce is key to Korea's long-term growth and prosperity. Yet 21st century international competitiveness is already proving itself to be remarkably different from what it once was during the last half of the last century. As such, a change in thinking may be required for Koreans to compete more effectively in the international marketplace.

EXAMPLES OF PREDOMINANT KOREAN THINKING

Let's look at some representative case studies of Korean thinking in the workplace.

Software vendors are expected to act as support system integrators, going beyond simple software sales to custom-develop or greatly modify software to meet the "unique" requirements of each Korean company. While software modification and adaptation is commonplace around the world, Korean companies take customization to a new level—often for idiosyncratic reasons premised on the special demands of the client company. In fact, Korean software providers often go through a bit of a charade, making a big deal of how much they are customizing their products, when most installations in fact require much less modification than the customers may realize.

This practice may seem quaint at first glance, but upon further examination, one finds that customers will often demand software changes that can in fact be extremely expensive to engineer, and ultimately costly to maintain. Client companies can be extremely inflexible about these unique requirements. Again, the official reason is that the information systems must conform to the preferences of senior managers in running their companies. Management approaches are often internally defined as the "one best way" by a specialist, an executive, the company's founder, or the current practices of the market. Suggesting alternative business processes for any reason can be hazardous to one's career, unless one is in senior management or has been asked to do so by a powerful executive.

In contrast, Western companies often reconsider their management processes. They can be remarkably open to package software that needs only minor software customization, but sometimes require significant business process modification for the overall cost effectiveness of the company's business. In other words, while the "not invented here" and "one best way" approaches can be found in Western companies, such prejudices are not nearly as strong as what is commonly found in Korean organizations, as the author will explain later in this section.

Let's look now at an even more common example of Korean decision-making: the way organizations traditionally evaluate options like major purchases or strategic decisions.

First, an evaluation committee is drawn up. These representatives consider their options by determining evaluation or selection criteria. As one of the first steps, it is common to turn to well-recognized "experts." These people may reside within the organizations, but often they are university professors or other outsiders recognized and respected by top management. As such, they are commonly regarded as possible or likely possessors of the "best knowledge."

While Western evaluators will also look to respected authorities for insight and guidance, those opinions are, at least initially, kept at arm's length, since the prior work of authorities or experts is considered at best to be only one source of information. Korean organizations, however, are more likely to immediately accept the findings found in the white papers or verbal opinions of "experts," usually due to political considerations. These findings are massaged into the evaluation criteria so as to make these experts' findings meet an evaluation committee's needs.

Having witnessed the Korean evaluation process as a competitor on numerous occasions, I have noticed that the initial evaluation conclusions, as evidenced by the selection criteria, seem to be based on the following questions:

1. How have other companies dealt with similar problems?

2. What are the personal relations between relevant committee members and others inside and outside of the organization—and how will the selection criteria impact those relationships?

3. What are the organization's overall and current political trends, and how do the selection criteria follow those political winds?

4. In what ways can the selection criteria be politically leveraged to gain a personal advantage with an evaluation committee member by using the opportunity to enhance the "politically correct" expert's position/image? In other words, what may be the opportunities for positive blowback by relying on the expert?

5. How may the final evaluation or selection meet the satisfaction/ego requirements of the top managers?

This is not to say there are no other relevant evaluation criteria. Of course there are. But I have seen that obscure selection criteria can be given remarkably heavy weighting due to political considerations—sometimes at the expense of much more relevant evaluation criteria.

Before proceeding, I should point out that it would be unfair to say there is no Korean rhetorical process. One can see it in some of the better editorials in Korean newspapers. A common format is a problem statement or question, followed by different points or facts and summarized by a conclusion. What is often lacking is a discussion of the pros and cons of the thesis or argument. In other words, there is rarely a checking of assumptions or serious consideration of alternative views or options. Furthermore, there are often points that, while sometimes interesting, do not lend themselves to the conclusion.

One long-term American resident of Korea who is fluent in Korean calls this form of thinking a "bucket of rocks." He described wading through countless reports over the decades so lacking in organization that it seemed like the ideas had been written down willy-nilly, similar to throwing rocks into a bucket. In other words, these reports seem to be a mishmash of observations, conclusions and opinions. Too often the final reports lack logical presentations, logical build-ups, and clear, logically supported conclusions.

For those who are lacking in Korean language skills, a first impression may be that Koreans are remarkably wordy in presenting their ideas. And as these foreigners develop their Korean language skills—or simply participate in meetings where Koreans state their opinions in English—the foreigners discover that their Korean counterparts seem to be pulling ideas from the air, rattling off ideas and opinions that may at best be only slightly relevant to the subject at hand. Koreans endure on a daily basis public speeches where the speaker covers the subject in many ways and from different directions, but often omits an introduction, body of logic and relevant conclusion.

Given their jumbled organization, these recommendation reports frequently lack adequate consideration of various possible scenarios, so there may be no self-checking of logic to justify the writer's positions. Rather, many report writers blindly "barrel down the runway" advocating the "one best solution." As a result, implementation plans rarely address many of the real, practical issues that could affect—and counter—long-term implementation and operational processes. The common practice is to quickly set off in an agreed-upon or authorized direction, and then deal with problems as they are encountered.

Now, there are some advantages to this approach. This type of thinking has allowed Korean organizations to be remarkably quick and nimble. But there is also a lot of expense and inefficiency being "swept under the carpet." So from a foreign perspective, Korean implementation can come across as chaotic. At the same time, much of the waste is not formally recognized by managers during the break-neck rush to get things done within a short time frame. The liability is that this approach works only if the evaluation criteria get it right on the first attempt and the implementation is fortunate enough not to encounter any significant problems. In addition, one would need remarkably capable and experienced people on the implementation team. Getting enough of these positive factors consistently in place, however, is not likely to happen for most companies anywhere in the world.

CREATIVE THINKING FOUND AMONG KOREANS

A common complaint—or should I say stereotype—held by Westerners is that Koreans lack in lateral, critical and creative thinking. At the same time, if one considers the mental capacity one needs to have to properly play a good game of *gō*—or as the Koreans call it, *baduk*—such skills are essential to win against a competent opponent. And not surprisingly, Korea has a sizeable population of capable *baduk* players—several at the master level.

So if there is in fact native critical thinking, one wonders whether Korean technology has been unfairly criticized as only being creative in terms of application rather than original development. Indeed, Korea has generally been thought of as lacking in the development of world-renowned generic products such as Xerox copying. But not even most Koreans know that the world's first MP3 player was created by Saehan Information Systems. Today, Korea's MP3 players are either being outmarketed by Apple or undercut by Chinese knockoffs. So the stereotype remains that Korean engineers adapt others' discoveries to the Korean market and/or improve on original foreign designs for local manufacture and eventual export. At the same time, we should also recognize that Samsung is number two in the world after IBM among corporations with the most registered patents.

So if there are so many who can think laterally, critically, and creatively, why don't we see as much of this thinking in business? Some observations suggest that younger Koreans who do have some or all of these thinking skills are stifled by the authoritarian cultures found in both private and public organizations, where even the brightest are rarely given opportunities to develop their lateral, critical, and creative mental skills. The exceptions are most commonly found in senior top management. Age as well as rank earns these few executives the intellectual freedom often found throughout the ranks of Western company management.

The worst example of suppressed thinking was the tragic Korean Air crash in Guam at the end of the 1990s, when the navigator dared not challenge the pilot's authority in the doomed cockpit. Much of this mindset can be traced to the educational system.

COMPARING KOREAN AND WESTERN EDUCATIONAL SYSTEMS

Many people, including South Korean President Lee Myung-Bak, are very critical of the Korean education systems when compared with those of other countries. When it comes to science and math, Koreans are near the top globally, but when measured in liberal arts and related subjects, students do substantially worse.

The 21st century is presenting many more choices of varying strengths. The traditional "one best way" approach taught in the Korean educational system and enforced in society is proving to be less feasible in the multinational world in which Korea must more effectively compete.

Consider the differences in education between the West and Korea. Western schools teach children essay composition from a young age, starting in grade school with summarizing information as the first, preliminary step. The two systems further diverge in middle school, where Western students learn to outline and prioritize information so as to organize ideas, facts, and known data into a logically structured form. In high school, students are required to conduct original research, where they find sources of information, evaluate what information is relevant, and faithfully cite sources, since plagiarism is considered a serious academic crime deserving severe penalties.

Meanwhile, in Korea children are taught correct answers and methods. There is little effort to teach composition, meaning that quality writing skills are often beyond the capabilities of many college graduates. In middle and high school, students learn by memorizing facts, dates and formulae so as to achieve maximum scores on multiple-choice exams—even in the case of foreign language testing. Assigned "research papers" require students to cite information sources, but they are generally not taught how to organize information into a logically sequenced format. Fundamental evaluation and analysis skills are frequently glossed over or not taught at all. Furthermore, plagiarism in Korea is not considered a very serious academic crime, and teachers even at the graduate school level will often overlook and not bother to check for instances of plagiarism.

Western university graduates, regardless of academic major, are expected to have the fundamental skills to analyze, evaluate, and organize all empirical data, facts, and theories in a logical order; develop and evaluate various possible objectives beyond philosophical ideas and personal prejudices; reveal and analyze all known influencing factors; consider potential future changes and secondary results; construct interim analytical "proofs" to check for gaps in logic; and clearly document all information sources for possible double-checking.

Many Korean university students, after surviving an academic hell of memorizing facts and figures in grade school, essentially take a vacation during their college days. Most have learned the "best" answers or ways of getting by—often uncritically accepting what has been fed to them by their teachers and seniors. There are even stories of Korean university students not being permitted or encouraged to question or develop ideas in front of their professors. The good news is that Korean universities are now beginning to recognize this problem. Several schools are attempting to foster creative thinking, such as by teaching students to summarize readings and critically answer questions rather than simply relying on rote memorization. But we don't know if these fixes are enough to correct the overall problem.

To be fair, as much as we may criticize the Korean education system, the overall Korean situation is nonetheless considerably better than that of America when it comes to student retention through high school and beyond. This may be more a reflection of a highly competitive Confucian society than the education system per se. Regardless, for the average student, the Korean system delivers fundamental education rather well. But when it comes to international competition between top players emerging from the two education systems, the weaknesses and strengths of education systems become obvious.

KOREA'S DOUBLE BLIND SPOT

Today, many, typical Koreans seem to operate with a double blind spot. The first is a lack of critical skills in the organization and prioritization of data, facts and theories; a lack of analysis of information that results in definite conclusions with options for solutions; and a lack of objective evaluation procedures that exclude concerns of what may best please their superiors. The second is the lack of awareness that such skills exist and, critically, that they are being applied by their international competitors.

To further understand this matter, consider the difference in logic between Koreans and Westerners. For example, Westerners—particularly North Americans—often ask, "Is that legal?" In other words, they place a high premium on empirical, relevant, and specific data. Koreans, in contrast, are more likely to ask, "Is that right?" That is, beyond what is factually true or false, Koreans give major consideration to personal, philosophical, and political issues during the logic-building process. Intangible personal and emotional opinions are continually interjected throughout the evaluation process, intermingled with empirical data considerations—often without a "building process" of logic.

This is not to say that one way of thought is necessarily better than the other, but the Western one is more likely to keep thought concentrated on organized facts and data. The Korean thought process is more socially aware and better for cohesive group thinking. But if tough decisions are to be made that extend beyond Korean society, there is something to be said for the Western frame of mind.

To give a recent example, consider what happened in early 2008 when American business professionals visited Korea to discuss leasing land for an engineering project at a government industrial zone. The lease contract being considered didn't specify requirements for a security deposit and maintenance fees. When the foreigners pointed this out, their Korean counterpart responded, "Are you saying you refuse to put up the deposit and pay the common costs?" The Korean then launched into a long, philosophical discussion on the justification of both costs and criticized the "show of bad faith" by the Americans in "questioning" the request for the charges. In other words, they failed to communicate given the differences in logic.

CURRENT KOREAN THINKING IN INTERNATIONAL ARENAS

The problem can be even greater. In a March 2008 edition of Newsweek, there was an excellent account of the Hyundai and Kia success story in America. Yet there have been some new, recent challenges as Hyundai attempts to move from only selling high-quality "econobox," low- and mid-range automobiles to marketing upscale, luxury vehicles in the US$25,000-plus niche.

For the first time in years, the company was substantially missing sales targets. What appears to be lacking in the company's approach is consistent marketing to add luxury value to the equation of basic features and price that has successfully sold the lower-priced cars. In sales, we refer to this element as the "value proposition," where the total value of the product or service is greater than the mere sum of the parts.

Nonetheless, just a year later, the Hyundai Genesis was named "Car of the Year" at the January 2009 Detroit Motor Show. The Genesis became the first Korean car and also the first Asian automobile to win the "North American Car of the Year" award in the large luxury sedan category. Even Hyundai will admit that the main reason for developing the Genesis was a push back against imported, primarily German, luxury sedans in the Korean market. In fact, much of the styling and key components originated in Germany. But all of this makes for a successful marketing strategy: emulate what works best from abroad, redevelop, refine, export—and sell at a lower price than the competition. Still more important, Hyundai created for the Genesis a totally new product development methodology, while spending more effort than in the past in getting both American and Korean driver feedback on prototype vehicles.

Here is one more example: Korean Aerospace Industries, together with Lockheed Martin, has produced arguably the world's best jet trainer, the T-50 Golden Eagle. It is also the world's most expensive. Given its high performance, extreme versatility, quality engineering, and manufacturing, the plane offers a superior value proposition, not only as the ultimate trainer, but, if need be, as a quality attack plane as well. Unfortunately, as of this writing, the planes have not found a buyer outside of Korea. The apparent difficulty is that the Korean sales team is having difficulty positioning this superior product, given that the Koreans may not have yet graduated from the "features, functions and price" school of selling associated with lower-level product sales, which is commonplace in the markets of developing countries.

At the same time, there are some exceptionally bright spots among Korean marketers. Specifically, Samsung Electronics comes to mind. In 2009, Samsung Electronics achieved higher brand equity than Sony, worth US$17.5 billion to the Korean corporation, according to Interbrand, a global marketing company. And that achievement was no accident. Years ago, the former president of Samsung Electronics made some excellent critical decisions. One directive was to consolidate all sub-brands into one "Samsung" brand. The other decision was to focus on "hero" products such as LCD panels, televisions, and cell phones. By "hero," the company meant both creating and marketing premium consumer products. That decision was partially premised on the concern that a large percentage of these products would be consumed abroad, so they did not wish to produce anything that could potentially damage the overall brand of the Samsung Group.

In this way, as Korean companies move up the food chain to create and market products that cannot be produced by competitors in developing countries, they are being forced to market using an advanced sales paradigm that emphasizes the overall value proposition. While some Korean companies are beginning to climb over this hurdle, this is not likely to be an easy task for many other corporations.

When one considers the thousands of young Koreans who live and study in Western countries each year, one would expect to see some of this internationally competitive thinking having a greater impact on Korea. But as we have so often witnessed, when these same young Koreans return to Korea, they are smothered by the *pohm seng pohm sah* ("live and die by form") approach common in lower and middle management. Too often, business measurement data is essentially made up to satisfy the "get it done on time" expectations of superiors. For example, all business students must study cost accounting. But the author has yet to find a Korean company to date earnestly using that and other professional business measurement criteria beyond, at best, going through the motions. Instead, personal politics—often in the form of departmental warfare—reigns supreme. As a result, the actual financial health of a company is often unclear.

To be fair, just as in the US, Koreans companies often succeed simply because their competitors are as ill-managed as themselves. However, American companies got a rude wake-up call in the 1980s when Japanese companies began offering superior quality assurance and inventory control management systems. After initially dismissing the Japanese threat, American companies "faced the music" and revamped important management systems to meet and sometimes beat the Japanese at their own game.

In other words, inferior management and related traditional thinking works well so long as there is no new competition. But that is not the case today, as the Korean marketplace continues to open up to some of the world's most competitive foreign companies and as Koreans companies are being forced by products from newly developing countries to compete more intelligently in advanced markets. Given this, Korean executives need to reassess the competitiveness of their organizations.

QUESTIONS FOR THE FUTURE

In the 21st century, many Korean companies are facing greater global competition. The planning shortcuts summarized above are likely to be costly, not least of all due to waste, and to result in a further drop in competitiveness.

Korean executives may do well to honestly ask themselves and their organizations the following questions:

- Are the academic processes and related business practices that once served Korea well now preventing it from moving up to the next level?

- Should any OECD country's primary industries compete with those from developing countries?

- Can Korean companies expect to successfully compete higher up the food chain, where value propositions can be much more important than simply price and features?

- How well can young Korean employees and their managers "think outside the box" to anticipate foreign competition?

- Can Korean managers develop and execute effective business plans based on the best of all known scenarios? Can they also consider what issues may remain unknown or impossible to define as a means of double-checking their preferred plan of action and developing contingency planning?

A POSSIBLE SET OF SOLUTIONS

Given the above, and presuming that the observations there are largely correct, there may be a need to upgrade professional business skills through training in critical and creative thinking. In the past, both public and private institutions have sent promising young managers abroad for business education. As invaluable as that experience may be, it can be wasteful if, when Koreans return, they are forced by senior management to conform to traditional thinking and traditional business processes once again.

Young college graduates may need some kind of re-education as they cross the critical bridge between their university and business lives. This business skills training program should provide specialized, experience-based training that stresses individual, creative, and analytical thinking that is channeled into critical processes to help future managers and leaders assess and evaluate operational strategies and options.

But before even attempting the above, the seniormost management needs to be on board with this kind of internationally competitive thinking—and fully supportive of this kind of training. So as a first step, executive training would be needed, followed by middle management training. At a minimum, this preliminary training would be required for ongoing operational understanding and appreciation of this new mode of thinking.

Naturally, the training would need to be in line with the organization's philosophies and yet still foster creativity and the freedom to help take the company to the next level. As such, the natural tendency among many Korean organizations may be to develop this kind of training internally. There are some strong plusses and minuses to doing so.

The plusses would include certain managerial control to ensure that young employees are keeping in line with the overall company philosophy. Also, if there is a sophisticated training group within the company, it may be possible to develop this program so that it effectively impacts all levels of managers and employees. Finally, this kind of internal education is more likely to be incorporated into the regular budgeting processes as opposed to special one-off training expenses.

The minuses of creating and facilitating this kind of program as internal education are as follows. First, there may be a lack of adequate internal experience and knowledge in this form of business skills innovation. Training should be done by a mature, world-class faculty—possibly recruited from the U.S. or Europe and possessing international experience, ideally matched up with local trainers who understand Korean education systems and managerial thinking processes.

Second, while the overall direction and content should be developed in concert with senior management, the program itself needs some autonomy, free from the many political influences that exist in any organization found anywhere in the world.

Third, the training program needs to develop its own integrity, based primarily on global thinking and competition—and away from the natural organizational trends generated by in-group thinking. The program's primary mission is to help young Korean managers to be globally competitive by being able to employ out-of-the-box thinking in their planning. If placed within the formal control of the greater organization, there may be a danger of the program's key mission being subordinated to contemporary political developments, when in fact the value of this kind of education is for the long-term well-being of the organization.

A Six-Point Development Program for Global Business Leaders is what the author specifically recommends to address the above concerns. This is just an example, but in any case, the core of any program would need to be based on specific training in analytical thinking and create problem-solving abilities. The following is an example of what might make up the curriculum's training modules:

1. World-Class Analytical Thinking and Creative Problem-Solving

2. Global Strategic Planning and Effective Implementation

3. Disciplined International Negotiation for Agreements and Results

4. Building and Maintaining Strong Global Customer and Employee Relationships

5. Optimizing Efficiency through Strong Multinational Team Leadership

6. Communicating Effectively in All Directions—At Home and Abroad

FINAL CONSIDERATIONS

Today, Korea's executives are reassessing international competitive pressures daily. These pressures are certain only to increase on both domestic and global markets.

The old saw of the last century was to "think globally and act locally." Increasingly, however, this shrinking globalized world is forcing everyone to "think globally and compete locally everywhere." Preferred work patterns and mindsets need to be regularly assessed as to whether they are helping or hindering organizational competitiveness, both abroad and now even at home. What is ultimately being advocated here is professional business skills training that focuses on critical and creative thinking.

Executives, when pondering whether and/or how much of this kind of training is really needed, could do worse than to ruthlessly ask themselves the following questions:

- Is my company at an internationally competitive crossroads where new strategies are essential for medium- and long-term survivability of the corporation?

- Does our company's decision-making adequately address our expected—and unanticipated—challenges?

- What are the real costs—not just the reported expenses—of our planning and implementation efforts in situations when we have to frequently react to unforeseen events?

- Do our products, sales strategies, and personnel seem to be in sync or out of sync with the rest of the global market?

4. UNDERSTANDING KOREAN MANAGEMENT

*T*he Korean business enterprise has accomplished an almost unduplicated feat over the last five decades. From the ashes of one of the most devastating wars in the early 1950s, an economic miracle has occurred that has won the admiration of both the developing and industrialized nations. With a multi-billion dollar turnover and tens of thousands of employees, once exotic names like Hyundai, Samsung and LG have become familiar around the world. Their prosperity and success are, no doubt, the result of the rank and file of those organizations.

A powerful drive motivates this teeming manpower in one of the world's most densely populated areas, a drive that has made them productive and loyal to the industrial team. There must be something unique that unifies and motivates the labor force of these huge organizations despite a relatively short history of modern management. The foreign businessperson must understand some of the underlying forces that make these industrial organizations work, and pinpoint some of the cultural patterns, psychological factors, and historical influences that have converged on the labor force at this point in history. By doing so, foreign business executives may understand how to harness the Korean labor force's potential.

ORGANIZATIONAL LOYALTY

Hard work and dedication to one's profession and organization are regarded as a virtue and have become a social norm. Anyone who is not in conformity with this value system is simply not accepted, sometimes not even by his own wife. She finds it difficult to understand the fact that her husband finishes his work at 6 p.m. every evening while other neighborhood husbands return home late in the evening, apparently because of important business activities. She wants to boast that her husband is involved in some important business, even though it may detain him with late working hours.

Many large companies on the growing edge require a working day that begins at 8:30 a.m. and does not end until about the same time in the evening. Some departments of these companies find it necessary during especially busy seasons to keep their office staff on the job until almost midnight, occasionally checking into a motel and burning the candle all night long. These extended hours are gradually decreasing in some companies. At the same time, somehow, the long workday verifies the sense of loyalty that the company expects and receives from its employees. It should be noted that there is no other force more powerful than peer pressure in formulating human behavior.

Another phenomenon that cultivates company loyalty is the equating of personal goals with company goals. With Korea being an export-dependent economy, all major companies export a large portion of their goods and services. The size of the nation and its population restricts the production level for the domestic market. The saturation point for many consumer products is quickly reached, so the survival and prosperity of the nation is inescapably dependent on exports. In such a firm, an employee's best effort will help to bring prosperity to the company and to the employee personally, and ultimately—and perhaps most importantly—to the nation. This strong form of patriotism—what foreigners may view as ultra-nationalism— manifests itself in pride in Korean exports and anxiety about consuming imports.

A sense of loyalty does not just happen. The traditional Confucian background, as well as humane and paternalistic leadership, provides the foundation for employee dedication to the company. Judging by the results in productivity and quality, it works. It's the bread and butter for the employee, the company, and, ultimately, for the nation.

This sense of loyalty and reciprocal evidence of company concern for its personnel even work at a Korean LG plant established in Huntsville, Alabama. Many doubted that the Korean management philosophy known as "*inhwa*" (meaning "human harmony") could be applied to the American labor situation. This two-sided coin of company loyalty and personnel concern has resulted in an absenteeism rate of around one percent, compared to the national average of 5 percent, and a profound improvement in the quality control rejection rate on the production line, which emphasizes the concern for excellence.

FOUNDER'S CONVICTION

As Korea's industrialization history is short, the children of most major corporation founders are still at the helm of their enterprises. Their fathers were noted for a strong will to succeed, contagious zeal, self-sacrificing dedication, and vision for the future—common traits evident among these pioneering, self-made entrepreneurs. Even today, the spirit of the first generation of founders remains fairly strong. It may not be like the past, when the founder's spirit was contagious and permeated every nook and cranny of their organizations, but the next generation of corporate leaders tries to emulate their fathers' examples by personally communicating to their workers. This is one reason for the driving force behind Korean organizations even to this day.

One almost fanatical general-turned-businessman, for example, built one of the largest steel mills in the world from scratch within a decade. Behind the build-up of the world's second largest shipbuilding industry, there was absolutely nothing but dogged determination and the tenacious will to succeed. It is common practice in these burgeoning corporations for every battalion of new recruits to be routinely drilled for months; this is where they are instilled with the founding father's philosophy and spirit.

Still, as these businesses have burst beyond the bounds of the founder's personal supervision and the new generations have come up without experiencing the hardships of the '50s and '60s, the founding spirit of the companies has become diluted. The initial zeal and the most conspicuous legacy that was left to influence the mental and psychological backbone of the oncoming generation have dimmed.

PATERNALISM

Companies tend to function like families: loyalty and long-term service are expected from the employee, in return for a secure position and a sense of belonging. In Western companies, paternalism by the company toward employees is considered objectionable by most people, particularly by upper-level management and higher-educated professional specialists. In Korean companies, however, it is expected and desired. The prospective new employee looks beyond the basic financial remuneration to what additional benefits, privileges, and allowances are offered.

Management demonstrates this by giving personal attention to the individual needs of employees and their families. Regular bonuses are proportioned to be paid at special occasions such as kimchi-making time and family occasions like Chuseok (Korean Thanksgiving). Special bonuses are paid for family funerals and school entrance fees. The employee would be disappointed and feel ill-treated if these paternalistic considerations were not provided—even though these practices have been considerably reduced as employment and compensation systems have become more transparent and contractual.

A number of companies provide recreational facilities such as tennis courts and dormitories for single employees working at factories. So paternalistic attitudes and activities are expected from management. Indeed, this may be a unique reason for the remarkable success of industrial enterprises in their approach to labor management relations.

HIERARCHICAL ORGANIZATION

In a Confucian society, each individual has a distinctive position in terms of rank in the hierarchy. The business organization is no exception.

Most firms, especially those employing large numbers of blue-collar workers, have adopted a military-style system in their organization. Almost all men are required to serve in the military. While this may be a hardship for the individual and undesirable or disruptive for the company, the positive legacy that this experience has indelibly carved on the national psyche is the concept of establishing a clear chain of command, which is suited to the Confucian social structure. Cultivating a sense of responsibility and training in leadership are outer by-products of this national duty for local managers and organizations. So companies have adopted this basic infrastructure essential for the administration of those large business organizations.

In actual application, this business hierarchy system has an extensive series of "*jangs*" ("chiefs" or "managers"). Though the numbers vary, there are as many as a dozen in some companies. The *jangs* on the lowest level, the *gye-jangs*, may each supervise fewer than ten people, and usually have very little decision-making authority.

In this hierarchical structure, the so-called seniority system is given greater consideration than the merit system, even though it has gone through some evolution due to rapidly changing technology and the shorter life cycle of products.

MODERN CHALLENGES TO FAMILY CORPORATIONS

Most medium-sized Korean corporations, and even some large-sized ones, are less than fifty years old. As such, most chairmen and CEOs are the sons and sometimes daughters of the companies' founders. While many members of this second generation are capable business professionals—

with a large percentage of them possessing prestigious advanced degrees from foreign universities—a large percentage work closely under the supervision of their retired fathers.

What struck the authors who have worked with several of these second-generation business leaders is how rare it seems that any of them can conduct a business meeting. Rather, by the force of their positions, these second-generation executives exercise a fiat-based management style that would be regarded in other countries as flippant and chaotic.

Much of the continued success of some of these family-owned companies is based on long-term business relations established by the founders. When the founders eventually retire, many companies are pulled apart by competing offspring, leading to large internal—and sometimes external—divisions.

Consequently, the common belief among many Koreans is that one really often doesn't know the true capability of an entrepreneurial family until the third generation. If a company can continue to build and grow under third-generation leadership, totally separated in time from the founder's direction and influence, then the family company has proven to the market that it is

| OFFICE WORKER TITLES |

English Equivalent	Korean Title	Literal Translation
Chairman, Board of Directors	*Hwoe-jang*	Chairman of Board
President	*Sa-jang* (*Dae-pyo I-sa*)	President (Representative Director)
Vice President	*Bu Sa-jang*	Vice President
Managing Director	*Chun-mu I-sa*	Principle Director
Director	*Sangmu Isa*	Standing Director
Department Manager or Section General Manager	*Bujang*	Department Chief
Assistant Department Manager	*Chajang*	Vice Department Chief
Section Manager or Supervisor	*Gwajang*	Section Chief
Assistant Section Manager	*Daeri*	Deputy Chief
Senior Clerk	*Juim*	Principle Job
Clerk	*Gyewon* (*Pyung Sawon*)	Branch Member (Ordinary Company Member)

TABLE 3.1

LIST OF JOB TITLES (IN RANK ORDER)
[ENGLISH PRONUNCIATION USING NON-STANDARD ROMANIZATION]

being properly managed for the long haul.

In any event, of course, companies largely succeed or fail due to the managerial and leadership skills of their executives, regardless of family connections. But as one interfaces with these family-owned enterprises, one should be aware of what may the underlining realities of current realities. Often, today's success may be the result of the current generation's business acumen. But sometimes, a family-controlled company could be living on borrowed time as the legacy foundations deteriorate.

CARROT AND STICK

While Korean companies may look more humane and considerate of their employees, the standard of performance is rather rigorously applied. The poor performers or non-performers are subject to harsh disciplinary action, while the winners are always pampered with generous prizes or various material benefits, as well as recognition or citations by top management.

Reward and punishment may be universal in managing people. They seem, however, to be more strictly and extensively applied in Korean business organizations. *"Shin sang pil bol"* (the Korean term for "carrot and stick") is frequently adopted as one of the major personnel policies by many companies emphasizing "reward and punishment."

The competitive spirit of Koreans, perhaps originating from early educational training as well as from their own higher aspirations, may make them more susceptible to such stimuli as recognition and incentives.

GROUP ORIENTATION

The Koreans, somewhat like the Japanese, are quite group-oriented. People tend to be identified by a group rather than as individuals, and their society as a whole is knitted together by ties and relationships in groups and organizations.

In large business organizations, rewards and punishments are even meted out collectively. Managers try to capitalize on this trait by developing a culture of belonging. One of the ways they do this is by encouraging workers to share a common value and commitment, sometimes creating some slogan or motto under which all employees can unite.

So it is not uncommon for employees to share their concerns and gripes together so as to attain group objectives and consensus, although each has different responsibilities. The resulting camaraderie and cohesiveness among employees always contribute to greater productivity in the organization.

PROMOTION OR TERMINATION

When the foreign visitor first deals with corporate bureaucracies, certain aspects may seem almost quaint. In time, however, the foreigner may conclude there are some illogical aspects that greatly affect overall organizational behavior, often creating what seems to the unfamiliar Westerner to be counterproductive behavior.

A paternalistic, family-type corporate environment works fairly well, so long as there is a constant demand for young, bright, malleable, and lesser-paid employees. As employees mature and assume greater responsibilities, however, there is the expected reduction in available jobs. Even taking into consideration voluntary turnover of employees as individuals seek their fortunes elsewhere, general management routinely struggles with an excess of middle-aged managers.

The solution seems to be a page out of the military. Ultimately, most middle managers are involuntarily retired before they hit age 55. Some corporations have an unwritten rule that a certain percentage (say, 10 percent) of all executive contracts are not renewed each January so as to allow a few of the best senior managers a chance to be promoted to the next, higher level. By the same token, many middle managers in their 50s find themselves with termination notices at the beginning of the New Year. Since most corporate managers generally hope to work until age 65, termination coming in their early to mid-50s is a traumatic event feared as many turn forty.

FEAR AND LOATHING IN DEPARTMENTAL POLITICS

Given the overriding fear of early retirement, individual reputations become of paramount concern for department managers and their bosses. Interdepartmental cooperation is minimized, since to ask for advice and assistance outside of one's work group or department is, in effect, to publicly admit to the rest of the company that there is some lack of expertise or knowledge within that sector. This situation is exacerbated by routine shuffling at least once a year. As a result, Korean companies are staffed with many generalists and relatively few specialists at the middle and senior levels of management.

Middle managers and even executives will therefore go to great lengths not to ask for direct assistance from personnel outside of their departments, unless such a request is routinely expected without fear of loss of face or damage to one's reputation. What may be considered a routine request by Western standards to someone outside of one's department may be viewed in Korea as an admission of incompetence.

As a result, if information or assistance is ultimately required from outside of the department, the request almost never travels horizontally, such as to a peer in another department. Rather, the request must travel upward to a senior manager or executive whose span of management control extends over to the other department. The request then descends to that other department from on high. If the request is acted upon at all, the reply traces its reverse course, and almost never directly over to the original party. Needless to say, this approach is hardly time-efficient, and it is often one of the main reasons why foreigners are confused about how simple requests take surprisingly long periods of time to be acted upon.

Another consequence of this dilemma is that projects are often done on time without critical input from other departments. Again, the fear individual managers have regarding loss of reputation preempts what other countries may consider rational action. At the same time, anything that may touch a department—such as a business transaction—demands visible action proving or validating that manager's worthiness to the corporation. Extraneous requests for information or demands for modification are routine. To allow a matter to pass through a department with minimal comment or action may be interpreted as an indication of the irrelevance of the department and/or the incompetence of the manager.

All of these matters may at times seem a bit irrational in the short run, but each senior manager and executive routinely frets how he or she may be viewed and what may transpire behind closed doors—particularly each December, as the top executives decide who is promoted, who stays, and who is terminated.

GOVERNMENT

The influence of the government is omnipresent. The nickname "Korea, Inc." is no exaggeration.

The government and businesses have worked together very closely to accelerate the industrialization of the nation. Without the sanction of the government such as preferential financing, technological supports, and administrative guidance, no business of any size could have expected to prosper. Close collaboration between businesses and the government has made positive contributions in efforts to ensure the most effective utilization of limited resources in the process of industrialization, even though there have been some inescapable side effects.

Even today, understanding the direction of general policy and maintaining close communication with the relevant branch of the government bureaucracy are very important to any aspiring entrepreneur. While Korean companies can normally count on building up long-term relations between their top executives and key bureaucrats, foreign companies often face a different problem given the peculiarities of starting up local operations. How foreign companies may effectively deal with this issue is discussed in this book's chapters on PR and dealing with bureaucrats.

A NEW STYLE

A perhaps unique Korean management style has evolved from the underlying Confucian culture as the nation has gone through rapid industrialization. In a country where people are the only major resource, more effort has had to be made on managing people. As a result, a distinctive management model that is essentially Confucian while trying to incorporate modern management techniques has started to take shape.

Korea's management practices and theories are subject to the test of time. Their applicability to other cultures is still questionable. Regardless, understanding them may help expatriate managers to develop more efficient and productive organizations in Korea—especially when trying to find a proper mix between the best of both national and corporate cultures.

5. GETTING A HANDLE ON INFORMATION

*T*he newly arrived business professional in the "Land of the Morning Calm" quickly discovers the initial orientation to be a bit less than a calm experience. If it is not immediately obvious, it soon becomes apparent that doing business in a strange culture, via new personal relationships and by a different set of rules, will be a challenge. The foreign businessperson must tap into information and develop expertise on how to do business in Korea. More importantly, he or she must know where to go for help. The author hopes this book may be a good start, but additional resources are, of course, needed.

The Korean marketplace is one of the most dynamic in Asia, with developments happening at Internet speed—and where, incidentally, Internet broadband is virtually everywhere. To illustrate, over 95 percent of households have broadband access. To add to the complexity of doing business in Korea, most of the information is in the Korean language—though English translations are quickly becoming routinely available. While most international business and economic news is available in English, most of the local business news remains only in Korean for the intended and primary benefit of the local business community. Very little is available in English for the foreign businessperson to learn about local industry and business procedures.

Information is a perishable commodity anywhere; however, it seems to be more so in Korea, where there is an especially rapid and profound transition constantly taking place. Much to the dismay of foreign researchers, various organizations often publish conflicting information—particularly statistics. It is also well known that Korean companies are reluctant to release information to outsiders, even if it is not considered confidential.

Given that this is the 21st century with its rapidity of change, it is somewhat useless to give a listing of telephone numbers and addresses in this book—especially when we are talking about one of the most wired economies in the world.

KOREAN GOVERNMENT

- KOTRA (Korea Trade Promotion Investment Association; check out the section on Invest Korea at www.investkorea.org)

• Seoul Global Center (this site offers Seoul resident foreigners some practical assistance that goes beyond simple business requirements. It may be found at http://global.seoul.go.kr).

HELPFUL BLOGS

The following is a list of helpful blog websites provided by a British PR director who uses these blogs to keep abreast of Korean current events beyond what is provided in the traditional English media. Since URL addresses change, one may have to employ a search engine to find a blog's name. Like all blogs, one has to take the information with a grain of salt, but the following will help one keep current on what's happening in Korea:

Coyners @ Home in Korea (www.tomcoyner.com) is an irregularly updated site, but its "Understanding Korea" offers a better-than-average collection of essays and articles collected over the years, organized by topic.

Korea Business Central (www.koreabusinesscentral.com). This is a new and very lively website that acts more like an online Korea business news service, focusing on local, primarily foreign businesspeople and others whose work impacts on business.

Marmot's Hole (www.rjkoehler.com) provides a robust collection of articles, photographs and commentary on Korean current events. Its "Korea Blog Aggregator" is particularly interesting.

GI Korea (http://rokdrop.com). Now known as "ROK Drop," it provides a series of worthwhile analyses, often from a military perspective, since the blogmaster is a career US Army officer

Brian in Jeollanam-do (http://briandeutsch.blogspot.com). There is much more to Korea than just Seoul! To get an ongoing perspective on what is happening as viewed from outside of the nation's capital, this is an excellent place to begin.

Korea Beat (http://us.asiancorrespondent.com/korea-beat). This is a subsection of an Asia-Pacific web site, Asian Correspondent, that endeavors to stay on top of things of interest in this part of the world.

Monster Island (www.monster-island.net). This Korea-centric blog is very deserving of a regular inspection.

Gusts of Popular Feeling (http://populargusts.blogspot.com) provides well-researched and thoughtful commentary on modern Korean history and is well worth the read.

Eclexys (www.gordsellar.com) is very eclectic, but it is done in Korea, and often there are some interesting pieces worth checking out.

Korean News Feeds (http://koreannewsfeeds.com). Wish to scan what is showing up in today's mass media, including popular blog sites, regarding Korea? One is likely to find it in a glance here. The site stays on top of 35 English language newspapers and blog sites, hotlinking to the most current articles.

One Free Korea (http://freekorea.us) is a well-informed but highly critical look at North Korea by a Washington-based attorney and North Korean human rights activist.

CHAMBERS OF COMMERCE

All chambers of commerce have their ups and downs depending on who is hired and volunteering for work within these business groups. It may be a "no brainer" to join the chamber of one's own nationality or the head office's. The membership fees may be cheap for firms just entering Korea; however, the real cost will be one's time, since only by active participation will any chamber of commerce be of real value.

Long-term foreign business professionals often belong to more than one chamber, since it doesn't necessarily follow that the chamber of their nationality will best serve their business needs. If one feels it only makes sense to belong to just one chamber, one may wish to survey which chambers are doing what and consider joining a chamber that best suits one's business area and not necessarily one's nationality. Most chambers look great on paper or on the Web, but it's wise to consult with established expats to get their impressions. If a chamber lists a committee that seems relevant to one's business, get the name of the current committee chairperson and contact that person to learn how often the committee has actually met recently and what kinds of activities the committee is actually doing.

Finally, all of the chambers of commerce sponsor business networking events. Understandably, the bigger chambers hold the biggest events, but be aware that these large events often attract large numbers of local businesses that depend on expats by providing services including personnel placement, relocation/moving, travel, and housing. These "camp followers"—who can be found at some of the events, since they often join the largest chambers—can be a bit of a nuisance in their excessive numbers. Conversely, since the smaller chambers are less attractive to these expatriate service providers, their presence is less noticeable, and the overall quality of business networking may be better.

ONE'S EMBASSY

Most Western nations have embassies with some kind of commercial service. As may be expected, the larger nations tend to have the better commercial services. Regardless, one should remember that while highly educated and dedicated personnel staff these commercial services, one would be dealing with people who have chosen careers in government rather than in business. No matter how wonderful their attitudes may be—and often they really do wish to be helpful—their perspectives and priorities tend to be different from those of business professionals. Rarely is their on-hand information as up-to-date and specific as one's requirements demand—but one can get lucky. On the other hand, the US, UK, Australian and other embassies can, for a very reasonable fee, commission special market research projects on one's behalf. So if other avenues fail, one's embassy may be of service.

SOCIAL ORGANIZATIONS

Private clubs such as the Seoul Club can provide premier environments to make the right connections—but they come with extremely hefty (refundable) deposits. Total membership costs may be higher than similar organizations in even Hong Kong or Tokyo. Nonetheless, they are exclusive and offer facilities and services that may be suitable for business entertaining as well as for expatriate family members. There are other membership clubs, but the Seoul Club is currently the best-known international club among Western expatriates and their families.

Interesting alternatives include the Seoul Foreign Correspondents' Club, which offers memberships for non-journalists at reasonable fees and is situated at a convenient location just behind Seoul City Hall on the 18th floor of the Seoul Press Center. The British Embassy has come up with a clever way to offer a very good venue for networking while ensuring that their diplomats are in sync with the business community. On most Friday evenings, they open up a pub called Broughton's Club in their basement, with their diplomats serving as publicans. Attendance and membership are by invitation by a current member only, but there are no fees to join, and the beverages at Broughton's are among the least expensive in town. Not all members are British, and many "old Korea hands" start their Friday nights here.

Public service clubs are remarkably common in Korea, including Lions, Kiwanis, and Rotary. However, only Rotary Club of Seoul (www. seoulrotary.com) is an English-language club, with more than three-quarters of a century of service to the Korean community. Rotary membership is two-thirds Korean professionals and executives and one-third foreigners, with Germans and Americans competing for the largest membership share among expatriates. Through the weekly luncheon lectures and public service activities with Korean Rotarians, many foreign executives and managers have gained special insights into Korea and its business culture.

For more than a century, the Royal Asiatic Society, Korea Branch, has offered somewhat academic yet very accessible insights into Korean culture, history, politics, geography, and natural science. During most months of the year, the RAS provides free lectures on the second and fourth Tuesday of the month at 7:30 p.m. The RAS is famous for its modestly priced non-profit tours led by knowledgeable subject matter experts on weekends and occasionally weekdays. For more information on this club—popular with academics, diplomats and business professionals alike—go to www.raskb. com.

Finally, there are a number of churches and religious organizations that conduct services in English or other foreign languages. Often, strong and valuable friendships with both Koreans and foreigners can be made within these gatherings that can serve one well during one's stay in Korea. The local English daily newspapers frequently list such religious bodies, as do the English-language monthly magazines, which are found in major hotels and restaurants frequented by foreigners.

ENGLISH PERIODICALS

Newspapers (three in English), economic dailies and business journals are excellent sources of information. The Economist often has decent updates and summaries on doing business in Korea, and this English magazine can be found easily in major bookstores and international hotels. Also, the three English newspapers, including The Korea Times, The Korean Herald, and the JoongAng Daily, have decent English websites worth regular scanning. Meanwhile, SEOUL Magazine is an English-language culture and lifestyle monthly that has valuable event information. Other magazines that can be good information sources include 10, Eloquence and Groove. Since Korea is one of the most online societies in the world, it takes relatively little effort to keep a lookout for articles in these periodicals and to develop one's own sources of information directly revelant to one's particular personal interests. With just a little effort, a foreign executive can take advantage of these almost-free resources.

CONDUCTING CROSSCHECKS

Most available information is collected and processed for different purposes, with different sets of criteria and definitions being used. It is essential to compare and check information from different sources against each other. To secure nearly accurate information, it is sometimes necessary to hit a median among a varying range of numbers on the same subject. For example, production figures published by a government agency may differ from those reported by industrial associations, due to the use of different sets of criteria.

As anywhere, one should weigh the source of information to determine whether the organization has some vested interest in making itself look good in the reporting of certain numerical information. It will probably be necessary to consult with other informed persons to help weigh the level of bias in a given piece of reporting.

DRAWING ON INSIDE PERSONNEL

The Korean personnel of any business organization are another valuable source of information. They can be an extensive reserve of information. By consulting with and inquiring of them, one can also increase rapport and develop working relationships. Sometimes, if one's staff does not have the needed information at their fingertips, they may still have access to sources through personal ties to whom they can refer the expatriate executive. At any rate, fellow workers will still have far more accurate information on a given situation than the new foreign businessperson relying on his or her own "guesstimates."

CONTACTING PROFESSIONALS

There are an increasing number of professional organizations that are developing a bank of information on national business and economy. In addition to CPAs, lawyers, and government-sponsored research organizations, market research firms and consultants cater to the needs of international businesses. Services offered by such research firms will undoubtedly prove to be more economical and accurate than if one were to ferret out this information by oneself. In addition, these research firms can custom-tailor research information to suit the particular needs of the client.

One of the common causes for regret is not getting professional advice early and only seeking it "after the horses have left the barn." Also, when it comes to compensation surveys like polling, there is a tendency for Korean respondents to give out "public" information, in spite of confidentiality assurances from surveyors. Consequently, the accumulated information can be a bit more sweet or sour than the actual, depending on circumstances.

"OLD KOREA HANDS"

Every port has its own, and Seoul certainly boasts its share of long-term foreign residents who range from the wise to the simply colorful. Many are conversant to near-bilingual speakers of Korean with in-depth experience. However, having said that, one must be careful. Like people everywhere, old Korea hands' views of reality are usually based on strong opinions that may or may not be current with the changing reality. While these folks generally have the better handle on what is going on, newcomers with unprejudiced perspectives can do a better job of picking up on the latest trends and changes in Korea. So our final advice is to listen well—but keep one's wits about one at all times. When in doubt, one should compare one's newly acquired wisdom with what one hears from other old Korea hands and Korean colleagues—then draw one's own conclusions.

UPDATING PERIODICALLY

In a dynamic environment, information becomes obsolete fast. As such, there are times when extrapolation of past data in future projections is not valid.

With increasing affluence and the development of mass communication and transportation, the lifestyle of the Korean people is changing rapidly. The pace of change is so fast and profound that extreme care must be exercised in developing a firm hold on the domestic market and industry situation.

HOW TO KEEP A HANDLE

To keep in touch with and feel the pulse of the throbbing business heart, gathering information and developing expertise are imperative. These can be gleaned with some time and effort. The above suggestions may enable the expatriate to know what resources are available and how to compile a mine of materials for business development.

The chart on the following page can also provde a head start on how to find one's way among professional organizations and the government. Most of these organizations have information available in English.

| INFORMATION SOURCES |

Information	Primary Sources	Secondary Sources	Sources of Specific Information
General Information on Korean Economy and Industries	MOFE, KIET, embassies	banks, accounting firms, foreign chambers	publications, (especially from such institutes as SERI)
Industry-Specific Information	trade/industry associations	KCCI, FKI, KITA, KOTRA	professional services
Trade & Investment Regulations	MOFE, SMIPC, KITA, MOFAT, KCCI, MOCIE	foreign embassies & chambers	professional services
Technology	KAIST,KDI, KIET, MOST	trade & industry associations	professional services
Distributor/Partner Company Backgrounds	KCGF, Banks	trade & industry associations	professional services
Marketing & Distribution	market research organizationsmarket research organizations	advertising agencies	professional services
Factory Locations	MOCIE, MOCT, provincial & city governments	real estate agents	professional services

Acronym	Full Name
KCCI	Korea Chamber of Commerce & Industry
KDI	Korea Development Institute
FKI	Federation of Korean Industries
KCGF	Korea Guarantee Fund
KIET	Korea Institute for Economics & Trade
KOTRA	Korea Trade-Investment Promotion Agency
KITA	Korea International Trade Association

Acronym	Full Name
MOFE	Ministry of Finance & Economy
MOST	Ministry of Science & Technology
SMIPC	Small and Medium Industry Promotion Corporation
MOFAT	Ministry of Foreign Affairs & Trade
SERI	Samsung Economic Research Institute
MOCT	Ministry of Construction & Transportation
MOCIE	Ministry of Commerce, Industry & Energy

© YONHAP PHOTO

PART II.
PUTTING YOUR BEST FOOT FORWARD

6. 11 COMMANDMENTS FOR DOING BUSINESS IN KOREA

I. THOU SHALT ALWAYS HAVE A FORMAL INTRODUCTION

If one is a Korean, it is most important and advisable to have a formal introduction to any person or company with whom one wants to do business. Meeting the right people in a company almost always depends on having the right introduction. Whenever possible, obtain introductions rather than making contacts directly or just popping in on a businessman. Use of the proper intermediary or go-between is desirable in business meetings. If the person whom one wishes to meet has respect for one's intermediary, chances are he or she will have equal respect for that person, too.

II. THOU SHALT NOT BE WITHOUT BUSINESS CARDS

In Korea, every person has a distinctive place in an organizational hierarchy. A businessman is not comfortable until he knows what company and what position the person he has just met is from. Therefore, the exchange of business cards in Korea is critical, a formal affair that plays a very important role in introductions.

One should have calling cards made prior to visiting companies and keep plenty on hand at all occasions. When exchanging cards with someone, one should try to hand the card to the other person with both hands. If that is physically awkward, one should hand the card over with the right hand—never with the left hand, even if one is naturally left-handed—and place the left hand at one's right arm or elbow or against one's chest.

Once the other person's card has been received, one should never place it immediately into one's pocket. One should always take a few seconds to study it in the other's presence, closely examining the card for the person's details, including name and title, as a way of showing one holds the other party in respect. It is good manners to always show interest in the other person's position. Particularly in a Confucian culture, the card signifies a person's status, and one needs to demonstrate interest. Given that, it goes without saying that one should never fondle or fold a person's card, as this is considered insulting. Traditionally it was taboo to write on the card, but these days writing a date is acceptable. After the exchange, one may place the card on the table in front of one and proceed with the meeting, using it for further reference.

While it is a good idea to have bilingual cards printed up with English on one side and Korean on the other, it is a terrible idea to use one's bilingual Japanese-English cards (unless one is based out of Japan). Though many Koreans can read Japanese, to casually or deliberately give them such a card is highly insulting, given Korea's lingering sensitivity from the Japanese colonial period.

III. THOU SHALT NOT ASSUME EVERYTHING THOU SAYEST IN ENGLISH IS COMPLETELY UNDERSTOOD

Remember that the real level of comprehension possessed by many English-speaking businessmen may not be as good as their courtesy implies. Their perception can be, and often is, surprisingly remote from what one thinks one is getting across to them. For one thing, out of consideration of "face," Koreans often will not admit they are not following one's explanation. Also, cultural barriers are sometimes bigger than they may appear on the surface. One should take pains to emphasize and repeat one's key points for their understanding. Try speaking in short, grammatically correct sentences using simple vocabulary. Sometimes it is a good idea to ask questions to verify the other person's understanding, while taking care not to embarrass that person in front of others. One should try diagramming one's points rather than simply using English. Exchanging notes after meetings is very helpful for this purpose.

IV. THOU SHALT REFRAIN FROM PUSHING THY POSITION TOO HARD

Korean businessmen are internationally believed to be good negotiators. Be prepared to be patient, gentle but firm, and as dignified as possible at a negotiating table. Do not try to push a position too hard. Sensitive issues and details may be skipped for future discussions—preferably left to a go-between or one's staff, if available. The use of go-betweens can be very valuable, especially in delicate dealings where financial negotiations are involved. One should allow sufficient time for one's counterparts to consider their options. Their decisions are usually made collectively and often require more time than one may expect. Often, the real decision-maker is not at the negotiating table, in spite of one's negotiating partner's business title suggesting otherwise.

V. THOU SHALT BUILD HUMAN RELATIONSHIPS

Legal documents are not as important as human rapport and relationships. Koreans do not like detailed contracts. They prefer, and often insist, that contracts be left flexible enough that adjustments can be made to fit changing circumstances. Therefore, it is very important to develop and foster good relationships based on mutual trust and benefit in addition to the business contract. To a Korean businessman, the important thing about a contract is not so much what is stipulated, but rather who signed it and the fact that it exists. Do not be surprised when a business partner immediately asks for exceptions to a recently signed contract due to unforeseen business circumstances. This is normal business, but, of course, it takes sound as well as flexible judgment to decide when to say "yes" and when to say "no."

VI. THOU SHALT RESPECT THY PARTNER

Koreans are extremely sensitive people. Never cause them to "lose face" by putting them in a difficult position. On the contrary, offer praise for a partner's business successes. Their state of good feelings, or *gibun*, can do wonders far beyond one's expectations. And, of course, one also benefits from the good mood created. At the same time, be aware that there are smooth "foreigner handlers" who flatter by insisting that one "understands Korea better than other foreigners" and that one therefore can see beyond sound business logic thanks to one's "cultural insight."

VII. THOU SHALT ENTERTAIN AND BE ENTERTAINED

Entertainment plays an important role in any business relationship. When offered entertainment, one should always accept and in some way reciprocate in due time. Parties are often drinking competitions. One's capacity of alcohol consumption may be one of the deciding factors that can lead to a successful business negotiation and relationship. One may be expected to get intoxicated, but one has the right to politely hold the line. Legitimate reasons for drinking little or none include personal health conditions and religious beliefs. At the same time, symbolic or token drinking can be done as a substitute when accompanied by a positive and friendly attitude. The giving of small gifts is also an accepted practice and is recommended. Golf is a popular form of entertainment. Join the game as often as possible.

VIII. THOU SHALT TRY TO KNOW THY COUNTERPART

Try to personalize all business relationships. An informal agreement with a trusted party can be considered far more secure than any written document. One should try to find out as much about one's counterparts as possible, including but not limited to details about their family status, hobbies, philosophies and birthdays. One should try balancing one's social life with regular activities with Koreans and not simply people of one's own and/or similar cultures. Even if one cannot speak Korean, there are a number of groups largely comprised of Koreans who are bilingual, such as churches, civic organizations and special interest clubs. Even if these extracurricular activities have no direct impact on one's business, one can gain invaluable insight into the Korean mind through active participation. Furthermore, since Korea is a tight-knit society, what may begin as an association for non-business reasons may evolve over time into valuable introductions to others important to one's future business.

IX. THOU SHALT TEMPER THE USE OF WESTERN LOGIC

Do not try to appeal too much to Western logic, but try instead to find "emotional common denominators." Feelings and "face" are often far more important in local business dealings. A willingness to compromise without giving up one's core values is an invaluable skill anywhere, but it is an ability that will serve one particularly well in Korea. Spend some time reading up on Confucianism. Then observe and inquire on how it operates in the workplace and elsewhere. The sooner one does this, the more natural finding appropriate points of compromise and knowing where to draw the line between Korean and Western logic will be.

X. THOU SHALT KEEP FULLY INFORMED

Be aware of the fact that many changes are taking place at an unprecedented pace in current society. With increasing affluence and the development of mass communication, the lifestyle of Korean consumers is changing rapidly. Changes in their fashions, diet habits, housing, and mobility are so fast and profound that one has to take extreme care to maintain a proper grasp of the market. Accurate market research and other advice concerning future trends are prerequisites for success in this ever-changing land. Remember: Korea is a world leader in the common use of broadband Internet communications, and consequently events and trends often change at Internet speed. Be particularly aware how heavily younger people use their multifunctional cell phones beyond simply making phone calls, as this crowd can easily outpace their "wired" Internet counterparts.

XI. THOU SHALT RECOGNIZE THAT FOREIGNERS ARE DIFFERENT FROM KOREANS

While the first ten commandments definitely apply to Koreans, foreigners are placed involuntarily on a different plane from other businesspeople. While this can work against the foreigner, it can often be an advantage. This is not to say that one should discount the first ten commandments, but it does mean a foreigner has a bit more wiggle room than his or her Korean peers. For example, as a visitor or short-timer, one may lack the necessary contacts in one's industry, which a Korean will probably already have. Does this necessarily mean one must find a Korean partner, even if one is working within a short time schedule? The simple answer is "no." Ideally, one should have someone on one's side who can help grease the introductions to key individuals. But turning a negative into a positive—being the "dumb" foreigner who "knows no better"—can often work, particularly if one is new to Korea.

However, whether one is a newbie or an "old Korea hand" going solo or in tandem with a Korean partner, some things remain the same. Preparation is key, as in all good business. Before making one's first move, it is essential that one does one's homework on the industry in Korea, including knowing who the players are and who has been successful and unsuccessful—and why. One's presentation needs to anticipate who will be in the audience and what they wish to know. One needs to seriously consider what to expect of meetings and presentations ahead of time to be mentally equipped to respond. One should have a portfolio of relevant detailed information on hand so that one can deliver it on demand (but do not volunteer it unless it is truly necessary!).

In any case, with care and patience, foreign business professionals—including those who speak no Korean—can make it and have made it on their own through the front door to get to the key officials. Furthermore, mature and well-prepared professionals have walked away with major contracts. This may not be the easiest way to do business in Korea, but out of necessity it has become the (unconventional) path to success.

7. GET OFF ON THE RIGHT FOOT: BUSINESS ETIQUETTE

*A*s an expatriate doing business in Korea, of course one wants to achieve success. One must know one's products and services; one must know one's business. There's no question about this.

But one must also be equally acquainted with the cultural delicacies and the etiquette patterns to avoid putting one's foot in one's mouth. A thorough knowledge of Korean etiquette will enable the foreign businessperson to "get off on the right foot."

Let's pose a horrible example:

A tall American businessman is on his first trip outside his home country. After an extensive seven-month period of correspondence, he is finally encountering the top executive of a small business firm in Korea. He is now being led into the president's modest office by an entourage of assistants who bow dutifully and respectfully. Meanwhile, the man feels somewhat ill at ease in the presence of awesome authority. The soft-spoken, grandfatherly president rises graciously and comes forward to greet the Western business associate.

The aggressive cowboy businessman greets the mild president with a vigorous, painful, pump-handle handshake that practically crushes the knucklebones of the poor president's hand. Overjoyed with this first personal meeting with his correspondence and friend, he slaps the president on the back like a "long time no see" college classmate and gives him a big bear hug, calling him by his first name out of unrestrained, exuberant friendliness. As his part of the ritual, the company president instinctively removes a name card and hands it to his foreign client, who apologizes because he cannot reciprocate since his have "run out" and are not yet reprinted. The client, in his haste and enthusiasm, plops himself into the single armchair at the head of the coffee table and launches into a boisterous torrent of conversation centered on the remarkable qualities of his own company and his own country. He expresses surprise to learn that Korea is only one-twentieth the size of his state, which makes the country's rapid economic development seem even more remarkable. This unbridled enthusiasm and monopoly of conversation continues for over two hours in their business consultation.

We now draw the curtain on this unfortunate scene.

Exaggerated? Yes. Improbable? Unfortunately, no. I leave it to your imagination to guess the outcome of this memorable business encounter, and of the conflict between two cultures.

Without intending to stereotype any person or situation, certain ground rules in business protocol and etiquette must be observed to get off on the right foot in productive business relationships. The bull-in-the-china-shop approach is bound for disaster and misunderstanding in future business connections. A brief survey of etiquette may make all the difference in positive business results between representatives of divergent cultures.

THE NAME GAME

American businessmen are commonly accustomed to calling each other by first name, often even referring in that way to top executives of at least small- to mid-sized businesses. However, the Confucian social structure is a hierarchical society where everyone has his or her recognized niche or position. Therefore, a Korean is referred to and called by this position label along with his or her name, and usually his or her full name or family name. only There is almost never any first-name basis in the name game—and certainly never from Korean company personnel toward management.

The name game is recognized and fixed by the perennial calling card, the exchange of which is an initiation ritual when two businesspeople meet for the first time. If one party is not able to present his or her card, the ritual is violated, and the greetings become a little strained and awkward. Remember, the second commandment of the suggested "11 Commandments for Doing Business in Korea" is "Thou shalt never be without business cards." (Refer to page 86 for more tips and information.)

In addressing a corporate executive, remember that his or her title is always affixed to his or her family name. Rather than as a prefix as in English, in Korean the title comes as a suffix. For example, "President Kim" is "Kim Sa-Jang." If an expatriate can learn to address the Korean counterpart in the Korean style with title, that person may be even more favorably impressed, which may in turn win the expatriate a warmer friend and business associate.

The executive's position also entitles him or her to a special regal throne—at the head of the table in his or her office, and in the right or rear position in his or her car. Great care must be exercised to avoid usurping the monarchical seating position in these circumstances. Even in a somewhat more informal dinner function, it is a wise strategy to let others direct one as to where one should sit.

NUNCHI—THE POWER OF EYE CONTACT

Nunchi is an important aspect of Korean society where form often seems to dominate over substance. Whereas the West proclaims, "The eye is the window to the soul," Koreans place much less stock in smiles and frowns than in the *nunchi*—or "eye energy"—that they pick up by literally and figuratively looking the other person in the eye. But this is actually a crude and limited understanding of this concept.

For example, *nunchi* entails the entirety of body language from the interacting parties. And yet most Koreans tend not to be expressive with their gestures, and so the misunderstanding among foreigners, since Koreans tend to focus on eye contact.

By Western standards, there seems to be a disconnect between what Asians express and what they do or mean. In the case of Korea, there are cultural reasons for trying to maintain an outward respect for one's superiors while getting on with what needs to be done, which may include taking actions contrary to the superior's "face." Consequently, it is critical for everyone to be on the lookout for subtle clues of the other party's intentions.

It is therefore important to look one's business associates in the eye with a sense of sincerity and, when appropriate, humility. In fact, one can learn a great deal by developing this silent talent, since with this developed skill one is often able to discriminate between a gentleman and a scoundrel. One may also be surprised to find by observing *nunchi* that some of the most elevated Koreans have a sense of intelligence and yet humility, while their subordinates may possess an arrogance of a lesser character.

Among Koreans, someone who is known as being "*nunchi bbareun saram*"—or "a person quick with *nunchi*"—is someone who is socially adroit and quick to read the immediate psychology of the situation. These people are among the most successful in society, since they are able to "read" people better than most. Conversely, someone who just doesn't get it when it comes to understanding where the other person is coming from is known as a "*nunchi eomneun saram*"—or "a person lacking *nunchi*."

As you can see, *nunchi* is an excellent skill to develop and put to use not just in Korea, but anywhere in the world. But whereas *nunchi* may be more an accessory elsewhere, in the Orient this skill is critical, and one should necessarily develop one's *nunchi* skills as one interacts among Koreans.

"THE MEANS JUSTIFY THE ENDS"

In Korean business activities, the "process" may be a bit more important than the "substance." How negotiations are conducted may determine their outcome. Protocol and procedural ways and means are of primary importance in conducting business in Korea.

The local executive feels more comfortable in a more relaxed, low-key level of business discussions. "Getting to know you" is a basic ingredient of business relations. If there is time, with the possibility of extended, multiple meetings, the first meeting might well be a courtesy call to merely get acquainted. If time does not permit, small talk should certainly be regarded as an essential prerequisite before serious business negotiations get under way. The Korean executive wants to gain some impression and sound out his or her foreign associate to gauge sincerity, trust, and reliability. This is harder to do across a cultural divide, so more time is needed for casual, preliminary conversation.

As business discussions reach the serious negotiation stage, it is usually unthinkable to expect the top executive to engage in these intricate matters. He will usually want his responsible, informed, and delegated personnel to handle the mundane details. It may be a fact that they know more about these details than the chief executive does. So expect to negotiate with these working echelon management people.

If the negotiations involve more serious issues such as financial arrangements or legal matters, an independent third party might be called in to mediate such discussions rather than having the chief executive deal directly with them.

In any event, the expatriate business client will get farther and faster by giving maximum attention to the "means" to make sure discussions are conducted properly. That is to say, it's important to be sure the Korean executive is comfortable without a risk of his authority that could result in "loss of face."

MONEY AND GIFTS

Like many other Asian countries, it is unnecessary to leave a tip for service in South Korea. A 10 to 15 percent service charge is automatically added to bills in most hotels and luxury restaurants. Normally a tip is not needed at all elsewhere. In a similar vein, it is very bad form to offer or give money to a Korean in return for favors that have been provided out of kindness.

Indeed, offering money can sometimes be considered offensive, since one is, in effect, demeaning the well-meant gesture as a mercenary act.

Also, as in Japan and China, which have the same associated homonym between the pronunciations for "four" and "death" in the local language, one should never give a gift where the objects can be counted as a set of four. The word for "death" in many Asian languages carries an almost obscene nuance, and this millennia-old cultural pattern shows up in various ways, including this phonetic phobia centered on the local language's pronunciation for the word "four."

There are times when gift money is appropriate and even expected. Money should not be simply handed over; it should always be given in a plain envelope. At special, once-in-a-lifetime occasions, such as a wedding or a funeral, there are special envelopes that can be easily found at stationery stores and even convenience stores. The actual amount of money one should give depends on one's relationship with the person and the current going rate given inflation. It may be best to ask a Korean for the appropriate amount after explaining one's relationship with the recipient. Finally, for the same reasons as explained in the above paragraph, do not give money that has a denomination of four (e.g., 40,000 won).

Having stated the above, the author should note some potential catches for a foreign business professional, since many countries have laws similar to the U.S. Foreign Corrupt Practices Act (FCPA). American and other foreign businesspeople have spent time in jail for "going local" because of this and similar laws.

We need to be mindful of the fact that while Korea is much less corrupt than it once was, it still has much room for improvement. According to Transparency International's 2008 Corruption Perception Index (CPI), among 180 countries surveyed, South Korea ranked 40th from the top. On a scale of 0 to 10, with 0 being viewed as the most corrupt, the nation ranked just 5.6. The good news is that these are better scores than in past surveys.

FTI Consulting's John Kim pointed out in the April 30, 2009 edition of The Deal Magazine that there is an apparent discrepancy between South Korea's economic achievement and its perceived corruption. For example, the top 20 nations by CPI rank are economically advanced, and all but two are OECD member nations. And yet Korea scores significantly lower in corruption than most of its OECD peers.

According to Craig P. Ehrlich and Dae Seop Kang in their 2002 paper "Independence and Corruption in Korea," published in the Columbia University Journal of Asian Law, there could be a few reasons for South

Korea's lingering corruption.

First, until recently Koreans have lived under various forms of authoritarian governments, so a culture has developed where unwritten codes of conduct have become more important than clearly defined laws. Also, Confucianism, with its emphasis on social and family obligations, gives legal compliance a secondary consideration. And finally (and the biggest factor in this author's opinion), there is the common practice of giving *chonji* cash gifts for special events such as the birth of children, weddings, graduations, and funerals in an increasingly affluent yet competitive society that invites abuse and corruption.

The Columbia white paper also notes that until 1998, undocumented confidential business expenses could be deducted for up to one percent of net worth plus 0.035 percent of gross revenue. That came out to a lot of "rice cake money" (as the local businesspeople describe slush funds) being spent. But again, referring to the first two points, a change in the law doesn't necessarily mean that traditional practices will follow.

Furthermore, up through the current ROK administration, it has been traditional for the President on special occasions to pardon not only large numbers of minor, first-time offenders, but sometimes major white collar criminals as well. While this tradition may be politically popular, one may say that the practice demeans the role of law in Korean society.

In time, the trend toward less corruption will likely continue. But in the meantime, as is the case with so much in Korea, essentially honest and ethical people will cut corners because the rest of society is perceived to do the same and because there is an anxiety that the company will be at a serious disadvantage when the competition is viewed as frequently flouting the law.

ENTERTAINMENT EATING AND DRINKING

Entertainment is an important aspect of doing business in Korea. While it is important to be punctual, traffic today can often frustrate even experienced Seoulites. Also, out of bad habit, some Koreans often tend to be unpunctual. Regardless, one is better off taking the other party's tardiness in stride, since during a later meeting it might be one's own turn being the late arrival. In any case, being intolerant of late arrivals is generally counterproductive to one's overall business strategy. So it is best to tolerate tardiness with a sense of equanimity so that one's business will not be sidetracked. By the same token, should one expect to be late, today's cell phone etiquette demands phoning ahead to apologize for one's anticipated tardy arrival.

Eating is often done sitting on the floor. Should one have a medical condition that makes it painful or difficult to do so, it is wise to alert the Korean hosts early, since not all restaurants have conventional tables and chairs. However, if one is capable of sitting on the floor but simply prefers to sit at a table, it is better to keep quiet and go along for the experience.

If the foreigner has never been to Korea, much of the food may appear quite unfamiliar—particularly if one is taken to a specialty seafood restaurant. If one doesn't know what something is, it is acceptable to ask, but it is more graceful to try a small taste first. Nothing on the table will kill, and it is unlikely anything will cause illness. Koreans do not really expect foreigners to like all of their food, but one may insult them by refusing to try something.

Drinking is both a frivolous and serious matter. As one might expect, the serious aspects degenerate into the frivolous as the evening progresses. Nonetheless, there are some basic rules that follow until the very end of the evening.

The eight pointers below are good to keep in mind:

1. Never give or receive anything with the left hand.

2. As with business cards, give and receive with both hands or the right hand, and with the left hand held to the forearm, elbow, or chest.

3. Always accept a new glass or a refill with a slight nod and expression of thanks, such as "*kahmsa hamneedah.*"

4. Never pour for oneself, but always keep vigilance to detect who has drained his or her glass so that one may have the honor of refilling the other person's glass.

5. Sometimes one may see someone drain his glass, place it in front of one, and refill it. In such a case, one should finish one's original glass, and hand the empty glass to the other person and refill it. (Upon seeing this version of the ritual kick into motion, one may take it as a signal that serious drinking is likely to begin.)

6. While one should always pour for the most senior persons first, it is very good form to make a point of pouring for the junior attendees as well. Women will often accept only token drinks, and one should respect them for holding the line.

7. In many Asian cultures including Korea, even if one wishes to receive something, it is impolite to readily accept it. So the first one or two refusals are often insincere. (This applies to all aspects of social interaction as well as drinking.) If one has had enough alcohol, expect that one will have to make one's point in good humor at least three times before being taken seriously.

8. If one cannot drink for religious or medical reasons, quietly and humbly explain the predicament to the Korean host prior to sitting down, with sincere apologies. One should accept a token first cup, however, and touch it to the lips during the various toasts. Soft drinks or water can be ordered afterwards.

THE MAGNETISM OF DIFFERENCES

In electric polarity, opposite poles attract, like poles repel. In culture as well, there is an attraction in divergent etiquette patterns. Kipling observed that "East is East, and West is West, and never the twain shall meet," but this doesn't always prove true in the world of modern-day business. East and West are confronting each other in dramatic convergences, and the accommodation of cultural differences is becoming an everyday fact of life.

The expatriate businessperson will have a much more relaxed and successful experience if he or she learns to recognize these differences as cultural factors rather than "uncultural" aberrations of behavior. Though it may never be possible to "adopt," it is quite essential to "adapt" and to accept these cultural variations. If the foreigner can acquire this state of mind, he or she will find the differences fascinating and interesting, rather than objectionable and annoying. It is worth keeping in mind that the Korean counterpart may find some of the Westerner's cultural finery to be distasteful and irksome.

One of the cultural patterns with which the expatriate must struggle is the slower process of decision-making. Korean business approval must usually go through an endless chain of command that may seem to take all the time in the world. The Western characteristic of efficiency and promptness may arouse an inclination toward pushing, but this usually delays rather than expedites. So the patience of Job is necessary to wait for a business decision to transpire.

Also, a blunt objection or a decisive "no" must be avoided by all means. By the same token, Korean etiquette does not permit such bluntness, so the local practice of "We'll study it further" or "We'll ask the top executives about it," or the convenient, "*Keul-seh,*" is a handy way of giving the meaning of "We'll see," or "We'll think about it." No matter how it may be said, the real meaning is often "no."

An indirect approach is much easier to accept and avoids a confrontation. When poles are wide apart, this can be a successful strategy.

"I THINK I KNOW WHAT YOU'RE SAYING, MAYBE"

The expatriate businessperson is almost never equipped to consult in the Korean language. But his counterpart is almost always forced to do business with foreign clients in English. Always be considerate of the fact that he is at a distinct disadvantage in the crucial necessity of communication. Remember, the third commandment for doing business in Korea is "Thou shalt not assume everything thou sayest in English is completely understood." The Korean counterpart may seem to be fluent in casual conversation and small talk, but when dealing with highly intricate technical, economic, or legal discussions, he or she may be less equipped to converse adequately in these terms. Keep the following in mind:

- Accommodate the client by putting a speed limit on one's rate of speech,
- Use common, uncomplicated vocabulary,
- Repeat, if necessary, in the same words,
- Speak deliberately and distinctly,
- Carefully repeat key points during consultations,
- Exchange notes at the conclusion of each meeting.

LET YOUR HAIR DOWN

Perhaps as much business is transacted in the informal setting of a dinner party as in the company conference room. The Western business professional should never regard informal entertainment as a waste of time or irksome. Such events can be great icebreakers, and as friendships warm during enjoyable dining and pleasantries, sensitive business negotiations can be drastically defused and eased.

Without a doubt, a Korean will grant an invitation for some informal entertainment. One must accept the offer and show that one enjoys it. Be sure to reciprocate. Some Western expatriates may be surprised at the degree to which a usually staid, conservative Korean executive really unwinds in such an informal occasion. Some may almost seem to come unglued. Try to be a bit more open-minded and informal than one may otherwise be. Although one may think that such "letting down of hair" is completely unrelated to business, to the Korean host it is all part and parcel of the same business relationship. Entertaining can contribute much to rapport, compromise and agreement. If one's host entertains in a Korean cultural setting for dining and entertainment, one may reciprocate by arranging the next event at a Western restaurant.

Remember, during such informal entertainment the Korean host is weighing his counterpart's sincerity, integrity and social graces—all of which are important to Korean business relations.

So without sacrificing principles and integrity, one should not be afraid to let one's hair down and enjoy one's time. This covers a multitude of difficult business negotiations.

A LITTLE HUMILITY GOES A LONG WAY

To many Koreans, foreign businesspeople from highly advanced countries sometimes appear superior, even somewhat arrogant. Therefore, a foreign businessperson will gain little ground in dealings without maintaining a sense of humility.

The impression of the Western business image is of self-confidence and self-assertiveness that may border on aggressiveness, an inflated sense of self-importance, and a know-it-all attitude. To succeed in Korean business, this image must be subdued at all cost.

The smart foreign businessperson remembers that he or she is confronting a culture that is more than 2,000 years old and consists of well-established modes of social behavior and interpersonal patterns. Korea's technical knowledge may have developed late, but this country has risen from the ashes of war within a half century to a level of industrial and technological development that is nothing less than remarkable. If the expatriate professional needs a reason to maintain some humility, he or she may contrast Korea to other countries that have experienced industrialization over many decades without the interruption of a truly devastating war. Unlike Japan, Korea was literally dirt poor even prior to the war.

If one comes with an inquiring, sharing, and open mind, the Korean counterpart will put out the welcome mat and treat one with respect, confidence, and generosity. Koreans are motivated by the desire to learn, to progress, and to catch up in becoming equal partners in world trade.

When a Korean executive apologizes or seems to demean or devaluate him or herself, one should not confuse cultural humility and apology with weakness and ignorance. This is a cultural etiquette pattern that by no means reflects negatively on his business skill or knowledge. It does, however, illustrate why the Western business professional must indulge in a new form of humility while doing commerce in Korea.

WISH LIST OF FOREIGNERS AND COSMOPOLITAN KOREANS ALIKE FOR IMPROVED KOREAN ETIQUETTE

In response to the International Cooperation Bureau of the Presidential Council on Nation Branding's request for suggestions on how Koreans could better interface with foreigners, a number of ideas were offered. While these suggestions are ho-hum for those people who have lived in Korea for some time or longer, the author is including this list for the benefit of the foreigner new to Korea. The purpose of doing so is to enable the Korea neophyte to quickly understand that the behaviors referenced below are not normally regarded as rude by most Koreans—and one should not take personal offense when encountering them.

1. Interrupting others in conversation, often without something equivalent to "excuse me."

2. Excessive commenting on physical appearance, both positive and negative.

3. Inquiring about age, religion, politics, or earnings.

4. Insisting on sharing the same glass when drinking.

5. Applying pressure or asking too many questions about marital status. Questions may include, but are not limited to: "Why aren't you married?" "When are you going to get married?" "What is wrong with you? Why can't you find a husband/wife?"

6. Asking questions about children. Questions may include, but are not limited to: "Why don't you have children?" "Is there something wrong with your wife?" "Is there something wrong with you?" "Why don't you have a second child?" "Aren't you disappointed that you have just a girl? Wouldn't you rather have a boy?"

SOME OBSERVATIONS ABOUT LEARNING KOREAN

Korean is often classified by the U.S. government as one of the "hard" languages, along with Japanese and Chinese. In China and Japan, however, medium- and long-term resident foreigners make a point of speaking much better than just "survival language" during their tenure there. And in all fairness, I have often witnessed foreign managers carrying on in Korean when dealing with simple issues such as asking for items and answering telephones. What is rare, however, is to see foreigners in Korea carrying on serious business negotiations or handling complex personnel issues in the Korean language. In Japan and China these days, if one has been in country more than a couple of years, one is generally expected to do business in the local language, with the possible exception of senior executives, who are frankly written off as being "too old" to learn a new language.

SO WHAT MAKES KOREA DIFFERENT FROM THE TWO NEIGHBORING COUNTRIES?

Over the past years of talking with polyglot expatriate managers who have fairly consistently given up on learning Korean, the author has found some common reasons, which I will lump into two groups—linguistic and cultural.

Linguistically, beyond the brilliance of the *hangeul* writing system, Korean is a very difficult language for two major reasons. First, while the grammar is similar to Japanese, it is not as consistent as Japanese. As such, it needs to be learned more in terms of sentence patterns than grammar. So while memorizing sentence patterns can be applied to new situations such as learning grammar, sentence patterns are not as readily applicable as grammar, since sentence patterns tend to be more situation-specific than grammar.

Secondly and much more significantly, Korean has fairly unique phonetics. The closest that may be found among Western languages may be German, but only as far as the vowels are concerned. Yet while there are many Koreans who speak German beautifully, there are few Germans who can do the same with Korean. Even worse is the case for other foreigners.

The reason is that many of the Korean language's consonants and vowels do not correspond to most other languages' phonetics. Consequently, if the ear and the tongue have not learned to differentiate correctly among the sounds of a foreign language, it is almost impossible for the brain to internalize and replicate new vocabulary. And even if new vocabulary is studied, if the foreigner cannot properly pronounce the words, he or she is quite understandably not going to make as much progress as hoped.

The second group of reasons for foreigners not really learning Korean—and this is a big one—is cultural, and to a degree social. With the exception of blue collar laborers who must speak Korean as a matter of survival, white collar foreigners questioning whether to speak English or Korean 7 find themselves in linguistic competition with Koreans who either speak or wish to learn English. This is also true in China and Japan, but what really sets Korea apart is the number of English-speaking Koreans at many levels of commerce. The sheer volume of bilingual or near-bilingual ethnic Koreans or Koreans who have studied abroad one encounters in business frankly diminishes the incentive for many foreigners to try to become truly conversational or better in Korean.

Unlike with the Japanese and Chinese languages, few students studying abroad choose to learn Korean as a foreign language. It is common to find people, such as this author, who studied Chinese or Japanese in university before coming to Asia. The few universities that teach the Korean language find that most of their students are ethnic Koreans who study out of family obligation and/or a desire to better connect with Korea. There are some notable exceptions of non-ethnic Koreans studying the language before coming to Korea, such as missionaries and military/government employees. But only a few of these make it into business; those who do generally do very well indeed.

One author, having gone through the elementary phases of learning Japanese in Japan and replicating the experience here in Korea, found the experience to be remarkably different. And from his conversations with other foreigners who have studied foreign languages abroad, his encounters with Koreans were not at all unique.

Even today, when one walks into a common restaurant as opposed to an international-class establishment, it is not unusual to get the deer-in-the-headlights panic stare from employees. While a few rudimentary words of Korean do work wonders in many cases, there are other times when it can be painfully difficult as a foreigner to struggle to be understood beyond ordering from the menu. While this is rare with younger Koreans, sometimes older Koreans can display a confidence-destroying reactive behavior to a beginning speaker's efforts by abruptly turning away, since they don't wish to deal with the hassle of communicating with a foreigner. The Japanese, on the other hand, may actually have the same feelings, but a strong cultural trait of *tatemae*, or social decorum, mandates that they smile and at least pretend to be nice, regardless of whatever they may be thinking. For the beginning Japanese speaker, this is a good thing, since it gives the foreigner, at worst, a false sense of competency.

So is there hope? Maybe. Back in 1970, no one expected foreigners in Japan to speak Japanese. Just saying "*Ohayou gozaimasu*" each morning earned foreigners undeserved accolades for fluency. Today, if one cannot carry on a reasonable conversation as a resident of Japan, one is regarded as being, well, culturally challenged, to put it nicely.

In spite of Koreans' fanatical drive to master English, will they expect others to speak their language decades from now as the Chinese and Japanese do today? We can only hope they may. We may likewise hope that future foreigners will resume the challenge of truly learning Korean for use in business and elsewhere.

NOW THE NEXT STEP

This is just a scant survey of the crucial importance of delicate etiquette. It may increase awareness of the differences, stimulate the reader to be more observant, and help the reader to understand and ask the right questions. Sensitivity to the Korean counterpart's etiquette patterns is one way to achieve success. So put your best foot forward—being sure to take off your shoes when entering Korea.

8. ADAPTING TO KOREAN BUSINESS PRACTICES

*F*or many international companies, adapting to the business practices of host countries poses a major challenge. The regulations of the Foreign Corrupt Practices Act of the U.S. and similar laws in other countries stipulate restrictions on the business conduct of their business citizens abroad. In addition, most companies have developed their own codes of corporate policies for dealing with sensitive legal and ethical business practices.

Multinational companies tapping lucrative Asian business opportunities, however, need to be especially ingenuous and flexible. Trying to conduct business according to the rules of the home country could invite business blunders or even no business. The multinational business executive must be in tune with the local business scene. That involves being in sync with official, regulated practices, as well as the unwritten and traditional customs and procedures. A strong personal sense of ethics is a real asset. There are times when passing up an immediate opportunity because of ethical concerns can be the best long-term strategy. At the same time, it is critical to be able to view business from the Korean perspective.

BACKGROUND

First, it is important to understand how the Korean regards his or her position.

Social Environment

There is a latent tendency for local businesspeople, as well as officials, to consider their office as their own private domain. Some exploit their posts to pursue their own private interests and "feather their own nests." Even though this is officially unethical, historically there seems to be a practical public acceptance of some degree of irregularities—if the scope is not too excessive.

However, following the "IMF crisis" at the end of the '90s, there has been remarkable corporate restructuring resulting from the demands of international stakeholders. At the same time, the Korean government has done much more than just give lip service in its push for greater transparency and better corporate governance. While old habits die hard, particularly in small- and medium-sized enterprises, the larger corporations—particularly the major *chaebol* business conglomerates—have been forced and/or motivated to tighten management controls. As a result, corruption has largely disappeared from Korea's largest corporations, but remains an issue with many of the smaller companies.

Nonetheless, there are broad gray areas regarding such practices. Even though they are frowned upon, such irregularities can still be found with some frequency and extent in many segments of society today. This tends to blur the moral implications. This phenomenon is not limited to Korea. It is an unfortunate and real situation that is more of a personal problem than a national one. Regardless, this reality must be recognized.

Personal Relationships

The majority of Korean business transactions are conducted by people who are bound together in some way through personal ties. When an intimate relationship exists between a vendor and client, the climate is conducive to breeding irregular dealings. Also, if a certain tie is established between an official and a business executive, bureaucratic sanctions and favors are more readily accorded.

Given this, the foreign executive needs to monitor his or her employees' relationships with their external partners—particularly so with sales and purchasing staff members. It is easier to crack down on a purchasing manager who lives beyond his recognized income than a successful sales manager who is enabling the Korean business unit to meet its revenue targets. The expatriate manager ultimately needs to operate like his or her employer—sticking to the core values—while being flexible enough to deal with local idiosyncrasies. How difficult this may be has less to do with Korea and more to do with how well the regional and head offices sincerely adhere to their corporate ethics policy, as well as their willingness to back the local expatriate manager when it is necessary to make a tough call.

Competition

Due to the domestic market's relatively small size and limited scope, Korean business is extremely competitive. That makes business more susceptible to irregular practices. For many, one simply has to win at all costs to survive and succeed.

Because of this keen business competition, an "ends justify the means" mentality has developed. Too often, the unethical means of past wins have been justified and rationalized as survival necessities.

This mentality has softened somewhat in the past decade as more foreign firms have entered the market. Some foreign firms have been able to change the game, given that they have something that is needed and not easily attainable from local firms. On the other hand, it can be exasperatingly difficult to change the "ends justify the means" game if one's product or service does not have a clear competitive advantage.

WHEN IN ROME...

Normally, foreign business executives should not expect to succeed in business transactions by going it alone or by attempting to apply tried and trusted methods from their own turf. The expatriates usually need to rely on others, particularly their own loyal Korean staff.

Local Expertise

Local experts know the language of diplomacy and the nuances of "rubbing the fur the right way" and "smoothing feathers." So the foreign executive would do well to rely—heavily, even—on local expertise in surmounting these complicated indigenous cultural structures and official red tape.

At the same time, the foreign manager should remain somewhat circumspect. Some Koreans working at multinational firms have well-earned reputations as expert "foreign handlers." One of the most common techniques is frequent or strategic flattery of the foreign manager's cultural/business insight over that of other, "less insightful" foreign managers. For example, one may hear something like, "Ms. Jones, you understand Korean business so much better than Mr. Smith and the other foreigners. So only with you can I explain this and expect your understanding..." Those words are not necessarily the signs of a trap, but that kind of praise should be red-flagged.

In all fairness, sometimes these foreign handlers are actually moving the business along efficiently for the overall good. Too often, however, these bilingual staff can be smart shortcutters who in the long run can unwittingly—and sometimes cynically—create some major headaches.

Third Parties

Another way to deal with sticky, questionable conventions is to take a step outside the company by engaging local organizations, brokers, agents, partners or consultants to handle the situation. By doing so, the foreign executive may seemingly remain aloof and intact from any potential problems.

It is necessary, however, to have a thorough understanding of and confidence in the agent, because there may be no control over what he is doing on behalf of the foreign company. There is a delicate balance in finding a local partner company that is well-regarded locally and that largely abides by the foreign company's code of ethics. At the same time, when it comes to understanding the deal's details, it is not uncommon for some of the most reputable foreign firms to take a "don't ask, don't tell" approach with their agents.

Lofty Causes

There are situations where special commissions are expected in order to consummate a business deal. In such cases, one company, rather than particular individuals, can propose benefits for the other company or group. These benefits may come in the form of scholarships, a welfare fund, office equipment, or furnishings for the organization. Sometimes, advanced educational training programs are provided for key staff in the organization, which will then benefit the entire organization rather than a few individuals.

Traditionally, one of the benefits of considering buying from a foreign company was traveling at the foreign vendor's expense to visit overseas reference customers. Most firms today prohibit their purchasing and decision-making employees from accepting such offers. If a foreign company hosts informative as well as recreational customer events as part of a regional customer relations program, however, many Korean managers are eager to accept such invitations as an alibi for traveling abroad, even if their own company foots most of the bill.

With some creativity, there are ethical ways to demonstrate one's appreciation that will have a lasting beneficial effect on the customer, while circumventing the questionable practice of "greasing individual palms."

Personal Ties

It may not be easy for a foreign businessperson to develop a genuine friendship with his or her business counterparts. Yet establishing informal personal contacts can significantly expedite business proceedings. This may involve lavish entertainment. But perhaps the more cost-effective and long-term practice is going out to lunch or dinner on a regular basis without a specific agenda in mind beyond simply wishing to build better personal relations. Often Koreans are impressed by the rare foreigner who is willing to go the extra mile in this regard. Sometimes it means informally letting the hair down, but ultimately, no matter how the foreign executive goes about it, the time and money invested in developing these personal ties are absolutely necessary.

Public Relations

A business venture in Korea must develop a strong, positive public image as a responsible, dynamic corporation among local consumers. After all, much can be said for buying from a Korean company that provides a truly localized product/service and usually offers superior after-sales support. Foreign businessmen should give prominent consideration to the public image of the company to balance buyer wariness. Many hurdles can be surmounted if a corporation uses PR to develop a strong public image. People tend to give a certain amount of credit to a company they respect. Contrary to the prevailing "ends justify the means" mentality, Koreans do not respect a company that has a reputation for irregular practices. (Please refer to this book's chapter, "Advertising & Public Relations—Korean Style," on page 280.)

Playing by Local and International Rules

The author referred earlier in this chapter to the old axiom of "When in Rome, do as the Romans do" as an example of practical wisdom. But sometimes that may not be your best option. First of all, going native is a pretty tough thing to do as a foreigner. Usually, at best, an expat can act approximately Korean and hope to get some sympathetic appreciation from the local populace. Other times, one can be in what seems to be a hopelessly disadvantageous position given the cultural and language differences.

At the same time, being a Korean in Korea hardly comprises a bed of roses. Often there seem to be more thorns than petals, given the various social and regulatory obligations and responsibilities. In this context, there are some inherent advantages to being foreign, since in being alien one is not inferior or superior, but simply separate from the mainstream. As such, one can work by slightly different rules.

Often these rules are technically in place within Korean business and legal parameters but are generally not observed due to overriding social and political concerns. As a foreigner—and even as a foreign businessperson—the expatriate manager may be surprised at how this can work in his or her favor.

For example, with some small Korean companies, oral agreements may be preferred to written ones. A foreigner's insistence on long, written agreements can be regarded as almost insulting. Nevertheless, it is imperative to have written agreements. Generally a foreigner can insist on this more easily than a Korean can. He or she has the option of demanding that negotiated agreements be as explicit as possible due to the differences in business culture.

This is not to say that one needn't be sensitive about practical considerations that may seem unique to doing business in Korea. A comprehensively detailed agreement drafted by a Western company's legal department may seem to cover all bases. Yet such a document can confuse and cause major problems during and following negotiations. The expatriate business professional should be prepared to redraft the head office's prepared document to say exactly the same thing, but in simpler language. Not to do so is likely to confuse the Korean counterpart with Western "legalese," which in turn can lead to major misunderstandings.

One simple approach is to break up long contractual paragraph blocks, with the sub-clauses presented in an outline form that is easy to search and understand. It is often a good idea to add hypothetical examples of unusual or complicated concepts or conditions to ensure not only agreement but also complete understanding by all parties.

Being culturally sensitive, one should be careful in discussing indemnification for malfeasance so as not to insult the other party. This issue normally does not exist in purely Western business, but often a Korean may take exception to how a Western attorney describes the other party as being liable for potential penalties. Still, addenda should be freely and fully included in contracts to specifically point out issues such as payment terms and timing so that there is no misunderstanding or possible variance of interpretation.

Now, all of this is a lot of extra work for the Western businessperson—but it's worth it, given the likely headaches and incriminations that may follow if one doesn't do this kind of preparation.

Not only are the business cultures different, but basic commercial concepts may also significantly vary in the details—or possibly not even exist within one's Korean counterpart's normal activities. So it can be dangerous to assume understanding. When in doubt, define in writing.

Furthermore, Korean employees are quite frequently transferred between the various departments of their organization. Rarely is there time for a decent handover of responsibilities. It is not uncommon for the exiting employee to neglect to mention to his or her replacement where one's contract has been filed. Consequently, an extremely detailed, heavily illustrated and well organized agreement, with full addenda, can be critical for getting the replacement employee up to speed.

This kind of document can also get the new employee off the hook with his or her boss should a disagreement arise. If the disputed matter is covered in the agreement and clearly explained as a contingency or possibility—complete with hypothetical examples—the new employee can report that the matter has already been contractually settled.

Keeping a Practical Balance

Now, should it not be already obvious, the important lesson is not to get suckered into the "cultural catch" of surrendering good business sense due to cultural differences. The Korean cultural trait of not wishing to put things down on paper or taking contracts as literally serious as Westerners do should be accommodated just so far. To repeat, the Westerner is not a Korean, and thus is not part of Korea's social web of obligations and potential penalties. As the Westerner regularly works across the "cultural divide," he or she must protect the company's interests by refusing to compromise the company's core values and policies.

It is critical to be as clear and as explicit as possible when negotiating a strategic legal agreement in Korea. It is also important to keep in mind that, ultimately, Korean contracts are fully enforceable. But be aware that these documents are literally as good as they are written. There are almost no additional legal safeguards beyond what appears on the paper.

So be prepared and be explicit. Most important, do not assume, but always confirm, genuine understanding, in writing, of all points with one's

Korean negotiating partner.

Business negotiation is an exacting and demanding matter, and particularly complicated when one is playing by a different set of cultural rules and business practices. The more the expatriate executive is familiar with the rules, the more there can be a meeting of minds—and the more success he or she can achieve at the bargaining table. It is all to the expat's advantage to be thoroughly familiar with the counterpart's set of mind and behavioral patterns. At the same time, consider what one's strengths may be—including those that may not strictly fit in the normal Korean cultural context. The fact that other, Korean companies may not have these qualities should not prevent the expat from leveraging those advantages in Korea.

To give an example, if one's company is challenged by a government regulator, one should establish a legal defense much as one would in one's native country. One should resist, or at least seriously question, advice from one's Korean employees—and even Korean legal counsel—to settle and compromise, if one is convinced that the company is totally in the clear. Even if there is indeed a problem, a Western legal defense can be the best course of action.

Korean government officials are accustomed to sometimes unfairly getting their way, since most Korean companies will quickly try to settle, even when they are completely innocent. If the regulatory challenge is unjustified, it is often best from the first moment to emphatically state that this is so and get one's legal ducks in a row. The regulator will probably not be amused, but will also realize that dealing with the foreign company is going to be more work, and it may not be worth the hassle. Even if the regulator decides to proceed, one should be prepared to act "un-Korean" and cite chapter and verse of the government's regulations, since they often can be used to one's advantage.

Keep in mind that Korean business practices, though often based on deep cultural foundations, are rapidly changing. The marketplace is becoming more open to international practices. Women and those Koreans who have lived for extended periods abroad are making their impact, along with the changes resulting from the wide application of broadband communications.

The points discussed above are what one may consider bedrock when it comes to doing business. Bear in mind that the rules are changing. Therefore, it is wise to occasionally review and test one's understanding with a Korean colleague, while being sure not to give up some of the advantages of being a foreign business professional.

9. WOMEN'S CHALLENGES IN KOREA'S WORK ENVIRONMENT

D uring the days of the U.S. Peace Corps in Korea, many volunteers' first encounter with Korea's sexual differentiation was during their pre-service training. Often, their most important survival skills were taught by experienced Peace Corps volunteer instructors. Without a doubt the most important lesson many new volunteers picked up from these folks was that when in the village, they should bow respectfully to the male elders—but watch out for the women, since it was they who really ruled.

Most Westerners expect and witness a major separation—and often discrimination—between the sexes in Korea. While men may dominate in society, again, the real rulers of Korea are the women—traditionally at home, often running the small family businesses, but almost always controlling the household finances. While everyone always bows first to the eldest male in the home, normally the real power can be the mother of the husband, who manages the affairs of everyone in the home, followed by the wife, who is second-in-command, with direct responsibilities for the welfare and education of the children and investing the family income. The financial difference between two similar male wage earners' incomes is often due to the business acumen or investment luck of the wife. Should all parents-in-law be deceased or living apart, the husband assumes the de facto authority of his mother. Still, in such a case, his wife carries on, controlling the home—which even includes managing the husband's discretionary money spending.

As strong as the superficial and real advantages of men over women may be, the yet stronger controlling factor is age. Even in the business world, an older woman can hold sway over younger men, which may be one of the reasons why Korean companies have traditionally urged women to retire when they become pregnant. Things remain simple with an older male manager supervising a younger female employee. The situation has improved to where today's young men are even generally at ease when reporting to female supervisors—provided the woman supervisor is older or, at the very least, has more years of relevant company experience.

Matters can become complicated within most Korean companies should a younger manager need to supervise an older employee, regardless of sex.

As Korean companies move more to merit-based promotions and away from seniority systems, this Confucian mentality often forces the early retirement of senior managers as a means of the company preventing discord caused by a younger employee managing one or more older staff members. Too often the first to go are women.

For example, in some corporations the supervising managers do not do performance appraisals. The overall distribution of appraisal scores and grades is fixed and can have a large-scale influence on the final individual appraisal results. Often the number of appraisals by grade is pre-ordained, such as by a predetermined bell curve. The best appraisals are reserved for senior and older managers, since for them not to get a high rating could quickly lead to early, involuntary retirement. Also, married men supporting families tend to rate better than single women. From an individual employee's perspective, this may not seem to be fair, but from the group's concern for the overall welfare of the employees, there is a rationale.

Many Korean managers are not anti-female, but they expect male employees to be shouldering or to eventually shoulder the majority financial responsibility of raising a family. Therefore, when push comes to shove, women employees often lose out unfairly.

And yet things are changing, even in Confucian Korea. Korean women are assuming wider and greater roles in business, so their presence is being felt more significantly than ever. For example, business entertainment or after-work dining/drinking is an important part of Korean business. Traditionally, women were often invited but not expected to stay on late into the evening. But even here, change is in motion.

Increasingly, Korean businesswomen are feeling free to invite people to and attend after-work entertainment occasions (*hoe-shik*). A proper evening out on the town starts with a restaurant and ends after visiting two or more bars. Attending the restaurant portion of the evening is no problem, and possibly the same with the first bar. Still, it may be wise for the businesswoman to be attentive if the guys are going to be ill at ease with her joining them at the second or third bar. Change does not happen overnight, and pushing the issue too hard can be counterproductive. On the other hand, Korean businessmen can be delighted that businesswomen wish to continue on. The problem, of course, is alcohol, and it is not enough that the woman alone is in control of her senses. So there are no easy words of advice on this topic, since the situation can vary considerably.

While most younger Korean men and women are much more

progressive about fair and equal treatment of women than their older male managers, the corporate bodies tend to be systemically conservative. In due time, many liberal-thinking men conform to the majority, and most women eventually give up any ideas of getting past what are often rather low glass ceilings. Consequently, women tend to be among Korea's least leveraged resources.

But the picture is not entirely bleak. One of the positives of the IMF Crisis at the turn of the century was the sale of major Korean companies to foreign corporations. Motivated by global commitments to employee diversity and recognizing the untapped potential of many Korean female employees, foreign-controlled Korean companies are implementing fair employment practices and proving to the rest of the market the competitive advantages of promoting competent female employees into responsible management positions.

Recently, local newspapers noted that of Korea Exchange Bank's recent 114 promotions to management, more than 40 percent were female. Two years ago, less than half of that percentage were female. What was not reported was that Korea Exchange Bank is now under foreign management. In contrast, only about 10 percent of Korea's overall managers are female. But even that is progress when one considers that nine years ago, less than one percent of Korean managers were women.

One of the challenges is for women to develop the self-confidence and image to take on serious management responsibilities. Even in junior grades, women often refuse to do less than pleasant duties, such as traveling on extended trips into the countryside and to smaller cities away from Seoul, which their young male counterparts accept as part of "paying one's dues." Undoubtedly, many young female employees cannot see the value in paying their dues when there is ultimately no real opportunity for extended career growth.

Also, as was the case in the West, young aspiring Korean female business professionals lack the mentorship that their male cohorts enjoy. If there is a woman in a senior position, too often she is in another department, and getting too close to a senior manager in another department can make for hazardous corporate politics. And as is the case anywhere, if a woman is to succeed in general and senior management, she needs to determine to what degree she can stay true to her intrinsic feminine values without being mistakenly viewed as incapable by her masculine co-workers. Until there are more Korean female executive role models, the current generation of women managers will likely have to suffer through an ongoing process of trial and error in the workplace.

While not an entirely happy picture, it is an encouraging one. Korea is opening its marketplace not only to new products and services but also to new management ideas. As more Korean companies discover the competitive advantages of fully engaging the capabilities of all employees, in time most other companies will follow suit, if only out of economic necessity. When that happens, Korean women will be stepping out from homes and family stores—and will finally be publicly acknowledged for their genuine role in this society.

OVERALL INSIGHT

Foreign businessmen in Korea will discover a business environment in which they must act with restraint, as well as situations where greater flexibility should be exercised. Only with good insight and discernment can they succeed and profit in this expanding market. Insight normally takes place from a steady position of self-knowledge and confidence as a business professional—as well as having the perspective and wisdom to understand changing local circumstances that may be foreign to the rest of their companies outside of Korea.

An open mind with personal integrity is a must. One of the joys and frustrations about doing business in Korea is that one never totally masters the subject—it is a never-ending, ongoing study for those with a curious mind and a desire to do better.

10. MANAGING—AND BEING MANAGED BY—KOREANS

*H*ad this chapter been written not so many years ago, the author would have written simply about how to effectively manage Koreans as an expatriate manager. But with the rapid development of the Korean economy, non-Koreans are finding themselves both working with and reporting to Koreans. Even if one does not have a Korean boss, it is strongly suggested that one also read the section intended for subordinates of Korean managers, as it may give important insights into the overall Korean corporate culture. Since so much about working with Koreans cuts in so many directions, regardless of one's job position, reading the entire chapter could be valuable.

For this chapter the author went beyond his own experience by interviewing expatriates of a wide array of nationalities working from the very top of their organizations down to the middle manager levels. Also interviewed were Korean executives working at foreign companies in Seoul. For anyone with more than a few years' work experience in Asia, some of the findings will not be surprising—but the author also uncovered some very practical suggestions and ideas for effectively moving from the theoretical to the practical when it comes to managing, communicating and just getting along with Koreans in the workplace. If the prose of this chapter is a bit uneven, it is because the author tried as much as possible to capture the words of advice from several experienced executives and managers. Finally, one must balance this chapter's pointers with one's own integrity, consisting of the core values of one's company and of oneself, while adapting to Korea's business culture.

EXPATRIATE EXECUTIVES

Success comes down to the personal things and touches. As an expatriate executive, one may have been sent abroad due to one's special expertise, but one's overall success will largely be premised on one's general attitude of getting along with one's Korean workers. It is important early on to have one-on-one meetings with one's staff to get individuals' views and concerns about themselves and the company.

Making this kind of extra effort is often not easy or second nature. But it is important to get to know one's colleagues on both a personal and professional level. One often has a choice of socializing with one's own nationals or with Koreans. While choosing to spend precious personal time with Koreans may not seem natural due to culture and language, one should make an effort to be part of Korean society and not just dwell in the foreign "ghetto." If one doesn't speak Korean, it can be critical to one's overall success to develop close friendships with Koreans who speak English or a common language.

There may be cases where it makes sense to hire a Korean partner who will eventually take over one's position. During the first years, one should consider having that person handle some of the more delicate Korean business cultural issues as well as serving as one's guide.

Often expats exclude Koreans from their personal social activities. It is a very good idea to include even some of one's employees in one's activities, including when hosting home dinners. And it may be recommended to introduce one's Korean friends to foreign friends as well.

It is important to find an entrance into any society in which one lives. If one is with a family, one should introduce them to Koreans whenever possible. Koreans love children, and one should try to bring them along whenever possible, including to employees' weddings.

Korean staff strongly dislike foreigners looking down on local practices and customs, including eating preferences. At work, Koreans still have a strong sense of community and resent the person who regularly retires early during a company dinner or frequently begs off a night out on the town with co-workers. In reality, they, too, would like to go home to their families, but they feel it is more important to the group's success to build strong personal relations with co-workers.

As one European president put it, "If I were to do things over again different than what I did when I first arrived, I would have done more face-to-face personal relations-building, such as over *soju*. For example, I worked a great deal of the first year on a deal that was never concluded. The customer would often come back to issues that I thought were agreed upon or kept niggling on agreed-upon clauses. I suspect the reason why they did this was fear of possibly being taken advantage by a foreigner." In other words, the expatriate executive had not yet learned the importance of building a personal relationship before expecting to close the deal. What applies inside of the company often applies outside the company, as in this case.

Those foreigners who have lived and worked in other Northeast Asian countries, or even Southeast Asian ones, generally have a much easier time adapting compared to someone who has never worked in Asia. Europeans who have never worked in the Orient, for example, often develop a negative attitude. One German was so alienated by a Korean worker's loud slurping of noodles one evening that from then on he had little to do with that employee during his tenure in Korea.

Unlike some Asian cultures, a small, friendly gesture like a touch on the shoulder and a compliment go a long way. Another small but effective pointer is for the foreigner to take the initiative each morning to greet his or her staff rather than expecting them to greet him or her first.

Leadership through employee bonding is an important trait of many successful Korean executives from which one may learn. For example, Samsung Data Systems CEO Min-soo Kim is well known for hiking thirty kilometers with his staff each New Year starting at 6:00 pm. Other Korean executives choose other physically challenging events, such as climbing with employees to the top of a mountain in winter—suffering, but also bonding in the process.

The wise expatriate manager takes special interest in his "problem" staff. One Korean executive recalls when he worked for an American company in Hong Kong. The young Korean manager faced a great deal of stress and difficulty due to his weak English language skills. No matter how much he prepared and rehearsed, his spoken English performance was below standard. His stress only accumulated. Finally, his aggressive Irish boss realized that something needed to be done. His boss took him out for drinks, during which they drained a bottle of scotch. The Korean manager candidly expressed his frustration with working in English and yet his desire to be successful. The Irishman realized the problem and put his subordinate into a six-month English tutoring program. Not only did the Korean manager's English improve, but he also developed a lifelong loyalty toward someone who appreciated the expatriate's concern and showed the understanding and willingness to help.

Never shy away from asking questions—particularly at the beginning, even if it seems the learning of all details is going to kill one. Don't sign off on things during the first days without a thorough understanding of what one is signing off on and the whys behind the procedure. If, in the process, one finds a major wrong, an experienced executive advised that one should "execute" the offending employee publicly; but if the wrong is a small infraction, one should have the offender make amends in a private way. If one wishes to retain the employee, it is critical to reprimand in such a way that he or she does not lose face with the rest of the employees.

Regardless of one's mandate, one should not try to change the organization overnight. It won't happen. It will always take more time than one or one's bosses may expect. The only exception may be if one is given the backing and resources to fire and hire replacements, with a reasonable amount of tolerance by one's senior management for the ensuing business disruption caused by the housekeeping.

If the foreigner works in a JV, it is very important for the expatriate to show respect and humility to the Korean counterpart. The Korean is likely to be able to teach the foreigner at least as much as the foreigner can teach the local manager—that is, if the Korean likes the foreigner and the expatriate gives the local partner the chance. The worst thing to do is take on an "I am the boss" attitude. If one's office is bigger than the other's, one should offer the bigger office to one's Korean peer. Such an attitude will be noted and respected.

Another observation by one of the executive interviewees is that the mental processing of data by Koreans and foreigners can be very different, so the level of understanding may also be very different. Often a Korean is unwilling to acknowledge a lack of understanding, as a means of saving face in front of other people—and even more so in front of other Koreans—so it is important to test one's explanation for proper understanding. One foreign executive has found it effective to use simple, graphic PowerPoint presentations and to use the whiteboard in his office to diagram concepts as a means of communication.

Younger expatriate directors often can be at loggerheads with experienced senior Korean managers when it comes to accepting the foreign manager's directives, especially since the Koreans believe they know better due to their longer experience. Management orders will be followed, but as a foreign executive, one should beware that sullen resistance comes easy to a people accustomed to being bullied over the centuries. So it is not enough simply being right. A better approach is to sell one's ideas to the senior managers by asking for their input on, say, how to possibly localize an initiative.

As always, communication is essential and incredibly problematic. Besides just dealing with the local business unit, one experienced expatriate advised incoming executives regarding how critical it is to manage the head office in terms of their expectations and understand how different Korean business can be. He really believed that if one is "to globalize, one has to localize."

One Korean working as country manager for an American corporation learned that the most effective way to communicate with the regional and head offices was to send an email followed up with a phone call. To send an email alone was very dangerous, since it could be easily misinterpreted. To simply phone took up too much time. To do both in the right order was both efficient and effective. This was particularly important since offshore staff had difficulties in understanding the differences in business cultures—and that required additional explaining. While business from the Western perspective was primarily a numbers game, Western visitors needed to understand that while numbers are important, there was a much larger factor in personal relations that dictated long-term success. The country manager felt it was very important for visiting managers to be introduced to customers, if only to get a feel for how business is actually conducted in Korea.

Flexibility and compromise beyond what may be appropriate elsewhere can be essential in Korea. One expatriate executive has discovered during his six years in Korea the importance of flexibility and making concessions that would not be acceptable overseas. Giving in at the right time, however, can be reciprocated in future dealings with the same negotiating partner. He further advised that one should keep in mind that signing a contract with Koreans is often just the start of the negotiating process—not the end. So the quid quo pro is an ongoing process, but it can be worked from one's end as well.

Whether it is a fair observation or not, the author has repeatedly heard how Western expatriates have been struck by how emotionally Korean business is conducted. One piece of solid advice, regardless, is not to become exasperated. Often this is easier said than done. But one should keep an eye on the bigger picture when doing business in Korea. It often makes for good strategy to make some major tactical concessions.

For example, a Western company had an expensive license for state-of-the-art software used in their outsourcing services. To get the deal, however, they had to agree to purchase what they thought to be lesser-quality Korean software that performed the same function. With that concession, the Korean customer extracted from the Western company an order that was substantially greater than the price of licensing the redundant software.

It is extremely important to be on guard as to what one says to Koreans, since like most people, they only hear the parts they want to hear, regardless of the caveats. However, this natural tendency is much stronger in Korea than in many other cultures—particularly if one is not communicating in the Korean language.

An example of selective listening by a Korean subordinate, albeit an extreme one, involved a top-producing Korean manager who kept thinking he was being denied a promotion that would effectively have him replace his expatriate boss, given his expectations from when he was hired. He had been told that if all went well, in the long run he might be considered as a possible replacement for his expatriate superior. The Korean manager tried to run the operation in his superior's stead until he was confronted in private and disciplined like an errant teenager. The Korean manager responded remarkably well and continued to be a top producer. So when the time of his next performance review came, the expatriate boss and the head office president were planning to promote the man to a director-level position. During the performance review meeting, however, the Korean manager produced a suggested organization chart with him at the top and demanded that he be promoted within his suggested organization. When he was denied, he lost his temper and pounded the table. As the head office president walked away from the scene, he turned to the expatriate boss and asked, "Are we here to promote or fire this man?" Three months later the Korean manager was fired, but only after a very difficult and expensive termination process

On the other hand, the author often heard from the interviewed foreign executives that it is very important to be very careful and specific about what one asks of Korean employees, since one is likely to get literally what one wished for. One German manager ended up with a half-meter tall stack of data with no summary or analysis when he simply asked for the background data on a project. Due to this and other cultural issues, including deference by Korean employees in not questioning their senior managers, it is worthwhile to make extra effort to get meaningful feedback beyond simple comments following one's issuance of instructions.

Another example of how personal and other relationships rule over conventional international business involves a foreign firm applying for a substantial loan via an established relationship with a local bank. All was going well until the Western firm suddenly learned that there was an unspecified obstacle. But two weeks later, things were back to normal. Afterwards, the expatriate managers learned that their contact in the bank's head office, a 38-year-old manager, had battled with the politically powerful 50-year-old branch manager of the loan's location. The branch manager insisted on getting credit for the loan in spite of the younger man having done all the work. The two bankers met over *soju*. After so many bottles, the younger man ended up assaulting the older man, so that the latter was physically and psychologically humiliated. Since the two men graduated from the same university, the older man let the whole incident go. The branch manager announced at the office the next day that he was sick and tired of the whole transaction and that he no longer wished to be part of it.

The point of the above episode, and much of this chapter, is that personal relationships and connections generally predominate over most business factors. From the Western perspective, Koreans may seem overly emotional and even juvenile. However, when viewing the same circumstances from within Korea's extremely competitive yet Confucian culture, extreme behaviors—while at times unpleasant—are more often not as juvenile as Westerners may dismiss them as being.

Top 18 Suggestions from Experienced Expatriate Executives:

1. When coming to a new country, it is imperative to be open-minded about the entire country and not just the new job.

2. Don't compare Korea with any other country; accept Korea for being what it is.

3. Understand the Koreans as a unique people. They are neither Japanese nor Chinese, in that the Koreans are more socialist, harder-working, more homogeneous and more suspicious of outsiders; foreigners will be well received, but until trust is developed, Koreans will tend to be skeptical.

4. Be prepared to compromise.

5. Don't be brash and try to steamroll over colleagues. One may get many "yes"es, but in the end one will get very little support. Be patient—things take more time in Korea than what one is probably accustomed to.

6. If one needs to convince a Korean in a higher position, one should not try to persuade him or her by logic alone. Better yet, one should feed the parts of the overall solution to the other person and then allow him or her to come up with the obvious decision on his or her own. That way it will be his or her "own idea." Too often, very good ideas are rejected primarily because the Korean executive did not think of them by him- or herself.

7. An expat executive is an agent of change, and as such, it is important for the expat to show how this change will benefit the Korean employees. At the same time, it is critical to have the ability to compromise.

8. Don't come with an attitude of educating the Koreans with clever Western ways, since one is not going to be successful that way.

9. Spend pre-arrival time learning about Korean history and culture and identifying its strengths and weaknesses.

10. If possible, before arriving in Korea, read up on Confucianism to understand its impact on society and how people interact. Not knowing Confucianism in Korea is like working in Europe without knowledge of Christianity.

11. Look for ways to socialize with Koreans to show that one is human.

12. Whenever possible, one should dine with one's Korean staff and customers; whenever possible, eat Korean food. The willingness to do so can generate surprisingly positive results.

13. Always ask for explanations before signing off on anything; one should not allow oneself to be relegated to simply affixing the chop while others run the business.

14. Always manage the disposition and use of the company chop or seal, particularly if one is under the illusion that one's Korean operations do not have one; it is almost certain that someone has created one in accounting or finance. Remember: a document with an affixed seal or chop is as legally binding as a signature from the representative director. More than once a foreign representative director has found himself or herself personally accountable for what someone had inappropriately authorized by applying the corporate seal without notifying the representative director.

15. It is easy for the expat executive to be set aside from what it really happening in the organization, so one needs to gently confront. Slowly, one will eventually be able to identify which employees are the potential agents of change who can be depended upon to make things happen and to report bad news early.

16. One should show that one is not a softy, but that one has one's own standard by which one will stand, all while being sensitive to cultural difference. But be careful not to be snowballed by the infamous line, "In Korea we do things different, so..."

17. Once one has earned one's employees' loyalty, one really has a dependable organization with which to get things done.

18. If one can come out and offer one's Korean employees an inspiring vision of the future where all may prosper, one has a special opportunity. On the other hand, if one comes here simply because one thinks one can exploit the Korean market, then it would be best not to come at all.

Let's first consider what the role of the expatriate manager or executive is. As an expatriate, the foreign manager has a very important and unique role in his or her Korea operations. That should be pretty obvious. But what may be less obvious is the unofficial role he or she is likely to be fulfilling: that of an agent of change.

If expats think they are not agents of change, consider this: thirty years ago, many of the jobs in their offices, currently held by Koreans, would likely have been filled by other expatriates. Back then, there was not enough local talent with the professional and language skills to fill those jobs. Today, however, there is a large pool of English-speaking Korean professional managers who very conceivably could be handling expatriates' jobs. But, of course, they are not: expats are. And often the reason an expatriate is assigned to Korea is either to upgrade the Korean office and/or to ensure that the Korean operation is not left behind as the company globally responds to pressures.

Regardless, if the reader considers himself or herself to be an agent of change, one of the biggest challenges for anyone holding a responsible position is selling change to the Korean employees—particularly when change may come unexpectedly and be unwelcome. Let's face it: most people don't like change, unless they are the initiators of such. But often regional or head offices require change for the overall benefit of the company, as well as the Korean branch.

To functionally pass on marching orders may be met with many "yes"es from the Korean employees, but an executive fiat will quite possibly also generate passive resistance, and possibly passive aggression—something the Koreans as a nation have hundreds of years in perfecting in the face of overwhelming foreign adversity.

To prevent that from happening, as well as to be a better manager overall during one's Korean tenure, consider some ideas that the author has picked up over the decades in the course of doing business in Korea.

First and obviously, doing one's homework is critical. As stated above, it is essential to spend the time and effort to learn the basics of Korean culture, history and society—and, above all, to get a grasp on how Confucianism operates in the daily lives of Koreans. While several decent books can be sourced at Amazon.com and major bookstores in Seoul, one of the best ways to get up to speed is to check out the Royal Asiatic Society, Korea Branch (RAS-KB), which also hosts cheap lectures on Korea on the second and fourth Tuesday evenings of the month at the Somerset Palace residence hotel in Gwanghwamun, as well as very inexpensive weekend tours. At the RAS, the foreign manager can find foreign residents and English-speaking Koreans who make a point of regularly upgrading their knowledge of this country. Besides offering the world's largest selection of English books on Korea, this is a very good venue through which to network with other businesspeople who have been in Korea for several years.

Speaking of networking, that brings us to our second point: develop mentors, both Korean and foreign. And, one might add, try to discover mentors both within the company and outside. A good mentor should ideally speak Korean fairly well or better, but above all should certainly have a good grasp of how this country operates in business circles. While "old Korean hands" may provide quick insights, the better mentor may be an experienced, English-speaking Korean business professional who takes a genuine interest in one's success. Though one may find such a person within one's company, I suggest that one also foster a relationship with a mature Korean outside of one's employ.

One way to do so is to get involved in a community service organization. The only such English-speaking organization, albeit largely made up of senior Koreans, is the Seoul Rotary Club. But the author knows of at least one European manager who has, at best, simple knowledge of Korean, but who has joined a local Lions Club as the lone foreigner. In any case, these organizations provide excellent opportunities to learn about Korean society and business while developing lifelong friendships with Korean business professionals.

Now, returning our focus to the office, the one piece of advice the author has heard over the years—almost as often as the need to understand Confucianism—is to develop sincere personal relationships with as many of one's employees as possible. That means taking a genuine interest in them as people, many with families, as well as co-workers

One of the most effective ways to accomplish these relationships is to regularly practice "management by walking around." The last thing one should do is stay holed up in one's office with a bilingual secretary acting as a filter. Of course, this is not unique to Korea. And as W. Edwards Deming once wrote: "If you wait for people to come to you, you'll only get small problems. You must go and find them. The big problems are where people don't realise they have one in the first place."

Try making it a regular point, at least three times a week, to walk about the office and ask employees about their jobs, how long they have been with the company, where they live and how much time they need to commute. Use such questions to inquire about their families, and try to get to know about their children's educational progress and the health of their parents. Also, for future political purposes, it may be helpful to know which universities they attended and where their hometowns are. In doing so, one should try to really get to know one's employees while demonstrating that one is genuinely curious about them as people and ultimately cares about their welfare as well as their productivity. Because when "crunch time" comes and one is called upon to be an agent of change, it is much easier to sell a development to good friends than to distant employees.

Also, it is important to keep in mind that Korean employees, including the well-intended ones, will often avoid bringing "bad news" to your attention if they cannot fully trust you and if you have not repeatedly gone out of your way to encourage the bringing of problems to your attention. Perhaps more than in many parts of the world, there is a strong desire or hope for problems to simply go away so that the subordinate need not endure the unpleasantness of reporting distressing or even potentially troubling information. Consequently, one should try to indentify and encourage Korean employees who are willing to pass on such knowledge while the problems are still small. If one handles one's relationship with them consistently and fairly, these same people can be one's own agents of change.

Finally, the toughest challenge can arise if one is younger than some of the senior Korean managers and also required to make unpopular changes. More than gender, Koreans differentiate on the basis of age. Under such circumstances, a bit of humility while maintaining one's authority—which includes accepting full responsibility—can go a long way. Specifically, ask for advice from your senior managers, stating that you recognize in part why the upcoming change may be difficult for some Koreans to accept, but after much discussions with your superiors, you have no option but to move forward. Given that you are lucky enough to have some senior Korean managers on your staff, you would like to know how they would handle the situation if they were in your shoes.

By asking for one's senior staff's counsel, one may learn that making the change can be achieved more easily than feared if done "Korean style," and one might even get some influential buy-in from one's senior staff. At worst, when the change is going to be tough, one will at least be given credit by one's local management team for asking their help before moving forward.

Let's now consider specifically what one may need to be aware of as the country manager of a small- or medium-sized foreign subsidiary or a middle or senior manager of a larger multinational business unit in Korea. Again, many of the suggested actions here can apply to an executive as well as to those in the lower ranks.

As soon as possible upon arrival, one must learn who is the real power broker—regardless of job title—in the local business unit. And it is, of course, important to discover how to get along with that person. While this piece of advice may apply anywhere, it can be more of a challenge due to cultural and language barriers. So the old wisdom of "when in doubt, don't speak, but listen" can be even more essential to the newly arrived expatriate manager.

One should do whatever one can to demonstrate cultural sensitivity from day one. No one expects mastery of Korean culture, but a positive attitude about learning will almost certainly earn appreciation and respect from one's new Korean co-workers. In the same vein, while one's co-workers do not expect one to master Korean, it is very important that one learns some courteous phrases to demonstrate an effort to learn Korean culture.

Again, as a new manager, one must attempt to learn Korean customs and get to know one's co-workers. Koreans are very shy about opening up to foreigners, so foreigners need to make a special effort beyond simply working amicably together. One needs to understand that personal relations come before business relations in Korea—both inside and outside the company. Therefore, it is important to learn about one's co-workers' personal and family backgrounds. One should consider inviting one's co-workers to one's home. The author doesn't suggest an open house, but co-workers should be invited on an individual basis or in small numbers. In turn, the co-workers may reciprocate, and one may be able to learn and appreciate one's co-workers' standard of living, such as by meeting their family members. An exception would be if one is younger than many co-workers and is living in what many Koreans consider to be luxurious expat housing. In this case, it may be wiser for one to host a number of dinner-and-drink nights at restaurants.

It is critical for one to understand the employees' personal problems and attempt to assist even with private matters whenever possible. By making an honest attempt to help, one should be able to build a strong bond and loyalty that will translate into greater productivity and quality of work from one's teammates. If this bond does not take place, over time one may get minimal or simply average output from one's staff, who will feel no particular obligation to go beyond what is nominally expected of them.

Recognize that certain management practices by foreigners are difficult for Koreans to accept due to differences in culture and language. Also, Koreans tend to prefer a vertical organization with top-down commands and are often uncomfortable with essentially flat organizations. They normally prefer a *hobong* (salary step) ranking of jobs, as it is more consistent with much of Confucian society's consideration of seniority and responsibility. Much of this mentality is starting to change, but many organizations—including multinational subsidiaries—retain this conservative mentality.

One should accept the fact that one will never fully fit in with the rest of the Korean employees and that one will be considered a relative short-timer who will eventually move on, leaving the Korean employees behind.

When it comes to motivating senior Korean managers, it is important to have discussions with them in formal and informal settings such as over meals and drinks, rather than simply in the office environment. It is critical to build a personal relationship, sharing personal information on family and background. To a similar extent, this may also apply to one's direct reports, but not necessarily to all employees in one's unit. But the point remains that it is important to develop this sense of trust and understanding before assigning goals and objectives to one's staff.

It is very important that the expat manager assume an attitude of humility. Ask for advice on specialized and technical matters, and learn from and show respect for another individual's expertise. The worst possible behavior is to strut around with an "I'm the Boss" demeanor and have a checklist mentality of checking up on one's subordinates' work, as that behavior does not generate genuine respect.

It is much better to be always asking and coaxing employees to offer suggestions on how to do things better. Often they know but are hesitant to offer their opinions. Also, this attitude of commonly asking for suggestions shows that one is willing to learn how to work effectively in Korea.

One should be aware that Koreans' English skills are much greater than they initially seem. Conversely, accomplished English speakers are often not as technically skilled as one may expect. There has been a traditional role for the English specialists, but those positions are disappearing as the availability of skilled employees with strong English language skills grows.

Foreign executives and managers need to be aware that no matter what their rank and title may be within their firms, they are subordinate to virtually everyone within their customer's firm. The customer is king and the king is always on top in Korea, no matter what he or she may be elsewhere.

Korea is a great place to do business. It is one of the best places to learn how to succeed in mainland Asian commerce. And perhaps best of all, if the expat manager makes the effort to build personal relations with his or her staff, co-workers will be more likely to forgive the foreigner for being only human if the foreigner should stumble, and be more willing to help him or her succeed the next time.

WORKING IN KOREAN COMPANIES AS A FOREIGNER

While foreigners have worked in Korean companies in Korea for decades, most of their job responsibilities have been limited to English language-related roles ranging from teaching business English to proofreading English translations. In the past decade, some of the bigger Korean corporations have recognized the need to bring in foreign specialists as a way to help move the pendulum from the current 80/20 mix of generalists and specialists toward more specialists. For that reason, besides internal development toward greater specialization, some Korean firms are hiring foreign specialists.

Often Korean managers have a good understanding of the rest of the world on an individual basis—but their organizations often are not well prepared to accommodate foreigners. Furthermore, where Korean firms expect foreigners to learn and adapt to Korea while in Korea, Korean managers are notorious for insisting that everyone in their offices abroad also act like Koreans. Again, this is not so much a reflection of individual Korea employees as it is of Korean corporations, which are at this stage struggling through the maturation process necessary to take them into the international arena.

Koreans can view recruited foreign executives as providers of "free" knowledge—but there is a price for that knowledge. One cannot expect to learn anything without changing one's behavior, one's perspective and possibly one's status. It is hard to adapt to change anywhere—and that is a price that many do not wish to pay. So one may need to temper one's expectations—even if one finds an enthusiastic initial reception upon one's arrival.

Often Korean staff members are uninterested in getting assistance from foreign managers unless such aid will clearly assist them in obtaining their next promotion. This is particularly true if that help is being offered from outside of the local manager's department. In fact, sometimes a foreigner's expertise can be viewed as a threat, revealing inadequacies in a Korean manager's knowledge—particularly if that expertise is coming from another department.

New foreign employees are frequently given impressive job titles. The titles have often little to do with the actual responsibilities and more to do with the pay. Human resources departments can be very bureaucratic and rigid in assigning job titles according to pay grade. Since foreigners generally need higher salaries to entice them to work for Korean companies, they are often given job titles above their actual job responsibilities. This can be particularly awkward if the expatriate is a young person and works with Korean staff of greater seniority, but with similar or even lower job titles.

In addition, the common case is for the foreign manager to arrive with a good salary and title, but discover that there are no reporting staff members. Those foreign managers who are viewed as being "lucky" by other foreign managers at Korean companies are those who are recruited to accomplish a specific mission, as opposed to upgrading the knowledge of the Korean staff, and who are assigned with reporting staff from the beginning to assist them in accomplishing their mission.

It is very important that if one considers working in a Korean firm in Korea, one gets a detailed job description with specific duties and a description of where one will be in the organization. Getting such a job description is no guarantee against being given a somewhat different job upon arrival, but it will minimize friction and misunderstanding from the Korean perspective.

Also, one should be aware of the motivations of one's non-Korean recruiter or reference people. Often, Korean corporate performance appraisals consist of "evaluation points," and some of the points can be based on the ability of the expatriate employee to recruit other foreigners. So if a foreigner approaches someone to work in his company, there is a good chance that the recruiter is at least being motivated to get a better performance evaluation.

For example, a 30-year-old American working in a Korean corporation was shocked by this reality when he arrived in Korea. Given the recruiter's explanations and descriptions of the job, he was not prepared mentally to deal with how the Korean culture operates on different age layers and how Koreans routinely interact differently depending on one's age.

Often the age barrier in Korean companies is the reason why younger, brighter employees are not promoted faster. One frequently has to reach a certain age to be eligible for higher responsibilities and compensation. It is often a shock for Americans who have strong, personal reputations for professional expertise and achievement elsewhere to find that they are not as well-regarded in Korea for their professional skills.

All of this can lead to feelings of alienation and frustration among foreign managers in Korean firms. The largest causes of frustration are:

• Routine exclusion from ongoing business activities. Sometimes this is due to the language barrier, and sometimes it is done intentionally for political reasons, since foreigners can be too eager to offer their expertise. Also, since foreigners are often given high-status job titles, the Korean natural deference to senior managers can make communication even more difficult.

• Korean managers are often awkward in accepting foreigners parachuted into their midst by the international human resources department. They are sometimes not sure how or where they fit into the day-to-day operations.

• The firm's recruiters further complicate matters by intentionally or unintentionally misrepresenting to prospective foreign managers what the nature of their work responsibilities will be. Most foreigners are recruited as subject matter experts, but find they are largely ignored by the rest of the company, partially for the reasons stated above.

• Often, foreigners get irritated by what seem, at times, almost daily requests to donate money to occasions like weddings, childbirths, and funerals. The fortunate expat managers can claim these as company expenses, but many find these to be constant drains on their personal finances. Koreans expect those managers with significant titles to contribute to all such requests. Among Korean managers, this form of personal charity comes with the territory and is a form of noblesse oblige that comes with personal success. For the parachuted foreigner who may be wondering whether he or she has any real authority, these obligatory donations can be viewed as insults upon injury.

One American was able to find a Korean mentor who counseled him that the first couple of years are like being in hibernation. It is important to keep a low profile, to not compare what one sees with what happens in the US, to keep generally to oneself, and to try to understand why some things that appear to be "wrong" are, since there is often a good reason within the Korean context.

A common breakdown in relations can be traced to contrary expectations between the foreign manager and the Korean employer. Many Korean companies do not expect miracles from their foreign employees during the first months, or even longer. Rather, they expect the foreigners to learn about the company and to make an effort to become part of the team. In contrast, well-meaning Western employees start feeling guilty after a couple of months about not adequately earning their salaries. They then often try to advance their unsolicited expertise into the organization. Compared to Koreans, Westerners tend to show off and come off as lacking a proper sense of humility—and that can be misinterpreted by Koreans as not showing a proper sense of loyalty.

From the perspective of many Korean managers', it is most important to not be a jerk, but to try to get along with folks as a nice person. During the first couple of years, mediocre or even worse performance can be overlooked if the person is genuinely trying to fit in with the rest of the team. On the other hand, employment contracts are sometimes not renewed due to nonperformance or inadequate performance by the foreign employee. So there is a balance that the foreign employee must learn or be advised of. In short, a great attitude will normally be one's best—but not only—attribute for success and survival.

Speaking of survival, one should get to know how one's Korean company conducts its—and one's own—performance appraisals. For example, the supervising managers largely do not do performance appraisals in some corporations. The overall distribution of appraisal scores and grades can have a large-scale influence on the final individual appraisal results. Often, the number of appraisals by grade is pre-ordained, such as by a predetermined bell curve. The best appraisals are usually reserved for senior and older managers, since for them, not receiving a high rating could quickly lead to early, involuntary retirement. Also, married men supporting families tend to rate better than single women. From an individual employee's perspective, this may not seem to be fair, but from the group's concern for the overall welfare of the employees, there is a rationale.

In many Korean companies, it is important for foreigners to speak Korean, as there are insufficient resources to be constantly translating and interpreting for the English-only speaker. There may be the beginnings of a sea change, where Koreans are coming to expect foreigners to speak Korean if they plan to be working for the long haul—particularly in positions that deal directly with Korean customers.

In any event, if a foreigner is promoted to a senior *sang-mu* directorship or higher, it can be important that he or she have good Korean language skills. The expat may have some great ideas and strategies, but he has to rely on the local staff to implement these ideas correctly—and that normally requires monitoring in the local language. In the lower management positions the responsibilities are fewer and the span of control less, and so is the need for monitoring in the Korean language.

If one works at a globally positioned company, one's English skills will be better appreciated. But for firms focused on the local market, Korean language skills become more required and English skills less needed.

Regardless of the language in which they are conducted, meetings in Korea often do not result in decisions. They are mainly for consensus building or gaining awareness of what the most influential or powerful members are thinking. The real decisions frequently take place in informal settings.

At times, it seems critical information is never given directly, but only indirectly—often over drinks and "under the table." It's not unusual when drinking for one to discover that there is another party or more parties with important influences or concerns. One must then schmooze with that person to develop a relationship for support on a project or an idea. Commonly, during the evening, that person is noncommittal, but often the next day he or she comes back in full support.

Because of culture, subordinates do not express their thoughts and opinions. Consequently, foreigners can mistakenly view their subordinates as incompetent when they are actually highly skilled.

It takes time for Koreans to get used to Western consensus-style management—as opposed to the special dynamics of Korean group decision-making. This apparent contradiction can trip up foreigners when, after hours of consensus building, top-down orders are issued in an autocratic or military fashion. Often the foreigner has been unwittingly party to the lengthy, behind-the-scenes consensus building, but only sees the orders being issued. Some Koreans never seem to make the transition to a Western, open-to-discussion management style, and some Westerners never really understand how Korean management decisions are being made.

Similarly, Koreans approach project development differently than Westerners. Westerners act and interact directly and logically, thrashing out competing ideas and opinions and then coming to a resolution. Koreans work things out more indirectly and socially in a prolonged consensus process. Consequently, something that may be resolved in an hour in the West can take a week—or longer—in Korea.

Regardless, if one is working in a foreign or domestic company in

Korea, drinking can be a big issue, and often a health hazard, for many managers, foreign and Korean alike. Depending on one's boss, alibis along health and religion lines may or may not be respected. A less tolerant boss might not say anything, but he may convey that he is making sacrifices in the form of regular drinking to build a stronger team, also insinuating that one is failing as a team member for not making similar sacrifices.

As a foreigner, one can superficially "get away with it," but if one is planning to work in a Korean company for the long haul, this issue can be an obstacle. Yet there are successful Korean teetotaling managers who have mastered the art of nursing a single shot of soju all evening after modestly explaining their religious beliefs or health restrictions.

It is all about working the web of personal relations. That is why it is so difficult to take business from another company even if one has a better business proposition. Often, the customer has long-standing, deep personal relations with the other vendor's personnel, receiving many personal favors for employees and their families from that vendor.

The real power in Korea is the *in-maek*, or "personal network." As a foreigner, one is not expected to have a good *in-maek*, but one can develop a relationship with a Korean mentor or partner within one's business who does and can teach one the cultural subtleties of being successful in Korea. In the end, it may be critical to find such a mentor or partner. With enough time and exposure, one may join the other foreigners who have been able to develop their own respectable *in-maek*.

KOREAN RETURNEES (*GYOPO*)

During the past two decades, Korea has largely benefited from a reverse brain drain. Young Koreans raised and educated abroad have returned to Korea to pursue their careers in both foreign and domestic companies there. Often, these returnees, as well as their families who continue to reside abroad, are called "*gyopo*"—a term referring to overseas or long-term expatriate (in the original sense of the word) nationals.

Korean-speaking *gyopo* are treated as 100 percent Koreans, so when they stumble by not knowing the exact, appropriate Korean term and perhaps substitute with an English word, they are thought of as being less educated or worse. But when a white foreigner uses English terms, then the white employee is often given special consideration, where his or her English terms are held in higher regard.

Korean staff members tend to be more lenient toward Westerners than toward *gyopo*, and sometimes their image of *gyopo* is not as positive as that of Westerners. The counterbalancing news is that *gyopo* managers are normally able to close the cultural gap faster than their Western counterparts. For example, *gyopo* can often pick up faster than other Westerners on staff attitudes and opinions on working conditions and workload—although, of course, even *gyopo* can make mistakes in this area.

On the downside, Korean staff members have higher expectations of *gyopo* regarding adaptation to the local culture. This can be unfair if the *gyopo* manager was born and raised in the West, especially in areas where there are few Koreans. Initially, such a *gyopo* does not have a genuine advantage over other Westerners, but faces a higher standard for acceptance.

If a *gyopo* has less-than-fluent Korean-language skills, the local staff members have high expectations that he or she will strive hard to upgrade his or her Korean language ability—unlike with other Westerners.

Many *gyopo* managers will not consider holding meetings in English, while foreigners may often do so, even if this causes inefficiencies. Even when dealing with bureaucrats, bad word choice by a *gyopo* can be disastrous, while with a white foreigner, in spite of the lack of *gap-eul* (the order or power of position), the foreigner may be given special, positive consideration.

So *gyopo* often have some inherent advantages over other foreign managers, but there can be several hidden cultural traps that the *gyopo* and their managers need to be aware of. Even the so-called bilingual *gyopo*, at least in the beginning, often lacks educated, current Korean language skills, since colloquial Korean is vastly divergent from business Korean. Nonetheless, those *gyopo* employees with the right attitude and commitment often end up being exceptional employees. However, no matter what, the initial cultural and even linguistic adjustment can be surprisingly difficult.

HANDLING EMPLOYEE FRAUD

We all acknowledge fraud exists. But as managers, how do we appropriately and effectively deal with fraud, especially as an expatriate or a local manager in Korea, and what must we keep in mind?

There is a strong tendency for Koreans to try to sort out fraud problems amongst themselves rather than raising the matter with the appropriate authorities within or outside a company. Since subordinates can be covering for themselves, their customers, or their immediate supervisors, general management often works with a false sense of security. Many hidden bombs lay ticking and eventually explode as small problems spin out of control.

As in other countries, there is an anxiety that a fraud problem, when discovered, may reflect poorly on the performance—and possibly the career—of the concerned employees. Consequently, as is the case anywhere in the world, management must do all that they can to assure that fraud will be handled fairly and confidentially when reported.

Given the historical lack of consistent and adequate internal control and management systems within most Korean organizations, many Koreans frequently do not trust, or have confidence in, their management that reported fraud will be handled justly.

To counteract all of the above, management needs to establish the appropriate infrastructure for a fraud-prevention corporate culture. At a minimum, there needs to be a clearly written code of conduct that details what constitutes fraud and malpractice, along with the penalties, including possible employment termination. This code must be given to and signed off on by all employees, starting on the first day of employment. Furthermore, managers must live up to the code of conduct themselves and not simply mouth the words. Finally, there must also be an effective "speak up" or "open door" policy that consistently affords confidentiality and fairness to those who come forward.

A fraud risk-control program that includes clear policy and procedures on reporting and investigation, a customer due diligence approach, employee sanctions, employee fraud awareness and training should be built within the company. Policies and procedures must be practical and clear, with consistent management enforcement. Too often employee fraud cover-ups are predicated on trying to protect the individuals involved, and even their immediate supervisors, when something goes wrong as a result of not following procedure or the law. Frequently, things have become dangerously lax under the alibi that "Korean culture" or "Korean practices" require corners to be cut.

Having said that, Korean culture can create real problems for otherwise ethical employees. There are stories of middle and senior managers feeling the financial squeeze caused by financially helping out subordinates beyond their capacities and then rationalizing some kind of embezzlement. Other war stories include too many bank loans being made to friends for too small amounts, especially given limited lending resources. This kind of lending can hurt the bank's overall performance, preventing focus on larger and more profitable businesses.

One additional example was of younger loan officers making loans to friends in other corporations and then privately borrowing money from those same friends. This would be considered a kind of corruption in many countries, but in Korea, this is almost expected behavior. In one extreme case, a loan officer even forged the signature of his friend in withdrawing money from the friend's account within the loan officer's bank. When the customer was confronted with the evidence, the response was, "No problem. He's a friend of mine."

So the challenges for general managers are often not so clear-cut at the outset. Even more so than in perhaps most countries, executives and managers in Korea must routinely demonstrate what one should do and consistently act appropriately when facing possible fraud. This includes openly and consistently enforcing a zero tolerance policy with clear forewarnings of penalties, while assuring that the disclosed irregularities will be handled with appropriate confidentiality.

Since fraud is a form of human behavior, an effective manager monitors his or her subordinates' activities, constantly being on the lookout for unusual or sudden changes in behavior. For example, if an employee is first to work and last to leave, while being eager to handle customer complaints, one might think the employee to be exemplary. While that may well be the case, such an employee may also need the very early and late hours to work unsupervised so as to work a fraudulent scheme while being sure to handle the customers whom he or she may be bilking.

While all of the above is important, perhaps more critical and in the end cost-effective is filtering out future employees who have been or may be tempted to commit fraud. During hiring, it is absolutely necessary to get the prospective employee to sign a confidentiality waiver to allow human resources to check prior credit, employment, and educational background. At that time, it is strongly recommended that human resources also obtain a copy of the employee's family tree, since fraudulent funds are often transferred to a close relative rather than kept incriminatingly within one's own household. Given Korea's very strict confidentiality laws, it may be virtually impossible to do background checks once the employee is on his or her way in a fraudulent scheme.

It is important to consider that fraud normally happens when the employee has the knowledge, the motivation, and the opportunity. So fraud rarely happens with junior employees, as they have neither the knowledge (having relatively simple needs or motivations compared to those of older employees with greater authority) nor access to systems and procedures. However, once they are faced with these temptations, this can lead to a change in behavior, where the fraudulent employee shifts to a new lifestyle that includes increased spending, more luxury, and a change in work attitude. Such a change, of course, is not necessarily a sign of fraud, but it should be taken seriously as a "red flag."

Again, because of confidentiality laws, gathering evidence can be more difficult in Korea than in many other countries. Fraud and risk control requires professionalism consisting of effective investigative procedures and employee interrogation. A competent internal fraud specialist should have an extensive personal network—ideally including people in the local police department. Officially the police are constrained due to confidentiality laws. But many police officers are very sympathetic to companies trying to remove corruption from within their ranks and can be surprisingly helpful after strong personal relationships have been formed.

If one cannot afford to have a professional fraud and risk specialist on one's payroll, there are outside resources available. While not all international fraud prevention firms have representation within Korea, they at least have Asian offices that subcontract out to Korean firms. One place to begin one's search online is at www.nafraud.com/dynamic/country.html. A good question to ask is whether the local firm is affiliated with any of the major, international fraud companies. Major auditing firms such as KPMG offer fraud control services and should also be considered.

11. KOREAN IMPRESSIONS OF FOREIGN BUSINESS

*T*he presence of foreign businesses permeates every nook and corner in Korea. Goods and services of foreign origin have made their way into the market along with economic progress. From soft drinks and cosmetics to drugs and fast foods, many of them are successfully established as household brands. Employing nearly a million Koreans, foreign companies have also emerged as an important factor in the local economy.

Foreign businesses should be aware of the general Korean attitude toward foreign products and businesses and make any adjustments necessary to counter possible objections or prejudices.

FEELINGS REGARDING FOREIGN DEPENDENCY

Foreign companies, especially from the major countries, are regarded with mixed feelings. While high technology and advanced products are admired and coveted, they are at the same time somewhat feared by Korean businessmen who perceive the possibility of having to depend on them.

Whether one is an individual or a nation, control of one's destiny is of utmost importance. People, especially those who have suffered under centuries of foreign domination or suzerainty, value independence very much. That the Koreans themselves did not liberate their country from Japan makes them perhaps more defensive about their independence than the people of many other nations.

In recent years, however, Korea has generally become more accommodating to foreign business—perhaps not by choice, but by necessity, as its trade and investment overseas have expanded rapidly. Even though most Koreans acknowledge that Korea's economy is highly trade-dependent, in 2004 it took seven months of deliberations and three failed attempts for the National Assembly to ratify its first-ever free trade pact with another nation, Chile, because of the overzealous and nationalistic agrarian-interest groups. Nonetheless, the trend of greater acceptance is evident in the gradually relaxed regulations on imports and foreign investments, though most foreign chambers of commerce would say the pace of deregulation is still too slow.

LINGERING DEPENDENCY

In relations with major trading partners, Korea tends to have a "poor country mentality." Just four decades ago, it was regarded as one of the poorest in the world, requiring much relief aid from advanced countries. Through the 1950s and 1960s, food grains granted or sold at concessionary terms under the PL480 Program helped alleviate hunger. In addition, grants by Japan as a part of reparations for the occupation of Korea also contributed to the process of capital formation. But even after attaining their present prosperity, Koreans still regard themselves as poor, expecting preferential treatment from trading partners.

Until fairly recently, the U.S. had been looked upon as a generous big brother with unlimited affluence and resources, while Japan continued to be regarded as a country that should eternally compensate for its colonial exploitation of Korea. Today, younger Koreans look upon the U.S. in less favorable terms—partly out of concern that America seems at times an economic bully, and partly because a large number of younger Koreans blame the U.S. for being an obstacle to unification of the country. In dealing with the ever-growing trade frictions with these two major trading partners, Koreans have maintained these attitudes. The readjustment of past relationships seems to be taking a long time—often to the detriment of cooperation with its allies. At the same time, there is growing recognition of a new relationship with China, which is increasingly becoming recognized as an economic giant at Korea's doorstep.

Even after becoming an OECD member in December 1996, South Korea feels a bit disadvantaged. Korea's 2002 gross domestic product, at US$898.7 billion, was tenth among the thirty member countries. The average GDP of the OECD members was US$962.4 billion. Perhaps by other developing countries' standards, Korea—even with its high-tech strengths—may be viewed as a "poor little rich country." Yet Koreans measure themselves by the standards of Japan, the U.S. and Western Europe. And from that perspective, they feel relatively impoverished.

GROWING NATIONALISM

Another aspect involved in foreign business is the strong spirit of nationalism exhibited by Koreans. As the nation's economy continues to improve, a sense of nationalism deepens, which may also be a latent legacy of President Park Chung Hee's infusion of positive thinking and somewhat chauvinistic sentiments. More recently with the Kim Dae-Jung government, and more so with the Roh Moo Hyun government, populism with a strong element of "*minjok-juui*"—which literally means "racism" but is actually more along the lines of the Spanish word "*la raza*," or prideful recognition of a common ethnicity—has become a key element.

A natural, if unfortunate, side effect of *minjok-juui* is a kind of generally benign racism that resents foreign influences on the fate of the nation. This is understandable, but at the same time, Koreans of all ages tend to put out of their minds the historical and current realities of being surrounded by considerably larger and more powerful nations.

Americans seem to be the greatest butt of this thinking. Today's large, if diminishing, U.S. military presence is insulting to many ultra-nationalists. But one needs to see Korean attitudes toward the U.S. not so much as a love-hate relationship, but rather as a partnership comprised of both high expectations and sorrowful disappointments over the past hundred years.

A century ago, the last royal government put a naïve sense of faith in its American relations to counter Chinese, Russian, and finally, Japanese encroachment on its sovereignty. The Americans were regarded as relatively pure, in the sense that they seemed to have no territorial designs on Korea and were reputed to be of high moral character, given the role of Protestant Christianity in American values at that time. It was true: the Americans of 1900 understood that Korea offered little economic or trade value, realizing that the small kingdom was a diplomatic minefield when coming to terms with the shifting powers within East Asia. Consequently, contrary to the pleas of a few American businessmen and many American missionaries, the US government turned its back on Korea and allowed Japan to colonize the country.

A half century later, when America accidentally came to the rescue by liberating Korea from Japan, Koreans once again looked upon it as a selfless savior, only to be again disappointed when the temporary division of the peninsula became permanent and resulted in a civil war that escalated into a major Cold War conflict, the Korean War.

Today's ongoing set of high expectations, often followed by disappointments, can be generally attributed to the Koreans' natural sense of being of strategic importance to the world in general and the US in particular – while the American often seem to be slow on picking up on the cues. So from the Korean perspective, America frequently comes across as "arrogant" in its failure to take US-Korean relationships adequately seriously, while the Americans are left scratching their heads and wondering what all the fuss is coming from a relatively remote part of the world.

At times, this "head in the sand" mentality generates what foreigners may regard as illogical outbreaks of nationalism over trivial events. Real or imagined national slights tend to yank Koreans' heads away from the sand, and they are often quite unhappy with what they perceive. So for foreigners, particularly from major Western nations, being in Korea can be a bit of a bumpy ride. The good news is that these outbursts are rarely directed personally at foreigners.

Those sensitive and idealistic young students who have not experienced the hardships of war or poverty have leaned toward more independent and nationalistic ideals. Their voice in the 2002 presidential election was temporarily loud enough to win the acceptance of the majority of students and the general public. With a nationalist, populist government in power, however, many of the weaknesses of this philosophy became self-evident. As a result, today there is an emerging moderate and practical moderate—at times even conservative—body of young people. In any event, nationalism remains a very strong, emotional factor in the daily lives of Koreans, and foreigners have no choice but to handle the matter sensitively.

CONSUMER BRAND PREFERENCE

The local consumer generally associates brands of foreign origin with quality and durability. That's why many manufacturers and marketers like to name their products with Western brands or write brand names in Western style, even though the products are exclusively for local consumers. A few examples are Kuraun Sando ("crown sand[wich]") cookies, Whaitu ("white") sanitary napkins, Bejimil ("vege-mil") vegetable milk, and Suitumintu ("sweet mint") gum. The government, however, encourages industry to develop indigenous and original brand names. In those cases where a local brand is written in Western style and easily confused with well-known foreign brands, the government encourages Korean companies to change the brand name.

Meanwhile, the local consumer has shown a strong preference for foreign brands. Even though nationalistic sentiment may indicate otherwise, nowhere is preference for foreign products more evident than in consumer behavior. Consumer preference for quality seems to transcend ideology everywhere. In reaction to this trend, some consumer activists have attempted to discourage the purchase of foreign-brand products, alleging that Korea has to pay high royalties to foreign licensers for using their brands on local products that have the same quality as foreign brands.

The general perception of foreign companies in Korea among ordinary consumers is rather favorable, again relating to their quality goods and services, as well as to the impression that foreign firms generally provide better working conditions for local employees. Instances of success by foreign consumer companies in assimilating to the local market have definitely helped in this direction.

At the same time, it may be helpful to keep in mind that there is no Korean word for "brand"—Koreans are forced to use the English word. And even when doing so, they can have a different view of branding. Historically, this has caused a problem with even some of the country's biggest firms, where marketing has not been their forte. Also, since the major *chaebol* firms are in seemingly every business niche proudly using the same corporate name, it often becomes meaningless to understand what, say, a "Hyundai" product may be. An automobile? An oil tanker? A credit card?

There are exceptions, such as with Samsung, which has strongly marketing-oriented management and was clever enough to overcome this problem by reinventing its image outside Korea. But even leading companies such as Samsung get caught up with family and personal dynamics. The company name often ends up being vastly more important than any ideas about branding. As a result, Korean firms are often indecisive in the use of international agencies abroad. At the same time, a purely Korean agency is likely to fail to detect offshore opportunities, while a multinational one is likely to find it very difficult to understand the different motivations of the Korean client.

What that means is that if a foreign company's products already carry a strong, well-recognized brand, the foreign company may have a major advantage in establishing a coherent image vis-à-vis the local competition, so long as that image is not inadvertently inappropriate in the context of Korean culture.

OFFICIALS: ELITE PERSPECTIVES VS. THOSE OF WORKING-LEVEL BUREAUCRATS

The attitudes toward foreign businesses among government officials and intellectuals may be more discerning. They usually have better perspectives with regard to the national interest—with the possible exception of lower working-level bureaucrats. The elite and officials in the finance and commerce ministries, who are aware of the highly competitive international environment where Korea has to chart its development course, are quite open-minded. Naturally, they can be more liberal concerning foreign investments and access of foreign goods and services to the local market.

The spirit of reciprocity is discussed more and more among those enlightened groups. For responsible officials, the treatment of foreign businesses, especially where it involves government sanctions and approvals, is often a delicate matter. There are always interested parties, either among local industries, which might be affected by the foreign presence, or activists and radical students with extremely chauvinistic inclinations. In rare instances, certain ministries have contradicted the decisions of more liberal ones. Under these circumstances, lofty causes of face-saving justifications can always help.

Yet most foreign businesses do not deal with the elite. Probably one of the most frustrating aspects of doing business in Korea is the inconsistent interpretation and application of conflicting regulations among the various government agencies at all levels. Naturally, government bureaucrats strive for a smooth and effective administration. Often there is a lack of clear communication with related parties, and this can lead to unnecessary requests for information. (Please see our chapter on "Relating to Bureaucrats" for a full discussion.)

For example, a number of foreign companies have looked into setting up large discount stores in Korea. Too often they were at the mercy of local politicians when it came to applying for a building permit—and that was after spending much time and energy trying to find their way through the bureaucratic jungle. In other words, while those at the top of the ministries may in fact be enlightened, too often it is the middle and lower levels that create the red tape. In doing so, they allow other outside "interested parties" to become involved.

Pressure by major trade partners to lift a certain trade regulation may cause a nasty political uproar, particularly if there is no good face-saving countermeasure. Such pressure is often referred to as "Gunboat Diplomacy," and such tactics with one's local embassy should be carefully and most conservatively considered.

BUSINESSMAN ATTITUDES

Korean business professionals are, of course, concerned with the protection of their businesses against foreign companies that usually enjoy such advantages as advanced technologies and products. Unless the advent of foreign business threatens immediate survival, Korean businesspeople tend to be more pragmatic, either pursuing coexistence or joining the inevitable force. With relationships established over the years with bureaucrats, businesses can also effectively block the entry of foreign companies into a certain segment of the local market.

EMPLOYEE FEELINGS

During the roller coaster years of the past, when the Korean economy was still in an early developmental stage, foreign firms were highly regarded as prospective workplaces by bright young graduates from good universities. They provided their employees with excellent opportunities for training and overseas travel. Additionally, foreign firms offered higher incomes and better working conditions than local firms could at that time.

Attitudes have changed, however. Many of those who joined foreign firms in the early '70s were disappointed by their limited upward mobility due to slow company growth. They felt the lack of long-term job security, as many foreign businesses that could not turn an immediate profit simply closed their doors and went home. Often, there was friction between foreign management and the local staff, where language and communication problems abounded, as did those "irritating differences" between the Korean and foreign "ways of doing things," particularly when home offices abroad were involved. This problem was exacerbated by frequent changes in expatriate managers. This last problem has become less of an issue as local hires have matured into taking on senior management roles and as Koreans have assumed top country management positions.

Nonetheless, some prevailing attitudes among Korean employees toward foreign employers remain. The biggest concern is the willingness of many foreign firms to terminate operations in Korea when things get tough, and this naturally spawns anxiety among prospective employees as to how certain their career prospects may be when joining a non-Korean firm. Rightly or wrongly, many Koreans view foreign firms as offering less job security than Korean companies. Also, there is a natural hesitation about working for a foreign boss who almost always does not speak Korean and may not have a good grasp of Korean business practices.

Though the political pendulum of late seems to be swinging back from ultra-nationalism to the center, there is an ongoing concern that working for a foreign firm is in some ways unpatriotic. In other words, many Koreans feel it is their nationalist obligation to build up the business of Korean firms rather than those of foreign or multinational companies. In a similar vein, foreign profits from the Korean market are too easily equated in many Koreans minds with profiteering from Korean vulnerabilities, and thereby offering nothing to the nation's welfare.

On the other hand, there are a number of well-recognized benefits to working for a foreign company. Foreign firms often bring along more progressive management systems and provide their staff with better technology to accomplish their work. While today's bright young prospects look more to major Korean companies for employment, other aspiring employees expect from foreign employers a benefits package better than what they can receive from domestic companies—a package that in some ways compensates for the anxieties and differences in ideology described above.

Depending on the company and job position, some employment opportunities with foreign firms can be very attractive, as foreign firms are often willing to invest in training to bring the skills of their employees up to levels of world-class competency. Much of this training is done outside of Korea, and that can be a major draw to prospective employees. Also, many young Koreans are aware of several Korean executives now in Korean firms who started their careers working for foreign companies, where they polished their English skills and gained business know-how that later made them more attractive candidates for outside executive positions with Korean firms. In any case, one of the striking differences between an office of a foreign firm and that of a similar Korean firm is the working environment. While constantly improving, Korean work conditions still tend to be relatively cramped and joyless. For some young Koreans, spending most of their waking hours in a more pleasant environment may be a strong incentive to join a foreign firm.

MIXED FEELINGS

Korea is becoming a more pluralistic society, with the voices of various interest groups growing. The presence of foreign businesses and products also draws reactions that are not necessarily uniform. Some college students are antagonistic toward anything foreign, while the majority favors freer trade and investment. The feelings are mixed.

Today, Koreans' sophistication allows the acceptance of foreign businesses as a "necessary evil," but they have also learned how to accommodate, as well as take advantage of, the opportunities for economic growth. The inevitable trend of internationalization in the economy is gaining momentum, possibly overcoming social and cultural obstacles.

© YONHAP PHOTO

PART III.
GETTING ALONG WITH KOREANS

12. NEGOTIATING BUSINESS

*E*veryone negotiates something every day as a means of getting what one wants from others. Negotiation is a two-way process designed to reach an agreement when two sides have some shared interests but also have differences. Although negotiation takes place every day, it's not always easy to do it successfully, especially when the parties are from different cultural, social, and legal backgrounds. These differences often add other dimensions to the negotiating arena.

DIFFERENT RULES

An acquaintance of this author once said: "Comparative international law is really simple. In England, anything that is not legally forbidden is permitted. In Germany, anything that is not legally permitted is forbidden. In Russia, everything is forbidden, even that which is permitted. In France, everything is permitted, even that which is forbidden. And in Korea, anything that is either forbidden or permitted is subject to negotiation."

Korea, with its long Confucian historical and more recent Japanese colonial background, has developed a business climate unique unto itself, and its businesspeople tend to play by their own set of rules and ethics. With these cultural differences setting the stage, foreigners often have difficulties doing business in this country.

PROBLEMS

One extensive study of skilled international business negotiators, involving 22 different countries and 55 nationalities, pinpointed where conflict is most often experienced in international negotiations.

A. Finding a Common Ground

All skilled negotiators recognize the necessity of establishing a common ground for reinforcing negotiations. The wider the area of common interest and concerns, the more negotiators are able to reduce conflicts and differences. This common ground must be determined and utilized, though it may not be readily recognized. Intense effort and research may have to be employed, but finding such common ground on which to build negotiations is a must, and the results are worthwhile.

B. Mutual Trust

Reciprocal trust is indispensable to the success of negotiations. Trusting those who think, believe and act similar to the way we do is not so difficult, but establishing a relationship with people in a foreign country whose values and behavior sharply differ from what we are accustomed to is much more difficult and takes much more time. It is incredible to think that we can fly into a strange country and in the first few hours attempt to negotiate with persons about whom we know practically nothing.

C. Communication Barriers

Language obstacles are formidable factors in impeding negotiations, even if one's counterpart speaks one's language fluently. It is likely that, while his words are in one's language, his thinking, psychological orientation, and business culture are bound to his own language and mentality. These elements are untranslatable, unless one really knows a new culture extremely well, which is very rare.

Conversational knowledge of one's language is not necessarily adequate for use in negotiations. The nuance of words is crucially important in communication. Negotiations communication can often be hampered by nuance differences and the lack of equivalent expressions. For instance, knowledgeable people cannot find a vocabulary concept corresponding to "sportsmanship" in the Korean language. Also, through the nuance of language one may casually send a signal of willingness to compromise if the counterpart does likewise, but he may miss this completely.

Case in point: one may say, "We would find it very difficult to make that delivery date," with the meaning of "...but it's not impossible." But one's Korean counterpart may interpret the statement as a polite Korean way of saying "no" and miss the attempted signal completely.

Misunderstanding can also occur in the reverse. In Korea, cultural nature does not permit an individual to say a flat "no." So one's Korean counterpart may state that something is "very difficult," an indefinite expression that will actually mean "absolutely impossible." In this way, the Korean language is much more indirect, indefinite, and evasive than

English, which is frank, direct, to-the-point, and sometimes interpreted as impolite and unkind by a Korean counterpart.

Both the Korean and English languages have the word "understanding" in their vocabularies. However, the Korean word implies "agreement" with the nuance of "understanding," whereas the English word can imply "disagreement" along with "understanding." The Korean language has a word for "compromise," but decades of authoritarian rule have permitted little practice of the concept anywher in society. In practice, "confrontation" is the form that has an effect on business and management negotiations as well. National differences within the same language can also hamper communication. To "table a motion" in parliamentary procedure has the exact opposite meaning in British English and American English.

Language is more than a medium of communication: it can be a symbol of national identity. One's negotiating counterpart may insist on negotiating in his own language, even though he knows one's language quite well. He may feel this affirms his national identity or gives him an advantage.

In this case, an interpreter is necessary. This opens a whole new box of potential problems. Great care must be exercised in the selection and use of an interpreter.

D. Cultural Business Etiquette

To say that business behavior is based on cultural roots is a gross understatement. Inadvertent impolite behavior has hindered or wrecked many negotiations. One's host may have some very special dining practices, which are based on cultural behavior. It is to the advantage of the expatriate negotiator to know about these. (Please refer to the chapter "Get Off on the Right Foot—Business Etiquette" for details.)

E. Legal and Practical Distinctions

Local culture determines what business conduct is proper or improper, moral or unethical, and legal or permissive. The difference between a gift and a bribe is not universally recognized.

Differences in legal codes also affect negotiations. Beyond basic differences in national legal codes, complications may arise in the different applications of those codes.

In some countries, oral agreements are preferred to written ones, and attempts to insist on written agreements are often, if not always, regarded as insults. A comprehensively detailed agreement drafted by one's Western company's legal department may be worthless in the courts of a developing country.

KOREAN CONCEPTS OF NEGOTIATING

For a Korean, negotiating is viewed more as part of a relationship, rather than specific terms of an agreement that happen to be written down on paper. A written contract among Koreans is not necessarily regarded as binding or important as it is in the West. To the Korean mind, commitments based on relationships or on a personal level are equally important.

It is commonly considered that "a contract is as good as the willingness of the parties to observe it." Perhaps Koreans are more concerned, even in the early stages of negotiating, that future enforcement of agreements can only be secured by personal commitments.

"Who's in charge?" is sometimes a baffling mystery to the Western negotiator. A dozen negotiators may sit on the opposite side of the conference table, but none may have decision-making authority. This can be the cause of the Western negotiator's frustration and impatience. This is especially the case with family-owned companies. Families still control many companies in Korea. When negotiating with a family-dominated company, the key family decision-maker usually does not attend the negotiations. Pinpointing the real decision-maker may seem to be impossible. In many cases, the absence of the real decision-maker can seriously delay negotiations.

Foreign businessmen are often puzzled and frustrated when Korean counterparts shy away from seemingly lucrative deals. Sometimes it is because the Korean party lost face or felt that he or she was patronized too much, or possibly that the setting of the negotiation was unsatisfactory. To a Westerner, this may be a denial of the process of logic with which he or she is familiar.

NEGOTIATING POINTERS

As negotiating situations can vary greatly, generalization is not easy. The following, however, are some suggestions that may help the foreign business professional sharpen his or her sensitivity to the local business environment and enhance his or her negotiating skills, thus contributing to his or her success in dealing with Koreans.

Build the Right Climate

Koreans prefer to do business with people they like. Profit alone is not always their first priority. Sustained growth and good personal relations are equally important.

Entertainment plays a major role among businesspeople in building a climate conducive to a better understanding of one another. To facilitate the negotiating process, entertain and be entertained. Behave as an uninhibited human being at a drinking party with local counterparts. Let the hair down. Koreans love to see a foreign opponent unmasked by his nationality, company, and position. One will be quite surprised to discover the different mood and rapport at a negotiating session the next morning.

A common concern of Western businesswomen is how they should interact in business entertainment involving professional hostesses and the like in Asia, including Korea. There are no easy words of advice on this topic, since the situation can vary considerably. Some general observations, however, made over the past decade may offer insight on how to play the next scenario.

Women—including Korean women—are assuming wider and greater roles in business, so their presence is being felt more significantly than ever. Foreign women—and most particularly non-Asian women—are given much more latitude than Korean women when it comes to joining in on traditionally male-only venues. Times continue to change, but one approach is for the foreign businesswoman to feel free to invite people to and attend after-work entertainment occasions. Often, a proper evening out on the town starts with a restaurant and ends after visiting two or more bars. Attending the restaurant, and possibly the first bar, is no problem. It may be wise, however, for the businesswoman to be attentive if the guys are going to be ill at ease with her joining them at the second bar.

Communication

Without communication, there is no negotiation. Whereas communication is not easy even between parties who have a considerable amount of shared values and experience in their backgrounds, cross-cultural communication is even more difficult. Negotiating under these kinds of conditions requires from both parties special qualities such as empathy, patience, and a good ear, in addition to proficiency in the language used.

Remember that local businesspeople prefer to express themselves in their own language, which is often vague and ambiguous. It may help for a foreign negotiator to repeat, in his or her own terms, what has been presented by his or her counterpart after each session. Exchanging minutes after meetings is helpful to avoid misunderstanding. Don't assume that all was understood by one's counterpart and therefore agreed upon.

If an interpreter is used, make the most of him or her. Brief the interpreter beforehand and provide any notes one has on the proposal one intends to make. Also, allow sufficient time for the interpreter to clarify points where he or she thinks the meaning is obscure.

Allow Sufficient Time

Typically, a visiting foreign businessperson will attempt to settle all his business dealings in a short period of time. He becomes impatient when he cannot secure a firm reply from the counterpart on short notice. This is, of course, an even greater problem when the foreign representative has reached a milestone in his overseas management. Consequently, experienced foreign businesspeople in Korea tend to underestimate results compared to their colleagues elsewhere.

Negotiation can be time-consuming in any place. Time must be spent, however, to assure that the decision is as close as possible to what one desires. For most local businesspeople, their exposure to foreign business is rather limited, and they naturally want to be more prudent in their decisions with foreign partners. Do not demonstrate impatience at a negotiating table, since one's counterpart will interpret this as weakness. Allow sufficient time to negotiate, and remember to be patient with the counterpart's deliberate and often slow decision-making process.

By not allowing sufficient negotiation time, it is more often the foreign negotiator than his Korean counterpart who unnecessarily concedes important points in order to catch the plane. Depending on one's relationship with the other negotiation team, one may wish to be precise or vague in offering one's flight departure date and time. If one is negotiating with an established partner, it is good to share the information so that the other side can negotiate in good faith at a pace to come to an agreement in time. On the other hand, if one is unsure about or unfamiliar with the other firm, one may give a general, expected departure date, but work with an airline ticket where one is certain one can extend the departure date if necessary.

Finally getting to a "yes" with the other side of the negotiating table may not be the same as coming to an agreement with the other firm. Often, the final terms agreed upon may require additional time to gain final approval when dealing with a large, bureaucratic firm such as one of the *chaebol* (business conglomerate) companies.

Be Innovative

To strike a deal in a dynamic country where nothing seems stationary, one must be quite imaginative. Be it a JV negotiation or negotiations with the government, a highly innovative mind is often required to forge an idea from an amorphous state to reality. During the course of negotiations, generate as many possibilities and present these alternatives as much as necessary to induce an agreement.

The reason one negotiates is to produce something better than the results one can get without negotiating. Knowing those results and all the possible alternatives or the BATNA (Best Alternative To a Negotiated Agreement) will definitely lead to efficient and productive negotiations.

In the compact, Seoul-dominated market, it is common for foreign firms to have Korean employees who may have personal, often long-term relations with employees of the other firm. Often the foreign executive can learn a great deal about the "lay of the land" via these personal connections. If the other firm has a sincere interest in coming to an agreement, one may be surprised to find "inside salespeople" in the other firm invaluable. These individuals are normally junior managers and above who are willing to assist the overall negotiation process by providing insight as to what the real priorities of their company are, which personalities are leaning towards and against a deal with one's firm, and even information on competitive offers.

Use a Facilitator

It is desirable, especially in the case of sensitive negotiations, to have someone to facilitate the proceedings either at the negotiating table or outside the meeting. A facilitator may help to keep the meeting on the right track, enforce any ground rules, and stimulate proceedings at the negotiating table. In this case, a third-party mediator or consultant may play a role. An interpreter can also perform on a limited basis. In case a mediator is not participating in the meeting, he or she can work as a go-between, facilitating the process of agreement. These facilitators may ask for a flat fee, but often payment is a percentage of the value of the deal. Obviously, it is important to understand up front what kind of remuneration the facilitator is expecting, as well as what kind of political and social leverage—and obligations—the facilitator may have with both negotiating parties.

If negotiations reach a stalemate, change the environment. Inviting the counterpart to one's home ground is one way to solve a stalemate problem, and replacing the negotiating staff may be another. And, as elsewhere, sometimes it is best to walk away and be prepared to come back another day.

Find the Right Fit

What is important for successful negotiations in Korea is the sensitivity and understanding that a different set of rules and environment are operating and a different fit to which both parties must be tailored.

Once the right fit is found, sincerity and a contest of wills usually decide the outcome. One should demonstrate one's strength and power when necessary, as in any negotiation. Local companies are generally in need of technology, export opportunities, and capital that will contribute to their sustained growth. Even though the advantage one offers is an ideal fit for the parties, it should be "sweetened with a personal touch" and accompanied with "attractive trimmings." The success of the deal can largely hinge on the personal relationship one establishes from the time of the initial negotiations. If the transaction is a large and complicated one, one's goodwill—or lack thereof—can make a difference. One is likely to find oneself in continuous negotiating mode as the two parties encounter the inevitable "speed bumps." One's personal relationship with one's counterparts can make the difference in determining whether this will be one's first contract of many other profitable deals, or a single painful Pyrrhic victory that one and one's firm may regret in the future.

Maintain Relationships

Do not leave hard feelings with the counterpart even if the negotiation fails. Even after the negotiation breaks off, one should try to establish a pleasant climate for one's potential partner. It will also facilitate one's next move. Sometimes, chauvinism can harm the game, too. A bad aftertaste will be long remembered by local businesspeople. This can be bad, since there is often a second chance to come back to the table—if not for this deal, then for a new opportunity. Also, it is important to remember that the Korean marketplace is a tight-knit one, and a reputation of any sort can precede one. As an example, it is not surprising to learn that strong sentiment against a major multinational, which divested from Korea after a controversial conflict when negotiations broke off, will remain very much alive among some government officials even after some years elapse.

Always leave the counterpart with something to feel good about. Otherwise, one may make an enemy. One should try to negotiate as though one will definitely have the occasion to deal with the same partner again. Given the escalation of mergers and acquisitions in the Korean marketplace—not to mention the fact that Koreans these days often change firms—it is important not to burn one's bridges.

Process Rather than Substance

Koreans also place value on the process as much as on substance in business negotiations. A common phrase in business that betrays the Korean sense of humor is "*pohm seng pohm sah*." This phrase, delivered with the same intonation as "*comme ci comme ça*," means "to live and die by form (*pohm*)." While even the Koreans can laugh at or be frustrated by this cultural pattern, everyone acknowledges it to be all too real.

Koreans also place value on the "process" as much as on "substance" in business negotiations. Foreign businesspeople are often puzzled and frustrated that Korean counterparts sometimes shy away from a seemingly lucrative deal, perhaps because the Korean party lost face, or felt that he or she was patronized too much, or possibly because the setting of the negotiation was unsatisfactory. To a Westerner, this may be a denial of the process of logic with which he or she is familiar.

Tough Bargainers

Koreans are frequently known as tough bargainers. From living in fiercely competitive and crammed environments, Koreans have developed strong qualities that are not necessarily consistent with the Confucian teachings of moderation. Yet if there is anything that may be construed as being Confucian, it is the principle that there is always someone on top of the other. Otherwise stated, it is an Asian application of the Golden Business

Rule—"He who holds the gold makes the rules."

It is not uncommon for a Western businessperson to be surprised when he or she finds that a counterpart who had appeared to be very calm and gentle in manner in reality has the ability to be very shrewd, tenacious, and even ruthless.

Normally, the seller is at a disadvantage, and "fair negotiations" from a Western perspective can be alien to the Korean side of the table. Koreans often approach negotiations with a "zero sum game" mentality. A "fair price" is the best the buyer can extract from the seller without seriously endangering delivery of desired goods and services. For example, one of the biggest causes of failure of Korean start-up companies is negotiating away too much—even with negative margins—so that their first deal often becomes their last. Accordingly, the Western negotiator may find it critical to keep his or her actual margins confidential.

PLAYING BY LOCAL AND INTERNATIONAL RULES

With some small Korean companies, oral agreements may be preferred to written ones. As stated before, a foreigner's insistence on long, written agreements could be regarded as insulting by a Korean. Nevertheless, it is imperative to have written agreements. And those negotiated agreements must be as explicit as possible due to the business cultural differences.

A comprehensively detailed agreement drafted by one's Western company's legal department may seem to cover all bases, when in fact such a document can confuse and cause major problems during and following negotiations. The expatriate negotiator should be prepared to redraft the head office's prepared first document to say exactly the same thing but in simpler language. Otherwise, one is likely to confuse one's Korean counterpart with the Western "legalese," which in turn can lead to major misunderstandings.

Long paragraph blocks should be broken up, with sub-clauses presented in an outline form that is easy to navigate and understand. Hypothetical examples of unusual or complicated concepts or conditions need to be included to ensure not only agreement but also complete understanding.

One should be careful in discussing indemnification for malfeasance so as not to insult the other party. This issue normally does not exist in purely Western negotiations, but often the Korean negotiator may take exception to how a Western attorney describes the other party as being liable for potential penalties. Addenda should be freely and fully included to specifically point out issues such as payment terms and timing so that there is no misunderstanding or possible variance of interpretation.

Now, all of this is a lot of extra work for the Western negotiator—but it is worth it, given the likely headaches and incriminations that may follow if one doesn't do this kind of preparation. Not only are the business cultures different, basic commercial concepts may significantly vary in the details—or possibly not even exist within one's Korean counterpart's normal activities.

Furthermore, Korean employees are quite frequently transferred among the various departments of their organization. But rarely is there time for a decent handover of responsibilities—often during these very brief orientation periods, the exiting employee neglects to even mention to the replacement employee where his or her contract has been filed. Consequently, an extremely detailed, heavily illustrated, and well organized agreement, with full addenda, can be critical for getting the replacement employee up to speed.

This kind of document can also get the new employee off the hook with his or her boss should a disagreement arise. Should the disputed matter be clearly covered in the agreement, especially if explained clearly as a contingency or possibility—complete with hypothetical examples—the new employee can report that the matter has already been contractually settled.

Keeping a Practical Balance

Now, should it not already be obvious, the important lesson is not to get suckered into the "cultural catch" of surrendering good business sense due to cultural differences. The Korean cultural trait of not wishing to put things down on paper or not taking contracts as seriously as Westerners do should be accommodated just so far. The Westerner is not a Korean and is therefore not part of Korea's social web of obligations and potential penalties. Since the Westerner is negotiating across the "cultural divide," he or she must protect the company's interests.

It is critical to be as clear and as explicit as possible when negotiating a strategic legal agreement in Korea. It is also important to keep in mind that ultimately, Korean contracts are fully enforceable. But be aware that these documents are literally as good as they are written. There are almost no additional legal safeguards beyond what appears on paper.

So be prepared, and be explicit. Most importantly, do not assume, but always confirm, genuine understanding, in writing, of all points with one's

Korean negotiating partner.

Business negotiation is an exacting and demanding matter, particularly complicated from playing by a different set of cultural rules and business practices. The more the expatriate executive is familiar with the rules, the more there can be a meeting of minds, and the more success he or she can achieve at the bargaining table. It is all to his or her advantage to be thoroughly familiar with the counterpart's set of mind and behavioral patterns.

At the same time, it is critical to keep in mind that Korean business practices, though often based on deep cultural foundations, are rapidly changing. The marketplace is becoming more open to international practices. Women, and Koreans returning from extended periods living abroad, are making their impact, along with the changes resulting from the wide application of seemingly ubiquitous broadband communications. The points discussed above are what one may consider to be bedrock when it comes to negotiating. But bear in mind that, while the rules are slow to change, they are changing. Therefore, it is wise to occasionally review and test these rules with a Korean colleague before entering the negotiating room.

13. GETTING JOINT VENTURES RIGHT

*I*t is an all too familiar scene: the shouted recriminations, the secret maneuvers, and a total breakdown in communications, ending in slamming doors. A marital spat? Sure. But the marriage is one of vested business interests: the international joint venture.

Such scenes, played out in executive offices around the world, have become the bane of multinational corporate life. They are indicative of a growing malaise that affects bottom-line corporate decisions: the cross-cultural partner conflict. Their resolution requires the wisdom of a Solomon, the patience of a Buddha, and a deep understanding of the culture involved.

Resolving conflicts requires neither mystical nor magic powers, but a deep understanding of cultural differences, with some streetwise business acumen to help dilute partner conflicts.

A PROFITABLE MARRIAGE

JVs are frequently seen as marriages between companies, and justly so. The similarities between personal and corporate relationships are striking. As in a marriage, cross-cultural business ventures demand a generous degree of give-and-take, understanding, patience, and forbearance. It has been noted that to regard marriage as a 50-50 proposition is a mistake; usually one side must go more than halfway. Marriage might be more properly regarded as an 80-80 proposition. The same is true of corporate partnerships.

Nonetheless, when looking for a prospect it is critical to know one's future spouse's limits before reporting home. As obvious as this may seem, often wishful thinking takes the place of doing one's homework.

Some years ago, one of the large *chaebol* companies was willing to go 50-50 on a JV with a large American company. When the assigned American VP went back to the executive board in the U.S., he was asked if the American firm could have a 51 percent share. He made the mistake of saying "I think that may be possible" when he should have said "No way"— or at least "I need to confirm." When he returned to Korea with the 51/49 authorized offer, the Korean company told him to get lost.

It was a loss for Korea and that expatriate. The plant that was to come from this JV would have provided a product for use in Korea and for export to the rest of Northeast Asia. Instead, the plant was built in Taiwan. And the American VP was later fired. The VP's blunder was agreeing to an impossible request because he did not fully understand the limits of his prospective partner.

One other common blunder comes from foreigners believing a *chaebol* prospect's overstated boast as to their capacity to sell to other companies in the same *chaebol* group. As enticing or logical as the claim may seem, the figure is hardly ever accurate, and the messenger who predicates setting up a JV on this exaggeration could be heading for some nasty turns in his or her career.

Nearly every JV in Korea has had some sort of adversity between partners at one time or another. Sometimes complete breakdowns occur due to severe partner conflict. In such cases, the unfortunate result is a traumatic divorce causing permanent damage and injury. Perhaps many of these situations could have been avoided or overcome with adequate counsel and understanding of the unique dynamics involved on both sides.

Several factors may enhance the sensitivity to cultural differences and bring about an awareness of potential areas of conflict and their prevention or resolution.

NATIONAL DOMINANT TRAITS

While they accept the internationalization of the economy as an inevitable trend, Koreans want to maintain their independence and self-reliance, free from any domination by foreign business. Remember, they belong to a nation that successfully maintained its identity throughout a history of repeated war and domination by neighboring powers. Therefore, in dealing with their foreign partners, it is natural for them to be sensitive and concerned about the degree of control that they can maintain. It should be readily recognizable that some of the justifiable reactions and behavior of local partners is due to their fear of losing control of the company.

As in any human organization or enterprise, control of one's own destiny is the name of the game. National sovereignty is an ideal for many people. This deep-seated emotional response is especially prominent in the Korean national psychology. History has made the people sensitive about their national identity and destiny, and they may, in extreme cases, behave quite chauvinistically in spite of their realization of the benefits of being more open and cosmopolitan.

Losing control of a firm, even in the U.S., is a traumatic experience for its founder. After he has poured his life's blood into it and suffered the growing pains of a developing business, the loss of supervision of the enterprise may be compared to the emotional trauma of a parent whose son is being adopted by an alien foster parent. While more and more JVs are involving companies managed by the second generation of the founding family, the sense of loss—or even feelings of betrayal to the deceased founding father—can create some significant, ongoing psychological burdens.

Often, a JV takes place between a foreign company and a company that belongs to one of the major Korean groups, or *chaebol*. In this case, the family ties to the founder may no longer be present. The common Korean employees, however, will certainly be paying close attention to which executives will have the majority influence on their long-term well-being. So the foreign director may have special challenges in obtaining the same level of loyalty and dedication as received by the Korean counterpart. Because of this general tendency of the Korean partner's employees to generally ignore the foreign staff and work around them, it is critical for the foreign partner to send someone who is mature in many ways and has superb people skills.

The biggest mistake is to send some young MBA or Ph.D hotshot lacking in excellent cross-cultural political skills. Generally speaking, the foreign representative really should be in approximately the same age bracket as the Korean counterpart. Someone quite a bit younger is likely to not be taken seriously by the Korean rank and file for this senior position.

EXPECTATIONS OF A FOREIGN PARTNER

Position and Status

Every businessperson is profit-motivated. Korean business people are no exception. Profit is not the only objective, however, that Korean business people seek from an association with a foreign company. They also want sustained growth and a larger market share via foreign products, technology, capital, and export capability. Small companies sometimes seem more interested in building their image with an affiliation with a reputable foreign company than in immediate profits.

In an association with a foreign partner, the national executive wants to occupy a position with a title that denotes status and recognition, even though the position itself does not necessarily accompany major responsibility in the company. Job title is important, since it signifies social standing in Korean hierarchical social structure.

The local partner usually finds satisfaction in a situation where a smooth relationship exists and, at the same time, he can meet his ego needs. In Korean psychology, "*gibun*" is an extremely important factor in ego fulfillment. This is the personal feeling, the attitude, the mood, and the mental state. Once the "*gibun*" is unpleasant or unsatisfactory and "face" is lost in a relationship with a foreign partner, the Korean partner might be willing to sacrifice any monetary benefit.

SOURCES OF CONFLICT

It may be beneficial to identify some of the possible causes of conflict. To be aware of these factors beforehand may help in avoiding confrontations. Just as in individuals, each organization has its own personality or culture, sometimes unique to itself. Commonly these traits can vary between different organizations.

Discovering incompatibility is not uncommon. Just as in human relationships, two organizations can be quite incompatible with each other. Many points of friction are related to differences in the culture and the flexibility of management styles. Incompatibility, both in its personal and organizational aspects, can lead to serious conflicts.

Priority Differences

Each organization has its own set of priorities. The global strategy of a major multi-national corporation may not necessarily be aligned with those of the host country or a local partner. The most common priority differences arising between Korean and foreign partners are:

- Profit versus market share,
- Dividend declaration and profit remittance, and
- Marketing strategy.

In the early stages of a JV, management control is usually contested, even in a situation where the contract stipulates that the foreign partner has full responsibility for managing the operations.

Management Style

Management style, especially concerning personal policies, is frequently a cause for conflict in such matters as:

- Employment and promotion policies
  - Salary increases
- Management information systems
  - Customer relations
  - Marketing and selling practices
- Transfer pricing (rare)

PREVENTION OF CONFLICT

From the beginning, joint operation partners should openly discuss and agree upon definite steps to be taken as preventive measures for minimizing conflicts related to management and organization.

Procedure Formula

A set of positive "rules of the game" must be established in the formation of the JV and maintained throughout the entire engagement. Some JVs have made it a point to have formal, annual review meetings to ensure that both sides are pulling in the same direction and, ultimately, to determine if it still makes sense to continue to partner. It is desirable to discuss and lay out as much as possible the management of the companies, anticipating some of the possible problem areas.

Records and minutes of negotiations and ongoing consultations should be kept in good order and detail for future reference. Since Koreans tend not to be very fastidious documenters, it may be wise for the foreign partner to volunteer to keep minutes and records, with the Korean partner reviewing the drafts before both parties sign the final documents. If misunderstandings arise, it is always helpful to go back to the record, thus avoiding uncertainty and doubt that could create instability and deteriorate the partnership.

Communication Channels

It is important to maintain regular, sincere, and open lines of personal communication between the partners. This is crucial in a marriage and in a family relationship between parents and children. It is just as important in the maintenance of an effective, productive, and harmonious business partnership. As long as there is dialogue, solutions can be found, even to differences of major proportions.

The issues that arise when working with a *chaebol* are completely different from those that occur when working with a medium-sized partner. While one can assume a *chaebol*-class company will have staff with the English language skills and background to communicate effectively and easily with foreign partners, that is usually not the case with smaller companies. Therefore, special diligence is needed to make sure that individuals with the appropriate language and communication skills are available when considering partnering with a medium-sized company.

The importance of emotional bonding with Korean partners cannot be overstated. The source of many communication breakdowns can be traced to foreign mangers treating their office relations as simply "business relationships." This "strictly business" compartmentalization of personal relations can come across as being exceedingly cold and cynical to the Korean partners—much more so than is the case in other cultures. If the foreign manager neglects this essential aspect of business in Korea, he or she may one day be surprised to discover that he or she is working in isolation and very much out of the loop.

To avoid this pitfall, regular sharing of meals and at least the occasional after-hours drink with one's partners, colleagues, and subordinates can do wonders. Even the foreign teetotaler can learn how to nurse a drink and still build the critical emotional bonds with co-workers.

Status Position

Another way to avoid difficulties with local partners is to be sure that they feel they have something important to do in the administration of the business and are busy and active in company affairs. They can be of invaluable use in areas where they have special skills and important contacts, such as PR, government connections, customer contacts, and labor relations. These are areas where the expatriate partner might lack skills, especially due to language and communication obstacles. The local partner can perform a strategic role with these contacts and can be a beneficial adjunct to the foreign partner, enhancing the whole joint operation.

Based on Confucianism, Korea's vertical social structure places great importance on position and status to satisfy the ego. Therefore, some conflicts could be avoided by appointing the local partner in the highest possible position in the company, such as chairman. In a Korean organization, a person on top of the hierarchy is not supposed to be involved in the mundane, down-to-earth details, so suggesting placement in a high honorary position can prevent him or her from meddling in day-to-day management decisions.

Extracurricular Activities

One very important way to develop harmonious working relationships is to share and develop a common interest outside the office. A shared interest in sports activities like tennis or golf can contribute greatly in building understanding, relaxing tension, and resolving conflicts. A great deal of business has been transacted and negotiations achieved while walking an 18-hole course in a relaxed, pleasant atmosphere. Likewise, a healthy, grand-slam volley just inside the right corner of the court produces more constructive results than a volley of words in the office conference room. There's nothing like a hole-in-one or a sliced smash just inside the alley to build a someone's respect for you. But don't win too often!

Mutual Family Interest

Interest in each other's families will go a long way in easing tensions and bridge barriers. Discussing children and discovering common problems and concerns elicit empathy and concern, which will likely transfer to business relationships. Every business partnership needs some time of relaxation and laying back, accomplished by sharing personal interest.

Mutual Respect

Another indispensable ingredient that must be prescribed for conflict prevention is for partners to have an unshakable mutual respect for one another. In a business partnership where there are conflicting interests, it may not always be easy to maintain respect for each other. If there is to be a working relationship, nothing must be allowed to interrupt this interflow of confidence and understanding. When partners start to slander each other, it will inevitably result in the destruction of the interpersonal relationship and, of course, seriously affect the operation of the business venture as well.

As important as personal relationships are, consideration for the effectiveness and productiveness of the business venture should demand the discipline required for maintaining a healthy mutual respect between partners. When respect is threatened, begin looking for the positive, strong points in the other partner, which will begin to outweigh the problem points of weakness or shortcomings. In this way, respect can be rebuilt and even become long-lasting.

In any relationship, differences in opinion and occasional misunderstandings that could result in conflicts are bound to arise; it's almost inevitable. But by anticipating possible conflict areas and taking measures to prevent the problem from arising, one can prevent many run-ins.

RESOLVING CONFLICTS

Conflicts are inevitable and rarely predictable—and each JV has a way of creating its own peculiar set of clashes. All of this makes it almost impossible to give simple precautionary advice. Nonetheless, here are some general ideas that may help in resolving future conflicts.

Personal Considerations

Western logic alone is not usually sufficient to influence a Korean counterpart. Simply reopening or referring to the exact stipulations of a contract may not work; it has been said, "Don't confuse me with facts." Such a factual confrontation will only raise the defenses of the local partner and even block any attempt at resolution. This is not to say one should let contracted terms and conditions slide. But it also very important to take into fullest consideration the interpersonal issues. Once again, the matter of "*gibun*" plays a subconscious role in the resolution of conflict. Try to appeal to the emotional common denominator.

Controlling Emotions

Showing one's emotions in a demonstration of anger can only exacerbate the situation; the foreign partner must always keep his or her own emotions under complete control, while appealing to the local partner's emotions. This is obviously easier said than done, but too often by "losing it" the person who loses his or her temper becomes the ultimate loser.

In the real world, it is not simply a game of winning and losing when it comes to controlling one's emotions. For example, information of a dramatically upsetting nature may reach the foreign partner first, without enough time for the foreign partner to share the bad news with his or her Korean counterpart diplomatically or in confidence. In the worst case, the Korean partner could learn of the news in front of other employees as well as the foreign partner and conceivably lose control of his or her emotions.

In such case, it may be wise for the foreign partner to give a nod or two of the head, signaling understanding or appreciation of the Korean's predicament or interpretation. If there is, in fact, a significant difference of views held by the two companies or partners, it is better for the foreign partner to wait and talk it out behind closed doors, hours later at least if not the next day, after the Korean partner has had a chance to cool off. This may be a much better tactic than simply standing in cool, stoic splendor—and thereby causing one's Korean counterpart to lose face. While there is no set formula to address all scenarios, this example may demonstrate the need to be flexible and alert when dealing with emotions—particularly when in front of subordinates.

Just as wise parents go to great lengths not to bicker with each other in front of their children, it is even more important that the top executives representing two companies keep at least a positive and pleasant façade for the benefit of the other employees. They still can—and should—let their hair down offsite or behind closed doors to get conflicting matters, no matter how small, out on the table to resolve them.

Compromise Diplomacy

In difficult confrontations, the use of some diplomatic procedures such as give-and-take or a trade-off may prove productive in resolving conflicts. It may require some innovation to generate alternative ideas in the resolving process.

A Korean JV partner agreed to concede the majority share in the company to the foreign partner, on condition that he be granted the right to veto the first executive vice-president appointed by the foreign partner. Though perhaps not ideal, it is an example of a trade-off.

The "tit-for-tat" procedure normally does not develop into a productive partnership. One wins only the battle and not the war. If a deadlock arises, however, a valid alternative may be to consider areas of possible trade-off in order to reach a compromise.

Home Office Support

A very important requirement for expatriates representing a foreign company is to secure the full support of the head office for what one intends to propose to the local partner. If such support is not firm, it will be more difficult to resolve differences.

Such consultation with and approval from the head office has several benefits. First, it offers the opportunity for counsel concerning the proposal. It also gets the foreign partner representative off the hook should the proposal be a difficult sell. The tough proposal will not be simply the representative's personal idea, but that of the foreign corporation. It also adds political clout to the foreign representative when presenting his or her company's case to the local partner. The stronger the home office support, the easier it is to deal with difficult conflicts. Such backing boosts the confidence that can influence the outcome of the consultation.

At the same time, the foreign representative stationed locally must be given the authority to make responsible concessions on the spot, if at least only tentatively, pending head or regional office agreement. In any event, if offshore management frequently overrules the representative, the Korean partner will likely conclude that the counterpart is either inadequate at his or her job, particularly in terms of home office confidence/politics, or inappropriate when it comes to international business acumen. Consequently, there needs to be an appropriate delegation of authority and a willingness to listen on the part of the offshore management team.

Confidential Negotiations

Keeping quiet is not an easy discipline, but still a crucial skill in resolving conflicts. Korea is a relatively small community. Word spreads fast, especially if it is undesirable, unfortunate news. In this case the problem of "blab" is not confined to any one segment of society. So it is important to keep one's mouth shut when partners are trying to resolve a conflict. During World War II, we were told that "Loose lips sink ships." As in war, loose lips can sink a business partnership.

Proper Protocol

Form, process, and setting—that is, protocol—are quite important in Korean business encounters. One must pay attention to the time, place, and general environment for important discussions between partners. It can be very helpful to choose a neutral place away from the location of the conflict—a place that is pleasant, relaxed, away from phones, and in the end more conducive for dialogue is highly desirable.

Neutral Moderator

In Korea, there is a saying that "Buddhist priests cannot cut their own hair—nor can barbers." When the going gets tough in dealing with the local partner, who in most cases has a definite vested interest and advantage, it may be wise to seek professional help from a consultant or prominent figure, preferably in the local industry.

A mediator or go-between has no emotional connection to the situation and can help to reduce tensions and defuse the volatile atmosphere between the partners. Third parties can be used to great advantage. When one is confronted with an uncompromising deadlock, replacing the negotiating party with another may lead to a solution.

EXPECTED CONFLICTS

Probably few partnerships have escaped at least some of these practical, crucial issues. At one time or other, strain or misunderstanding has disturbed every business relationship. Particularly with cross-cultural ventures, such differences are inevitable. So the fact that they arise should be no surprise; how they are handled is the crux of the matter.

Sometimes, however, the conflict goes beyond personalities. Fundamental differences in priorities between two mother companies can and do take place. When the conflict of interests becomes so obvious that most middle managers and above recognize the problem, in extreme cases it may be a good strategy not to make a futile effort to hide the matter, but to amplify the matter. Ensuring in this way that the issue reaches the board of directors and over to the next shareholders' meeting may prevent the matter from being dismissed as a mere personality disagreement. Obviously, this is an extreme case. But sometimes this magnitude of conflict can occur beyond the control of the current representative directors—however adroit they may be at handling the issue locally.

Top 10 Pointers (from an Experienced Foreign JV Director):

1. Whenever possible, make sure one's firm has the CFO position. Try to avoid giving up control of the position. In the end, no matter how tempting it may be in the current situation to negotiate away that position, one will regret giving it away.

2. The Korean CEO is likely to be a god in the eyes of the Korean employees. Never underestimate one's counterpart's power, and be extremely careful not to cause him or her to lose face. It is not easy, but one must determine how to walk the line between not being belligerent and being a pushover.

3. The wrong motivation to enter into a JV in Korea includes forming a partnership simply out of necessity or ease in entering the market. There needs to be a genuine, ongoing, and mutual reason for maintaining the JV with the Korean partner.

4. The expatriate director must have a clear-cut mission and genuine backing from his or her head office to be successful. Too frequently, the overseas head office loses interest in the Korean operations, and the local expat director takes on an attitude of resignation from not making a real contribution. This sort of matter often appears in JVs created out of convenience rather than shared purpose with the Korean firm. When that attitude sets in, it can be the beginning of the end for any chance of a successful JV.

5. It takes at least eighteen months even for a fairly experienced and competent foreign director to become truly effective, since it is so difficult for any foreigner to understand the Korean game.

6. As soon as a new person comes in as the new foreign JV representative, the Korean partner will almost certainly try to revise the relationship, with the disappearance of a number of regular meetings, reports and information procedures. It is therefore important that the new representative director arrive with a clear agenda as to his or her role and what information he or she is to receive, as well as clear delegation of authority, such as spending authority and investment authorization.

7. Most Westerners want about a month to ease into a job before putting their foot down. In Korea, one is not normally given that luxury. It is much better to approach the job as representative director with even a dogmatic sense of authority. Otherwise, the Korean organization will likely marginalize the new director, and he or she will be endlessly trying to chase down critical information.

8. It is critical in Korea to immediately establish one's authority to be included on important—particularly negative—information. By culture, Koreans are loath to speak up, especially if there is bad news. One really needs to make it clear from the beginning that one needs and welcomes bad news, preferring preemptive notification over waiting until a bad situation festers into a crisis.

9. Networks of relationships are critical. Regularly the real communication and secrets are shared over beers (and/or even soju!) after work.

10. Consider hiring a bilingual Korean or even a gyopo (Korean returnee) who is completely on one's payroll, but works within the JV. This person can be much more than an interpreter. For example, one may hire a bilingual Korean who has a relevant degree or experience, preferably an MBA. This person can serve beyond his or her official responsibilities by offering invaluable reports as to what is happening in the company below the surface, offering insights on cultural issues, and suggesting advice on how to rebuild damaged bridges.

14. HIRING AND FIRING

*I*t is not uncommon when the new expatriate manager reviews his or her local staff to find that some departments need expanding, while others require pruning. The expat must now undertake one of the most delicate operations in Korean business—the hiring and firing of local staff.

In addition, it is critical to know the legal lay of the land. While it may seem a bit unfair at times, Korean authorities are known to have more consistently enforced foreign companies' violations of labor laws and regulations than those of local companies. Nonetheless, on balance South Korea's code of labor regulations is technically reasonable. Given that the nation's Labor Standard Act has been properly translated into English and may be found on the Internet (www.ilo.org/dyn/natlex/docs/WEBTEXT/46401/65062/E97KOR01.htm), the foreign manager has no defense of claiming ignorance of the legal basics when it comes to personnel management.

First, however, let's take a brief look at the Korean office, its social structure, and attitudes about working for foreign companies.

PERSONNEL INTER-RELATIONSHIPS

In the average Korean office, staff members are bound in a complex web of personal ties and relationships. Small groups are formed primarily on the basis of kinship, regional origin, school affiliations, and military friendships. Each group strives to extend its power within the office. Expatriate managers should not be surprised to find, for example, that among their staff members, the graduates of Korea University are in fierce competition with the "boys from Yonsei."

Given these conditions, it is easy to see that the addition or removal of a single staff member can create profound changes in the status quo of office politics. Late into the night, involved group members discuss such changes, evaluating possible group—as well as individual—power gains or losses.

The practical consequences of this social system are immense. Since hiring is done largely through personal referrals, taking on a man from Daegu may, a few years down the line, result in an office that speaks with the accent of the Gyeongsang Provinces. The prospect of firing him then becomes a sticky issue, as this may, over time, spark a mass migration of the

"Daegu boys" to their leader's new office. Making changes in the local staff can thus require a great deal of tact and diplomacy.

VIEW OF FOREIGN FIRMS AS EMPLOYERS

During the roller-coaster early years of the Korean economy's development, foreign firms were highly regarded among the bright young graduates of Korea's more prestigious universities. Such jobs provided employees with excellent opportunities for training and overseas travel. Additionally, foreign firms offered higher incomes and better working conditions than local firms could afford at that time.

Attitudes have changed, however. Many of those who joined foreign firms in the early '70s were disappointed by their limited upward mobility due to slow company growth. They felt no sense of long-term job security, as many businesses that could not turn an immediate profit simply closed their doors and went home. Often there was friction between foreign management and the local staff, a problem that was aggravated by frequent changes of expatriate managers. Language and communications problems abounded, as did those "irritating differences" between the Korean and foreign ways of doing things.

All this has led to a certain amount of disenchantment with foreign firms. Today's bright young prospects look more to major Korean companies for employment. This change in attitude has made the recruitment of local staff for foreign companies somewhat problematic in recent years. Fortunately, "problematic" does not mean "impossible." Let's consider some of the most prevalent methods of staff adjustment.

HIRING

While the biggest challenge for foreign employers may be retaining talented Korean employees, the biggest headache can come when it's necessary to terminate a Korean employee. Many foreigners believe it is virtually impossible to do so, but that is not the case.

Too often the cause for termination starts during the hiring process. For example, it is not uncommon that a Korean employee is hired for qualifications such as his or her English language skills and very little else, eventually resulting in that employee's position in the company being more of a burden than a benefit. This is but one good example of some of the most common causes for termination: improper hiring practices. So let's briefly look at some ways to avoid making a hiring mistake that can lead to a difficult termination.

RECRUITMENT

ClassIfied Advertisements

For lower-level jobs such as clerks, accountants, and secretaries, classified ads in local newspapers and Internet job sites may be the best way to recruit. There are a dozen popular job sites that offer free placement of recruiting ads. The response rates to these Internet job site postings are quite good, if the position does not require highly specialized qualifications. The ads, however, must be specific in describing the position and its requirements. Otherwise, the arrival of hundreds of applications can make screening extremely difficult. One also has to bear in mind that advertising in the major dailies can be quite costly. Considering the expense of classified ads, one may take advantage of a lower-priced product or company image ad as an opportunity to include notice of employment opportunities along with the ad's primary message.

Referrals

Korean society operates within a complex network of interpersonal ties and relationships. If two people unacquainted with each other find themselves in a situation where they must speak together, they will attempt to establish some sort of link between themselves, whether through extended kinship or school, military, regional, or other ties.

Such a propensity favors a system of referrals as a primary recruitment method. Here, the referral source is all-important. In the case of an established company, staff members can introduce candidates. One runs the risk, however, of office politics playing too large a role in the candidate selection.

A way to avoid the complications of staff referral is to consult a neutral third party, such as a friend or business associate. An important advantage to this method is that traditionally, the person consulted carries at least some degree of responsibility for the success of his or her recommendation.

One must be aware that Korea's confidentiality laws are quite strict—which is a bit ironic, since it is often amazing how much personal information one can find through informal channels. Officially, though, getting personal information can be more difficult than in most countries. Even public information may be denied to prospective employers at the whim of whoever controls that data. Consequently, it is critically important to get a written waiver signed by each prospective employee that will allow one temporary access to otherwise closed-off information. Be sure to also get a copy of the family register, since it may be critical later on to know the names and locations of the employee's close relatives should fraud become suspected. It is a common practice for Koreans to transfer ill-gotten gains into their relatives' bank accounts.

Executive Search

The executive search profession has become quite developed in Korea. Both international and local organizations provide search services in addition to their other activities. The number of successful placements of top executives by these firms is growing rapidly, especially for foreign companies. An advantage to using this hiring method is that, when conducted properly, executive search makes effective use of referrals while preventing, or at least minimizing, the burden of obligations inherent in Korean society. This is true because the referrals are made "out of office," or one step removed from the hiring company. The search firm assumes the obligation of referral within its own network of business associates and contacts. As Korean business management continues to modernize, the executive search business is expected to continue to assume an increasingly prominent position among hiring practices.

Common Pitfalls

Within the wide selection of search firms, there is a lot of criticism heard from clients and, in private, from the search firms themselves. Clients often complain that search firms shove unqualified candidates in their direction, and search firms grouse that their clients really don't have a clear idea of what kind of candidate they are seeking.

There is much truth in both camps.

The problem, in part, comes down to most foreign operations having weak or nonexistent HR functions within their Korean operations. Worldwide, the HR function remains the least-developed function within most corporations. Very few HR professionals have an adequate understanding of their employer's business. As such, many line managers often give lip service to the HR department, and essentially try to hire with minimal HR participation. The problem is that the line managers often lack training or adequate experience in direct hiring. This issue only escalates when a foreign hiring manager is involved, such that he or she often becomes bewildered by the Korean candidates that he or she must choose from. Too often, the best English-speaking candidate is chosen—to the organization's later regret.

Search firm representatives generally maintain their composure, but they are often frustrated by clients—the worst tending to be the aforementioned foreign hiring managers—who only vaguely state the qualifications of the job, later flip-flopping in their hiring criteria as they slowly discover what types of people are most likely to succeed in their Korean operation.

Experiences with foreign firms can be so bad that some Korean search firms tend to shy away from assignments dealing with foreign hiring managers. After all, search firms can make the same amount of money dealing with Korean companies at a fraction of the cost and frustration. There is also a stereotype among Korean search firms that it is not worth the bother to cultivate long-term relations with the hopes of eventually placing top executives at foreign companies. According to this old Korean saw, top executives placed at foreign companies will thereafter only deal with prestigious international executive recruiters, in the hopes of eventually endearing themselves in preparation for the time when they themselves must change horses. Well, that certainly may happen, but what may in fact be the case is that an international search firm could be better skilled at helping their clients in determining what kind of candidate is needed.

All of which leads us to this fundamental of hiring: it is critical to clearly understand and define the vacant position's requirements. To do this professionally, there should be a clear and concise position description that is properly evaluated vis-à-vis the other position descriptions in the overall organization to assure proper compensation, management, functional responsibilities, and ultimately career-pathing. Now, this sort of thing is old hat for most Western professional HR departments, but even corporations that have a top-class HR department in New York or London may be at a loss when it comes to how to assist a small startup operation in Seoul. And often the startup country manager may not realistically expect the home office HR staff to be of any meaningful help.

Given this potential conundrum, it may make sense when shopping for a recruiter to qualify possible search agencies by reviewing how they help their clients define what the position's requirements are. A good search firm may suggest candidate evaluation procedures for their clients to use when trying to fairly compare interview candidates who could be spaced over a month or more in time, so that neither the first nor the last interviewee is given undue preferential consideration.

Alternatively, it may make sense to look at investing in a management consultant to set up an internal hiring procedure and possibly also act as one's temporary, part-time HR function during the course of the employee search. The management consultant may even know of someone worth serious consideration upon completion of the position-opening evaluation.

Selection

First, foreign employers need to be aware of the cultural and legal differences when hiring, disciplining, and terminating Korean employees. For example, Koreans place a much higher value on privacy than freedom of speech compared to, say, Americans, where freedom of speech is constitutionally guaranteed. Koreans have a constitutional guarantee of privacy, but less guaranteed freedom of speech.

As a result, past employers are usually noncommittal in saying anything negative about a former employee. The Korean definition of criminal defamation includes simply communicating anything—including the truth—that may damage an individual's reputation.

So when a former employer sandbags employment reference queries, it doesn't necessarily mean something is being hidden. It is probably just company policy. Naturally, it is very dangerous to rely on a single reference check. In spite of defamation liabilities, some Koreans will give away nuances implying negative references, sometimes due to personal spite.

In any event, finding out the true background for any candidate can be extremely problematic. Koreans, therefore, often hire people whom they or their trusted employees have known for years. As a result, it is very difficult to check out an unknown prospective employee using public records and sources. An extreme example of where this can lead may be found in the Shin Jeong-ah scandal, where a professor built much of her career on a bogus Ivy League university degree. As a result, many people were scandalized by her false representation of academic credentials.

Korean employers—and even search firms—often don't verify employee backgrounds. Other employers, including foreign ones, use background investigators to search both private and public information sources. Ironically, although discovery of information through public, third-party sources is usually not possible due to privacy concerns, the employment interviewer can legally ask almost anything of the job applicants—including many questions that are illegal in the West.

Some even go to the extreme by recording—and in a few cases, even videotaping—employment interviews and other important human resources meetings. In connection with this, it is important to understand that verbal or witnessed accounts are not legally recognized as evidence. Even written, contemporary notes are considered too self-serving to be admissible as evidence.

But audio or visual records—including those made without the knowledge or permission of the other party—are admissible as legal evidence, since mechanical recordings are considered to be legally "disinterested." While some employers secretly tape meetings, it is generally much better to be open and selective about recording, since good employee relations anywhere are based on trust.

Getting back to hiring, a practical approach may include having job applicants respond to a written questionnaire that requires them to sign and date the document. If one's rules of employment state so, one can justify a false answer on this questionnaire as grounds for legal termination.

Given this environment, there are some basic principles. It is most important to have stated the hiring requirements in one's written rules of employment so that it is clear that all of one's requests are a matter of procedure, and not personal harassment or suspicion. These same rules of employment should also describe other terms and conditions of employment, as well as stating conditions and processes for employment termination.

For example, the rules of employment might state that a potential employment candidate will be required to go to the local police station to get a letter certifying that he or she has never been convicted of a crime. Another good idea, particularly for those handling or having access to money, is that all such finalist candidates must submit a copy of their family registers as a condition of employment, since just about every case of embezzlement involves a relative—usually a brother—as an accomplice.

While the civil code does not require written employment contracts, the Labor Standard requires an employee to receive written notice of the company's adherence to minimum standards regarding terms of employment including hours of work, vacation, termination, and welfare benefits. As such, even small companies should prepare written rules of employment. But should these rules not exist, the same matters should be covered in detail in employment contracts.

Starting Salaries

With young, inexperienced employees, starting salaries are less problematic than when recruiting experienced professionals. For example, in Korea's Confucian, age-centric society, there is a strong sense that those with advanced degrees will likely progress faster than their less qualified peers, but only after they have proven themselves with real work experience. Consequently, as of 2010 many inexperienced university graduates have commonly started their careers at 28 million won per year, regardless of their level of post-graduate education.

When hiring experienced Korean employees into established Korean operations, the common rule of thumb is not to pay more than 20 percent above what a recruited employee may be making elsewhere, with the target being closer to 15 percent. Naturally, there is the expected need to keep the new employee's compensation in line with those of other employees. However, the starting salaries may have to be higher for startup Korean operations, especially when the foreign firm has yet to establish developed Korean benefits and may still be viewed as a bit of an employment risk for successful Koreans working elsewhere. (For more detailed information about employee compensation, please refer to Chapter 15, "Compensating Your Employees.")

Restrictive Covenants of Employment Contracts

It is becoming increasingly important for employers to protect their intellectual property in the form of trade secrets, as well as to protect themselves from competitors drawing away employees for the primary purpose of unfairly obtaining propriety information and technology. To that end, many employers around the world institute restrictive covenants into employment and other agreements with employees. The ongoing question anywhere is how enforceable these covenants are.

In Korea, non-disclosure, non-competition and non-solicitation agreements have been upheld by the Korean Supreme Court. Such cases have successfully met reasonably concrete legal standards. But before trying to understand those standards, one needs to understand the legal foundation of such standards. That is, enforceability of these standards is governed by the "catch-all" clause of Article 103 of the Civil Code, which provides that "matters contrary to good morals and social order shall be null and void."

In addition, there are specific laws that protect trade secrets, such as the Unfair Competition Prevention and Business Secret Protection Act. By its very name, the law suggests the problems of competitors soliciting employees for the purpose of gaining access to another company's trade secrets. On the other hand, Korean courts have denied trade secrets protections under special circumstances where a covenant may unfairly prevent an employee from making a living free of the current employer. That is, if a trade secret was developed by an employee—as opposed to simply obtained by the employee—the developer's employer cannot restrict the employee from using his or her knowledge and skills to work elsewhere, including applying experience and know-how central to an earlier employer's trade secrets to a later job.

In a similar vein, an employer may not enforce unreasonable non-compete clauses on an employee. Just what is "unreasonable" is vague and varies considerably from case to case, and often it is ultimately decided in the courts. Usually, however, a six-month to one-year non-compete clause is generally considered reasonable, depending on the nature of the job and the job incumbent's access to privileged information.

At the same time, one should keep in mind that a "trade secret" is confidential information that the company intends to keep confidential indefinitely, whereas a patent is something that is proprietary but is publicly published for the purpose of legal protection. As such, a trade secret that is discovered by reverse engineering is legally obtained, whereas a trade secret disclosed by a competitor's former or current employee is usually illegal.

Also, the definition of a trade secret includes how conscientiously and consistently a company protects its trade secrets. In other words, an employer cannot willy-nilly declare anything and everything about the company as a "trade secret." Legal defenses for trade secrets include restricting access to a few designated staff; marking such information "confidential"; limiting digital and/or physical access to privileged information with passwords and/or locks; specifying how long something will stay "confidential"; and keeping records of the use and access of confidential information. Furthermore, a company can further strengthen its defense and reduce the likelihood of trade secret loss by continuous education of and regular warnings to its employees.

Finally, the best advice is to consult with a competent attorney both when drawing up restrictive covenants and when implementing surrounding protections into one's management systems. One should make sure one's attorney expressly states the negative consequences of violating the covenant. And unlike cases in some Western countries, it is possible for a skilled attorney to draw up restrictive covenants for current employees as well as new hires to sign as a condition of employment.

While there is a fairly rational thought behind this body of Korean law, one really should get qualified legal assistance when forming legal protection from restrictive covenants.

New Employee Probation

Under Korean labor law, employers are generally permitted to put their new hires on a probationary period of up to six months. While the employer may not terminate the employment without "just cause," firing is generally easier to justify. Also, during probation, the employer is not bound to give prior notice or payment of 30 days' ordinary wages in lieu of notice.

Non-Regular Workers

Non-regular workers are defined as part-time, fixed-term and dispatched workers. The government encourages employees to use non-regular workers. The immediate benefits of hiring non-regular workers include greater flexibility, since upon termination they are generally entitled to compensation only for the remainder of their respective terms.

There are, however, some potential employment "catches" with non-regular workers, as embodied in the Non-Regular Workers' Act of 2007. Specifically, discrimination between regular and similarly situated non-regular workers, as in work conditions and hours, is prohibited; and after two years of continuous employment, non-regular workers must be automatically converted to permanent or regular employees. Both Korean and foreign employers have found themselves in significant legal jeopardy from failing to observe these requirements.

Employee Performance Evaluations

Employee performance evaluations comprise a basic human resources management procedure that applies anywhere in the world. Still, it is often surprising how many foreign companies lack regular, systemic performance appraisals and do not keep performance appraisals on file. Consequently, when these employers seek to terminate low performing employees, they find themselves lacking the necessary documentation. It is not unique to Korea, but evaluations can also be inaccurately positive, making it remarkably difficult for a third party to distinguish good performers from inept ones. Good management includes evaluating employees in a consistent and transparent manner, and Korea is no exception.

DISCIPLINARY ACTION

While there are cultural issues to take into account, if one has ever managed in a litigious environment such as California or New York, one will find the basic rules of discipline there also apply to modern Korea. The reasons for administering discipline may vary between the U.S. and Korea, but the methods end up being pretty much the same. Whatever the method, in both the West and Korea, hasty actions are for the foolhardy. Managers need to be extremely self-disciplined as they undertake disciplinary action.

Again, the employee should sign a well-documented set of work rules and employment regulations at the time of employment. Any foreign organization, whatever the size, should have such a document to serve as a guideline for employees. The rules usually stipulate that such undesirable behavior as poor performance, absence without notice, insubordination, and misdemeanors is subject to a series of actions that include but may not be limited to a letter of apology (*shimal-seo*) by the employee, a warning by the company, and, in the last resort, dismissal. Naturally, managers must also obey these guidelines as they manage their staff.

An employee may be requested to submit a letter of apology for any undesirable behavior he or she may have displayed within the company. If an employee's behavior results in, say, three incidents that require action, it can be grounds—according to company policy—for dismissal. The difference with many Western countries is that rather than having the supervising manager issue a letter of reprimand, the Korean employee may be asked to write a letter of apology. Most Koreans consider the *shimal-seo* to be the lightest form of formal disciplinary action. Essentially, the statement is a start-to-finish account of an event, noting the error made and promising not to make the same error again. Normally, a single *shimal-seo* will not damage the employee's career. But if one's company feels more comfortable with the letter of reprimand approach, then that approach is an acceptable alternative to the letter of apology.

The above methods are commonly exercised in lower and mid-level management, but often they are not appropriate for high-level executives. In such cases, given the potential legal and financial liabilities, it may be better to get outside help, such as from a human resources consultancy or a law firm.

Another method of disciplinary action Korean managers often administer is deprivation of responsibility. The employee continues to come to the office, but is not given an assignment. This is a very Korean approach to discipline and may not be appropriate for many multinational companies. Furthermore, in smaller operations, this approach is obviously impractical. Still, from the employee's perspective, killing eight hours a day without any duties can be worse than torture.

Demotion

In a hierarchical society such as Korea, each person has a well-defined position in the organization. As such, if one is left out from annual promotions either in the salary table or in title, it is an almost unbearable situation for the employee. One may endure it once but not a second time, even though one's livelihood would be threatened by resignation. A bad performer may be left out of promotions, and if he or she still does not improve, that employee may be again excluded from either promotion or salary increases the following year.

Traditionally, nine out of ten terminations have been "voluntary." The above-stated method may be time-consuming and costly, but it is without unnecessary ruffles. The downside to this traditional Korean approach can be a disgruntled employee who causes problems until he or she is able to find acceptable employment elsewhere. Furthermore, the likelihood of a problem employee working with a chip on the shoulder increases each year as the number of younger employees increases. Problem employees are more likely to vent their frustrations on these subordinates.

Regardless, hanging on to the low-performing company member can put overall employee morale at risk. Retaining a problem employee, rather than letting him or her go early on, can be expensive in the long run. Also, management may in time be deemed incompetent by the rank and file for ineffectively dealing with this difficult issue, which may impinge on the other employees' performance and welfare. When that happens, the in-house union may fill a power vacuum; or a once union-free company may soon find itself dealing with a union knocking on its door.

Transfer

Another universally popular method is transferring the unsatisfactory employee to another position or location. Here again, the work rules can be handy, if there is a stipulation that any employee may be transferred to another location.

However, if the employee is generally undesirable as a member of one's operations, it is usually a big mistake to transfer "bad news" from one department to another, since in the end, general management is not facing up to its responsibilities both to the company and even to the problem employee. Furthermore, if the employee endures the transfer with no improvement and management eventually has no choice but to terminate him or her, the prolonged employment record will work against the management's case should matters go to litigation. So if an employee is not working out, it is best to do the right thing—for both the employee and the company—and send the employee back to graze in the job-search pasture, where he or she may have the chance to become a more productive and happier person elsewhere.

Firing

This brings us to the topic of firing employees. Although there is no system of lifetime employment in Korea, employees are expected to remain with their companies for a long period of time. Loyalty to a company and long-term employment are generally regarded as virtues, a sentiment that is eloquently expressed in the Korean adage, "One must be devoted to the digging of a single good well." On the other hand, employers are expected by society to secure employee long-term well-being. It has also been government policy that business organizations shoulder the major responsibility of social welfare. In this climate, the firing of employees becomes a sensitive and delicate task. One has to be extremely cautious and prudent in handling the situation. When employment termination is inevitable or necessary, it is critical to protect the employee's face, since a mechanical and public dismissal will almost guarantee depressing the remaining employees' morale and seed causes for future employee relations issues.

Some considerations may help expatriate managers to be more successful in this area. Though situations involving the dismissal of employees vary greatly, firing in the Western fashion is rare in Korea. It is done rather discreetly, preserving the "face" of the dismissed employee. One should not expect to be able to fire a local staff member overnight. This should be done with a well laid-out plan, employing various indirect means, over a period of time. If at all possible, the actual contact and communication should be handled through a local executive.

One special consideration worth mentioning is employment termination payment. The legal minimum has been one month's pay for each completed year of service. However, for various reasons, an employer may pay more than that—sometimes substantially more. This extra money may be paid in consideration of special, potentially awkward circumstances surrounding the termination. In any case, the most important strategy is to get the terminated employee working satisfactorily elsewhere. Until that happens, it may be best to have the terminated employee be aware that he or she is better off not burning bridges with the terminating organization. Terminated employees' temptations for possible retribution can be tempered if money beyond the legal minimum, which must be paid out in a lump sum, is paid out in increments on a scheduled basis instead. During the extra severance payout schedule, the terminated employee can have a stipend to live off while looking for the next income source. At the same time, a potentially volatile former employee may have a cooling-off period during which time his or her good behavior will be rewarded by the extra, non-legally binding severance payments.

Whenever possible, one should gradually establish the psychological setting to allow the employee to fully comprehend why termination is required and give the employee a chance to submit a written and signed letter of resignation. When possible, give the employee some time to think it over so that he or she is not necessarily pushed or rushed into resigning. In any case, some kind of signed document verifying termination of employment is a must.

A common Korean practice—one that may not jibe well with one's international human resource policies—is to keep the terminated employee in the office for two or three months without pay while he or she looks for new employment. This applies best when there is a business slowdown and the employee is not working out professionally despite good intentions. Obviously, this does not apply to an employee who has intentionally harmed the company's interests, and particularly those employees who have access to finances and sensitive information. Again, the reason to consider this form of internal outplacement is to help the terminated employee save face to improve his or her chances of finding work elsewhere. Otherwise, the employee will likely be much more traumatized, as may his or her co-workers, who may well wonder how they may be treated if future business conditions mandate headcount reductions.

When following this Korean practice of delayed physical departure, one's rules of employment should probably stipulate that certain job categories require immediate physical separation from the company premises upon termination. Alternatively, terminated employees could be transferred to a "subsidiary company" that actually does nothing other than hold terminated employees until they find their next employer.

In 2009, many companies were forced to reduce their headcount due to the global financial crisis. While companies tried to hang on to their top performers or superstars by letting go of support staff members, some of the better performing and better paid employees moved on to safer pastures than those offered by some of the foreign firms. Later, when the economy began to return to normalcy, some foreign employers found themselves vulnerable to their competitors picking off the truly invaluable and yet underappreciated support staff who had once made it possible for the former top performers to be superstars and whom the company had let go—at the time without hesitation. In other words, employment terminations can create additional, unforeseen liabilities.

Whatever one's company philosophy may be, it is critical to consider one's legal exposure and protect one's Korean operations with well thought-out and detailed rules of employment. Wrongful termination in Korea can potentially lead to criminal prosecution of the CEO or managing director— particularly if the wronged employee is not reinstated.

Temporary and Contracted Employees

One of the most controversial causes of termination involves temporary employee contract non-renewals. Often, these employees are referred to as "contracted employees," and they may work as such for as long as two years.

Some employers try to get around the three-month employment probation maximum by asking new hires to agree to a six-month probation. Often, eager new employees will accept this term of employment, but employers should recognize that if challenged later, probation beyond three months is not likely to stand legally. It is possible for an employer and employee to agree to an extension of a three-month probation, but such cases are in fact very rare. Other employers, in lieu of or in addition to a three-month probation, initially hire employees and place them on a one-year contractual basis.

Upon successful completion, the employee is normally hired as a so-called permanent employee. This strategy may seem to make a lot of sense, but there are drawbacks. First of all, contracted employees often demand—and receive—higher wages in lieu of uncertain short-term employment, while not receiving the full benefits of permanent employees. Upon conversion to permanent employment status, it is virtually impossible to reduce salary levels.

Also, there is often a psychological divide between contracted and permanent employees. This difference may cause teamwork, diligence, and overall morale to suffer, leading to a high turnover even among good contracted employees, who may look upon themselves as second-class employees while working as temporary or contracted workers.

Separations: Settlement and Potential Returnees

An employee with many years of service may be requested to change his or her position to that of part-time advisor as a means of gradual retirement. A generous separation payment, in addition to some form of recognition—such as a citation or a plaque—may be presented. In many cases, a long-serving local staff member in a foreign organization has accumulated considerable leverage, and this should not be overlooked. In the settlement, the compensation for separation must exceed, by far, the minimum requirements of the labor law. This not only benefits the departing staff member, but stands as an example of good will to the remaining staff.

While many foreign and Korean companies have a written or unwritten policy of not rehiring former employees, some foreign employers have rehired "prodigal" employees who have discovered that the grass was not in fact greener on the other side of the fence. One foreign executive very experienced in the Korean business world said that in the cases of worthwhile employees, he has successfully rehired staff members. However, he offered a few guidelines.

First, beyond checking with human resources to ensure there is nothing negative in the person's background, this foreign executive informally checks with his team on a one-on-one basis to ensure that the prodigal employee will be accepted and welcomed back into the fold. And second, should that person be rehired, the foreign executive ensures that the returnee return to the same rank and pay grade that he or she left—there must be no real or presumed reward in coming back, since coming back into a higher position is bound to create resentment among the other employees. The foreign executive also says he has noticed that rehiring seems to be less problematic among female employees than their male counterparts.

TRAINED AND SKILLED HUMAN RESOURCE MANAGEMENT IS ESSENTIAL

When one considers the fact that most major labor grievances can be traced back to incompetent management, it is critical that managers be trained beyond their operational tasks. Today's manager—local or expatriate—needs to be trained in supervisory skills, including progressive discipline and coaching. While a good human resources department can be invaluable in this area, it is a mistake to leave everything to personnel, especially if a manager badly mishandles his or her staff. In-house training by qualified HR staff, or possibly outside HR consultants, can be a very prudent investment to prevent expensive business disruptions and legal fees resulting from poor personnel management. Good personnel policies can provide for fair and consistent employee treatment only when all managers are properly skilled and compliant in disciplinary and termination procedures.

So in consideration of all of the above, legal and managerial preventive thinking—and well-considered hiring and termination procedures—are crucial for running a successful Korean operation. Making staff adjustments in Korea is not easy—especially for the expatriate manager who may be used to quicker methods of effecting the desired changes. It is good to remember that one is dealing with another social structure that views hasty action as imprudent. In both hiring and firing, the expatriate manager will have greater success if he or she acts patiently and moves methodically, step by step, through a well thought-out plan, preferably with the help of a local associate, or a consultant when necessary.

15. KOREA'S CORPORATE MIDDLE MANAGERS

BUSINESS BACKBONE

The middle managers of Korean companies are the backbone of business organizations. Loyal, dedicated, creative, and relatively prone to risk-taking, they are the ones who make things happen—in the fiercely competitive marketplaces, in the research laboratories, in the factories, and in the piles of documents required for bureaucratic approval procedures. They are also the ones who passed the most strenuous competitions in entering the universities and their respective companies afterwards. In recent years, more and more senior executives, including CEOs, are appointed from among those who were recruited in an open competition, and they are quickly joining the main stream of the corporate power base.

IDENTIFYING THE MIDDLE MANAGER

Even though there is no clear definition of a middle manager, it may be better to refer to the whole spectrum of the management hierarchy; from the lowest-level supervisor (*daeri*) to the full manager rank (*bujang*) (refer to the "Office Worker Titles" chart on page ##). This spectrum will cover those who have served in the company for a period ranging from three to four years to approximately 15 years.

Actually, the first three to four years consist of a training period. During this time, the young managers develop the basic professional knowledge and skills necessary for mastering corporate objectives and policies. They also learn how to effectively network with others within the company's hierarchy. Only after this initial period are middle managers ready to be fully productive. Most of those who pursue this career track, especially with the corporate giants, regard this as a once-in-a-lifetime opportunity for their success.

Korean middle managers view their career as a long-term, nearly lifelong sacrifice to meet their personal objectives. They devote their days, nights and even Sundays to fulfilling their company's professional and social responsibilities. They will even give up what little personal time they have left to spend with family and friends for the company, especially if it will benefit their position and status within their company. In this way, they seem practically married to the organization, and they are an inseparable link in the corporate chain.

Why is it that Korean middle managers work so hard and give so much for their company? What are they after?

Korea's middle managers, like managers everywhere, are looking for the fast track to organizational advancement. Competition is keen in the corporate workplace, and one's position title and rank determines one's status within the hierarchy. A middle manager who does not get a promotion while his colleagues advance feels a great deal of frustration and loss of face. He must stay on the treadmill if he expects to get ahead in the organizational mosaic.

Advancement within the company is very important to the middle manager's progress. Each promotion guarantees not only an increase in pay, but also a better status position within the organization. If an employee is fortunate, he can climb the corporate ladder to become a manager (*bujang*) in a minimum of 12 years. But it usually takes about 15 to 16 years for a Korean to reach the upper level of management. A few of the large Korean companies pay top salaries to their middle management, but the competition to obtain positions in these select companies is intense. The major firms accept only about one out of every 10 applicants.

On a personal level, most middle managers have similar objectives to achieve, needing to afford 1) a home for their families, 2) a car to compete with that of other successful colleagues on the streets, and 3) a premium education for their children. However, such goals are not so easy to obtain in modern Korea. Housing costs in urban areas, especially in Seoul, are skyrocketing. Rental rates are extremely high, and the cost of ownership can put a family into debt into the next generation. Owning an automobile is a trendy status symbol that can easily eat up ten months or more of a manager's salary, even without the cost of gas and maintenance. Education becomes more expensive every year, especially with the pressure to afford the best cram schools for high school and university entrance examinations in addition to standard schooling requirements.

Financial pressures on the successful middle manager can be backbreaking, since they must "keep up with the Kims" while struggling to address the demands of various standard social obligations.

COMMON PROBLEMS

Middle managers sacrifice a lot of time with their families and to themselves to reach their professional objectives. What this means is spending many long hours, often six days a week, in the office or with office colleagues. The workplace becomes a "second home" where the environment creates a multitude of frustrations and unnecessary stress.

Promotion

A major source of frustration stems from the all-important promotion within the company. In the early 1970s, when Korea was undergoing rapid industrialization, opportunities for advancement to higher management positions were abundant. Companies sprang up nearly overnight, and with them came a wealth of management positions and quick upward mobility. But as the Korean economy has matured, large and established companies have gradually adjusted their structures to better resemble those of firms in other industrialized economies. As a result, the room at the top is less accommodating for those managers aggressively pursuing an upward career.

Position Limitations

Today, many companies are reaching their saturation point. The growth of new business is not as rapid as before, and the turnover of upper management is slowing down. Chances for advancement are therefore slower in developing, and harder to obtain. Many middle managers are now looking into other employment opportunities, such as moving to another company or starting their own businesses. According to a survey of Korean managers, twenty-four percent of those questioned stated that they would like to start their own businesses. If anything, this problem has become exacerbated. The result can be dysfunctional communications within major Korean corporations. (For further discussion of this problem, please refer to Chapter 4, "Understanding Korean Management Style.")

Aptitude

Another common problem faced by middle managers is the feeling of being in the wrong place, of not being "one of the gang." Many managers are not satisfied with or doubt their own aptitude for the positions that they hold. Due to personality reasons or being part of a corporate merger, some managers even have difficulties acclimating themselves to a certain corporate culture, which makes them feel like they don't fit in.

Long Hours

Working conditions are difficult in Korea. The early mornings and late nights five or even six days a week add up to many long hours of burning the candle at both ends. This is a tiresome burden not only for the middle managers, but for their families as well. Though they acquiesce as dutiful wives should, many women are not satisfied with being "corporate widows," especially younger and more independent females relegated to playing the role of "waiting wives" while their husbands gallivant around on late-night "corporate sprees." A surprisingly large number of middle managers, recognizing in part that they are not able to play an important part in the upbringing of their children, have gone along with the idea of their wives and children living separately and abroad as a means of instilling their children with bilingual English skills. This may seem like a rather desperate means of "keeping up with the Kims," but given that the rest of the family sees very little of the breadwinner, it is an easier proposition to consider than in many other countries.

Rotations

Another situation that creates stress is the frequent rotation by some companies of the middle managers into new positions. While good for expanding the knowledge and experience of the managers, on technology-related jobs, which require years to learn, frequent rotations (perhaps every six months to one year) put the manager into a position where he or she knows less than the "*sa-won*," or junior employee. So the manager must be dependent on and be taught by his or her supporting staff for knowledge about his or her job. Ultimately, the middle manager must sign off—or not—on various matters as they pass his or her desk. Given the lack of in-depth experience in understanding many of the issues, too often the middle manager either blindly relies on the advice of his or her trusted subordinates or makes decisions based primarily on departmental and corporate politics—often surprisingly unaware of the long-term consequences of those decisions.

A BRIDGE TO CROSS

In the end, holding the various positions within middle management is not easy. And yet middle managers are extremely necessary, since they are making the critical decisions for their organizations. Advancement to this kind of position is much desired and sought-after, but the position does entail formidable difficulties—including demands on one's own time and personal activities—as well as sacrifices by one's family. The position is a combination of wider benefits and risky dilemmas. Nevertheless, it is the backbone of Korean corporate structure. Also, it is the indispensable bridge to cross for all aspiring Korean managers in their drive up toward the coveted but relatively scarce executive positions.

16. COMPENSATING EMPLOYEES

*I*n the past decades, Korean employee compensation practices have evolved with the overall economy. Like employers elsewhere, superior Korean employers are constantly upgrading their compensation schemes as a way to attract, retain and motivate their human resources. Unlike employers in long-developed countries, Korean managers have had to revamp their thinking more often than most.

At the same time, Korean traditional practices, such as guaranteed bonuses, remain a strong part of the culture and the consumer economy. Given this, the expatriate manager faces a multi-ball juggling act of dealing with worldwide corporate standards, Korean traditional standards and expectations, and new, emerging local compensation practices. This juggling act may not be something new to the experienced expat manager, but the dynamism of compensation changes can make Korean management a special challenge.

For Korea's foreign organizations, it has not always been easy to conform to these patterns. This has been partially due to the Western concept of rather impersonal economic relations between the company and employees, and partially due to the relatively short-term Korean business connections, such as frequent expatriate managerial turnover.

Problems in local employee morale arising from improper compensation systems and other sociocultural differences can be major causes of a foreign firm's failure. Staff compensation plan considerations are a challenge for any executive, East or West. But it is more difficult in a completely different social environment. Proper compensation requires balance. To recruit, retain and reward local staff has always been important. Increasingly, expatriate executives need to review local operations' general compensation practices to counteract potential local employee irritations.

COMPENSATION PRACTICES

Let's first look at some of the past practices that either continue on to this day or at least have influence on modern compensation practices.

Salary and Bonuses

The multiple pay components of an ordinary "salary man" in a major company can be confusing to a foreign executive. In addition to the basic monthly salary, defined or guaranteed bonuses (actually a form of deferred compensation) are paid, ranging from four to twelve months' pay per year, usually timed to coincide with major holiday expenses, depending on the company's policy, the rank of the employee, and performance. These regular bonuses help the family to save, as the family usually intends to live on the assumption of receiving only a basic salary. Bonuses are also often used for special occasions, such as purchasing major household appliances, a new dwelling, a vacation, or annual kimchi preparation.

Some employees have a leveraged compensation program, but often these additional performance bonuses are allocated to groups or teams rather than on an individual basis—although individual commissions do exist. Additional allowances can be based on elements including position, family size, transportation, housing, overtime, professional licenses, research, and foreign language ability.

Salary Table

In the past, almost all large Korean companies adopted salary tables for their employees. In a social environment where seniority is important, such a salary structure was a necessity. Given the nature of Korean social relationships and obligations, which mandate candor among friends, local company salaries could not be kept secret. So an "open" system seemed best in the long run in traditional work environments. The advantage of this system was that it appeared fair to the employees. As long as there was a relatively clear policy for annual cost-of-living adjustments, employees could anticipate quite accurately the following year's salary. Since a person's salary is no secret in this country, such an open system, conforming to a table structure, was desirable.

Today, the salary table is still a common fixture in the manufacturing industry—particularly for low-skilled employees in positions with little career growth. In these work environments, seniority can be recognized and compensated beyond the annual cost-of-living adjustments of the tables. In a lean year when a major adjustment is not possible, the uniform revision of the scale upward by a percentage point or two is possible, saving responsible executives a lot of headache.

The salary table is relatively easy to establish, since the level and range can be determined by guidelines suggested by the government. Thus, the basic salary is practically on par with similar companies in the field and on nearly equal footing with the basic industry average structure for beginning employees.

As of 2005, however, less than 14 percent of Korean employers were still using this traditional compensation scheme. In many (usually white-collar) industries, these tables have been replaced by more sophisticated performance-based schemes.

However, both the salary table and its replacement are insufficient by themselves to determine adequate compensation, since some employees may actually be more deserving of better compensation. Therefore, the system of various additional allowances can add flexibility to the system.

"Perks"

Local companies try to develop a family-style atmosphere where employees feel quite comfortable and secure. Usually the manager, and often the CEO as well, develops strong paternalistic bonds by expressing various personal concerns for the employees and their families. These concerns can include visiting an employee's home when a death has occurred locally, participating in an employee's wedding (sometimes even officiating), attending the 100th-day celebration for a employee's baby (one of the family's important milestones), or visiting a home or hospital when an employee or his or her family member has taken ill.

In a similarly paternalistic vein, potentially substantial personal benefits may be extended to employees in addition to their formal, basic compensation. For example, many companies grant scholarships for tuition and school entrance fees for employee's children, which can be sizeable and thus very desirable. Some companies provide housing allowances or interest-free loans for key money or down payments.

In the case of higher management, a transportation allowance, a company car, or (more commonly these days) some reimbursement for operating a private car is provided.

Most companies have, or had, a separate payment system beginning with a legally mandated minimum of one month's pay per year of employment, and often increasing through longer employment, such as 15 months' pay for 10 years' service. Due to government pressure to support the financial industry, private pension programs are replacing this traditional practice.

The traditional system also had serious problems. The total of all employees' accrued severance pay, for example, was almost always carried on the books as a liability, but at the same time was almost never specifically funded.

Traditionally, foreign organizations have been at an inherent disadvantage as employers. Aspiring young business freshmen tended to regard foreign firms as lacking room for upward mobility, lacking long-term security, and lacking a certain culture in which comfortable, congenial personal relationships thrive. They had the impression that Western business organizations were sterile and somewhat impersonal. On the other hand, foreign companies offered more in the area of professional training. Overcoming these handicaps required higher salaries, a better working environment and attractive benefits.

While some of the above concerns have disappeared as Korean managers have matured into multinational executive positions, some of these anxieties remain to this day.

CONSIDERATIONS WHEN COORDINATING COMPENSATION PACKAGES

To groom satisfied and loyal staff, the expatriate manager needs to give serious thought to a compensation plan that is well-structured and designed, with serious consideration to the local staff's needs and cultural values.

Economic Rewards

A major part of compensation management is economic rewards management. Korean compensation professionals who investigated the economic rewards phenomena of Korea's business corporations discovered that both the level and the structure of economic compensation are more often based on traditional factors, such as seniority, rather than rational, motivational ones. However, these practices have not been effective tools of compensation management. Progressive employers have since recognized an urgent need for improvements in efficiency, flexibility, and satisfaction.

In terms of the efficiency of compensation management, Korean corporations have depended largely on simple seniority, with little or no heed paid to the quality or quantity of labor. Therefore, this simple seniority compensation system led to deterioration in motivation and productivity. This system often functioned in management, where trivial matters were handled promptly while important matters were never solved.

In terms of compensation management flexibility, the simple seniority compensation system presented many problems in satisfying employees' needs. According to case studies, in most companies and job classes, employees wanted rewards distributed by ability rather than seniority.

To increase efficiency, today's Korean managers are using evolutionary methods to migrate from a seniority-oriented compensation strategy to ability- and performance-oriented strategies. In the future, we may expect the norm for Korean companies to be promotion policies based on ability and performance—without consideration of birthplace, educational background or seniority. In the short term, however, Korean employers are trying incrementally to incorporate performance-based factors in determining compensation and to balance them with seniority.

Foreign managers may learn from Korean strategies for introducing ability- and performance-based compensation management. Often, multinational companies need to develop a hybrid compensation package that is in line with the international corporate standard while still recognizing local workplace peculiarities.

The evolutionary example below may provide some ideas for what may be appropriate for a multinational corporation in Korea.

- **Flexibility:** For an expatriate executive wishing to develop a compensation system to foster satisfied, productive employees, the key word is flexibility. It can be very difficult for the foreign business manager to keep up with Korea's changing compensation practices, particularly with respect to benefits. This kind of compensation, however, is the very foundation of Korean business practices to which the local employees are accustomed and responsive. If a business applies the Korean style of paternalistic consideration in compensating employees' efforts, then the employees may reciprocate with loyalty, productivity, and excellence.

  It is imperative, therefore, that the expatriate manager be very familiar with this Korean style of compensation and seek creative and constructive ways to initiate similar forms of reward.

- **Salary Trends:** The 2008-09 global financial crisis reversed annual wage increase trends. Dropping from a positive 2.6 percent growth at the end of 2008—which was a significant drop from earlier in the year, when it stood at 5.1 percent—the second half of 2009 witnessed a negative 1.2 percent delta in annual wage adjustments. Earlier in 2009, wage adjustments were averaging a minus 1.6 percent, so the Korean Labor Ministry is expecting the average wage increase for 2010 to be a positive 1.4 percent.

In a late 2009 survey, the Korean Employers' Federation discovered that smaller companies (fewer than 300 employees) were planning larger wage increases, averaging about 1.8 percent, while the largest companies were adjusting only 0.6 percent. On the other hand, starting wages in larger companies are generally higher than those of smaller companies. The highest-paid sectors, according to the survey, were the financial and insurance industries, followed by construction, manufacturing, transportation, storage, communications, and wholesale & retail.

More recently, Mercer compensation surveys of 300 to 400 Korea-based organizations found budgeted salary increases for 2010 to be 5.3 percent on average, with 3.2 percent actual increases paid out in 2009. The double caveat for these statistics is that this survey did not include the very large *chaebol*, which tend to pay higher—and surveyed budgeted figures tend to be a bit higher than actual numbers. However, a budget average of plus 5.2 to 5.3 percent seemed to have been well accepted as the market standard at the outset of 2010.

Prior to the global financial crisis and since 2003, annual salary increases have been averaging about 7 percent. That has been approximately twice the national GDP and CPI growth after the correction period following the Asian financial crisis of 1997-98. Depending on the industry, however, yearly pay adjustments have varied as much as 3.2 percent in net annual increases among industrial sectors. Employees of the general consumer goods industry tend to have the best salaries in light of recent salary increases averaging about 7.7 percent annually, while industrial, health care, and service employees averaged about 5.9 to 6.7 percent. High tech and financial sector employees tend to fall within the overall national median between 6.9 percent and 7.3 percent.

In recent years, we have seen some industries be much more consistent in compensation than others. The financial industry seems to be the most consistent across the board, while health care and high tech have the greatest variances—possibly due to the regular supply of and demand for experienced financial analysts and even financial software programmers—compared to the irregular supply of and demand for medical device engineers and pharmaceutical scientists.

• **Pay Structure by Job Grades:** Today, most large companies use the so-called "fan" midpoint regression in which the range from minimum to maximum pay broadens as the pay grades get higher. For general staff (*sa-won*), for example, the maximum pay is 44 percent higher than the minimum pay, while for executives (*isa*) that figure jumps to 141 percent. That minimum-to-maximum spread averages 53 percent for associates (*daeri*), 73 percent for supervisors (*gwajang*), and 80 percent for managers (*bujang*).

To give a ballpark idea of national average annual incomes, let's assume "annual income" is defined as salary plus defined or guaranteed bonuses alone. The following paragraph's generalized statements are based on that definition.

As of 2006 , general staff employees were paid about 20 to 25 million won per year. Their immediate supervisors, or *daeri*, were often paid from the mid-20s to mid-30s (mid-50s in the big *chaebol*) in millions of won. Supervisors, or *gwajang*, tended to earn from about 35 million to 55 million (70 million) per year, while their managers, or *bujang*, make from the mid-50s to mid-60s (nearly 100) in millions of won per year. Executive positions, or *isa*, encompass many grades influenced by a wide range of factors, with a variable pay portion such as special allowances and bonuses averaging about 17.5 percent to 20 percent—compared to 12 to 14 percent for lower grades—figuring into the final calculation. Korean executives are thus currently paid from as little as 70 million won to as much as 180 million won per annum. Again, top executives of the most successful *chaebol* companies can earn significantly more. (Refer to "Office Worker Titles" in Chapter 4 for more information.)

- **Benefits Philosophy:** Additional allowances may be provided in some areas where larger compensation is necessary. What matters most to the employees, of course, is the net benefit they receive—not simply the basic salary. The higher the salary, the more they pay in progressive income taxes. So various other benefit plans may be instituted to motivate employees and promote organizational stability. Some of these are scholarship grants for employees' children, housing loans, progressive separation payments, and allowances for transportation—even informal compensation counts, such as confidential expense accounts or other discretionary funds, although these are starting to disappear.

An example of this philosophy may be found in a Korean company in the U.S. that pays supplementary wages for perfect attendance over a short period of time and for exceeding a reasonable production goal. This has resulted in an absentee rate of only one percent compared to the national average of five percent. It also achieved a rejection rate far below the average on the assembly line, increasing excellence and quality control—all thanks to this extra compensation provision.

From a financial perspective, the biggest benefits liability for most Korean companies is their severance pay or pension program. Traditionally and statutorily, a departing employee has been entitled to the equivalent of one month's pay at the current pay rate for each completed year of employment. According to a recent benefits survey, half of Korean firms are self-funded or carrying the liability unfunded on the books. About a third were funding anywhere from a very small percentage up to 50 percent of their liability externally through insurance companies and banks. Fourteen percent were funding from 51 percent to 80 percent through such external institutions, while just four percent were doing the same at the rate of 81 percent to 100 percent of the total severance pay/pension liability.

Employee Funds

Some companies' employees organize their own employee fund like a company credit union or cooperative. Besides the employees' allotments into this fund from their pay, the company will often make its own contributions to the kitty. This pool or fund may be drawn on for various employee welfare purposes. Sometimes this fund may provide a loan to an employee when some urgent need arises. In case of a death or wedding in the family, the fund may offer a grant to the employee.

Such in-house services usually help to make a company more cohesive, respected, and productive. When the employee feels such concern and consideration from the company, these activities serve to intensify company loyalty and on-the-job excellence. Consequently, these provisions can be very effective for both management and employees.

KOREA'S EVOLVING PENSION PROGRAMS

More than ever, Korea's employers are facing a wider variety of opportunities—and challenges—when it comes to creating retirement

---

2. Please note that some of the top performing chaebol companies can pay significantly higher; those figures appear in parentheses. Obviously, this is just a rough guide, and one should participate in relevant salary surveys or employ the services of a professional compensation firm to provide timely and relevant salary and benefits data for one's operations

3. Again, the additional figures in parentheses are the averages of the better paid chaebol employees.

schemes to attract, retain and reward their employees.

Traditionally, employers were legally obligated to provide a lump-sum severance scheme that paid out at least one month of average salary (averaged over the last three months), regardless of whether the employee leaving—through a voluntary or involuntary termination—had worked one year or more than thirty. Though this scheme was supposed to be funded, in actuality it was often simply carried on the books. The fragility of this deferred income benefit became too apparent during the IMF crisis when many employers went bankrupt, and especially daunting for older employees who were left without any funds for their retirement.

Mr. Edward Eun of Watson Wyatt pointed out that in December 2005, Korea's first corporate pension law, the Employee Retirement Benefit Security Act (ERBSA), took effect as a means to ease the 45-year-old severance system described above out of existence. Related tax laws provide rewards of tax credits for defined benefit and defined contribution schemes, and in time will diminish the tax benefits to employers who continue with the current severance payment schemes.

The changeover to these new schemes requires majority consent of employees or, if the majority of employees are unionized, agreement from the union. As such there has been a good deal of resistance from the unions, especially when offered a defined contribution alternative. The larger corporations have been taking their time within the legislated three to four years until 2010 to make the transition, while the small- and medium-sized companies are moving faster upon analyzing the risks and benefits of these new alternatives. The year 2010 is significant, since after 2010 the external funding vehicles of the current severance pay schemes will lose their tax benefits.

Regardless, there is likely to be a major shift among several companies away from the severance schemes around the end of this year. Many employees like the idea of external investing of money, coming to at least one month of their annual salary, to third-party investments.

As such, many pension providers (insurance companies and banks) today are inundating HR managers with a mind-boggling array of schemes and marketing materials. But be aware that many of these new Korean pension providers will merge or simply disappear in the next few years.

Employees and employers are now looking at three major types of retirement funding—each with its own advantages and disadvantages. The employer can continue to operate the traditional severance program, albeit with decreasing tax benefits. This option is easy for both employee and employer to calculate and to administer. But the employer must properly handle its responsibility so that the program is not compromised by future liquidity requirements. Yet this is often not the case even today. Still, most employees wish to stay with the current scheme so long as they have faith in the overall welfare of their company. At the same time, however, older employees, with their huge accruing severance liabilities, become increasingly less attractive for employers to retain.

The employer-funded defined benefit schemes are more complicated for the employer to administer, but, like the severance program, are easy for the employee in appreciating or calculating future benefits. They are also much safer for the employee should anything happen to the employer—though the employee has to trust the third party to act responsibly.

The defined contribution schemes may be most attractive to younger employees who want to have some say as to how the pension money is being invested. Employees can invest additional funds to these schemes beyond employer contributions and can even receive tax deductions of up to 3 million won. Also, unlike defined benefit plans, defined contribution schemes are transferable as employees move among employers. But one must remember that defined contribution schemes are quite new to Korea and as such require a great deal of employee education. All countries go through this kind of learning curve; based on past experience, while this kind of scheme is currently not so attractive, we can expect its popularity to skyrocket once younger employees catch on to its benefits.

Nonetheless, with salaries inflating roughly 6 to 7 percent per year as of this writing—albeit slowly lessening in percentile increases year by year—the rate of growth in pension program benefits remains higher with the severance payment schemes and defined benefits than defined contribution offerings. In time, this is likely to change as the Korean economy matures and average income increases come in line with most modern economies.

Given all of this, changes are taking place. When employees terminated in the past, very few used the lump sum from the severance program to purchase an annuity program. Much to the government's concern, many former employees basically blow their sudden, temporary wealth on real estate, vacations, cars or small businesses—only to find themselves in great financial difficulty a few years later. To offset this, there are now special tax advantages to encourage the purchase of annuity programs.

Within this context, the government has scheduled in tax benefits and penalties to move employers away from the severance payments and on to these safer pension programs. Amazingly enough, there are no formal pension trustees in Korea who carry the liabilities of fiduciary responsibility. The closest to such are designated pension program custodians, such as banks and insurance companies, who act on the employers' instructions. The reason for this is that the new pension options are based on the Japanese model, and in Japan there are no pension trusts. Also, during the new law's formation, the big pension providers lobbied heavily against the establishment of trusteeships so as to maintain greater control of these funds.

Several human resource professionals in Korea think that while the government is pulling the market in the right direction, the tax incentives to wean employers and employees from the traditional severance program are inadequate. At the same time, the pension programs need to better address the current investment mentality of most Koreans, which tends to address investment opportunities within the three- to five-year horizon, rather than, say, the 35-year time frame of a full career ahead of a young employee. Nonetheless, most Koreans will in time become savvier in spreading their long-term, personal investments out into more diverse instruments. It's all a matter of Korea eventually moving up to the next level of advanced market sophistication.

IT'S A MOVING TARGET

Having a snapshot of Korean compensation, the reader may find a disconnect between what may seem to be optimal compensation policies on the one hand, and current, local pay and benefits practices on the other—not to mention what one's international human resources department may consider to be appropriate. Even if one's Korean operation is flexible in accommodating local compensation practices, it may turn out that the head office is not sufficiently elastic to satisfy local labor market requirements. The good news is that Korean personnel practices are evolving toward being more in line with many Western practices.

Traditionally, Korean compensation management dealt with pay for direct labor. Today's requirements—including comprehensive compensation with both direct and indirect rewards, cooperative labor-management relations, corporate administration, and the adaptation for growth—dictate that compensation management should encompass traditional economic rewards, current social remunerations, and now even performance pay. Effective and strategic compensation management is also required. Korean and expatriate employers must diagnose current trends, discover the issues, and develop new strategies. As a result, Korea's compensation practices are in greater flux than ever, creating additional demands on foreign and local managers alike.

Korean Evolutionary Compensation Strategy

Considering an evolutionary compensation strategy can give one insight into traditional Korean compensation schemes, as well as an understanding as to which parts of a legacy compensation program need to remain essentially unchanged and which parts are open to modification to meet modern business requirements. The following is one such example.

First, the simple, traditional equity grading system needs to be changed into a multiple-equity grading system. The compensation structure should be designed in terms of an efficiency cycle of an employee's tenure in each position and the employees' overall career.

Second, seniority-based bonuses and incentives that are considered to be salary and wages should be transformed to ability- and performance-based bonuses and incentives as a way to motivate employees.

Third, a recognized skills- and career development-oriented compensation strategy and management should be aggressively pushed to increase organization and individual performance. That is, seniority or career management should be based on the job's efficiency cycle of tenure and skills attainment. Each employee's career development and knowledge accumulation are needed to strengthening the organization's competitive power, which can be designed through timely and efficient job rotation plus promotion based on each job's efficiency cycle.

Thus, linking pay management and status management can establish an efficient compensation management system. Compensation management need not limit itself to material rewards. By incorporating intangibles such as rank and recognition beyond simply money, a new compensation management strategy can upgrade personnel management.

LOOKING AT KOREAN COMPENSATION IN DEPTH

So far the reader has been given a fairly descriptive review of Korean compensation. Many readers may wish to skip to the next chapter from here. For those readers who wish to know a bit more, the rest of this chapter covers much of what we have reviewed but in more depth. Much of this may come across as typical human resources guidelines. The below, however, is written from a Korean perspective, albeit heavily influenced by Western management ideals. A couple of decades ago, this kind of advice was considered leading-edge management strategy. Today, much has been incorporated into the better-managed Korean companies. What that means to foreign operations is that the below is no longer considered radical, so these approaches are no longer out of line with the market. At the same time, however, many traditional Korean companies are still slowly evolving toward the strategies recommended below.

Adaptability

Korea's corporate economic rewards management needs to be diversified for adaptation to rapidly changing situations and the demands of pluralistic organizations. To increase flexibility, economic compensation should be diversified based on a company's product technology and product life cycle. For example, companies producing unit-order products, such as in the construction and shipbuilding industries, should have more flexible wage structures and wage systems than companies producing standardized products, such as personal computers, machines, and automobiles.

Like most countries, wages for production department employees need to be systemized based on some relative efficiency standard, such as a time-based wage. The wage structures of marketing departments, however, need to be systemized in a relatively non-standard and flexible way, such as with performance-based pay. Also, within a department, compensation structures for difficult jobs should be different from those of less demanding jobs.

Social Compensation

The major impending task in social compensation management is raising social compensation levels. This means that in developing a corporate community, social rewards should not be viewed as less important than economic rewards. For example, social compensation could be defined as "low-level benefits strongly linked to labor-based wages."

The significance of social compensation benefits is often very minimal. Major components include retirement allowances, which function much like economic rewards. In one survey, respondents were asked to select three important benefits, and the results showed that retirement is a major component of benefits. In a few large companies, scholarships are sometimes offered. From these results, we expect that the benefits system of Korean business companies is limited to welfare benefits based on need, such as additional compensation based on the number of an employee's dependents.

Benefits

When benefits systems were analyzed by industry, such as wood products, coal mining, chemical and petroleum products, and plastic products, these industries recognized benefits as being more important than those of other industries. When the systems were analyzed according to company size, small businesses emphasized benefits more than large companies did. This meant that the work environment and other perks, such as working conditions, of small businesses were inferior to those of large companies.

Strengthening productive benefits as an alternative development goal to improve social compensation practices is often recommended. A benefits strategy should be executed on the premise that benefits are productive investments for increasing effectiveness. A benefits strategy based on the attitude that benefits impose costs or losses will probably never translate into increased productivity.

The following tasks are recommended to execute a strategy that strengthens the management of productive benefits.

First, benefits should be managed based on modern management schemes that include corporate community ideology and goals. As Korean corporations reached maturity, some companies broadened their goals, including labor-oriented goals. As they strived for broader social and personnel goals, managers also upgraded their management benefits strategies and investments.

Second, company benefits for management should be adjusted not only to specific conditions such as company size, industry, organization structure and company culture, but also to the social, economic, technical, and political environment. That is, benefits should be managed to maximize management performance, particularly in order to improve labor quality. For example, management may design cafeteria-style benefits that both consider the employees' needs and improve benefits packages. An additional approach may be to further joint decision-making or joint consultation of labor and management to gain improved benefits ROI as well as employees' trust, all based on cost-benefit analysis.

Compensation for Participation

Traditionally, Korean business corporations have shied away from systems of compensation for participation. The first such systems had various formal compensation structures, but in practice they were short-term, direct financial compensation systems. Korean companies' participation compensation management can generally be characterized as low-level compensation-labor.

To improve this situation, some Korean compensation consultants recommend that emphasis be placed on the goal of reinforcing compensation for performance and participation. To establish a compensation system that increases an employee's long-term income, it must retain employees in the company and have the flexibility to compensate based on management performance. Korean companies have for some time been urged to introduce participation compensation systems and support these programs with institutional schemes.

Ideally, management compensation strategy should raise the proportion of participation pay distribution, and that may transform from an attitude of conflict to one that highlights the common interests between labor and management. The major goals and tasks of participation compensation management are to balance profit participation (i.e., organization performance distribution participation) with capital participation (i.e., properties distribution participation).

Analysis of the compensation management practices of Korean

companies has revealed some problems. The schemes suggested below may rectify these problems, inferred within the sections below. Regardless, it is critical that one be aware of the goal, the structure, and the functions that integrate various schemes.

Corporate Community-Oriented Compensation

A rational goal in developing compensation systems is to establish a corporate community-oriented compensation system. To accomplish this objective, labor should seek to improve the quality and the quantity of products through a diligent and honest attitude, which will effectively boost productivity. Employers should design profit participation, keeping in mind the welfare of the employees.

Thus, compensation strategy and management aimed at corporate community building are required, and it requires special effort to initiate this strategy and management. Considering the Korean work environment of today, it is clear that labor and management need to build confidence with each other prior to establishing and preserving the community. Management must take into account not only capital-oriented goals but also labor-oriented goals. That is, when employers do not view profits as an objective but as a result, and when employees do not view compensation as an objective but as a result, labor and management can together build a trustful climate.

Employers should not view profits as only a return on their capital, or as investment payoffs for risk-taking and risk management, but also as a result of the joint efforts of labor and management. In addition, employees should not view compensation only as a return on labor and a payoff for supplying labor, but also as a result of the joint efforts of labor and management. From this kind of cooperation, a company can develop unity and team-orientation based on the employees' duties and responsibilities. In turn, executives can foster a trustful organizational climate and culture between labor and management.

Performance-Oriented Compensation

An ability- and performance-oriented compensation system (APOCS) should be considered. To establish an APOCS, compensation criteria based on social ability should be changed to criteria based on organizational ability rather than social status, or job-related ability rather than seniority and status. A rational compensation system should be developed incrementally based on performance rather than seniority. Generally speaking, the development of a rational compensation system for Korean companies requires a functional ability criterion that improves organizational fairness and performance criteria. Also, intensifying job grade-differentiated pay, implemented as prudently as possible, will strengthen fairness. This ultimately requires increasing the number of job grades vertically and job classes horizontally, and widening the payment gaps among different job grades.

In addition, a job qualification system with various qualifications and job responsibility allowances is necessary. With the above measures, management can reduce the impact of seniority while increasing the ability factor in compensation considerations.

To strengthen the performance-differentiated criterion, a compensation system should be designed to pay employees fairly according to performance by ability and by effort.

For pay according to ability, pay-for-job values based on job-level abilities have theoretical validity, but present more difficulties in objectively measuring job value compared to paying for seniority. This is not impossible, however. A well-developed pay-for-the-functions system and pay-for-the-qualification system integrates advantages into each pay system mentioned above. To attain this goal, management must strengthen job responsibility allowances and qualification allowances.

Ultimately, whatever the compensation system may be or evolve to be, the compensation system should be designed to satisfy organizational fairness and balance. Given that this is Korea, to be fair, pay-for-ability should be balanced with pay-for-seniority. To achieve this kind of fairness, compensation should go beyond monetary consideration. Less tangible compensations such as recognition with awards, office space allocation, and vacation/overseas training for outstanding workers are but a few examples that may be considered.

A final word of caution: even in "modern" companies with APOCS, gender discrimination remains a serious issue. The rationale for many Korean managers is not that they are anti-female, but that they expect male employees to be shouldering or to eventually shoulder the majority financial responsibility of raising a family. Therefore, when push comes to shove, women employees can unfairly lose out—particularly when there are predetermined numbers of performance ratings per grade and promotions. As an expatriate manager, one should be aware of this paternalistic prejudice among many Korean managers favoring head-of-family male employees over single female employees.

RECENT MULTINATIONAL CORPORATE COMPENSATION TRENDS

As we all know, a good compensation program anywhere nees to attract, reward, and retain good employees. Executives crafting compensation programs within foreign companies in Korea, however, need to consider a great deal more than their peers in their home countries.

First, Korean traditional payment schemes, while fading, still have a strong influence on employee expectations. Second, even if Korean employees are attracted to foreign company employment to pursue more individualistic career goals, they remain very much part of Korean society, which still influences their overall expectations. Third, foreign employers recognize that they are often not the first choice, as they may have been in the past, and accordingly need to offer attractive compensation packages while striving to be reasonably profitable in Korea.

During the past five years, wage increases across the board among expatriate firms have been hovering in roughly the seven percent range, while the GDP has averaged out to about four percent. While wage increases are expected to drop closer to the GDP and CPI averages, even this year the anticipated wage increases could be as much as 7.4 percent on average.

| KOREA'S ECONOMIC GROWTH AND SALARY INCREASE |

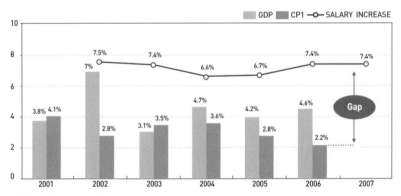

SOURCE: HEWITT SALARY INCREASE SURVEY 2001-2006

Part of this gap between GDP and CPI with substantially higher wage increases was blamed on management anxieties regarding labor unions. Though the enrollment rate of organized labor is dropping close to the 11 percent mark, the disputes, though fewer in number, have become more disruptive, with more days lost.

Hewitt Associates noted that as much as Korea's multinational corporations (MNCs) would like to institute broad salary grades, only about 20 percent are able to do so. About a quarter have adopted seniority-based systems, possibly because of the acquisition of Korean companies. But more indicative for most small- to medium-sized operations here, 37.5 percent have pegged their compensation on individual job market points in order to recruit and retain hard-to-hire specialists.

One of the more interesting philosophical issues for MNCs here is how to deal with bonuses. Bonuses were a genuine necessity some 40 years ago, when employees were paid minimal wages. There was the paternal responsibility of employers to provide extra cash so their employees could have enough for special occasions, including New Year's and Chuseok. This practice became so ingrained that most Korean employees expect substantial semi-annual bonuses, regardless of their base pay and even their personal performance.

Some years ago, a couple of MNCs attempted to roll these guaranteed bonuses into the regular salary and only pay out bonuses based on group or individual performance. What they discovered, however, was that even with the larger salaries, the employees found themselves in financial difficulty around the major holidays without the bonuses, as this benefit had become a kind of forced holiday savings plan. In the end, the MNCs ended up reverting back to the semi-annual bonuses— but now at higher base salary levels.

Nonetheless and understandably, many MNC executives feel uncomfortable with the regular semi-annual bonuses, associating them with a message of "We give you a bonus even if you do nothing," despite trying to think of bonuses as simply deferred compensation plans. And that leads us to the frustrations of trying to implement effective variable payment plans.

Communication is always near the top of any management issue, but it comes right out as the second biggest cause of difficulty in implementing variable pay schemes. At times, executives and their HR managers face a daunting task of communicating through long-held pay perceptions when explaining what new compensation plans offer. And not surprisingly, the largest challenge is that at least a fifth of employees don't trust the performance appraisal system or other matrices on which the pay variances are based.

One of the more unique aspects of Korean compensation surveys is that many employers ask for data on compensation by title. To many Westerners familiar with Korea, this may seem to be counterintuitive. After all, a *gwajang* or supervisor in a large company may have the same level of responsibility as a *bujang* or general manager in a much smaller company. Nonetheless, the demand was large enough to force Hewitt Associates to comply with client demand.

Hewitt found a very strong correlation with position title and overall compensation. Only when one compares senior management and above does the payment disparity between smaller and larger companies become pronounced. Consequently, it is no feigned interest that Koreans display when they closely examine each other's business cards, since they are sincerely interested in how well others are doing in this fiercely competitive society. (Refer to the "II. Thou Shalt Never Be Without Business Cards" section on page 86 for more information.)

In some ways, this tie-out between title and compensation is a throwback to the seniority-based, traditional compensation systems that are still hanging on in many Korean companies. In fact, even if an employee does not deserve a substantial salary increase, he or she may be promoted in position title based on his or her number of years in the position, although not necessarily with the full salary increase given to more competent peers.

As a result, some MNCs have attempted to get away from position titles altogether, or at least minimize the position titles to, say, "team leader" for those positions that actually supervise others, and "manager" for senior specialists. Sometimes this approach works; often, however, expatriate managers discover that an unofficial assignment of traditional position titles has emerged, as old ways, particularly in the larger social context, die very slowly.

Bucking a traditional trend not to provide long-term rewards to individuals, many MNCs are offering incentive awards, such as stock options, primarily to retain and motivate key employees and, to a lesser extent, to give these important staff members a sense of company ownership. What is unique about Korea, compared to the rest of the Asia-Pacific region, is that top management receives an overwhelming amount of this kind of benefit compared to other levels of management. Why this is so is not clear, but I would surmise that stock options are often necessary to recruit and retain top Korean executives in MNC operations.

So pulling all of this together, we may make the following conclusions. First, in spite of the economic slowdown, MNC salary increases continue in a competitive game where top players offer above market to get the best, while the rest of the pack plays catch-up so as not to be out of the game in attracting and retaining talented employees.

Second, while unions and traditionalists tend to preserve the seniority systems, MNCs are striving to move to performance-based compensation systems. Be it the execution, communication or both, many performance appraisal systems are not living up to expectations. Many Korean employees doubt the fairness of these systems. More work is clearly needed on management's part to make these systems fairly applied and appropriately understood by all ranks of employees. At the same time, these and other performance-based systems are needed to attract, motivate and retain top Korean employees.

Third, there remains an ongoing struggle between the ideal—compensation plans that support the business strategy—and the legacy—entitlements predicated on fixed bonuses, job titles, and seniority. Many MNC executives need to do a better job in persuading employees that their long-term welfare is best served by compensation schemes that underwrite the overall success of the company, rather than simply skimming the cream off the top.

RESULTS ARE WORTH THE COSTS

So there you have it—the lay of the land, an overview of how many Korean companies are trying to manage change in the employment marketplace. Whatever one's final approach may turn out to be, one should know that devising an equitable and balanced compensation system for the local staff is of utmost importance for successful business in Korea. Any foreign executive with this responsibility should be alert to the changing local practices and to the attempts to blend in new schemes to benefit companies.

As anywhere, in addition to the basic salary, other monetary benefits, personal attention, and humane treatment of local employees will ensure the sustained success of your business venture.

17. MOTIVATING PERSONNEL

Over the last few decades, Korea has earned a reputation for being one of the most dynamic economies in the world. The driving force behind this story of rags-to-riches has been Korea's hard-working people. Once properly guided and motivated, they are willing to make self-sacrificing efforts for the betterment of an organization, and ultimately the nation.

Foreign firms as employers are, however, sometimes placed at a disadvantage. For a potential recruit, foreign firms pose some serious questions from a career standpoint, despite the apparent advantages offered: 1) limited visibility, as most top management positions can be occupied by foreigners—though this is much less of an issue today with many Koreans now staffing top local positions; 2) uncertain business prospects; and 3) relatively less secure employment in foreign companies—again, this is less of an issue since the IMF crisis of 1998, as many Korean firms have been forced away from traditional, more secure employment models.

In addition, shortsightedness and insensitivity of expatriate managers and/or offshore executives often exacerbate personnel and morale problems that can contribute to general business failures. With true leadership, empathy, and tact, however, one may be able to harness the positive attributes of Korean employees to the company's benefit. The expatriate manager needs to be thoroughly familiar with the unique aspects of Korea's employment system. The foreign manager must learn how to be successful in cross-cultural business.

UNDERSTANDING THE EMPLOYMENT SYSTEM

One may find Korea somewhere between Japan and the West with regard to the mobility of employees. While loyalty and long-term employment are important, there is no such system as lifetime employment in Korea. Changing jobs is common, especially among the sales force and lower-level employees. But job-hoppers, whatever their qualifications, have not been generally welcome at many local companies, given the strong emphasis on company loyalty. Still, in view of the increased competition of the post-IMF crisis at the turn of this century, there has been an increase in companies recruiting top talent amongst themselves.

Recruiting in most large companies is done directly from colleges and universities. Clerical and blue-collar workers may be recruited from high schools and trade schools (i.e., non-academic institutes), but candidates for white-collar positions are almost always selected from the ever-increasing pool of university graduates.

Compensation depends largely upon seniority and the length of service with a particular company. Of course, there can be exceptions, and if so, one can be additionally compensated with various allowances and bonuses, leaving the basic salary scheme intact. While every employee, in theory, appears to move up in compensation as his or her service with the company advances, responsibility can vary considerably with ability. After several years, sharp distinctions are made regarding ability as judged by the company's senior members. The winner is often characterized, in addition to other capabilities, by his or her ability to endure. In many Korean companies, as the white-collar employee approaches fifty, employment often comes down to annual promotion or termination (see the "Hiring and Firing" section in Chapter 4).

DEALING WITH JOB MOBILITY

Having seen cases of rags-to-riches stories in Korea, young people tend to be ambitious and entrepreneurial. Some want to see big things happen within a short period of time, thus contributing to a higher turnover of the labor force.

As many new technology-intensive industries emerged, there was a chronic shortage of scientists, technicians, and skilled workers. Today, Korea has the highest per capita number of Ph.Ds. While many doctoral degrees are in soft disciplines and attained primarily for social and professional status, Korean universities graduate a larger number of students with advanced degrees in the science and engineering fields. Also, a surprising number of Koreans go abroad for graduate school and return to lucrative jobs. While the job shortage has been greatly alleviated in recent years, job-hopping has, if anything, increased. Rapid evolution of the economy also causes some industry sectors to stagnate and, in turn, leads their employees to seek alternative opportunities. In a dynamic economy, labor mobility may be desirable for facilitating structural change, but the excessive turnover can cause many Korean firms serious difficulties in training staff and retaining skilled workers.

MAINTAINING A GROUP SPIRIT

While Koreans are sometimes regarded as more individualistic than the Japanese, they are still very much group-oriented. The whole society is knitted together by ties and relationships among groups and organizations, some of which may be unique to Korea. Clans, schools, companies, the military, and regional adherence are some of the more important groups. It is generally accepted that the more cohesive a group is, the more productive it tends to be.

Any manager should try to develop a culture of belonging where there is sharing of a common value and commitment. For this, firm leadership is necessary, and many corporations have a company slogan or motto under which every staff member can unite. Most Korean companies have regular and intense company-wide training or indoctrination sessions. In addition, many firms have company-wide sports events as a way to strengthen group spirit.

DEVELOPING GOOD COMMUNICATION

As mentioned in "III. Thou Shall Not Assume Everything Thou Sayest in English Is Completely Understood" among the "11 Commandments for Doing Business in Korea," the real level of comprehension of English-speaking Korean staff members may not be as good as their courtesy implies. But communication is more than just language. Cultural barriers may also be bigger then they appear on the surface. Another difficulty facing a foreign businessperson is the "logic gap"—a gap in values, thought processes, and patterns—between East and West.

Experienced foreign managers have learned to pay particular attention in confirming that what they want to get across to their employees is properly understood—and vice versa. It is important for the expatriate manager to take pains to somehow overcome communication problems by trying to learn some of the Korean language. Reading the Korean alphabet (*hangeul*) is the first, surprisingly easy step toward this end. (Incidentally, in Korea one speaks "*Hanguk-mal*" and writes with *hangeul*. Only Korea's semi-sophisticated foreigners and some of their Korean sycophants use the weird phrase "speak *hangeul*"—such phrasing would be similar to saying "speak alphabet" when referring to someone learning English as a second language.) Enjoying as many informal occasions with the local staff as possible is also an excellent way to improve communication.

Not unique to Korea, but also true in some other Asian cultures, there is a strong reluctance to pass on bad news—particularly upwards. Often the reason is some kind of fatalism, mixed with unfounded optimism, anticipating that the situation will somehow correct itself and the subordinate will therefore need not have bothered his or her superior. Consequently, it is important to stress by word that bad news is in a sense welcome, and to reinforce by action, such as profuse thanks to the local employee for bringing bad news to the foreign manager's early attention.

ADAPTING TO LOCAL NORMS

Local adaptation for many large multinational firms can sometimes mean a sheer violation of the principles of the parent corporation. In the area of personnel policies, however, there are many benefits to be gained from being a touch flexible.

In a Korean organization, such non-monetary values as status, title, face, and recognition are as important as monetary benefits. Hierarchical harmony based on seniority and rank is another factor in making an organization work smoothly. Recognition and generous separation payments for resigning staff are highly regarded by local employees.

Visible, non-monetary status symbols such as placement of desks by rank can be extremely important, and placing the wrong employee in the wrong desk or at the improper work location can wreak havoc with the business unit's morale.

BEING SENSITIVE TO PERSONAL MATTERS

Be it East or West, a manager showing personal attention to his or her personnel will definitely boost morale. In a Korean organization, with its Confucian and paternalistic inclinations, the competent leader has multi-faceted responsibilities. One of these includes being present, such as by officiating or even arranging weddings for employees. In Korea, it's not uncommon for a president to visit the sickbeds of employees with flowers. The presence of an expatriate manager at a 100th day party for a newborn child may be remembered and cherished by the employee for a lifetime. At the same time, the expatriate manager should be prepared to make regular personal donations whenever an employee marries, a child is born, or there is a death in the family. The other employees base the amount one should pay on one's rank and perception of one's income. Since these events are fairly common, however, a single payment is not particularly large, as there are surely many more to follow at other occasions. If the custom comes across as a bit irritating, rest assured that the Korean employees largely feel the same way. But it would be unthinkable to put a stop to the practice, as it is a traditional and important means of building group solidarity.

Arrogance and impatience are known to be the most common shortcomings found among expatriate managers in Korea. A leader who is gentle but firm, has an aura of authority, and generally possesses the traits of a so-called *yangban* (an educated gentleman in traditional Korea) is normally respected and liked by Korean employees. Open criticism of the host country and conspicuous alliance among expatriates before local employees are not desirable. It is important to foster a climate of openness and fairness in daily dealings with local staff and employees.

In extreme situations and behind closed doors, however, a bit of emotional theatrics combined with explanations of how the offending employee's behavior has damaged the morale and well-being of the entire company and his or her co-workers—followed by an immediate regaining of composure— can be effective. Needless to say, this tactic should be used sparingly and strategically.

MAINTAINING CONTINUITY

It is often found that the whole philosophy of an organization changes as a new manager takes office or key local staff are replaced. In Korean companies, this most commonly takes place in January, when there is forced turnover by executive fiat. Consequently, Korean staff members are usually well experienced in this phenomenon with other, former supervisors—and often have specific expectations for the incoming manager's behavior. Criticism of a predecessor by the new manager may weaken the stability and continuity of the already volatile relationship between the local and expatriate staff. Especially in a small organization, tradition and convention should be preserved, and any desired changes induced gradually. To maintain continuity, a long-serving senior local employee may be appointed to an honorary position or retained as an advisor.

DELEGATING AND GUIDING

When guided tactfully and wisely with a relatively strong hand, Koreans can be incredibly resourceful and productive. Managers should give as much guidance and direction as possible. They should try to remain aloof from details and trivia and leave implementation to local employees. Many American and European managers, however, often err toward the other extreme. Too often, foreign managers insist on consensus management as a means of developing their staff. While this management style can work, initially it often causes confusion among the local staff, who are more accustomed to top-down orders. In the worst--case scenario, the local staff may openly question the foreign manager's competence. Consequently, it often comes down to a delicate balance of administering skilled direction while establishing one's credibility without getting one's hands unnecessarily dirty with the details.

Deviations should be corrected only through key supervisors. Here, saving "face" is equally important even to the lowest-level employees. Wise managers don't try to look over their subordinates' shoulders. The ties established with the key Korean staff, based on a sense of trust, can bring results far beyond one's expectations.

GROOMING KOREANS TO SUCCEED EXPATRIATES

For long-run successful operations, it is desirable to have local managers whenever possible. Once they are properly equipped with professional knowledge and skills, their commitment and local expertise can enable them to outperform expatriates, and at much lower costs. This change need not be implemented overnight. It may be planned over a three- to five-year period, and should be made known to local employees. It will make a big difference in their attitudes about their jobs and, of course, their productivity.

At the same time, it is often not entirely wise to leave the Korean operations 100 percent in the control of local staff. This is for two reasons. First, it is important that foreign staff members, even if in subordinate positions to Korean managers, work in the Korean business unit so that the rest of the company can have a better appreciation and understanding of what business is like in Korea. Second, if Koreans alone run the local operation, there is a very real danger that the Korean operation can start moving out and revolving in its own peculiar orbit, to the point that corrective measures to bring the Koreans back into the rest of the company's fold may be extremely expensive and painful. Korea is a very insular and nationalist society. So it is critical that "we Koreans" vs. "they foreigners" does not become too strong a facet of one's corporate politics.

MAINTAINING MOTIVATION

Maintaining a high level of motivation among company personnel is a top priority for all managers, but it is particularly challenging for many foreign managers. Job productivity, employee harmony, and work satisfaction depend on this essential dynamic. The expatriate executive must develop superb motivational skills to achieve a productive, profitable business organization. While this is still a challenge, there are more tools and opportunities to do so than in the past. Some of the foreign chambers of commerce hold regular human resource committee meetings that specifically address these issues and offer a chance for managers to share advice. Also, there are more business seminars in English that deal with this subject and are taught by local experts. Finally, there are now many bicultural Koreans who were either born or raised abroad and have returned to Korea. Although these individuals may make invaluable employees, some may also be less adept at fitting back into Korea, so hiring of such individuals is both a special and perilous option.

Ultimately, it is possible to lead and manage local employees through practical, if at times unusual, employee motivation strategies, such as by building close mentor-like relations with Korean and foreign managers.

INSCRUTABLE KOREAN LOYALTY

Korean employees are world-renowned for being industrious, self-sacrificing and persistent. At the same time, newspapers and television are quick to report militant union strikes. Yet only 11 percent of all Korean workers are unionized, with only a small fraction of these belonging to militant unions. So how loyal are Korean employees, really? One might consider that in certain sectors—such as manufacturing, where Korean workers are generally regarded as quite productive—efficiency may be a reflection of company loyalty. Or is it?

In 2003, British commercial pollster TNS conducted a global employee attitude survey of some 1,000 employees in 35 countries. When the results were tabulated, even TNS's long-term Korea resident North Asia Regional Director David Richardson was floored with the results. Only Bulgaria surpassed Korea in having the least company-loyal employees. Mr. Richardson was so shocked that he even temporarily delayed the survey's global announcement to check if something may have been in serious error. But the TNS survey did in fact accurately reflect the sentiments of the interviewed, including the Koreans.

Interestingly, Japan also scored among the lowest, while countries such as Israel, New Zealand, the Netherlands and Mexico scored among the highest in loyalty. Among the low-ranking countries, the former Soviet bloc weighed heavily. Given general worker attitudes developed over decades in inefficient, centrally planned markets, this was not at all surprising, since most observers expected a correlation between low productivity and low company loyalty.

So it came as a surprise that the two Northeast Asian advanced economies, with their high productivity, ranked so low. Immediate speculation considered the fact that, as with the Soviet model, Korean and Japanese workers have traditionally had relatively low job mobility. Since childhood, these Asians have been force-marched into studying at the right schools and cram institutes so as to get into the right universities and later enter the best companies—with relatively little freedom in selecting their careers. While comparing Japan and Korea with the Soviet bloc may be a bit of an exaggeration, the parallel is arguably a strong one.

Actually, on a worldwide average, 19 percent of all employees were "drivers" who were satisfied and motivated. Another 12 percent were "critics" who were motivated but dissatisfied. An exact third were "residents" who were satisfied but not motivated, while the bottom 36 percent were "detached"—dissatisfied and unmotivated.

A further breakdown of the Korean employee results indicated that there was an unusually wide disparity between the top two "engaged" groups— the drivers and critics—and the bottom detached group. Given that there was only a very small resident group, when averaged together the national average was lower than what one may expect. Also, it was noted that most of the engaged employees were males aged 25 to 49. In other words, if one is female or in the majority of middle-aged men with increasingly fewer chances for continuing promotion and employment, there may be much less of a chance for one to be engaged or very company-loyal.

Dr. Vince Conte of Korean Management Association Consulting (KMAC) has pointed out that survey results of the same people can vary significantly if the survey is taken at the work site, away from the comfort of their homes, or by private telephone conversation. In other words, if interviewed away from the work site, results tend to be more individualized, whereas surveys conducted at the work site often reflect more of a group perspective. Many people adopt a very different mentality once they set foot on the factory floor or in the office, and this attitude can greatly color a survey's results.

Dr. Conte has further suggested that many Korean employees are emotionally detached because they realistically expect to be with a given employer for only five years or less. There may be a subconscious anxiety that if one invests all one's heart, soul, and mind into one's work, one's own true values or feelings may inappropriately come into conflict with the views of one's superiors. Thus, out of cautious self-preservation, many employees behave differently in the workplace than their true feelings would dictate.

In addition to expressing skepticism about their company's motives, Dr. Conte suggests that Koreans receive more emotional reinforcement and comfort from their family and network of friends than Westerners do. For the average Korean worker, long-term security is less a matter of success on the job and more about having friends and family who will help when one is in trouble. The late 1990s made people realize that companies go out of business, and even great employees can lose their jobs

So in Dr. Conte's opinion, the TNS data was much more insightful with regard to, in his terms, "private Korea" than "professional Korea." It seems that, as in many countries, Korean employee attitudes shift each day as they walk in and out of the workplace.

Mr. Richardson has noted that Korean employees seem to shy away from taking personal initiative for self-development beyond English language classes. They tend to be more group-oriented, and generally only follow the suggestions and directions of their superiors. One other Western executive concurs, noting that when an expat manager suggests taking evening classes to an employee as a way to further qualify for possible advancement, too often the employee's immediate response is "What is in it for me? What guarantee of reward—such as a promotion—can I procure by doing so?" Since most managers lack complete clairvoyance, they generally cannot make any real promises, and as a result the employee loses interest. Another executive has noted that many Korean employees seem to be more concerned about the negative impact to others in their group of one person's advance.

Dr. Conte suggests that the old rules of the manufacturing-centric economy worked well, but as the Korean economy morphs into a more serviced-based one, much rethinking will be needed to foster new behaviors suitable for future markets and industries. He allows that while a nation's fundamental culture never really changes, processes within a culture can be modified to be in sync with new paradigms.

For example, Dr. Conte points out that Korean HR departments are less focused on individual development and more on team building—often including sophisticated social engineering to help an optimum number of individuals to work well in groups. Given that, one may expect less in HR policy changes but more in adjusting the work environment, including a great deal of future work dedicated to easing individuals and groups into more efficient, service-centric work environments via social pressures and structured social interactions.

To dig deeper into this issue, consider the 2008 Korean General Social Survey of 32 countries. Koreans were the least satisfied with their jobs, scoring 62.5 points in job satisfaction out of a possible 100. When the same questions were asked of other countries' workers, Switzerland came in first at 78.6, followed by the U.S., Ireland, and Denmark all scoring above 75.

Not surprisingly, Koreans were also the least interested in their work (56.5 points). Why this is so is unclear, but some think major restructuring following the IMF Crisis at the end of the 20th century may have been responsible. Naturally, as morale falls, so does productivity. According to the OECD's 2008 statistics, Korean workers worked the longest among member countries, while their productivity ranked last among 55 countries, as measured by the International Institute for Management Development in 2007.

As described elsewhere in this book, company loyalty is often rewarded with forced, early retirements when employees in their early 50s and older can least afford it. So it does not surprise that Korean workers ranked job security and income highest on their list of what they wanted from a job. A job security satisfaction rating of 54 points and income satisfaction rating of 39 points clearly indicates that they are unsatisfied in both categories.

Still, among the 32 advanced countries, Korea ranked in the middle, at 16th, in terms of loyalty to employers. Perhaps for these reasons, about two-thirds of Korean employees hope to run their own businesses. It is not clear how much of this is a natural inclination and how much a resigned belief that they will be someday given the pink slip regardless of their company loyalty. Korea ranked 29th in wishing to be employed until retirement, with only a third indicating such a wish.

Research by Marsh Mercer Kroll has found similar issues while conducting surveys over the past decade regarding job satisfaction among Korean employees. Somewhat disturbing was the finding that approximately 20 percent of surveyed employees liked their jobs but disliked their companies. More unsettling was the discovery that as many as 12 percent of the employees disliked both their jobs and their companies, but hoped to remain with their employers until retirement.

So what conclusions can we draw? If a manager wishes to keep his or her employees intellectually and emotionally engaged, that manager must communicate some kind of vision that employees can internalize, especially with regard to personal growth and benefit from working for the organization. At the same time, if Korean organizations are to effectively become fully productive in the service-oriented Korean economy of the 21st century, employers must remove overt and subtle threats of employment termination based on gender and age.

18. GETTING LABOR MANAGEMENT RELATIONS RIGHT

*F*rom the 1960s to the '80s, one of the major reasons for Korea's rapid industrialization was the absence of labor disruptions. But during the late '80s, the situation began to change. As genuine democracy took root in society, labor unions finally had the opportunity to strike without fear of government oppression. Like precocious teens finally getting their driver's licenses, some unions behaved responsibly while others did not. Those who acted up the most naturally gained the greatest press coverage at home and abroad.

Some reasons for the comparatively long period of labor stability in the past were:

- The Confucian social structure of ascending acquiescence to authority,

- Government policy of limiting labor unrest, and

- Rapid improvement in both salaries and benefits during the prior decade.

In recent decades, however, labor disputes have increased. Some of the causes have been:

- Slower salary increases due to the nation's decelerated economy,

- Rising worker expectations of a larger slice of the economic pie,

- The salary gap between white- and blue-collar workers,

- The subsistence wage level for unskilled and semi-skilled workers,

- Work force reduction due to business decline in some industries, such as overseas construction and small- and mid-sized manufacturing companies,

- Mergers and acquisitions causing a decline in job security, and

- High technology and information technology expanding via heavy capital investment, with diminishing reliance on human resources.

HISTORY OF KOREAN TRADE UNIONISM

Though actualized organized labor rights are a relatively new Korean phenomenon, today's unions share an important heritage in Korea's nationalism. It is therefore important for the expatriate manager to have a basic understanding of the background of Korea's trade unionism.

In 1886, the first strike by Korea's labor movement took place at Chosan Station in southern South Korea. Laborers protested against government officials, rather than against their employers, regarding harsh treatment on the job. Ensuing labor strikes, such as those at the Unsan gold mine and Wonsan Harbor, were not against Korean businesses, but against foreign capitalists and Japanese colonial authorities. In fact, at the time there was no indigenous Korean capitalism.

At the turn of the century, Korea's labor union movement had begun. By the 1920s, a national federation of trade unions was organized, although its primary objective was to fight against Japanese establishments and their colonial government. Perhaps the uncompromising and sometimes violent nature of Korea's current trade unions may be rooted in this tradition of resistance for the sake of political independence.

Post-World War II

Following the Second World War, trade unions resurfaced under the U.S. military government. Although the U.S. government intended to encourage unionism, patterned after the American three-party dispute settlement tradition, in Korea, there was little resemblance between the Korean and the American systems. Local labor union leaders were generally more interested in political activities than in the laborers' bread-and-butter issues. Among them were a number of left-wing communist agitators working in conformity with Pyongyang's directives.

Daehan Nochong, predecessor of the current Federation of Korean Trade Unions (FKTU), was formed to compete with the communist-led National Council of Trade Unions, called Jeonpyeong for short in Korean. By 1949, Jeonpyeong had been completely dismantled. In the process of fighting against Jeonpyeong, Daehan Nochong gained strength by cooperating with the government. Thus did the government begin exercising its influence on union affairs. After that, trade unions and national politics became entangled, and they remain so today.

Western Legislation Copied

At the close of the Korean War, President Syngman Rhee's government enacted three major pieces of legislation that have had lasting effects on South Korea's labor relations policies:

- The Union Law, which guaranteed workers the right to organize, to bargain collectively, and to engage in collective action,

- The Labor Standards Law, which stipulated in detail the minimum labor conditions employers had to provide, and

- The Labor Dispute Adjustment Law, which prescribed the administrative procedures to be followed in dispute resolution, including national emergency procedures.

The legal framework of collective bargaining was set, but actual operation and administration of collective bargaining did not materialize for a long time. The labor policies promulgated in 1953 had little bearing on daily labor practices. Labor standards were set so high that if an employer observed every condition of the statutes, he could not run a business. These laws were copied from the West via Japanese labor statutes (often complete with mistranslations made by the Japanese when they copied and translated the statutes from Germany). In fact, the laws were really designed as "window dressing" to show that the South protected laborers better than the communist North. As a result, delinquency in labor law enforcement became commonplace and still exists today.

Government Intervention and the FKTU

In 1960, workers participated in demonstrations that led to the fall of the Rhee government. Following his coup in May 1961, General Park Chung-Hee placed a ban on trade unions. Under close government supervision, the ban was lifted shortly thereafter. A new FKTU was organized, and unions were structured into industry-wide, national unions affiliated with the new FKTU.

In December 1971, President Park issued an Emergency Decree on National Security that suspended free collective bargaining practices that had been in operation during the 1960s. The decree was not revoked until

1981. During the 1970s, under the Emergency Decree, unions were required to secure government approval before engaging in wage negotiations. The Labor Dispute Adjustment Law was later suspended and replaced by direct government intervention in all labor disputes, but all collective labor actions remained prohibited. These practices have profoundly affected contemporary labor-management practices, so much so that even after the suspension of the decree, the government's interference in disputes deprived the parties of the opportunity to develop free collective bargaining processes.

During that time, of course, there were a number of major, illegal labor disputes that were harshly put down by government authorities, while all other disputes were resolved with management having overwhelming dominance almost all of the time.

On June 29, 1987, democratization was announced. The labor movement was quickly reactivated. In 1987, free from government interference, 3,749 labor disputes erupted. While the numbers of labor disputes slackened in the following years, the Korean labor movement was considerably more confrontational than in previous decades with its newly achieved freedom.

Korean Confederation of Trade Unions (KCTU)

In 1995, a more aggressive competitor to the FKTU, the Korean Confederation of Trade Unions (KCTU), was illegally established. This umbrella organization consists of unions from a wide array of service and manufacturing industries, including public sector unions. In the last days of 1996, the conservative party passed a law that effectively made it impossible to have a second umbrella trade organization. In early 1997, the KCTU achieved de facto legality after instigating with its half-million members the largest nationwide strike since 1946. In 1999, the liberal government of President Kim Dae-Jung recognized the KCTU.

The Asian Financial Crisis, or "IMF Crisis"

The economic crisis at the end of 1997 resulted in emergency measures by the government and employers. Earlier that year, the Trade Union and Labor Relations Adjustment Act was enacted, providing that a union could be formed in virtually any workplace with no minimum requirement in terms of the number of employees or the proportion of the workforce represented.

Korean companies called for labor market flexibility that allowed layoffs of redundant employees during much-needed corporate restructuring. These needs were contrary to employment traditions that were in many ways patterned on the Japanese example of lifetime employment.

In early 1998, under pressure from the IMF's conditions for assistance, the National Assembly reduced restrictions on employers' rights to lay off employees. In February 1998, the newly elected Kim Dae-Jung administration established the Tripartite Commission on Labor, Business and Government (TC). This consultative agency was set up to support the president's economic restructuring drive, which included legalizing layoffs in light of unions taking direct action to protect jobs. The long-term goal of the TC remains to arrive at a social pact among the three parties for an employment system that may address the requirements of Korea's economic development.

Developments Today and in the Near Future

At present, the level of labor unrest can be problematic even within well-managed companies. Regardless of intention, the mass media greatly exaggerate the severity of the issue. Only 12 percent or less of Korean workers are unionized—lower than in most industrialized democracies. For example, the proportion of organized workers in Germany is more than one-third, and in Britain nearly one-third.

As South Korea's economy continues to become more open, unions are finding themselves increasingly challenged. Some union leaders think that labor should redefine itself as a protector of social welfare. Union leaders are understandably most concerned about layoffs that are likely to affect middle-aged men. Unemployment in late middle age causes a double jeopardy for workers suddenly finding themselves without work, with few or no job prospects in a society prejudiced against older workers—and facing the additional, near certain expenses of putting their children through college.

In any case, unions are in danger of becoming sidetracked by short-term gains. In 2004, President Roh Moo-Hyun, a former labor rights attorney, outlined a new labor-management model. Still, all of this can make some union leaders feel a bit insecure about the future, and thus motivate them to look for or create issues to better ensure their organization's survival.

But one needs to find a proper balance for the entire matter between what most foreigners perceive from the mass media and what most managers face in daily commerce. As one of Korea's most respected expatriate executives aptly put it, "One definitely should not believe the perception of Korean industrial relations and employee relations one gets from the mass media. While there is no smoke without fire, most journalists focus on the sensational parts rather than covering the whole story. There is a lot of misinterpretation of Korean culture. For example, the wearing of red headbands or bandanas is meant to be much less aggressive than as understood in the West. The wearing of those headbands is basically a way of conveying group solidarity. Even salespeople in sales meetings don the headbands on occasion."

Korean democracy is a new and recent development. Many Koreans feel it is natural to demonstrate as part of their newfound freedom. Marches and protests are part of daily life and less intense than would be the case in more mature democracies. Only a small percentage of these demonstrations ever get out of hand, and only on relatively rare occasions do some Koreans act unruly and out of control.

The press tends to focus on what makes up only one percent of the story. But as one resident foreign CEO contended, if the reality was as represented in the media, why is Korea doing so well compared to many other countries? The fact is that 99 percent of the real story is about a highly educated, very hard-working labor force that is fiercely loyal and committed to company goals, he said. If there were a fair comparison, rather than only comparing Korean work stoppages with those of German factories, a more accurate comparison would be of total costs. One would find that Koreans are often doing much better overall due to fewer indirect costs (e.g., maintenance and supervision) than, for example, the Germans.

In the face of the global recession of 2008, the KCTU found key unions walking away in 2009, complaining of over-politicization at the expense of members' needs and expressing a general disgust at a number of public scandals involving KCTU leadership. Furthermore, as of this writing, ROK President Lee Myung-Bak has refused to meet even once with KCTU leadership, demonstrating his disapproval for their illegal activities and apparent disregard for the well-being of their members' companies. While the KCTU's future is not in doubt, it has so far failed to adequately adjust to the political pendulum swinging back to the right.

The KCTU faced new challenges a decade later as some big enterprise unions, including the Korea Telecom Trade Union, disaffiliated themselves. At the same time, both the KCTU and the FKTU faced the upward trend of independent trade unions and a move to form a third national trade union center.

As of March 2010, two new labor unions were being formed. Both are attracting workers who are fed up with the FKTU and KCTU. As of this book's writing, neither has been recognized by the Labor Ministry, on the grounds of so-called political bias. But their initial popularity is based on hopes that these unions might be politically neutral, seeking mutual benefit for both labor and management.

If recognized, the Youth Community Union would be the nation's first labor union that applies a rigid age limit to applicants. It would focus on teenage part-time workers and job seekers in their 20s and 30s. Regardless of employment status, only those aged between 15 and 39 are eligible for membership.

The second of these new labor unions, New Hope, was established in March 2010 by labor activists who broke with the two major umbrella unions over what they call "ideologically biased, anti-business and anti-market lines."

As of this book's writing, there are two potential amendments scheduled regarding the Trade Union & Labor Relations Adjustment Act (TULRA). The first involves no-wage payments to full-time officers from July 1, 2010. The ROK government is expected to provide some guidance on how this will actually work some time as early as April 30, 2010. At issue is a new concept of "paid time off," where under certain circumstances union official employees will in fact be paid for their time in administering union matters, but will not be viewed as receiving payment for doing company work, as once was the case. As of this writing, there remain some unresolved matters regarding how, if at all, this accumulated time off will impact matters such as pension and severance calculations.

The second TULRA amendment is an allowance for multiple unions at a single shop. This is scheduled to go into effect as of July 1, 2011. Until then, multiple unions are permitted at a single company only if there are conspicuously different classes of employees. For example, white-collar administrative workers may belong to one union and manufacturing employees may belong to a different one. Also, from July 2011, manufacturing employees, for example, may be represented by more than one union. However, multiple unions must negotiate with management via a single bargaining channel. Who actually represents union demands will be determined by the unions. If no representation agreement can be made, then the union representing the majority of union employees will be the single bargaining channel. If there is no majority union, than there will be combined representation coming from each union that represents at least 10 percent of the union members.

This second TULRA amendment, based on Koreans' Constitutional right to organize in any fashion, was created under the labor-friendly administrations of the Kim Dae-Jung and Roh Moo-Hyun administrations. As such, this change was designed to breathe new life into union-organizing efforts. At the same time, the various unions have become rather savvy at creating "how to organize" instructional web sites.

For managers wishing to maintain a union-free shop or to keep the number of unions to one, the following advice may be considered:

1. Create a "risk assessment task force" among managers to review and identify all potential root causes for multiple unions. It is obviously critical for management to identify and address these root causes before an organizer does. Otherwise, the organizer will take credit for bringing these matters to management's attention.

   a. In the case of an existing union, resolve minor issues so that the union and management team focus only on important issues. Don't allow small issues to fester and thereby create organizing opportunities for new union organizers.

2. Establish a communications program that will ensure that management speaks with one consistent voice.

3. Try to identify and deal with potential union organizers. Look for employees who starting taking Fridays off inexplicably. Often this change in behavior is a red flag indicating that employees are being trained in union organizing.

4. Train managers in order to avoid creating "triggering events" that may drive employees into organizers' arms. Middle managers are more likely to create these triggering events, so consider training that stresses pride in being part of the management team. It should also include a legal overview of dos and don'ts in addressing suspected organizing efforts, while stressing proper workplace management practices. With executives in a unionized shop, collective bargaining skills training as well as legal briefings can be excellent investments.

Still, the prudent manager needs to pay more attention to employee sensitivities. This applies especially to foreign businesses that lack deep roots in Korea and are therefore more susceptible to labor problems among their potentially skeptical national employees.

To acquire a basis for dealing with some sensitive labor issues, it may prove beneficial for the international executive to have a summary of potential management responses to important issues in the local labor situation.

LABOR REALITY

Compensation Package

Employers are expected to go beyond the basic monetary compensation by providing various benefits that satisfy employee psychological needs. These provisions can satisfy employee concerns and act as preventive measures against potential labor agitation. At the same time, it's important to put a cap on anything that is negotiated; one should never leave anything—for example, unlimited education assistance—open-ended. Don't dismiss this as common sense, as it has happened. The real danger comes from expatriate manager turnover, where some managers may be tempted to negotiate an easy close to a collective bargaining agreement (CBA) session and let future general managers deal with the problem years later.

According to the law, each company's collective bargaining agreement with its union must be renegotiated every two years. There is no legal requirement, but by established, nationwide practice, wage negotiations are annual events, and a procession that can be very company resource-draining.

Also by law, the union must vote for new leadership every two years. This makes things difficult for everyone. It means starting all over on a regular basis. Management has to build new trust with the new union leadership team, which often comes in with a mandate to be tougher than the previous leadership. This forced turnover of leaders often creates factions within a company's union. At best, union leaders have just two years in office before they must return to the work floor to wait two years until the next elections. Though wage agreements do pass on the first vote in some years, one can expect the first vote to fail due to union factionalism rather than the contents of the agreements.

Social Ties

Another stabilizing factor in labor relations is the recognition of personal ties among the personnel. The strongest of these are clan, school and military associations and regional roots. Informal as they may seem, these links conform to a strict hierarchy based on seniority. They often form the basis for corporate or office politics. At the same time, these ties provide efficient, informal communication channels up and down the hierarchical organizational structure. Employers may use these ties in resolving the inevitable organizational conflicts.

According to the authors' interviews with expatriate executives, however, the truly effective manager is the one who personally takes the initiative to learn about his or her employees by walking around and asking questions about them both on a personal and professional level. Korean employees sincerely appreciate senior managers taking a genuine interest in them as human beings, and they are often proud to demonstrate their expertise in their given company roles. Often the difference between a foreign manager who instills strong employee loyalty and the remote manager who is often at odds with the Korean staff is whether that executive takes the regular initiative to spend time really trying to get to know the employees and learning from them about how they are making a corporate contribution.

Company Rap Sessions

Official channels exist as well. Recognizing the importance of a stable labor environment, both in the economy and in politics, the Labor Ministry has instituted the Labor-Management Council to be set up in local business organizations, and the Ministry recommends that all private industries have regular sessions. Employee representatives and chief executive officers are to meet every month for face-to-face discussions on current labor issues. For many companies, this has proven effective in resolving sticky labor irritations and providing, under a controlled situation, a vent for labor discontent. Such up-front consultations can serve to defuse an otherwise explosive labor issue. In some instances, however, they are held as a matter of formality, as in some government-sponsored organizations.

Company Training

Another element in the Korean labor scene is the company-wide training session. Almost without exception, Korean corporations provide training to strengthen group spirit and sharpen employees' professional skills. Whenever possible and appropriate, expatriate managers should join these shared experiences. The resulting camaraderie can serve as another deterrent against disruptive disputes.

USEFUL IDEAS

As the atmosphere becomes more conducive to labor tension, management needs to develop greater sensitivity. At the same time, management must possess the negotiation skills and know the preventive methods to avoid and to resolve growing labor unrest issues. An effective mediator should have a number of measures at his or her command.

Communication

Maintaining lines of communication with employees is of the utmost importance for a responsible executive. This requires both formal and informal channels of communication. If already established, the Labor-Management Council is an effective, official channel.

It is also necessary, particularly for an expatriate manager, to open natural but discreet communication channels with the local staff, preferably at different levels and departments. A deliberate avoidance of bureaucratic protocol will make the head office more accessible to the employees, allowing lines of communication to develop. As long as there is a conscious effort to remove all obstacles and restrictions to a free flow of communication between labor and management, disputes can be prevented or defused.

In communications with labor, however, management has to preserve a benevolent but firm and consistent position. Koreans have learned how to respect authority. When privileged information is shared with union leadership, it is not unreasonable to try to get some kind of quid pro quo agreement from the union leader. The skillful manager maintains with his or her union counterpart a relationship of mutual respect and trust and a sense of give and take. It is critical that the senior-most executive maintain his or her composure—no matter how exasperating the situation may be—by demonstrating maturity and sincerity while still being crystal clear when consistently communicating and upholding the company's principles. This may require the patience of Job at times, but no one said managing at the top is easy.

A Leading Edge

Another way to dilute possible labor conflicts is to provide employment benefits that are superior to those of other companies. If an employee is sure he or she has a better compensation package than is possible elsewhere, that employee will have no basis for pressing demands for additional compensation. Thus, he or she will be less inclined to rock the boat when he or she obviously has the best deal attainable.

For sustained growth and success, it is imperative for a company to have a competitive compensation scheme. For many foreign businesses of relatively smaller size, it can be difficult to find out what the competitive salaries are for their national employees. Therefore, some are below par in compensation, and sometimes they lose key workers to other companies with higher pay systems.

Some foreign managers rely on survey reports published outside the country that may be out of touch and unrepresentative of a truly objective picture due to distorted sampling. Sometimes these surveys do not take into consideration the various informal benefits in the compensation package.

Things have improved in recent years. Some of the international human resources consulting firms have established Korean offices and can provide assistance, including compensation advice. Also, the larger foreign chambers of commerce have committees focused on personnel issues, and these groups can offer invaluable help.

If budgetary restraints do not allow companies to provide a basic pay system on the upper end, unique supplementary benefit schemes can be devised. Such benefits, such as stock offers, can be novel and attractive to most white-collar workers.

The Personnel/Labor Relations Manager

Sometimes labor disputes are caused or exacerbated by a manager's clumsy handling of labor issues. Resolving sensitive labor tensions requires a great deal of skill and diplomacy in personal relationships. Companies do not always have a suitable moderator among the office staff who can adequately deal with labor problems.

A company needs to have an appropriate officer who has special personal sensitivity and recognized ability in mediating labor conflicts. A senior officer respected by the employees may be an ideal candidate for a combination personnel/labor relations manager. In some cases, a retired senior manager may be considered for this position. Such a person would probably have extensive experience in negotiating some sticky labor problems. Particularly in this traditional culture, an older person has a decided advantage in being respected for the wise counsel that he or she has to offer.

At least one expatriate manager of a foreign company that has taken over management control of a Korean company has also learned the hard way of the limitations of hiring a human resources manager with experience only in other multinational corporations. Particularly when dealing with the dynamics of a long-standing labor union, the newly hired, English-speaking HR manager, who had dealt only with the relatively mild unions of smaller multinational business units, was at a loss at "crunch time." So hiring the right HR manager with the right kind of union experience can be critical.

In dealing with labor unions, such a manager has to be fully aware of the union's methods and tactics and should be able to anticipate union demands. He or she must always be one step ahead of union officials and hold the employees' needs in high regard. This type of manager can be successful in labor negotiations.

Interpersonal Company Activities

A positive preventive tactic to ward off possible labor disruptions is to build a community or family-like atmosphere through company-sponsored activities, such as picnics and sports events. There are specific instances where these have proven quite successful in building morale and productivity. A satisfied employee pursuing a personal interest as a company activity will probably not have the time or motivation to instigate labor problems.

There are numerous possibilities for such activities, from editing a house organ to flower-arranging, from *baduk* (*go* chess) clubs to mountain-climbing groups. Such diversions are far more productive and economical than lost time from strikes and sabotage. One astute local labor relations manager was successful in channeling a union activity into the beautification of factory premises: "Keep 'em busy with something worthwhile!" Again, the astute foreign manager joins in whenever appropriate to build personal bonds with union and other employees.

Fair Treatment

A way for employers to inspire confidence and respect is to always be fair and reasonable in dealing with employees in every situation. It is sometimes necessary to go beyond the stipulations of labor law, adapting to various local conventions and unwritten practices in rewarding an employee. All employees will share in the good will for a retiring employee if the company shows great deference and honors someone who has served loyally for a long period of time.

In any case, all employees should be treated equally at all times, regardless of the manager's natural preferences. Absolute consistency and fairness must always be maintained, especially in cases where family members of top executives are involved in the business organization.

Without compromising standards, the manager's handling of a staff member's mistakes requires a great deal of diplomacy and understanding to prevent the errant one from losing face. To avoid office tension and belligerence, the manager's fair and just treatment is crucial. Proper treatment creates manager loyalty and raises the degree of desired care and work quality.

Document Work Policy

Employment regulations, office procedures, and work rules, if put in written form, will prevent many potential problems. Such details as work hours, benefits, compensations, vacation period, job description and expectations should be in document form and signed by the new employee to alleviate later misunderstandings and possible disputes.

These documented, signed regulations serve as guidelines for employees and stipulate their code of conduct and compensation policy. This way, it is clear what is expected of them and how, in turn, they will be compensated for their services.

Once an employee files a complaint against company executives, the mediating labor authorities tend to support the employee rather than the company. So a signed document can save an employer many unnecessary problems.

An Ounce of Prevention

Even when labor matters are well in hand or seemingly nonexistent, particularly in an organized shop, it is essential that both expatriate and senior local management build personal relations not only with the union leadership but also with local police and government officials. And this needs to be done well before there may ever be a problem.

Police and labor authorities normally hesitate to get involved in union matters even when there are clear legal violations and management is calling for outside intervention. The prevailing bureaucratic attitude dictates not intervening in private disputes until things get out of hand.

On the other hand, if management has built and maintained personal relations with local police and labor authorities, there is a much better chance that local authorities will quickly respond to a request from their friends at the outset of a potentially major work disruption, so long as there is good legal cause to do so. Otherwise, management may face union leaders unabashedly thumbing their noses at labor law for some time, demonstrating their power to the rank and file, before the government moves to enforce its own laws—after which, of course, it will take much more time, effort and expense to resolve the matter.

UNLIMITED POTENTIAL

The Korean labor force has a tremendous usable energy potential that, if properly motivated, can unleash an incredible capacity for productivity and excellence. All, however, hinges precariously on personnel attitude and morale. If the worker has satisfying work conditions and compensation, the manager will have little concern about quality and productivity.

Therefore, the sensitive manager needs to pay much attention to labor issues. Even if additional expense is involved to provide adequate compensation and pleasant working conditions, the resultant level of production volume and quality will more than compensate for the costs.

It is also important to remember that Korea's largest corporate group, Samsung, is union-free—as are some of the largest foreign companies, such as Merck. One need not resign oneself to having to deal with a labor union. If one is ahead of the curve in treating one's Korean employees well and competitively—and, probably most importantly, taking an ongoing sincere interest in their welfare by building close relations with the local staff whenever possible—it is possible to be union-free.

If one does have a union, however, it is important to help it to be reasonably strong and responsible. A weak union is more likely to look for issues—no matter how fantastic—as a means to justify and strengthen its existence among the employees. Also, a common tradition in some industries, such as banking, is to encourage responsible union leadership by routinely promoting union leaders into management upon completion of their union duties. With the lure of a likely promotion in the near future, union leaders are more likely to consider the longer-term results of their activities and negotiations.

What one should not do is emulate the example some years ago of a certain expatriate representative director. The executive had come up through the ranks on the technology side of the business with relatively limited personnel management experience. As such, rather than building personal relations whenever possible, he stayed in his office and "ran things by the book," frequently relying on outside legal counsel in making decisions. The net result was that the employees considered him remote and hostile to the union. That in turn led to three years of major labor friction, causing serious damage to the company's Korean operations and running up major legal expenses.

Top 20 suggestions on union relations offered by experienced expatriate senior executives interviewed for this book:

1. At all times, show the union respect—even when things get rough. It is critical to protect the union negotiators' "face" whenever possible so that negotiations remain focused on legitimate matters.

2. Don't try to demonize or humiliate the union; don't duck issues or play games.

3. Don't try to weaken the union. A weak union looks for problems, whereas a strong union focuses on truly important matters. In an unstable environment, most problems with a union are a reflection of internal or intra-union issues; few are matters that are at-hand business issues.

4. Sharing of information is critical for trust building.

5. Communicate frequently and openly about the real situation of the company to both the union leadership and employees so that in time, informed employees can differentiate between company business concerns and union political concerns.

6. Athletic and social events are very important as a way to signal to the rest of the employees that the union and the management are getting along with mutual respect.

7. Put in all the time that is necessary with the union—even if it may seem excessive compared to one's past assignments.

8. Sometimes the real union influencers are not on the negotiations team, so it can be critical to identify these people.

9. Often the real deals are made outside of the formal CBA negotiations; it's important to build personal relations with union negotiators.

10. One should spend at least three times as much time communicating with one's management team about dealing with the union as one spends directly communicating with the union. One bad manager can destroy a great deal of union bridge-building.

11. Senior local managers often harbor grudges and prejudices against the union. One may find that 90 percent of the Korean management's thinking needs to change. It is equally important to work for change with Korean managers as with one's union.

12. Recognize that in most instances that management has much more power and resources than the union. If one is a certain distance apart between labor and management, management should travel 90 percent and labor 10 percent—and then, together, the two can move on and steer back to the center.

13. Negotiations in Asia are not by nature win-win activities, but win-lose. Western negotiators tend to not recognize this point.

14. Negotiations are not limited to the time of CBA renegotiations. A skillful general manager is always negotiating. Sometimes he or she will try for a major union concession shortly after a CBA has been signed and when the union leadership may be emotionally worn out.

15. Unions are like adolescents in that they are constantly probing to see what their limits may be. It is important to clearly and concretely communicate one's limits and governing principles.

16. One of the common problems with foreign companies is to allow unions to have a voice in promotions. Promotion is a key management control vehicle. Koreans highly value promotions for social as well as economic reasons. Management should have full control in this area as a way to keep employees in line.

17. Since only one demonstration can legally take place at a time at a single venue, management may wish to schedule a "demonstration" with the police at sensitive locations during upcoming CBA negotiations, prior to the union attempting to schedule its demonstrations.

18. A common mistake is that foreign companies do not give adequate authority to their negotiating representative. Often the chance to successfully conclude a CBA takes place at weird times such as 2:00 a.m. If the company negotiator needs to first check back with the head office, too often the delay will allow the opportunity to slip away.

19. Another common error is that foreign firms do not allow themselves enough time or are too impatient to come to a CBA agreement. In their rush, they weaken their position, and that can be very expensive. Union leaders often try to learn the negotiators' return flight reservations so they can plan their strategies accordingly.

20. Try to outsource as much of human resources as possible to reduce the power and influence of the union.

19 . COMPANY TRAINING

*E*veryone agrees training is important, but too often training loses its priority as executives face more pressing matters. Still, training can make the critical difference in the success of one's Korean operations. Koreans expect training. One's company needs training to integrate the Korean staff into one's international operations, as well as to provide necessary skills.

Korean workers' loyalty and dedication are often cited as contributing to the nation's rapid-growth economy. That loyalty very much stems from the "naturalization" of company personnel through rigorous training programs.

Korean training programs for new employees vary in duration, but may continue for two or three months—some as long as five months. Orientation training can be extremely rigorous, including techniques that border on "brain-washing" and "survival training." This is mainly geared to prepare and mold the novices into a particular organizational pattern and company culture—in other words, to make them into "organization men and women." One's operations may not be prepared to make this kind of commitment, but one needs to be aware what the local competition is doing.

CORPORATE JOB TRAINING

Korean companies tend to place much more emphasis on employee attitude training than professional skills. Employers consider company and work attitudes to be of the utmost importance. Traditional managers believe that a dedicated employee can always learn job skills, so loyalty, teamwork, and commitment to the corporate or founder's philosophy are top priorities in training.

Job-seeking Koreans highly value training opportunities. For the company, this intensive orientation is intended to instill in recruits a strong, positive attitude—and to weed out those who cannot conform and assimilate to corporate culture.

TRAINING ASPECTS

Training requirements vary from company to company, but a few general ideas may help the expatriate manager plan an adequate training program.

Team Spirit

In addition to professional skills, local employees should be trained in corporate culture and teamwork. For local employees with a penchant for individualism in a foreign organization with shallow Korean roots, team cohesiveness and group sensitivity training can result in a stronger organization and higher productivity. A sense of belonging and a shared common destiny will promote team spirit and company loyalty.

If one has a limited training budget, another way to achieve this kind of team spirit for a larger number of employees is to organize a day trip or weekend trip out of town on an annual or semi-annual basis. These trips should not be a substitute for formal training, but they can act as complements covering employees across multiple departments.

Professional Trainers

There are several effective local training organizations. Some organizations specialize in sales and marketing training. Others offer general management and cross-cultural training. As we will discuss later, however, the quality remains very uneven. For cost-effective results, training by an outside organization may best be done on a continuing basis rather than as a one-time, big event.

As elsewhere, professional trainers run in quality from expert to dilettante. Korean society's rapid development has made it easy for charlatans to thrive. In certain training disciplines, the lack of understanding of the curricula by all parties sometimes results in low standards being the norm. Therefore, when checking the references of a trainer, one should also take special care to qualify the competency of the references. While all of this may seem potentially exasperating, consider the consequences of committing time and resources to an incompetent trainer.

Product vs. Sales Training

Sales-experienced foreign executives are soon aware that most experienced Korean sales professionals have received little or no formal sales training other than sales manners and similar light subjects. To confuse matters, Korean sales managers often confuse product training with sales training and use the terms interchangeably.

While it is possible to hire Korean sales professionals with the "right personal contacts," foreign firms often introduce products new to their targeted sectors or unknown to the entire market. Consequently, legacy personal networks necessary for schmoozing existing and prospective customers often are less effective when employed by a foreign firm than with established Korean companies in pre-existing markets. Proper professional sales skills training tend to be more critical for many foreign firms than established Korean competitors.

Strategic selling, including cold calling, may be needed to get even seasoned salespeople to expand outside of their comfort zones—especially if one believes one's products may apply to additional, untapped market sectors. However, don't be surprised if older salespeople offer resistance. They normally take pride in their past achievements and are skeptical about the need to change. Yet at the end of the day, sales is a numbers game. If the numbers are not sufficient, sophisticated sales training may be required.

Keep in mind that sales training is still an underdeveloped discipline in Korea. Many "sales trainers" build their careers by providing sessions that are often light in content and heavy on entertainment as a means to get positive training evaluations. If one does not have a sales background, one may consider asking regional or head office training staff or a competent sales manager to help evaluate a good sales training program.

Parent Company Training

For a foreign business's local personnel, training at the parent company is always regarded as an incentive. Besides foreign travel, which is still uncommon for ordinary employees, these occasions serve to strengthen company ties and loyalty. It may be costly, but the results can more than offset the expense. Equally important, by acquainting Korean employees with employees in other business units, the Koreans will strengthen their identity with the overall company rather than simply considering themselves in the Korean branch, separate from the rest of the world. Since we all work in a shrinking world, it could be critical for one's overall business that the Korean employees develop early on a strong rapport with other overseas staff members.

Language Training

As foreign language skills become even more important, many companies provide in-house instruction—sometimes with native instructors, other times sending personnel to English language institutes. Company personnel will value these opportunities to expand their language skills, which will improve their chances for future advancement. For a foreign organization, provision of such opportunities can serve as a local staff incentive while also improving communication between Korean employees and expatriate and offshore staff. The HR department can use a good, well-recognized English training program as a recruitment tool to attract ambitious Korean employees to one's company.

Speaker Programs

To help nurture the minds of local employees, regular lecture programs may be organized with prominent professors as speakers. Since some retired university professors are quite popular, bookings for this purpose may have to be made months in advance. "Positive thinking," "reorientation toward life goals" and "career objectives" are sample topics.

Other Options

More than ever, there are a number of outside programs that range in cost from free to relatively modest. In recent years, Toastmasters Clubs have been established in Korea. While these public-speaking clubs have so far been English-speaking, most members are Koreans who use them to develop their English language skills and multilingual public speaking skills. Well-regarded but localized, international training programs such as Dale Carnegie and Franklin Covey have also set up shop in Seoul. While these professional programs are not cheap, they may be a good option to consider if one needs to train only a few employees.

START TRAINING!

Both orientation and on-the-job training are becoming a primary necessity in most Korean companies. Management has discovered that productivity is increased through company training programs. Personnel look at the extent of training in a business organization not only to determine the desirability of employment with that company, but as an incentive to their future development as well. One of the most effective means of reducing staff turnover can be a good training program, as Korean employees look for more than the immediate paycheck.

Training is not an option, but it is often treated as if it were. A common temptation is to squeeze extra training into a program, such as three days' training into just two days. Almost inevitably, this ends up being false economy, with a day saved and a training event severely compromised. Such tactics can convey to employees that management may not be sufficiently dedicated to the company's development.

In any case, there are now more opportunities than ever to appropriately develop one's staff in Korea. In other words, there is no longer a valid reason to not do what is necessary for success in Korea

© YONHAP PHOTO

PART IV.
MAKING IT IN THE KOREAN MARKET

20. DISCOVERING THE CONSUMER

K nowing the market ultimately comes down to knowing the consumer. Obviously, the nature of one's products and services will define the target consumers, but as one may imagine, the Korean consumer also embodies unique characteristics. Understanding and adjusting to these peculiarities can be essential to one's overall success in the Korean market.

This is even more important for international ventures. In Korea, consumers are often asked to purchase products that may be unfamiliar to them or that are totally alien to their culture. So prior to promotion, some basic questions similar need to be asked:

- Who makes the decision to buy?

- Why are some new products accepted and others rejected?

- What is the best way to approach a target market?

To answer these questions, consider some major factors of the Korean market.

OVERVIEW

A Young, Volatile but Maturing Population

Taken together, Seoul, Busan, and Daegu represent 67 percent of the nation's urban population. The greater Seoul metropolitan area, including surrounding Gyeonggi Province and its port of Incheon, accounts for some 23 million people. In other words, almost half of Korea's total population lives within an hour's commute of Seoul. Numbers such as these in Korea's largest cities indicate a process of rapid urbanization.

The nation is young; almost 19 percent of the population is 14 years old and younger. The median age—33 years today—is expected to climb to 43 by 2030, but currently over 60 percent of the population is under 27 years old and displays all the characteristics of young consumers. In terms of buying power, the Korean consumer has never been better off.

Disposable income continues to rise. With a per capita income topping approximately US$20,000 in 2008, South Korea has a large middle and upper class. Individuals with annual household income or consumption rates ranking in the top 10 percent of those wealth categories make up 25 percent of the population, while just 2.9 percent of all Koreans have an income ranking in the poorest 10 percent.

At the same time, not all news is positive. While Korea ranks 13th worldwide in gross domestic product (GDP) at US$890 billion, its per capita gross national income (GNI) ranks only 41st. Even prior to the 2008-09 global recession, only a bit more than 63 percent of the population was economically active. Much of this can be accounted for, since some 80 percent of high school graduates go on to college, and males are also obligated to perform compulsory military service. There is also a major misalignment of many highly educated people for relatively few suitable employment opportunities.

Not unrelated is the fact that South Korea leads the OECD nations in suicides, with 24.3 of every 100,000 people committing suicide a year (about 35 suicides per day). In 2008, suicide was the biggest cause of death for Koreans in their 20s and 30s. That year, those who took their own lives accounted for 40.7 percent of those who died in their 20s, and 28.7 percent of those in their 30s. Among other causes, experts attribute the rapid rise in suicide in Korea—with susceptible groups including young professionals and senior citizens—to the rising unemployment rate among the young and the weak social safety net for the elderly.

The "new rich," Korea's middle class, have also displayed a fascination with foreign brands and concepts. Since there is very much concern about keeping up with the Kims, Koreans are quick to replace items with the newest and most advanced. In other words, Korea is a nation of early adopters. Korea is also a nation of major consumer debt, as witnessed by its world-class credit card bills. Faced with a marketplace of ever-increasing variety, the Korean consumer has the means with which to make his or her choices.

The Graying of Korea

As of 2000, more than 7 percent of the Korean population was 65 years old or more. By 2019, that figure is projected to rise to more than 14 percent. Japan is already there, with the 65-and-overs accounting for more than 17 percent of the population. Looking at what is working in Japan today may give insight into what may be successful marketing in Korea of the future.

In 2002, according to the July 24, 2003, issue of the Far East Economic

Review, more than 56 percent of senior citizen respondents to a government survey reported they were living apart from their children. The magazine went on to say that considering that fewer than 12 percent lived on their own as of 1998, this is a major shift that is fueling new demand for goods and services for the more independent elderly. Indeed, the so-called "silver industry" catering to these older South Koreans was estimated to be worth about 27 trillion won in 2005, compared with 17 trillion won in 2000.

Korea's cybermalls are frequently associated with Korea's youth, but they are not exclusively for the young. There are also cyber-shopping malls that sell medical and other products online for elderly Koreans. Bestselling items include clothes and adult diapers specially designed for use by the elderly, telephones with big buttons, and games designed to help Alzheimer's patients.

Still, there may not be as much silver in this market as in other Asian or Western economies. Compared to their overseas peers, Korea's wealthy seniors are tighter with their spending, a reflection of their earlier lives of deprivation caused by the Korean War and the long struggle to rise out of poverty. Another factor in this frugality is that South Korea lacks the social welfare system of more advanced countries.

Nevertheless, the demographic shifts and the change in lifestyles to living apart from one's children have created major business opportunities that are expected to continue to grow for the next three decades.

Who Do You Trust?

More than ever, proper branding in the Korean marketplace is essential. According to the 2006 Edelman Trust Barometer survey, 84 percent of South Korea's more well-off consumers considered trust in well-recognized brands as part of their purchasing decision-making. The manufacturer's financial stability was also a major concern.

Korean consumers are among the most trusting (or gullible) when it comes to how much of print and Internet news media content they believe. The Edelman survey reported that a full 49 percent of all Korean consumers trusted what they read in the news, especially business-related content. In fact, consumers tended to trust the media slightly more than businesses themselves (46 percent), and much more than NGOs (39 percent) or the government (29 percent).

This Internet-centric market, in which 70 percent of the population today has high-speed connections, puts more trust in information on the unregulated

Internet (26 percent) than in what they view on television (22 percent). Many have noticed the power of the Internet in whipping up public opinion. Korea boasts the world's highest ratio (66 percent) of consumers reporting they have shared negative opinions about a company over the Internet—almost double the rate for American consumers. And a recent survey suggests as many as 40 percent of Koreans believe what they read on others' blogs.

"South Korea is the leader of the rise of citizen journalism in Asia by a wide, wide margin. The younger generation has really embraced blogging," said Robert Pickard, then President of Edelman, Asia-Pacific. "The media is seen not as the 'voice of authority,' but as the voice of the people challenging that authority."

Make Mine Digital—At Internet Speed

Koreans are among the world's most computer- and telecommunications-literate consumers. In 2004, there were more than 26.5 million landline telephones, but there were also more than 36.5 million mobile cellular phones. In the same year, there were almost 40 million Internet users, representing 62 percent of Korean households (72 percent by 2006) being served by more than 5.4 million Internet server sites.

Ninety percent of the country has broadband at about 3 megabits per second at home and similarly high-speed wireless connections on the road. The telecom companies are fiercely competitive, and broadband service costs the consumer less than US$20 a month.

Korea has about 20,000 PC *bang*s, or Internet cafés, that collectively provide more than one million desktops, where the consumer can rent a super-fast PC for US$1 an hour. Ninety-five percent of students and Koreans in their twenties, collectively, use the Internet; the figure jumps to 98 percent among students alone. Research has found that about 76 percent of the male population (17 million) and more than 64 percent of the female population (14.5 million) use the Internet. A recent survey found that 70 percent of Korean Internet users depend on the Internet for information searches and more than 15 percent use the Internet for shopping information.

During the last few years, smart phones or 3G phones have become remarkably popular. After a series of prolonged regulatory and telecommunications carrier negotiation delays, Apple's iPhone entered the Korean market on November 28, 2009. Contrary to many Korean media forecasts, initial sales were startlingly impressive, averaging 4,000 per day. By early March, there were some 400,000 phones in operation in Korea. Of that number, 70 percent of users were men, about half of users were in their 20s, and about 30 percent lived in the wealthy southern districts of Seoul.

Competing Korean 3G phones have also sold well, but the introduction of the iPhone as well as the prior year's entry into the Korean market of the Blackberry have put local manufacturers and service providers on the defensive, though Korean phones and services still overwhelmingly dominate the entire market. For example, mobile data downloads surged by 122 times in December 2009 and January 2010 following the iPhone market entry, compared to the entire period of January to November 2009. In other words, software content is driving this demand—a product category in which Korean technology providers have almost consistently proven to be less competitive.

Meet You at the Cybermall!

Korean consumers are arguably Asia's most enthusiastic. But the South Koreans are not satisfied with simply blogging, and have gone a step farther than the rest of the world. From a base of an estimated 33 million Internet users—more than half of whom have their own web sites—the Koreans have come up with the new concept of Social Networking Service (SNS).

Korea's biggest telecom company, SK Telecom, which pioneered the first form of this kind of service in 1999, owns the premier SNS provider, Cyworld. Two years later, Cyworld began offering next generation mini-home page services like "Mini Home-Ps"—apparently a Korean transliteration of "Mini Home Page." As of 2007, Cyworld was Korea's leading SNS, allowing some 18 million Koreans to express themselves online as individuals—and as often as not, in creative, non-serious ways. The penetration is remarkable. About 90 percent of all South Koreans in their twenties have signed up for Cyworld.

The attraction of SNS is that consumers can create avatars (virtual but visible representations of themselves) and visit each other to share ideas and opinions. Hosts decorate their virtual spaces by purchasing decorations such as furniture with cybercash, called "Dotori" (acorns). And these are serious acorns. As of early 2006, Cyworld[1] denizens were spending US$300,000 in Dotori daily, which would come out to almost US$110 million annually. This

---

1. An interesting aside is that Cyworld attempted to create a Cyworld USA, but had to close down American operations in November 2009, having drawn only 112,000 monthly visitors. Cyworld was apparently unable to cross the cultural divide; its awkward Korean-style English email that delivered the closure notice to its American user base served as additional evidence as to why that venture may have failed.

means that on average, each Cyworld denizen spends about US$7 per year on Dotori—whereas at about the same time, the average American user at MySpace was spending less than a third as much at US$2.17 per user.

Marketers are discovering that Cyworld and other virtual markets are increasingly becoming as important for a number of products and services as the physical markets. One estimate has as much as 90 percent of all Korean teenagers and twentysomethings registered with Cyworld alone—and they are uploading over 6 million photos to that site every day. What once was a mall experience for American youth is now replicated in cyberspace for Korea's younger set.

As of early 2010, other forms of social networking were catching on in Korea. Cyworld still commands the lead with as much as 67.1 percent of young people using the service. But recently, Twitter, Facebook and me2DAY, a Korean microblogging service, have all claimed over 100,000 users in Korea, with me2DAY announcing it had registered its millionth user in March 2010. However, in terms of active, ongoing use, Cyworld led in a February 2010 poll with 67.1 percent of young Korean users, followed by Twitter at 30.8 percent, Facebook at 20.9 percent, me2DAY at 17.9 percent, and MySpace at 5.1 percent. Users were also reported to use multiple social networking services.

But recognizing that not all consumers are purchasers, the question remains:

WHO WIELDS THE WON?

To discover who controls the purse strings, one must enter the Korean housewife's domain. Also, more recently, young single adults and kids have become significant purchasers as well as consumers.

Housewives

To those familiar with traditional society, it comes as no surprise that the housewife does most of the purchasing. In the past, division of labor cast this role upon women. Today, the custom continues in many industrial societies such as Korea—even when more and more women are working full time.

Research has shown that housewives make as much as 80 percent of supermarket purchase decisions—in addition to selecting household durables such as electric rice cookers, microwave ovens, and washing machines. For accessory items such as televisions, PCs, and audio equipment, they split the decision-making with their spouses. Since many Korean housewives are not in the job market, they have ample time for daily shopping. In addition, the media bombard them with vast amounts of commercial information. Beyond traditional advertising channels, Korean housewives spend a good deal of time checking for bargains on the Internet and watching TV home shopping networks. The result is a consumer who is alert to marketplace conditions and who determines purchasing by quality as well as by price.

Children and Young Adults

Another major influence on Korean housewives' purchasing is the degree to which they favor their children. It is common in patriarchal societies for the female to derive considerable power from child upbringing—especially of sons. Consequently, children—especially males—are pampered. Korean families will make great sacrifices for their offspring's welfare.

In many circumstances, it's the children who dictate the buying decisions for various consumer products. They are quick to adopt new and novel products, concepts and styles. One should remember that approximately 19 percent of the nation's population is under the age of 14. And for good or evil, minors often get a hold of their parents' credit card information to purchase goods and services over the Internet.

Moving from adolescence to young adulthood, Koreans adopt new consumption habits that reflect their times. Young people, for example, are increasingly putting off marriage. That means those singles in their 20s and early 30s often have substantial discretionary spending money, allowing them to be among the nation's most aggressive consumers.

Focusing on Young Adults, Housewives and Children

Since a great deal of purchasing power is in such consumers' hands, they are quite naturally among consumer marketers' prime targets. This simple fact propels, for example, the variety, quality, and circulation of women's magazines and similar Internet web sites and blogs. At the same time, the marketer needs to know as much as possible about the Korean housewife—her wants, needs, and purchasing motives. Marketing appeals directed at the housewife emphasize her comfort requirements and her self-image.

It also pays for the marketing manager to keep abreast of the latest mobile phone and Internet trends. Top marketing professionals try to anticipate which leading-edge wireless consumer technologies are likely to succeed and how consumer patterns will be impacted by them. They also need to have quick turnaround time, as fashions and tastes increasingly change at Internet speed.

A SPENDTHRIFT SOCIETY?

Getting a handle on consumer debt in Korea is much easier than understanding and agreeing upon a definition of consumer saving. While the National Statistical Office has recognized homeownership to be as high as 62.9 percent in 2004, most observers concur that the rate tends to stagnate closer to 55 percent. Whatever statistic one believes, it may be fair to assume that around 40 percent of Koreans live in rented housing. This is where defining savings becomes problematic.

One prominent form of building rent consists in part or entirely of *jonse*, which is a totally refundable payment, often at the rate of 50 percent of the money to purchase the property. This money is used or invested by the landlord and returned to the tenant at the end of the tenant's occupation of the property. So it's important to keep in mind that Korean bank home loans cover at most only 60 percent of the home value. In other words, virtually every Korean family has, in a sense, paid off at least 40 to 50 percent of their mortgage.

But looking at conventional savings in isolation, the news is not particularly good. For example, in 1988 the South Korean household savings rate was 25.2 percent. Today, savings have dropped, with a new low of 3.2 percent projected for 2010. Some observers blame the government, saying its policies have encouraged borrowing, but one must also consider other factors. For example, Koreans, with their status-conscious insecurities, are remarkably brand-conscious, be it for Louis Vuitton handbags or Ivy League degrees—a very costly mentality indeed.

Anxiety about falling behind the pack is a national obsession, bordering on a national religion. If one's family is falling behind in income, greater sacrifices must be made to give one's offspring as competitive an education as those of wealthier citizens. And if one cannot afford to educate and cultivate two or more children, then it makes sense to limit one's family to just a single child. To not keep up with the Kims by sending one's child to the right cram schools, driving the right car, wearing the right clothing and living in the right apartment is tantamount to losing face for many Korean families.

This all translates into a great deal of stress and heavy use of credit cards. So it is fairly commonplace for families get trapped in debt, while continuing to live beyond their means. For that reason, speculation is not only attractive but seductive—and from an economics perspective, that is why apartment prices in the more desirable parts of Seoul continue to escalate, regardless of the nation's overall economic circumstances.

It is common for parents to give or loan newlyweds the needed cash for down payments for their first homes. But in so doing, money that otherwise would have been kept in the banks for later retirement requirements is being flushed into a speculative real estate market. What concerns some economic planners is that the elderly may end up with inadequate funds and without the traditional filial piety from their children that was once demanded of them by their parents.

Due to these and other factors, average savings per household have dropped from about US$3,300 to US$525 during the past ten years, according to the Bank of Korea. During the same period, household debt as a percentage of individual disposable income has risen to 140 percent. The consequences of South Korea's collapsed savings rate are beginning to register in the country's slowing rate of growth, economists have said. For nearly 40 years, growth galloped along at between 6 and 8 percent, as banks were flush with household savings that fueled business investment and research. But growth slowed to about 4.5 percent after 2000, when the savings rate dipped below 10 percent.

While this may be good news for consumer products and service companies, Korea's economists worry. Some fret that the low savings rate will diminish Korea's growth capacity, leading to credit delinquencies. In addition, this spending/savings trend could cause greater income disparity with dire social consequences, including fewer resources for an aging population. Traditional means of savings have become less popular as the government-provided social safety net slowly grows. At the same time, most people think it foolish to place their savings in bank instruments, considering the windfall gains possible from real estate and stock market speculation.

INFLUENCING CONSUMER BEHAVIOR WITH CAUTION

By what mechanism does a consumer group come to accept corn flakes over rice for breakfast? No one knows for sure. One fact, however, is certain: Korean society is undergoing a rapid transformation, accepting many foreign concepts relative to life's basics, including food, clothing and shelter. Given these conditions, it is far better to ride the tide of the changing currents than to invite disaster by attempting to divert trends too quickly toward one's objectives.

Consider the introduction of sanitary napkins into Korea. They were virtually unknown here until female U.S. Peace Corps volunteers introduced them in the 1960s. The timing was right, where household incomes were rising and could cover expenditure on this product, and the products were a huge success.

In contrast, foreign companies have tried to change Koreans' breakfast menus for years. But enormous advertising and production investments have generated disappointing results, with only a minor percentage of Korean households adopting simpler Western-style breakfasts. It is difficult to say why most have resisted the change. Perhaps it has been a case of too much, too soon. On the other hand, how many typical Americans substitute Japanese instant *miso* soup for corn flakes each morning, or place a helping of kimchi alongside a cup of coffee to start off the day?

ADAPTING YOUR PRODUCTS TO YOUR CONSUMERS' TASTES

History is rife with cases of marketing managers forgetting that their mission's success depends heavily upon their products' ability to satisfy local customers' needs. Often they find themselves caught between the competing demands of the local market and the distant head office. Expecting the local market to conform to the dictates of predetermined policy is, in many cases, a sure path to frustration.

That frustration can often be avoided simply by adapting to local tastes. A slightly sweeter soft drink or a spicier tomato ketchup has often saved the day. Such modifications to suit Korean consumers' tastes and needs in design, color, size, and flavor has contributed to marketing success.

DOING CONSUMER RESEARCH

Marketing in rapidly changing Korea demands solid market research. Consumer research is no longer a developing area in Korea. The number of its practitioners is growing steadily. One economical way to gather information is to use the omnibus studies from a market research company. For a minimal investment, one can get a considerable amount of information on market as well as consumer behavior. In any case, today the top international market research firms are active in Korea, along with small, local agencies.

THE TAIL NOW WAGS THE DOG

Today, major retailers demand—and get—additional discounted pricing and promotions from manufacturers. No longer do suppliers call the shots. About 25 years ago, major discount and convenience store chains appeared in Korea. Things did not really change, however, until after the IMF crisis, when both groups' sales began to skyrocket. Today, they dominate the supply chain. The tail is now wagging the dog. More recently, home television shopping channels and Internet cybermalls have also created important large retail groups capable of winning special concessions from suppliers.

Korea has marketplaces that are hundreds if not thousands of years old. Yet in the past ten years, Korea has also proven to be a world-class leader in consumer marketing on the cyber frontier. Competing in the Korean market is not for the fainthearted. But for those marketers willing to address old, traditional buying habits while also using new, leading-edge retail channels, Korea can be one of the most exciting environments in which to compete.

21. MARKETING IN KOREA

"**D**ynamic Korea" was one of the government's slogans for promoting international tourism within the nation. But this may also apply to doing business in the Korean environment—and no facet of Korean business is more dynamic than marketing. To compound matters for the expatriate manager, there are significant cultural factors that may either be in play with the market or represent a distraction when trying to get a marketing strategy right. And for many foreigners, even with "helpful" advice from their Korean colleagues, it can be frustratingly difficult to differentiate between the cultural differences germane to developing a strategy and what may be interesting but essentially just a red herring.

In the following pages, we will recognize that while flexibility and pragmatism are key to any marketing development program anywhere, the basic skills are of an even higher premium in Korea. As one would expect, one requires a systematic approach that overrides "winging it" in a country where on some days everything seems up for grabs. At the same time, cultural awareness, including monitoring how quickly the popular culture is changing in relevant areas, is essential. Advertising may be critical, depending on one's product or service, but one should be prepared to encounter some major differences in how advertising is strategized in Korea compared to Western countries. This chapter will cover the basics of selling and what to expect from market research. But first, consider some of the political risks of entering the Korean market.

HOW RISKY IS IT TO INVEST IN SOUTH KOREA?

When considering the political risks of South Korea, it is undeniable that North Korea plays a role beyond the expected domestic considerations. Within the brevity of this chapter, I will attempt to cover the two major of many possible risks, namely possible reunification with the North, as well as the impact of Korean nationalism on foreign business.

North Korea and the Possible Reunification of the Two Koreas

When considering the two Koreas, one must also consider the sometimes contradictory interests of surrounding powers. While Pyongyang must be mindful of China's likely long-term hegemonic interests in its territory, the North Koreans appear primarily concerned with maintaining face with their southern counterparts. Yet the North Koreans need to worry that their northern border is weakened from both directions—by their refugees' northward exodus, and potentially by another onrush of Chinese "volunteers," as happened during the Korean War and prior wars over the centuries.

North Korea's fundamental irony is its dogmatic commitment to unifying Korea under its undisputed control. But in so doing, the ruling oligarchy has forced that impoverished nation onto a constant, delusional war footing, which has further weakened its economy. During the past decade, North Korea has had to increase its dependency on Chinese good will and direct investment, as well as on unilateral aid from the South and the West. In short, Pyongyang has devised a survival strategy that can do naught but buy time, its likelihood to indefinitely maintain its de facto sovereignty diminishing each year in the face of creeping Chinese power.

The North's ruling oligarchy appears blatantly prepared to let millions starve during the short term, and quite capable in the end of turning the real controls of state over to Beijing via Chinese-manipulated proxies in exchange for the long-term welfare of elite families. Consequently, the eventual reunification of the nation may have already slipped from the Koreas' hands.

From the foreign investor's perspective, there is an increasingly smaller chance of chaos from intra-Korean reunification damaging one's investment. Should North Korea suddenly implode, the Chinese have indicated—reasonably and expectedly so—in private circles that they would assist the North Koreans if called upon by Pyongyang, but only with multinational permission such as from the United Nations, or possibly by members of the six-party talks.

The question is what the Chinese might do if denied international approval. Some Korea watchers suspect the Chinese would move into North Korea, if only because they may feel they would have no other practical option, given the spreading chaos on their lightly defended border.

What is most likely not to happen would be the South Koreans moving northward, given the chances for initial misunderstanding by the North Korean Army and the certainty of taking on North Korea's recovery, which would cause both Korean economies to quickly nosedive for years and probably for decades. This is not to say one cannot find many South

Koreans who strongly disagree with the idea of essentially just standing by. The South Korean education system and ongoing propaganda have indoctrinated South Koreans with a conviction that they may eventually have to unify the country at great cost. But so far, this has been only rhetoric. Considering that many South Korean families emigrate each year in hopes of better lives for their children, it would be a tough call for most Korean families to deal their children a major economic setback that may take decades from which to recover—particularly as a sacrifice to a northern population that for decades has threatened to destroy the very economic system that has raised the southern half of the peninsula to where it is today.

The U.S., of course, has no stomach for an optional escapade into North Korea that may escalate into a major clash with China. And that brings us back to the Chinese solution—whether the parties involved like it or not.

South Korean Nationalism

For real-life examples of South Korean ultra-nationalism, one need look no further than recent newspapers. One key, unforgettable incident involves Lone Star Funds, a Texas-based private equity firm that in 2003 acquired Korea Exchange Bank (KEB), at the time underperforming. However, it faced national criticism and even legal action when it tried to sell the asset, which it had nurtured into the fifth largest bank in Korea.

In 2007, Lone Star was delivered a setback on its plans to sell its shares of KEB to HSBC when its local office chief was initially found guilty of manipulating the share price of KEB's card affiliate in 2003. Given the presented evidence in court, the Texas company's legal team had been understandably confident of an acquittal. This is not to say with all the smoke there was no fire, but more likely the flames came from outside of the accused party's control—not from Lone Star. But it didn't matter. The Korean public wanted—and finally got—a guilty verdict. Eventually the guilty verdict was overturned, but for the few years until a higher court reversed that decision, a shiver ran through potential foreign direct investors.

Ultra-nationalism can be strong. As the nation's economy continues to improve, there is a growing sense of nationalism, which may also be a latent legacy of President Park Chung-Hee's infusion of positive thinking and somewhat chauvinistic sentiments. More recently with the Kim Dae-Jung and Roh Moo-Hyun administrations, populism has become a key element with a strong element of *"minjok-juui"*—which literally means "racism," but is actually something more along the lines as the Spanish word "*la raza*," or prideful recognition of a common ethnicity.

The good news is that Korean consumers generally associate foreign-manufactured brands with quality. Even though nationalistic sentiment may indicate otherwise, nowhere is Korean preference for things foreign more evident than in consumer behavior or buying habits. Consumer preference for value seems to transcend ideology everywhere. In reaction to this trend, some consumer activists have attempted to discourage the purchase of foreign-brand products, alleging that high royalties have to be paid to foreign licensers for using their brands on local products of the same quality as foreign brands.

The general perception of foreign companies in Korea among ordinary consumers is rather favorable, again relating to their quality goods and services, as well as to the impression that foreign firms generally provide better working conditions for local employees. Examples of successful assimilation by some foreign consumer companies into the local market have definitely helped in this direction.

What this means is that if a foreign company's products already carry a strong, well-recognized brand, the foreign company may have a major advantage in establishing a coherent image vis-à-vis the local competition, so long as that image is not inadvertently inappropriate in the context of Korean culture.

Regardless of any potential foreign brand advantage, it is highly prudent for foreign business professionals to be aware of nationalist sensitivities. The Prosecutor's Office often reacts to general public sentiment in its effort to be of service to the common sense of justice. Consequently, if the uninformed media takes the wrong cue about a foreign company, the situation can spiral downwards into an investigation by the Prosecutor's Office. More than most markets, it is essential to have an effective PR component within one's Korean operations. This is particularly the case if a foreign company is visibly successful. It is critical to demonstrate that the foreign company is also contributing to the overall welfare of Korea. For example, Lone Star employed a well-regarded PR firm when it attempted to sell Korea Exchange Bank, but had there been similarly effective PR prior to its attempted sale of the bank, much of the pain, one may argue, could have been minimized if not avoided.

In short, Korea is an underrated market compared to its neighbors, with many hidden potential profits. But as is the case anywhere, one needs to get a handle on the risks.

THE CULTURAL MARKETING TRAP

The experienced expat international marketing manager may have worked somewhere resembling Korea. As a trained professional, he or she thus looks for signs by which to classify potential problems and opportunities in a new country and culture. These signals can give the marketer clues as to whether the company's products are properly positioned within the new market. Yet encountering the Korean marketplace can be confusing. For example, if the marketing manager concludes the sales force is doing its job well and sales results are still disappointing, marketing managers may have to determine whether the cause is simply a matter of product positioning or another hidden factor such as a cultural difference.

There may very well be a cultural "catch," but foreign marketing professionals have too often prematurely jumped to that conclusion. It seems that a "cultural wand" is waved about whenever there is a need to explain why sales are not up to standard. Foreign managers can be sorely tempted to pigeonhole the cause of their problems as "Korean culture" when there may in fact be a lack—or misapplication—of marketing diligence. If one wishes to ruthlessly interrogate the cultural alibi, one should simply ask what the cultural pattern is specifically and how it affects the marketing strategy. Then one needs to let both the brain and gut determine whether the explanation makes sense. More often than not, one is not going to be satisfied with the conclusion.

This is not to say there is no cultural impact—of course there is. However, the cultural issue tends to be overblown by both business professionals and academics, when in actuality there has been a lack of fundamental marketing analysis. At the same time, "doing one's homework" does not mean implementing the same market analysis one might have done in Los Angeles or London. It may be a good starting point to let go of MBA jargon, such as "product life cycle" and "market penetration," and consider what factors truly define success criteria in Korea. For example, "positioning" may presuppose that the Korean consumer will evaluate products or brands according to a single dimension, when there may in fact be multiple dimensions. And quite possibly, dimensions that are important to customers in North Carolina, such as performance or convenience, may be of little relevance to buyers in Busan.

Product life cycles may be much shorter in Korea, as the country is still, in many ways, a rapidly developing society. However, Korea is no longer a "developing country," and there are many facets of the market that are rapidly catching up with—if not expanding faster than, especially in the case of broadband Internet applications and services—those of other advanced economies. A "mature market" or "mature product" phase seems to last only a few months before it declines in the face of the next worthy competitor.

"Market share" may be similar in definition to other nations' markets, but in Korea it can be critical to differentiate between foreign products' market share and total market share, as in the case of luxury automobiles. Given that strong prejudices—and even social penalties—can influence consumers' selection of a foreign good or service, it may not be appropriate to apply a "one size fits all" market share analysis.

All the traditionally important marketing analysis matrices may also need to be recalibrated to effectively measure the Korean market. To cut to the quick, analyses and assumptions need to be tested before one bases one's marketing and promotion resources upon them. Yes, this may take more up-front time and money, but the long-term cost savings can be significant.

COMING TO GRIPS WITH THE CULTURAL COMPONENT

Though there is the danger of declaring culture as being the primary issue without doing adequate marketing spadework, culture remains a legitimate factor. While marketing does involve adjusting to market reactions, if one can get most—or at least some—of the critical factors right at the beginning, one is more likely to achieve one's targets.

In Korea, there are different approaches for different companies. One model is to start with the expectation that people react according to their environment—translated into marketing as a mixture of promotion, distribution, and prices. But just how this model responds depends on the target group's general tendency in a given market. If all factors are fairly equal in weight over the targeted demographic, then one may say that the model is not out of sync with any deviating cultural factor.

A market as ethnically and financially diverse as the U.S. can form a pretty flat, evenly distributed population when graphed, given a balancing portfolio of a very large number of consumers who constitute huge averages. For example, Harley-Davidson sells motorcycles to both the Hell's Angels and retired citizen cycling clubs in the U.S. The two market segments may have different and even conflicting consumer factor sensitivities, but the two segments can be averaged out to summarize the American motorcycle market. In that sense, one may say that on the whole, the U.S. motorcycle market could be expected to be fairly stable given the wide diversity of consumers.

When dealing with smaller, ethnically homogeneous populations, however, one can expect less diversity in tastes and acceptance of products. Furthermore, consumers tend to be more sensitive to how other consumers may respond to a product or service. As a result, we often see the "herd mentality"—be it with cheap consumer products or multi-million dollar capital expenditures. Once the lead purchasers take on a new direction, it is quite likely the rest of the herd will follow.

Another aspect of this herd mentality is "keeping up with the Kims." If consumption of a product or service is associated with the "right" kind of consumer or social stratum, there is a very strong urge by the rest of the market to follow, with consumers regularly spending beyond what other societies may consider to be prudent.

Consequently, sales trends or fads are not limited to low-cost or even consumer products. These fast-appearing and disappearing shifts are characteristic of Korea's tight-knit society.

While "word of mouth" advertising is most highly valued anywhere, it is extremely powerful in Korea's close-knit society of large, extended families and affinity groups, where extensive personal networking is a matter of basic survival. The impact of branding on this vibrant network has yielded some surprising developments for foreign marketing professionals.

For example, Korean consumers in the lower economic levels often have a better knowledge of high-end luxury brands than their American counterparts. At the same time, the sophistication of those consumers who can easily afford luxury brands is often decidedly less than that of their Western peers. The result is a Korean market that continues to be flooded with counterfeit products. Consumers apparently make little effort to differentiate between the luxurious quality found with genuine goods and the simple social status of a luxury product's brand—counterfeit or real.

The marketer must often contend with the horizontal factor of a homogeneous population that consumes in a relatively herd-like fashion and with the vertical factor of wide brand awareness across economic classes. Particularly when it comes to established (as opposed to new) products, one may try to identify some kind of consumption function. To determine whether a cultural factor is present, one first needs to determine the non-cultural factors. Foreign marketers too often ignore or disregard basic factors, such as distribution, and rush to blame poor sales on "culture." Following an analysis of all relevant conventional factors, such as pricing, product quality, and promotion, if any other non-marketing factor still remains, then one may identify it as possibly being "cultural." If one can't satisfactorily do so, there is a good chance one has missed something in one's prior, conventional marketing analysis.

The importance of this exercise is this: simply "recalibrating" one's market analysis tools may not be enough. One may still come up wanting. In such a case, one needs to ask if one has done enough to adjust one's analytical tools for the market. If the answer is "yes," then one should consider whether one has done an adequate analysis in one or more non-cultural factors. Only after answering "yes" once more should one focus on a cultural factor.

HOW TO AIM AT A MOVING TARGET

Virtually all markets are moving targets. But how many markets both count among top-end "developing countries" and lead the world in broadband Internet access and use? Either factor by itself would propel the Korean market into overdrive, but the two in tandem make Korea's marketplace one of the fastest in the world. Whatever the analogy or explanation, marketing professionals are facing rapidly moving targets that often make market analyses quickly obsolete. Still, all is not lost. There are factors one can monitor to gauge where the market may be moving in the near future.

Retailing has been a relatively hodgepodge aspect of an economy that traditionally comprised small, side-by-side retailers that serviced a surprisingly wide array of economic classes from the same location. Today's department stores are collections of small, independent shops placed under a common roof with shared points of sale. Some shops cater to the wealthy, others to the frugal, and many to the middle class, but most shops cater to those willing to indulge in real or perceived luxury items. Some large Korean retailers have attempted to differentiate by market segmentation, but most have given up and accepted that they need to have something for just about everyone to survive. So given the above, it may make sense to have as general a market appeal as reasonably possible.

The biggest retailers are large discount stores, convenience store chains and department stores. In addition, there are also online shopping channels, either as independent retailers or as extensions of the large discount stores and department stores. With most online retailers, one can find something for everyone, regardless of income level. So having a full-range portfolio of products may be the right strategy, but one must be on one's toes to have the newest and "best" products at all pricing levels if one is to succeed.

The Power of Rising Income

As Korean per capita income has stretched into the five-figure range, whole new classes of products and services are now within the eager reach of many Korean consumers. By Western standards, Koreans appear to be living beyond their means. Besides taking full advantage of various means of financing large purchases and ongoing spending, the Korean consumer often has access to money from family loans on a scale that is generally deemed exceptional by Western standards. The most obvious example or result of this form of family financing is the ongoing spiraling of prices in residential real estate. Those individuals who are unlucky enough to not have access to family capital and go without buying real estate doubly suffer, in that they are not able to purchase expensive products and services financed by borrowing off of the expanding equity of their properties.

Impact of Changing Lifestyles

While Koreans are still known for their extended families, as the country goes increasingly urban and financially upscale, the nuclear family is becoming stronger at the expense of the extended family. Women today are marrying later, have fewer children, and have a 50 percent chance of divorce—all three issues virtually unthinkable only a generation ago.

The post-Korean War generations have grown up in relative ease, accustomed to packaged and fast foods, labor-saving devices, credit cards and Western foods—albeit often heavily localized. While children's consumer products once filled small niches, today the child consumer represents a major opportunity for purveyors of food, clothing, entertainment, and educational goods and services. Reflecting these changes, new retail channels are matching the changes in demographics and spending patterns. Procter & Gamble, for example, has been quick to recognize the value of convenience stores to target customers in their teens and early 20s.

With couples having just over two children on average and average household income rising, money is being spent lavishly both in a loving manner and in a competitive way to meet or rise above the rising generation's social standards. The family's overriding anxiety about being "left behind" can be an overwhelming motive to invest extraordinarily in their children's formal and extracurricular education, in Korea and even overseas.

Since 2002, the Korean government has been pressing companies to work more and more within five-day work weeks instead of the traditional five-and-a-half-day week, which was effectively a six-day week. Together with rising affluence, more time and money are being spent on recreation. Big winners are products and services that promote health and offer both domestic and overseas travel. This, in turn, has created new demands for related apparel, hospitality services, and sports and recreation equipment.

Open Acceptance of Foreign Goods

Traditionally, goods made in advanced countries such as Japan, the U.S. and Germany have been valued in Korea, if often in a discreet manner. Between the 1960s and 1980s—as Korea matured through its export-oriented, industrial economic phase—overconsumption or conspicuous consumption of foreign-made goods was frequently challenged in openly hostile public scuffles as being "unpatriotic." Part of the counter-balancing attraction was the prestige of being able to afford foreign goods made expensive by their large duty-inflated pricing.

While some of that mercantilist/patriotic fever yet lingers, the times have changed. Today, foreign products are often priced only slightly higher than like Korean products, while Korean products have often improved to comparable quality. Rather than being shielded by a wall of protectionism, Korean products are now competing—and changing—along with foreign products. In other words, changes or advances in products abroad often are soon found within competing domestic products.

The biggest differentiating factor of many foreign products is still the fact that they offer prestige in the high-end categories, along with better design and manufacturing quality. Korean consumers are often willing to spend more for a foreign product. But when after-sales support factors into the equation, there may be a reluctance to buy, particularly if the foreign product is not backed with good, local "A/S" (after-sales) support services.

At the same time, some of the largest multinational consumer product companies in Korea offer both internationally and locally branded items.

As one American executive put it, "Most of our brands have Korean brand titles. The key is to become a Korean brand—become a part of the culture, constantly meet local consumer needs. Many companies come to Korea and try to force a global brand name on Korea consumers. Sometimes it is better to launch a Korean brand name or buy a Korean brand."

The Velocity of Technological Change

With one of the highest per capita technical/Ph.D holding rates in the world, matched by a rapidly rising consumer spending average, Koreans are among the world's fastest adopters of high technology. While local product quality may not always be world-class, Koreans are usually among the first to adapt new innovations to their daily lives. In an increasing number of automotive and electronics firms, Koreans are now starting to achieve top honors for product design and quality. Therefore, it is wise for foreign companies to stay on top of changing government policies pertaining to intellectual property protection and government support to R&D centers, and to keep tabs on who's who in the Korean technology leadership community.

NGOs and the Market

Many NGO leaders were once part of the democracy movement during the nation's prior dictatorships. Today, some of them have graduated to the top echelons of political power. They can now offer various forms of support to former colleagues active in, say, consumer rights and environmental protection or "green" groups. Often these groups carry a very strong nationalist or patriotic agenda. Woe to the foreign firm that trips up on labeling or is perceived as marketing via misleading advertising. The same goes for those who offer products that real—or self-appointed—experts declare to be harmful to the environment or to the consumer. While these NGOs tend to be vocal and relatively easy to track, their political and market influence should never be taken for granted.

Big Name Branding

"Brands don't exist in Korea," Miles Young, Ogilvy & Mather's Asia-Pacific co-chairman, was quoted as saying in the June 2004 marketing trade periodical Media. By Western standards that may be a fair statement, but one should recognize that in Korea, branding is handled differently. Korean companies spend a great deal on corporate branding, but while there is strong public brand recognition, there can be little brand connection to sales—or, at least, so it seems to many Western marketing professionals.

In the West, brand differentiation by product is the rule. For example, when it comes to potato chips, Procter & Gamble will market the Pringles brand rather than the P&G brand. In Korea, there is strong loyalty to the Big Name, such as LG or Samsung—regardless of the product. Koreans generally feel security and trust in a well-recognized name. Often, someone living in a Samsung apartment may feel better about buying a Samsung television—also given the trust in the Big Name.

This thinking also applies to the earlier example when it comes to celebrity endorsements. The bigger the name, the less important it is for the celebrity to have a connection with the endorsed product. In fact, just as one may see LG branding with a very wide array of products and services, a major celebrity at his or her peak in fame can be seen pitching totally unrelated products and services. In other words, there is a Korean consumer comfort factor to go with the Big Name, since the group mentality encourages conformity by being associated with widespread name recognition. This is not unique to Korea, of course, but this Big Name "halo" effect seems to be a bigger factor than in most developed, Western countries.

As noted, to the Western marketing manager in Korea there seems to be no connection between what a brand represents and why one should buy a branded product. Many Korean consumers are happy to buy counterfeit luxury goods becausee they like the brand name, but are not too concerned with how the luxury brand name is supposed to represent high-end quality.

As with most things in Korean business, however, branding philosophies could be changing, as companies such as Samsung Electronics discover the advantages of product-specific branding abroad. To date, product-specific branding overseas has been mainly managed by non-Koreans. The open question is if and how some of these lessons will be carried back to Seoul. There is a very big comfort factor inside Korea's largest firms associated with being part of a Big Name, and many Korean managers feel uncomfortable building new brand names that may emotionally take away from the common well-being of being part of their corporation's Big Name. Foreign companies lacking the Big Name of a *chaebol* continue to build on their global product brands in Korea as elsewhere. Whether this product-specific branding truly catches on in Korea, given overseas *chaebol* and domestic foreign firm successes, remains a matter of time and debate.

Test Marketing

In order to avoid a marketing catastrophe, it is advisable to test-market a new product or concept in a limited market prior to a major launching. One can learn a great deal from such an effort regarding the general consumer, distribution, and the media, as well as a particular product's regulatory climate—especially if it is new and somewhat novel to Korea. Seoul and its greater metropolitan area, which usually represents roughly half of the consumer market, may be targeted. However, a smaller city like Daegu or Busan may be more suitable for the test market, as these cities represent many characteristics of the nation's market, especially since they possess their own TV stations and distribution structures. There may be no shortcut to learning one's way around the Korean market, but this kind of trial may help to level out an otherwise costly learning curve.

COMPANY POSITIONING AND USER-CREATED CONTENT (UCC) MARKETING IN KOREA

In Marketing 101, we studied the Four Ps of Marketing: Product, Price, Promotion and Place (i.e., distribution). Later, Ries & Trout added a fifth P: Position, a concept anchoring the four aforementioned Ps to a single point of the market. And yet there is of course much more to marketing: there is also trust or credibility. Without it, the five Ps of marketing strategy crumble.

Customer trust is a requirement in any market, and this creates some of the unique aspects of doing business in Korea. A business professional must maintain a sensitivity toward the public's awareness and causes of attitudes regarding companies and their products and services. Korean consumer trust is vested more in a company's solid products and services than in the softer social issues. According to Edelman, high-quality products or services head the list of reputation drivers in Korea. But transparency and honest business dealings tie this attribute for first place as key drivers of business reputation. Open and honest communication has shown a significant increase in importance as a driver of reputation in Korea (50 percent in 2009, 66 percent in 2010). The most trusted business sectors are technology, automobiles, energy, health care, and banks. The levels of trust expressed regarding these sectors are, on average, substantially higher than the levels seen for the same sectors in the U.S.

Yet employee relationships, and the public's perception of a company's employee relations, can be a major driver of the company's reputation. So external communications might be best focused on business tangibles—and social programs should be clearly linked to core competencies. For example, an international carrier may donate its shipping services to special disaster relief efforts, highlighting employee participation and volunteerism.

Today, traditional top-down media still retain high credibility in Korea, but as one may expect, the Internet is now on a par with news sources such as newspapers and television. While hardly unique to Korea, User-Created Content (UCC) is a hot trend. Young Koreans aged up to their 20s are very comfortable interacting in web- and cell phone-based two-way, dialogue-driven promotions. Many, in fact, prefer UCC promotions over traditional one-way communication.

While UCC may be a great way to go, credibility does not automatically accrue from the process. The wise marketer in Korea looks for ways to incorporate company-positive third-party web content into local web sites. In so doing, one needs to recognize up front that there is a tradeoff between message control and credibility. Therefore, one should be prepared to cede some control over the message in favor of dialogue-rich relationships with influential stakeholders.

It's important to remember that when one forms an opinion about a product, service, or company, one is likely to hear various messages about it from different sources. Some of these sources are ignored because of lack of awareness about the source itself or negative experiences with the source in the past. Traditionally, word of mouth has been most heavily relied upon. Perhaps the next most trusted commercial sources have been outlets with perceived business expertise—analysts and business magazines. Today, increasing volumes of personalized information are obtained from sources including email, blogs and cell phones. These messages are not personalized per se, but they are much more targeted to suggest that the messages are from "a person like me."

Refer to the graph, titled "A Person Like Me" on the next page, configured based on Edelman research on factors that increase an individual's trust of sources of information on a company.

According to PR specialists at Edelman, the top three characteristics most likely to increase Koreans' trust in someone sharing information about a specific company are "shares common interests" (61 percent of those surveyed), "is of the same profession" (46 percent), and "holds similar

| "A PERSON LIKE ME" |

ALL OTHER THINGS BEING EQUAL, WHICH OF THE FOLLOWING CHARACTERISTICS ARE MOST LIKELY TO
INCREASE YOUR TRUST IN SOMEONE SHARING INFORMATION ABOUT A SPECIFIC COMPANY?

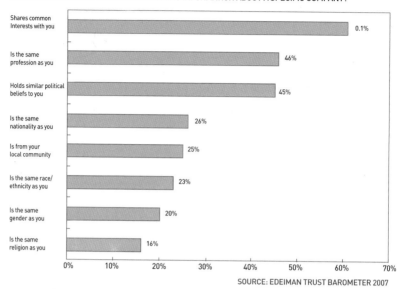

SOURCE: EDEIMAN TRUST BAROMETER 2007

| CREDIBLE SOURCES OF INFORMATION—CORPORATE |

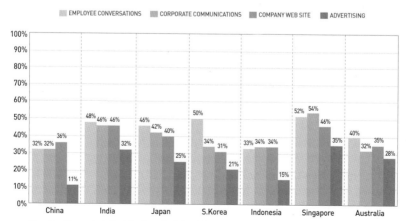

Bars placed by country in the following order, left to right:
• Employee Conversations
• Corporate Communications
• Company Web Site
• Advertising

SOURCE: EDEIMAN TRUST BAROMETER 2007

political beliefs" (45 percent). Perhaps surprisingly to many foreigners, commonality in nationality, race, religion, and community were substantially less important credibility factors in Korea. "A person like me" is rapidly becoming a highly credible commentator on one's company— aided by the rise of social media such as blogs and UCC promotions. This trend has only increased over the past two years, 2008 to 2009. According to Edelman research, the importance of social media as a source of business information has gone up.

Still, to minimize the risk inherent in having highly credible third parties talking about the company, it is critical to find ways to build trust-based relations with multiple stakeholders, given the second tradeoff—the balance between message reach and message credibility. In Korea, non-aligned commentators such as NGOs are becoming increasingly credible. Trust in government has rebounded strongly from 2009, while trust in business has made a modest improvement (up, but not significantly so). Trust in NGOs increased significantly during 2009, while trust in the media appears to be slowest in recovering from the roller coaster ride of the global economic slowdown, showing little change from 2009. The latest Edelman findings suggest that Korean consumers would be a little more likely to trust a company that partners with NGOs to battle global issues such as climate change (61 percent). This suggests that a good marketing program should build highly tailored communications channels aimed at different stakeholder groups using different third party spokespeople.

An interesting twist is for domestic communications campaigns to include international media as effective routes via which to reach key stakeholders in Korea. Sometimes international media coverage may come across as being more credible in Korea. Needless to say, outreach to international media needs to be based on a very different story angle from a Korean media campaign, but if done correctly, international media may offer a special kind of validation or credibility.

For example, when Korea Exchange Bank hired a new foreign CEO, the bank orchestrated its Korean media campaigns to focus on how well the new CEO appreciated Korean culture and how he would work to sell KEB in the most Korea-beneficial way possible. At the same time, the bank focused its international PR more on the new CEO's background and what may be his immediate business goals for the bank.

Turning to employee relations, Edelman has increasingly noted that the most important characteristic of companies in Korea that stands out in public perception is the way they treat their employees. This is partially because the past decade has seen a restructuring of employee and labor laws, as well as welfare and benefits systems. That is, there is a new emphasis on employee rights.

Therefore, it is becoming more important to develop communications campaigns from the inside out, particularly in terms of buy-in from internal stakeholders. Corporate reputation starts with employee relationships. That means building strong relationships with employees, who are among a company's most credible commentators. Since one's employees are prone to talk and send messages over the Internet, it is more critical than ever to foster internal feedback processes. Keep in mind that Koreans are the world's leaders in sharing negative, credible opinions of companies, products, and services over the Internet.

While the Korea Tourism Organization once proclaimed that "Korea, Sparkling" summed up the country, this author maintains that "Dynamic Korea" was the better nomenclature. The rise in social media—such as blogs, UCC and cell phones—is being matched by increased credibility of third parties such as NGOs. While it is certainly premature to disregard the importance of traditional media with a focus on business tangibles, one needs to recognize that communications channels are becoming increasingly fragmented, with non-traditional media channels becoming more prevalent.

The days of "one size fits all" are not completely over in broadband Korea; the most competitive and capable companies are using messaging and channel strategies effectively as they gain better insights into their increasingly narrowly defined target audiences. And if it is not enough to appreciate the benefits of learning to surf Korea's cyber waves, consider the potential cost of getting it wrong. As stated earlier, Koreans are more likely than any other nationality to complain online about companies they don't trust.

22. ADVERTISING & PUBLIC RELATIONS—
KOREAN STYLE

Getting advertising right in any market is always a challenge. To do so in Korea as a foreign firm can be particularly baffling when looking at how other Korean firms advertise. For example, one aspect of Korean advertising is to have a single celebrity momentarily endorse an unbelievably wide array of products. In the U.S., a very high-profile celebrity will charge very high rates to endorse one or a few products, so as to create a premium supply of endorsements in the face of high demand. In Korea, however, a single celebrity will be able to charge high rates to endorse many products from many different companies, since many marketing companies want that person to make an endorsement. And that is just one example among many in how Korean advertising differs from many other countries.

There is no simple reason as to why promotion is more difficult. It is perhaps the particular mix of supply-side and demand-side interactions that complicate the management of these marketing tools. For advertising, there are many institutional stumbling blocks that impede advertising management, ranging from KOBACO (the Korea Broadcasting Advertising Corporation, through which all television and radio ads must be sold) and other advertising regulations to the differential economics. Other headaches can include availability of media, advertising research data, and types of agencies and services.

To make matters worse, many of these factors are constantly changing. Again, marketing managers must aim at a rapidly moving target. Some of these changes, however, represent opportunities for foreign managers. For example, changes in the review code have paved the way for relaxing some of the restrictions on Korean ad production, such as the use of foreign models. The use of Hong Kong actor Chow Yun Fat had an immediate impact for Lotte's Milkis brand soft drink.

One of the problems that some foreign observers see in the Korean environment is what may be called the "uncreative creative tendency." "They [the *chaebol*] have huge strengths in every area—except creativity," confirmed Miles Young, then Ogilvy & Mather's Asia-Pacific co-chairman, in the June 4, 2004 edition of Media. One may be struck by the similarity of competing advertising campaigns for some product categories. Consider, for example, the past "Humantech"and "Technopia" campaigns from Samsung and LG, respectively; the "in-concert" campaigns for many soft drinks; the ads for Taster's Choice and Maxwell House Mocha Gold; and all the memorable ads for ethical drugs.

If one were to apply the standard test for creativity as being the degree to which an ad is capable of standing out, all of these candidates would not pass. Why. then. do trained advertising managers design creative campaigns in such similar fashions? There are several possible reasons:

- One may be the need to conform among sellers (similar to conformity among consumers). This may also have to do with the advertising client, who often has the final say in creative decisions. If a campaign has proven acceptability (e.g., the McColl in-concert ads), then they may think it is safe to follow in one of the following ways: 1) riding on the coattails of a popular advertising campaign by creating a primary effect for the product in general, and 2) negating the appeals of the leading company—or as the Koreans say, "watering it down."

- A lack of faith in the "creative" process. The feeling is that advertising is a "trial and error" activity. This leads again to reference to formats with proven track records. Another observation about Korean advertising is the high reliance on advertising gimmicks. A few come to mind: the trend toward using baritone American-accented reiteration of the brand or parent company (e.g., Golden Tex, GS1).

- Gimmicks. One gimmick in Korea is the way everything nowadays is "high-tech" or "state-of-the-art" (choe-cheom-dan in Korean). Especially as a foreign manager, one is faced with question of whether or not to conform. When in doubt, a "middle-of-the-road" approach may be best. The foreign manager is generally not better off going out on a limb and attempting a totally unfamiliar advertising format, especially given the potentially negative perception of a foreign company advertising in Korea. Instead, the creativity should be attempted within the generally acceptable confines of what Koreans expect to see in advertising.

- Awkward translation of advertising copy—especially in print advertising. This applies to both Korean-to-English translation and vice versa. This is often a result of agencies hiring nonprofessional semi-bilingual or student Korean-American translators. Given the importance of communicating effective campaign messages, one may wonder why agencies are so stingy in paying for translations.

- Inability of translated messages to capture the "essence" of the original prose. Literal translation is not enough—what is needed is a "creative" translation.

Finding bilingual translators who also possess copywriting abilities is, of course, very difficult for the agencies. Fortunately, the problem is being recognized, and more Korean and foreign managers are availing themselves of many proven techniques in international marketing that ensure the equivalence of translated campaigns. The foreign manager, however, should be especially on top of this issue.

As one might expect, appointing the right advertising agency in Korea is almost as difficult as choosing the right business partner—especially for a JV company or wholly owned subsidiary. Some things to watch out for:

- Does the agency have any international experience?

- Is it associated with any of the major American agencies?

- How strong is the association?

- Do they have an ongoing program of training and transferring information, etc., or is it a "name-value-only" relationship?

Review the work that they have done for other clients carefully, and be sure that the same "best" people who made the presentation are also working for one's own account. Remember, concepts and copy that one may think are clever and creative may go over like a lead balloon with one's agency people, and vice versa. Note that if agency staff feel they are being forced to do things the "foreign way" without regard for traditional customs and culture, they will quickly lose interest and motivation to do quality work.

PUBLIC RELATIONS

During the past couple of decades, Korean firms have recognized the necessity of corporate PR. As elsewhere, sometimes the image that a company intends to project is quite different from the one the public actually perceives. Modern business practices involve an intense degree of competition, advertising hype, and sometimes cutthroat tactics, and the general public can become skeptical, cynical and supercritical. All this contributes to the tarnishing and marring of a corporate public image.

Therefore, businesses have to pay more attention to appearances, applying the right kind of makeup to show their best possible face. Even businesses that operate with high ethical principles and fair practices may be subject to misunderstandings and misconceptions regarding their intentions and strategy. Corporate image is of the utmost importance in influencing consumer response anywhere. But in Korea, it figures as an especially major factor in consumer decisions. So the benefits of having a reputable and reliable image are simply not optional.

In addition to consumers' decisions to patronize companies with a good image, the brightest young people gravitate to them for employment opportunities. When such businesses seek approvals and permits, government officials are likely to be favorably disposed. Also, companies with a strong public image tend to inspire a higher level of employee morale, which, in turn, usually generates a greater level of productivity. In other words, satisfied and proud workers turn out superior commodities. A good corporate image is directly related to product excellence and quality.

Yet the reality can be substantially different from what has been described so far in introducing this topic. When pronounced by Korean speakers, "PR" comes out as "*pi ahl*," and to many Koreans in the profession, the "*pi*" stands for "*pihada*" ("to avoid") and the "*ahl*" for "*allida*" ("to inform"). In other words, PR avoids discussion of the shady matters and informs only the positive attributes, perceivably. While this may come as no surprise to PR professionals, it is also problematic. For effective PR, the PR agency needs transparency with its client to effectively understand and represent that client to the public. Many large Korean corporations who harbor this "*pee ahl*" mentality when dealing with their PR firms have seen it work against them in the end. But companies making enlightened use of PR have reaped the benefits, particularly during recent nationwide drives for greater transparency in business and government.

For a foreign business enterprise, it may not always be easy to have a consistent PR policy and to properly implement it. Even though these activities do not require large resources or expenses, it is often difficult to measure their effect, and some managers are reluctant to make any investment that may not produce results except over a sustained period of time. It is important, however, for foreign business organizations to build a healthy local corporate image for sustained growth and profitable operations.

When entering Korea, one should write down the key messages one needs to send out to one's target audience and use those messages as anchor points for external communications. One should consider what resources one might have at one's disposal—these may include newsletters, web sites, and community activities. Let's consider some of the aspects that need to be considered in the promotion of a positive PR program for a foreign business.

Korea Orientation

Good will begins with close identification and association with the local populace. Fraternizing with business counterparts, and government officials and nationals in general, will play a large part in developing a healthy image. Make the effort to create social contacts outside the foreign ghetto; this, in turn, will melt walls of exclusiveness and divisiveness, and build bridges of friendship, mutuality and understanding with the local community. Informed foreign observers have noted that Koreans are very outgoing and warm, so some very meaningful friendships may be cultivated from the little effort exerted to break out of the comfortable shell of socializing primarily with other foreigners.

To facilitate this interaction, some expatriate executive candidates enroll in formal orientation programs or workshops to become more thoroughly prepared for cross-cultural relations. The better the executive is informed about the cultural traits of his or her co-workers and customers, the better the business between them.

Business organizations in some countries require their expatriate executives to participate in such cultural exchange programs for the obvious reason that it helps them to be better businesspeople. Some of these programs are informal, like a live-in situation for a couple of weeks with a national couple from the host country. In these situations, all phases of personal, family and business life are dealt with. Another approach is to hold seminars and workshops presenting various aspects of the culture, society and business of the host country. Alternatively, the Royal Asiatic Society has a very active Korea Branch in Seoul that holds free or inexpensive lectures on various aspects of Korea twice a month. The presenters are preeminent in their fields, and the lectures are conducted in English. In addition, the RAS conducts informative and inexpensive tours throughout Korea almost every weekend. (For more information on the RAS, visit their web site at www.raskb.com.)

These all pay off in a positive PR image, so that some very successful foreign JV companies are not identified as foreign companies at all by most Korean consumers. Genuine concern for people's welfare will be highly regarded by the general public and will promote a good image in the minds of the business community and consumers. Participation in various local business associations also helps to promote a good corporate image and PR program. Social clubs, chambers of commerce, and business seminars offer good opportunities to meet clients and customers on a personal, friendly basis. A wholesome, healthy friendship can quickly dispel erroneous, distorted impressions of a business organization while fostering strong community relations.

Concern for the protection and conservation of natural resources can go far in furthering good PR. Foreign companies can often take the lead in demonstrating ways to preserve the air and water purity that so many industries today are frequently accused of violating. A foreign JV paper company that demonstrated real concern for natural resources through an extensive reforestation project earned both a good reputation and high profits. A foreign beverage firm has been recognized as a leader in wetlands conservation sponsorship.

Foreign business ventures must demonstrate a close orientation to the needs of the general population. Sensitivity and concern for community and national interests is a basic building block in the construction of a positive PR program and corporate image.

Issues

Publicizing issues of public concern is also a factor in developing a good image. To take advantage of it, the expatriate manager must keep his or her eyes open to such issues and have someone on staff to keep him or her aware and informed.

Some of the issues that require a keen, sensitive awareness are related to market demand, product features and technical expertise. Corporate image is greatly helped if product features are consumer-oriented and meet consumer needs, and if manufacturing technology is sufficient to guarantee product excellence and durability. The cliché of "new and improved" has been exhausted, but consumers are responsive to a company that actually does improve the features of its products, keeps up to date, and makes household appliances better and more economical. These consumer benefits should be publicized without hesitation.

But there are less tangible but still important issues related to corporate image other than those having to do with products, such as employee benefits that boost personnel morale. Here are just a few examples of newsworthy items that can enhance the public image of a business enterprise:

- Praise of the accomplishments of local employees,

- Extension of an innovative benefit to employees,

- Announcement of the executive promotion of a local employee, and

- Company participation in a community activity.

Some company achievements should be reported to promote corporate public image:

- Head office sales, profits and new product research,

- Reporting on how the company exports benefit the national economy,

- Transfer of technology to improve product quality,

- Scientific seminars sponsored by the company for technology sharing,

- New product developments,

- Product improvement to increase efficiency and convenience, and

- R&D projects to focus on future prospects for a better life ahead.

Media

There is a variety of ways to publicize company news and developments, but one area that requires more skill than budget is the public news media.

Access to the major mass media is not easy. There must be lines of communication that a capable employee can tap. A person with an outgoing personality will be a great asset in promoting this kind of relationship. Continual communication with the media contact is necessary not only to promote company image but also to avoid the reporting of negative news.

In any event, it is critical to have an understanding of Korean journalism. Despite relatively low professional journalism standards, with comparatively little regard for corroborating the facts in the hurry to meet deadlines, Korean journalists are very well educated and highly motivated. They are also very influential, regardless of the degree of their understanding of the topic matter they are reporting. Like other employees, they are often and routinely rotated among their beats, so it is rare that a single journalist covering a particular area of the news remains long enough to become an authority.

On the other hand, a good journalist will do much homework to try to get on top of a topic. But study is second best to long experience. In this aspect, wise companies may find special opportunities. If a company gives the appearance of being aggressive and open in providing information beyond simply what is going on in its business, for example by also providing information on the market niche in which it operates, grateful journalists will be happy to quote the firm as the information source. This strategy often works well for foreign investment firms in developing Korean market awareness of their services and overall expertise.

There is also a host of professional journals and publications that reach a select but limited audience. These are important, too, as a means of publicity. Trade and industry associations usually provide a meeting place for these reporters on a regular basis. A local staff member may distribute media releases to reporters at these locations.

Using this kind of publicity will increase the possibility of access to mass media for PR communication. It must be noted, however, that all company news releases must be in the Korean language to reach the general public. Acceptance by the news media will be more likely if these are skillfully and professionally prepared, so a person with good writing ability should be selected for this assignment. Until recently, media releases were best delivered in person, with the next best approach being by fax. Today, many reporters request that media releases be sent by email. But the trick is consistently and constantly following up emailed media releases by calling reporters on their cell phones.

Skillfully implemented, inexpensive use of the news media can be a valuable asset for a business PR program. To those firms offering the appropriate products or services, major successes have been found by connecting with the 18- to 25-year-old age group that is very wired and fashion-conscious, has large amounts of disposable income, and—like many young people elsewhere—is very trendy and cliquish. Korean companies sometimes employ university students part-time to participate in opinion-leading blogs as a means to influence the market. More and more, the key is to connect without using "mainframe" advertising.

In 2006, the major newspapers began facing a sea change that may ultimately force changes in their advertising practices. Traditionally, the major dailies have run a de facto cartel with similar, pricy advertising rates. Even during the recessions, they have sold expensive ad space, with most marketing done through relationship selling. Recently, however, things have begun to change. The national government has started to talk about deregulating television advertising, which may give the newspapers greater competition. In addition, the government has begun exploring how to give financial aid to smaller publications so as to create a more competitive print marketplace.

Despite this, KDD (or Hangul Data), Korea's adex monitoring body, reported that print's share of advertising expenditures dropped from 40 percent in the early 1990s to 24 percent in 2005. Since 2002, terrestrial television has made substantial advertising gains, and by 2006 had as much as 30 percent of South Korea's overall annual adex. At the same time, cable and online media, though smaller in terms of customer base, have shown solid growth. For example, during 2007 online advertising was close to 630 billion won, a remarkable increase from the 480 billion won in 2006. Much of this has been at the expense of broadcasting and print advertising, which dropped during the same period. Indeed, for the foreseeable future, some analysts are expecting as much as 30 percent annual online advertising growth until 2008. While Internet advertising is—and is expected to remain for the foreseeable future—number three in advertising spending after television and newspapers, its growth will be at the expense of the top two's market share, although modest growth is still forecasted with the two top market leaders.

In other words, media options and costs are rapidly evolving, and the expanding influence of Internet-based media in this broadband-centric market is just beginning to be understood.

Mobile Marketing

As in Japan, the relationship between mobile operators and their affiliated advertising firms is very close in Korea. Thanks to that, mobile advertising is on the rise. Some analysts are even expecting Korean annual mobile advertising and marketing expenditures to pass the half-billion U.S. dollar mark in the coming few years. Like Japan, Korea has a well-established 3G-based handset market, so Korean consumers have become familiar with content-rich advertising on their mobile phones and PDAs. While SMS messaging is pervasive, it is proving to be less effective, as many Koreans have begun to view SMS ads as spam.

So for many young Koreans, using SMS ads is "so last week." New ideas being explored include future phones that can read the radio-frequency identification tags that will eventually replace the barcodes attached to goods to check the expiration date of fresh produce. Other ideas under development include mobile phones that can pick up a signal from a poster advertising a new movie, which would then prompt one to download a preview.

As new ideas come into practical implementation, there seems to be little doubt that South Koreans will flock to many of these services. As they do, smart marketers will find new ways to reach targeted consumers.

Publications

Besides the public news media, there are numerous publications a business organization can use for publicity. Many companies have a periodical newsletter or house organ for this purpose. Web sites are a matter of course in today's Korea. What impresses many foreigners upon their arrival in Korea is how many firms—including the smallest—have bilingual web sites. Korean web sites tend to be very professional in appearance and, on average, a bit less so in organization. Nonetheless, Korea, with its high Internet literacy levels, has produced many web designers who are of the first caliber in professionalism. Special oversight is in order in allowing English and other non-Korean language text to appear. Unfortunately, misspellings and poor grammar remain common features of many Korean web sites as well as print media.

For a positive corporate image, it is imperative that these publications be executed with a professional touch. They should be attractive and colorful and contain interesting content. If a company tries to cut corners on this, the publication will probably not exhibit the professionalism it needs to. Sufficient budget must be allotted if a publication is to achieve its desired image.

In addition to the style and appearance of the house organ, the postal mailing and emailing list are also important factors. Both for clients and customers, as well as for PR purposes, distribution should cover government officials, trade organizations, universities, and, of course, the news media. Publications should be sent to as wide a range of contacts as possible for maximum exposure. Print and electronic media make up strategic channels for disseminating information for corporate PR, so they must be used skillfully and professionally.

BUILDING A GOOD COMPANY IMAGE IS ESSENTIAL

Company image is a major factor in consumers' perception of quality. A good name goes a long way, especially in the selection of household durables. In the pharmaceutical industry, many over-the-counter drug purchases are based on perceived manufacturer reliability. Consumers develop strong product and brand name loyalties. A strong company image offers an additional benefit: subsequent products tend to enjoy favorable consumer reception as well.

Consider how, back in July 2009, the South Korean Fair Trade Commission (FTC) slapped an American company with a record-breaking 260 billion won (US$208.2 million) fine for "abusing its monopoly market status," even though it was the provider of a technology essential to one of the nation's industries. By U.S. standards, one may argue that the Californian company did nothing wrong other than to offer special discounts to those companies who wanted to buy both the chips and the software rather than simply the CDMA software.

But Korea is not the U.S., and contrary to many suspicions, the American company was not singled out as a foreign company by the FTC. In fact, a number of Seoul-based American, British and Korean business professionals agreed that the U.S. company stumbled by not playing by some of the basic, unwritten rules of doing business in Korea. These rules can be divided into two categories—legal doctrine and basic marketing.

Like many countries, Korea has a legal principle stating that if society becomes dependent on a product or service provided by monopoly, eventually the monopoly party needs to relinquish its monopoly control of the good or service, if only for the overall good of society. At the same time, the FTC first and often foremost considers the welfare of the big players, such as the cell phone manufacturers, with their thousands of employee households and hundreds of suppliers who rely on the overall welfare of these giant companies. Smaller Korean companies— or small local operations of multinational corporations—generally stand to lose when up against the large domestic companies. In a sense, if there is discrimination, one may say it is more likely to be a matter of size or clout than nationality.

Whether or not the American company violated the above legal doctrine, it clearly failed in its prior marketing as a highly successful corporate citizen in Korea—at least in terms of perception by the Korean public, and by extension the Korean government. Specifically, there is a concept in Korea that may be translated as the "Law of Public Sentiment" and is generally considered to be of a higher standard than enacted laws and regulations. It is Korea's law of the land. A foundation of this concept is *daebeop*, which may loosely be translated as "mob rule," but the word's nuance suggests a strong sentiment rather than simple anarchy.

And this is where proactive PR plays a much more critical role than in many other markets. A solid PR strategy is often the first and most important legal defense any company may employ in Korea. The second defense for both domestic and foreign companies is to have executives with high-level communication skills to deal with government officials and the media. To buttress these two defenses, any successful corporation must impress upon the Korean community that it is a generous corporate citizen and not simply in the market to reap maximum profits. Again, perception is key. How the company is regarded matters more than how substantially it gives back to society.

For example, if one asks the Korean on the street about this American company, one may expect to hear, at most, that the U.S. corporation is a monopoly provider of a technology key to Korean consumer products. But even though the company had invested in corporate social responsibility (CSR) projects in Korea, their Korean operation was woefully under-recognized. Instead, it was viewed as a cynical corporation that held the Korean industry over a barrel, milking large profits without giving anything back beyond the contractual obligations. Not good.

Similarly, one can find parallel examples with other foreign operations in Korea, where they may have acted in a perfectly legal and, by most Western standards, ethical manner. The problem often comes about when the foreign company suffers from negative public image ensuing from making huge profits without giving anything back to Korean society. It is not enough, for example, that during the IMF crisis foreign investors took significant risks in turning around failing companies, thereby saving thousands of Korean jobs. To most Koreans, that is just basic business. There is the fundamental expectation of any successful individual or company that they will give something extra back to society. Those who do not donate from their profits only invite social—and eventually official—retribution for their perceived greed.

The takeaway from these case studies is that Korean laws do not fully encapsulate shared social values. Simply obeying the law and regulations is an inadequate strategy for avoiding harassment and punishment—particularly if one is visibly successful. That factor is in play regardless of nationality.

Nearby Professional Help

During the past two decades, international PR firms have established branch operations in Seoul, and local PR firms have matured substantially. Besides providing the expected PR activities, several are quite professional in providing crisis management services, as well as special event planning and execution. Unlike the past, when foreign companies tried to explain their needs to offshore professionals, Korea now has mature PR specialists—both foreign and local—who understand the needs of the foreign firm and the perceptions of the Korean market.

That does not mean one should be lazy in selecting a firm. One of the most common, serious mistakes foreign firms make when selecting a PR firm in Korea is basing the choice on a pleasant, English-speaking representative. While having an effective bilingual interface with the agency is very important, in the long run that factor is not the most important criterion. In fact, very few accomplished, English-speaking Koreans are also highly accomplished PR professionals. Many excellent English-speaking Koreans have a tendency to put on social airs based on their bilingual abilities, which grates on many professional journalists' egos. Consequently, Ms. Kim who sounds as if she is a U.S. native may be worth it from the foreign client's view, but a pretentious lightweight in the journalism community. It may be wise to rely on a Korean staff member to help with selection of the PR firm and its representative.

Thus rests the case for the importance of a strong PR program for companies doing business in Korea. But there is no rest for the promotion of PR programs to develop a positive corporate image within Korea. Due to cross-cultural differences and varying multinational corporate policies, misunderstandings and misconceptions are bound to arise. But they are not insurmountable, and with an effective PR strategy and program, it is possible to develop successful and profitable business activities in an unfamiliar cultural environment. Many companies with informed, concerned expatriate executives have proved this fact.

ADVERTISING

Using a Variety of Approaches

Given its population and income level, Korea is regarded as a major market for consumer as well as other products. Accordingly, advertising billings in Korea are the third largest in Asia. Twenty-five years ago, reaching consumers nationwide required at least a million-dollar advertising budget per year. Today, one can spend a quarter of that amount on a one-week promotional campaign in a major newspaper alone. This level of expenditure may be beyond the pale for many smaller companies whose products have smaller potential markets. In such cases, direct mail/email advertising to a select audience may be considered. Other options include advertising in specialty publications and with special campaigns. Targeting select audiences is not an easy task, especially under budgetary constraints. Imaginative marketing managers, however, will find all the necessary tools at their disposal in Korea.

Advertising Spending by Industry

Korea's biggest advertising spenders belong to the communications and information technology sector. In 2006, 535 billion won was spent on pitching high-speed Internet, mobile phone and telecommunication services. The finance industry places second, spending 513 billion won in 2006—an increase of almost a quarter over the prior year's advertising spending.

Industries that spent less on advertising in 2006 were in the service sector, which spent about 437 billion won; construction and real estate, at just over 378 billion won; and food and food services, spending 346 billion won. Though they are relatively small sectors, rapid advertising growth was witnessed in 2006 for fashion, at an annual increase of over

21 percent, and for education and welfare, at an increase of just short of 19 percent over 2005 levels.

A WORD OF CAUTION

To maintain a consistently positive public image in a foreign country, there are several points on which to exercise restraint and caution.

The first is to maintain absolute neutrality on political issues and party affiliations. Sometimes it may even be necessary to state publicly that the company does not interfere or take sides in national political issues or conflicts. To express approval or disapproval on political issues is only to invite the ire and antagonism of one group or another, and that will only impede the business success of the company. Political neutrality is a must.

There may also be incidents of conflict between the global PR policy of the multinational company and local convention or business practices. In such cases, it is necessary to persuade the senior home executives to follow the local practice, especially if they wish to preserve a positive corporate image within the environment in question. In the current environment, where Korean sentiment toward America is changing, minimizing identification with or approval of official homeland policies is recommended.

By a similar token, the message must always be "localized"—that is, centered on Korea. There is a famous story of a local newspaper in England in 1912 that had a headline reading "Local Man Dies in Sea Tragedy" when reporting on the sinking of the Titanic. The same mentality is prevalent in today's Korea. The national media that dominates the nation is Seoul-based and has a very strong nationalist, Korea-centric focus. It is essential to get a Korea hook in virtually every story and media release.

When it comes to cultivating government relations for foreign firms, the scenario can be a bit dodgy. For example, after several years of developing a relationship with one's man in the government, he may be suddenly transferred to a position that is of little consequence to one's company. Furthermore, if the goal is to develop a senior-level bureaucratic relationship with one's country head, it can be even more problematic if the country director is an expat on a three-year Korea assignment. It may make more sense to contract a government relations consulting firm that specializes in developing and maintaining close relations with government officials on behalf of its clients. (Please refer to Chapter 25, "Relating to Bureaucrats," for more details.)

23. SELLING IN KOREA—MYTHS AND REALITIES

SELLING OR ORDER-TAKING?

A couple of years ago, a British engineer in his late 50s who had been working with one of the world's largest computer companies for most of his career came to Korea to help with a major project at a local bank. His corporation's sales acumen was internationally respected, and the firm's name was synonymous with the ideal in professional selling. Having worked in many countries with his corporation, he was struck by what he found in the Korean operations. "The lads aren't really salesmen—they're just order-takers!" he quipped. "Bingo!" replied this author.

Selling in Korea is frequently described as personal selling or relationship selling. In Korean consumer markets, personal selling can be seen in the marketing of books, insurance, automobiles, cosmetics, and imported toys. Lower wages for salesmen partially explain the higher incidence of personal selling even in consumer goods. Sales management in Korea is difficult because of the many factors that a company has to consider, especially with regard to compensation. Getting the right mix of a seniority system with an incentive system is not easy. On top of that, companies are constrained by requirements imposed by Korean labor standard laws, such as those regarding minimum wage.

In general, selling is an individually oriented function that obviously presents obstacles in the group-oriented working environment more typical of Korean society. Thus, it is not surprising that people with related experience in this field assert that Koreans desire job security and advancement more than higher short-term incentives in their selling jobs. This may explain, for instance, why in many large Korean corporations, this function is called "business" (*yeong-eop*) and not strictly "sales." Of course, the generally negative perception of the "selling" occupation plays a part in this as well. The latter issue also hampers the ability of companies to recruit prime candidates for these jobs.

Another aspect of selling in a close-knit society is that interpersonal relationships can be critical in establishing leads and sales. In the life insurance market, salespeople tap into their extended families to get their initial sales; in industrial markets, salespeople latch onto their school friends to get entry. So-called "cold-calling" is less common than in countries like the U.S. But while use of personal networks frequently produces results that may look good in the short run, it must be monitored, as it encourages passive personal selling and does not promote the accumulation of selling know-how. Getting Korean salespeople to try to sell outside of their comfort zones normally takes strong management ability. This can be critical if one's marketing strategy determines the opportunity or necessity to extend one's sales outside of traditional market segments into niches where the sales force has few personal contacts.

BUSINESS ENTERTAINMENT

It goes without saying that entertaining customers and prospects is a big part of doing business in Korea. But since the enactment of various overseas anti-corruption laws in the North America and Europe, many foreign businesspeople hesitate trying to understand this topic. Many believe it is better to allow one's Korean partner company, which knows the market, culture, and language, to handle this part of the business process. They also believe it is legally prudent to pursue a policy of "Don't ask, so my Korean partner doesn't tell" should anything hit the fan down the road with their home office auditor. But as prudent as that attitude may seem, a Western business professional may hesitate come time to make a quick decision, such as on pre-authorized payment for business entertainment for one's Korean sales managers. Foreigners who don't understand Korean business may find it safe to reject the claim, which can frustrate a Korean salesman (understandably, sales turns into a man's game at this point) if he needs it to win a major deal.

At first glance, all of this business entertainment seems like an expensive way for Korean men to expand livers, kill brain cells, and generally have fun under the guise of developing relationships that lead to sales. That may be the initial attraction when one is young, but by one's mid-thirties, serious entertaining actually becomes hard work.

To put all of this into proper perspective, let's consider how a traditional Korean salesman uses various forms of entertainment to capture a major business-to-business sale. While personal introductions are critical, even with such introductions the Korean salesman often starts out dealing with strangers. The second sales call is frequently scheduled just before lunch, so that the salesman may take his or her prospects out to a modest meal. If the sales process is going well, later sales calls will be scheduled in the late afternoon. Sometimes, the salesman may offer to take the prospects out to a modest dinner, followed by a few beers. As the sales cycle progresses and personal relations improve, dinner may be followed by the reservation of a private room, where the parties drink beer while playing card games. Alternatively, a salesman may take his guests to the local sauna.

Based on this, a good Korean salesman should be earning the trust and candor from his prospects to pick up "insider information." Indeed, it is often startling how much intel salesmen can pick up through these informal sessions, especially compared to markets like Japan and the U.S. The salesman can learn not only who his or her competitors are, but also how they are viewed by the prospects and even what the competition's price offerings are.

When the schmoozing continues to and past contract signing, the serious business entertainment begins. Contrary to many foreigners' claims, expensive entertainment is not rampant. When serious money is spent, both the seller and buyer take such opportunities seriously. On the seller's part, it is naturally important not to inflate the cost of sales. But it is equally important on the buyer's part not to mislead vendors. Corporate auditors for buyers consider acceptance of excessive entertainment to be a form of corruption. In fact, there is the unconfirmed possibility that a seller that believes it has been misled by a buyer may notify that manager's auditing department. So offering—and accepting—a night out on the town is not a casual affair.

Take note of some common errors in this process. For foreigners, a common error is to pick up a prospect after dinner for drinks: entertainment always starts with dinner and ends at any hour, depending on the circumstances. A much bigger error can be entertaining the "foreigner-handler" rather than the real decision-maker. Once that mistake has been discovered, the foreigner will probably need to entertain once more, but at a more expensive level, since the foreigner handler is almost always of a lower rank, and to entertain the decision-maker at the same level would be considered a slight. Junior Korean salesmen can almost always correctly identify the right person to entertain, but misgauge the proper timing for doing so.

So timing is important, but so is frequency. Actually, the frequency of major entertainment has decreased. Prior to the IMF crisis, the common pattern was to conduct major entertainment two or three times prior to contract signing, followed by one very big celebratory entertainment upon consummation of the deal. These days, however, most companies expect one major night out on the town prior to signing the contract, and one more time if the deal comes to fruition, often including the buyer's team members as well as key decision-maker.

Timing is predicated on when the salesman is most sure he will not be turned down. At other times, a suggestion to go out together can be part of the sales qualification process. A buyer is unlikely to allow itself to be competitively wined and dined by two or more vendors; this can be considered unethical. It is also good to remember that decision-makers have seen and done it all long before reaching that position. This is not to say there is no enjoyment to be found in entertainment, but after a certain point it becomes, at best, one of the more pleasant forms of, well, work.

So let's start climbing the formal entertainment ladder. The bottom rung of entertainment includes the humble stand bars and *noraebang* (karaoke bars). In the latter case, female entertainers can be included at the additional charge of 20,000 to 30,000 won per hour per entertainer. Beverages are normally limited to beer and soft drinks. This is a relatively cheap and clean form of entertainment, where the young women are quick to admonish handsy clientele.

The next level up consists of "business clubs." The lower rung of business clubs is the *danranjujeom*, essentially a *noraebang* with private rooms that serves hard drinks such as whiskey and vodka. Here, too, there is the option of ordering female companions to join the fun. The difference with the *noraebang* is the higher price and women who are much less inclined to protect their physical privacy. The added surcharge or "tip" comes roughly to 200,000 won per companion.

Meanwhile, the swankier business entertainment clubs are called simply "business clubs." These are actually what some consider to be a light version of room salons, the next rung up. Clubs work on a pre-determined number of hours—usually two or three for a set room price that includes drinks and snacks at about 300,000 won or more per guest, with a 200,000 won tip for each de rigueur hostess per guest. One should budget at least 500,000 won per visitor.

From this point of the ladder, personal physical privacy becomes even less of a concern with the ladies, while the option of spending more money on these women elsewhere afterwards is available. Room salons are no exception. Room salons are occupied by women who are generally younger, prettier, and more well-educated than those employed at clubs. Many have college degrees and/or can speak multiple languages. Prices vary considerably depending on location, but generally one does well to get away with paying as little as 500,000 won per person, including tips; the tab often comes out to 700,000 won or more. An added plus of the upgraded venue is that there are no real time limits on entertainment at this level.

Next are the *yojeong*, which are combined restaurants and clubs. Traditionally, these were the *giseng-jip* (similar to the geisha houses of Japan) of yore. Today, the women tend to be beautiful and often well educated, but still generally lack the cultural refinements of *giseng*. These establishments are disappearing, since fewer Korean businessmen are using them among themselves. Those *yojeong* that survive are often the scenes of Korean businessmen attracting foreign buyers. The price per person runs roughly between 600,000 won to 700,000 won—considering that one gets a nice dinner thrown in, this makes for a pretty reasonable option compared to the values offered by the immediately lower establishments. The catch is that there is normally a four-guest minimum.

At this lofty height, what is left to entertain at the top? The rule of thumb is that any place that deals with professional female entertainment is appropriate to the *bujang* level or below. Entertaining executives is usually a different ball game altogether.

That ball game is none other than golf. An ideal golfing experience takes place at a golf club not too far out of town—ideally, the course should not be much farther than an hour from the departure point. Tee-off timing should be predicated on 18 holes, including a light lunch; the entire experience should not take more than five hours. One additional hour should be devoted to showering and relaxing before piling back into cars and arriving back at the point of origin by early evening. From there, an acceptable option is to carry on at a *yojeong*.

But a word of a caution regarding golf and government contracts: sometimes senior bureaucrats may decline golfing invitations if there has been a recent scandal related to golfing involving a minister and senior corporate executive. It is not uncommon for a golf course to be the venue for discovered corruption. So while there is normally no problem, it is wise to keep apprised of current political events.

Finally, one last detail should probably be addressed—namely, kickbacks. As with many things in Korea, standard kickbacks are different than in most countries. For example, there is a standard money-back rate that comes to approximately one kickback won for each U.S. dollar of sale. The money is paid in cash, of course, but it is done in a manner open and transparent to the purchasing department. The money doesn't go into any one person's pocket, but into a pool of like money. When special holidays rolll around, such as New Year's or Chuseok, this money is used to buy gifts for the purchasing company's employees. So in a sense, one may say these sales rebates are a form of entertainment, and they are certainly included in the costs of sales.

Foreigners may do well to better understand what happens during after-hours business activities, especially those who may be taken aback by how much money is used in this regard. One can debate the merits and faults of the system, but when all is said and done, the system is in place—and it is business entertaining that keeps Korea's business world turning.

SALESPERSON RECRUITMENT

Some Korean firms try to safeguard in personal selling by being more selective in recruiting. The educational level of potential candidates is usually just one of many criteria on which salespeople are screened. Some companies may include psychological compatibility with a list of selling attributes to ensure that people with the right mental profiles are selected. While these efforts may be aimed in the right direction, they usually miss the target.

The best and brightest of young recruits are generally career-tracked into marketing, with little or no real exposure to actual selling. At best, a very short time of working with the real sales team may be assigned, but these short tenures reinforce the image that the smart and talented are tracked to take on truly executive roles, whereas the lowly salespeople can only hope to achieve large bonuses if they are particularly successful. In fact, sales engineers often have a much better chance in high-tech firms to move beyond the realm of sales into general management, as they are generally regarded as smarter than their pure sales peers.

Korean managers often views salespeople as mercenaries. Their traditional strength is not professional sales skills or even product knowledge, but rather their personal connections. While Korean sales professionals are highly praised for their successes, they are also commonly stymied in their professional growth. This dilemma sometimes motivates the best-connected salespeople to walk out the door to greener pastures as they approach forty—taking a good portion of the business with them to a competitor. This frequently creates a vicious cycle of general management suspicions and limited career advancement for their sales force.

FOREIGN COMPANIES SELLING IN KOREA

Foreign firms have on occasion been able to turn a traditional negative into a positive, such as when foreign firms enter the Korean market with products and services that are greatly improved—or even totally new competitive offerings. At the same time, it is often difficult to recruit experienced Korean sales professionals with wide arrays of contacts—either because such individuals are not attracted to the foreign firm or because the market is so new that traditional contacts may not be as readily employable for closing sales. It is at this point that professional sales skills training finds traction in Korea.

Consider what traditionally happens with many sales cycles for capital purchases. A salesman (and most often they are men) hears from his personal contacts that a firm is thinking of buying a product or service. A good, traditional salesman will find an opportunity to get in the door before the formal, publicly announced bidding process begins. Often the prospective firm has defined or at least recognized a problem, but more often than not it does not have a good handle on what may be a good solution. Consequently, the first sales call seems to hark back to "Market Day," when buyers would stroll through the outdoor markets and see what the vendors had displayed on their mats and tables. With very little qualification, the salesman gives a company a high-end, all-product overview presentation, then waits for questions from the prospective buyers in the room. If he is successful, the buyers conclude that the seller may have something of potential value worth exploring in a follow-up meeting.

The important point to note is that right from the beginning, the salesman has assumed the role of a lowly order-taker and is purely at the beck and call of the prospect. There is very little or none of a problem-solving partnership, since the buyer holds the gold and therefore determines the entire solution selection process. And of course, the salesman is in competition with one or more other salesmen who have their own personal contacts with the same prospect. They, too, normally go in and spread their wares, so to speak, for the buyers to glance at.

Since the salesmen specialize in developing, maintaining and schmoozing key people at various accounts, they are usually not well versed enough to provide advice as to which solutions are best for the customer. When possible, they will bring with them product specialists such as sales engineers. But since the salesmen are responsible for orchestrating the sales cycle from the vendor's perspective, with only a sales focus and no strong solutions orientation, the salesmen often reinforce the "checklist" process mentality of product selection.

While personal relations can indeed be a major factor in making the final selection, inclusion among the finalists frequently comes down to which firms score the most checkmarks on the product selection criteria list. The irony is that the buyers often make up the selection list in the blind. Good salespeople, like their peers elsewhere in the world, will attempt to influence the selection criteria. Sometimes they are successful, but often another salesman has overriding control of the checklist. Regardless, there is usually only minimal interactive discussion between the salesman and his customer during which to effectively develop an understanding of what is the real—as opposed to immediately perceived— problem. The net result may be that the solution offered by one salesman's firm may actually be the best fit, but one is seconded by a competitor's product that better fits the selection checklist, without adequate consideration being given to the nature of the problem or the attributes of one's solution.

To counter this problem, multinational firms have been developing their sales forces by training in consultative selling in one form or another— both in terms of individual professional sales skills and in terms of up-to-date sales management systems. Frankly speaking, local firms—and one may include some foreign firms that have been in Korea long enough to be considered quite localized—normally display minor, real interest in consultative, professional sales skills training. Now, the legitimate preoccupation may be that local firms know something that foreign firms do not. Perhaps, but often that attitude results simply from the satisfaction of being in the market first and developing a dominant market share.

The danger to any firm is that by simply holding the largest market share and being smug about sales acumen that is based more on place-holding or account-farming than new account sales, sales managers and their general managers may assume they have a great sales force. Too often today's revenues are based on incremental sales from initial selling a decade ago.

As the market and the entire economy change, the smug and complacent are likely to find their slice of the pie growing thinner year by year as hungrier and more aggressive firms encroach. To say that replacing a legacy vendor is extremely tough in Korea—and probably more so than in most advanced industrial markets—is no light statement. This is because of the close personal contacts between key people—particularly salespeople—and their customers, where after-sales service often goes beyond what may be considered normal post-sales support, such as in terms of personal favors. In some cases, particularly with leading-edge technologies, the legacy vendor alone may know how his provided technology interacts with other systems the customer operates, thus making it almost impossible for a competitor to replace him. At other times—and more commonly—the customer alone may know how a system or technology has been uniquely applied within his or her environment, but without adequate documentation. Consequently, if the customer's resident guru is not well disposed toward a new vendor, successful implementation of new products can be virtually impossible.

SALES TRAINING

All of these situations cry out for consultative selling, since professional selling is not just about getting the contract signed, but also ensuring that a consummated deal translates into a profitable business with a satisfied customer. Too often, "sales training" is effectively product training, and what comes close to sales training is simply business courtesy training and simplistic ways of trying to define who the "key person" is. Moreover, when the key contacts on either end leave their companies, there goes the contract!

Today, larger multinational companies are training their Korean sales forces by contracting with multinational training companies, or sometimes by using their own international training departments. There are Korean sales training firms, including ones with bilingual managers, if not trainers. To date, however, very few of them have a sophisticated knowledge of world-class selling skills. Rather, they tend to focus on schmoozing with positive training evaluations—often predicated on the entertainment factor of the sales trainer's humorous storytelling and passed off as case studies—rather than imparting advanced selling skills.

As one may imagine, selling in any market is a topic large enough to devote a whole book to, rather than just a chapter. While there are no shortcuts in getting a basic understanding of successful selling in Korea, hiring a good sales professional can be the key to one's success. What constitutes a "good sales professional" is largely dictated by one's product niche, of course. However, one general warning is that while a traditional sales manager may quickly deliver results, he or she may also run out of steam as one's company's products move on to new markets or as one's products more or less saturate the soft market niches. A sales manager with the experience, professional sales acumen and flexibility not to be wholly dependent upon personal contacts is usually a hard individual to find and recruit.

Developing a mature and bright sales professional through quality sales training, however, is always an option that should be considered. Korean sales professionals are usually enthusiastic about learning how to increase their sales. By investment in their professionalism, one's firm demonstrates strong commitment to these salespeople as key employees.

As one gathers intel on selling in Korea, one may wish to consider the following:

SMASHING THE SEVEN MYTHS OF KOREAN SALES

Myths—every country has them. Be they the myths of Korea or the tales of ancient Greece, myths are considered collective "wisdom" formed and adhered to over a long period. In the business field, too, myths exist, and some remain unchanged even after the paradigm has shifted. While cultural myths may have little ill effect, in the fast-moving business world myths often become obstacles—which, unless countered, can hinder successful commerce.

Below, the author identifies seven of these myths dealing with sales in Korea that need to be recognized as not only outdated but also potentially devastating to a company's bottom line.

Myth #1: "Price Takes Precedence Over Value"

Value in sales terms means either tangible or intangible parts of the product or service that give the buyer a unique advantage. The seller must define value in a business proposition, such as by product differentiation, customization, or added services that provide a solution to the customer as valued in his or her own terms.

Until very recently, Korean companies created and provided products or services where the customer easily understood value. There was little product differentiation, and the product or service normally did not require a customized solution. Creating value had very little monetary reward. Therefore, reducing price or simply providing additional products or services free of charge became the natural solution when faced with competition.

For example, a salesperson takes a customer's interest to the proposal stage. The customer tells the salesperson that he or she has heard of a better price from a vendor of a similar solution. Instead of finding out how the competitor's product solution will meet the customer's critical business needs compared to his or her own solution, the salesperson starts price negotiations.

A better approach is for the salesperson to take early, proactive measures to gain the customer's agreement on the quantifiable value of the product or service. This approach gives the salesperson control not only with the immediate buyer, but also, when properly strategized, in more effectively dealing with the purchasing and finance departments for large sales.

Myth #2: "Focus on Product Knowledge Rather Than Selling Skills and Business Knowledge."

This problem also involves Western salespeople—especially inexperienced and unsuccessful ones. It seems, however, to be more predominant among Korean salespeople. One can think of two reasons for this.

One is that most products and services Korean salespeople sold in the past did not require in-depth knowledge of buyers' needs because the value of the products was self-explanatory. For instance, there's no doubt that a buyer needs an air conditioner with basic functionality in the summer.

Another reason seems to be related to Korea's Confucian order and "rote education" system. From kindergarten to university, teachers instruct students on the textbook facts. Students absorb and recite them in their exams. There is only one correct answer to each question, only one way of looking at things: the teacher's way. No questions allowed.

Korean companies, whose main focus until recently was simply on producing and selling, train their sales force in product features. Salespeople dutifully memorize all the facts and recite them to customers. As a product changes, the sales force receives updated product training. The practice continues. This product knowledge gives salespeople the basic ability to pitch the product.

But in a value-oriented business environment, it is the salesperson's insight as to how the product or service will meet customers' critical needs that will open the door to a successful transaction. To prevent burnout, some companies provide their sales forces with motivational-type seminars, where star salespersons relate their war stories. While some pick up hints and produce better results, many are only momentarily motivated.

Myth #3: "Emphasis on Personal Relationships Rather Than Business Relationships"

Anyone who has been in Korea for some time realizes that Korean society operates on the principle of familial, scholastic, business, or regional connections, rather than on egalitarian principles. Underlying this is the psyche called "*jeong.*" ("*Jeong*" is similar to the English word "heart"—as in the song from the Broadway hit *Damn Yankees*, "You Gotta Have Heart!")

For Koreans, having *jeong* and being seen to have *jeong* are crucial. Someone with no *jeong* will be categorized as "selfish" or even "inhuman." So it is a common practice for Koreans to make business decisions based on *jeong* cultivated through relationships. A young CEO of a prominent Korean IT company once commented, "The Vice Chairman who used to be my mentor taught me this: 'If you want the customer to buy from you rather than from your competitor, have one more bowl of noodle soup with the customer than one's competitor does with him or her.'" Maintaining a good personal relationship is important no matter where one does business. But more important is the degree to which it influences business decisions.

As Korea moves toward becoming a more egalitarian society, business methods thus become more practical, with accountability and transparency becoming more important. Buyers will have to choose business partners who understand their organizational needs, achieve solutions and can perform to the organization's objectives, rather than simply leveraging relationships.

Furthermore, as technology and business innovation only quicken in pace, existing networks of personal relationships may not be able to keep up with genuine and pressing business needs. Certainly many legacy relations will be leveraged forward, but not all. Given this gap between old friendships and immediate business requirements, gaps are formed where the astute and trained sales professional can find new opportunities that were once not available.

Myth #4: "Spend Money on Clients"

As in many Asian countries in which a gift-giving culture is predominant, bribery is a problem in Korea. To get things done, the beneficiary will present money to the benefactor. Though this is considered tasteless in egalitarian societies, in Korea it is matter-of-fact.

In a business environment where one seller's solution is little different from others, the question as to who is the beneficiary and who is the benefactor becomes crystal clear. Many bad scenarios occur—for example in the pharmaceutical industry, where it has been almost customary for companies to pay off doctors in the form of rebates to get business. But American firms, partially motivated by federal overseas anti-corruption regulations, have been changing the game.

Unfortunately, the perception that this practice is "undesirable but necessary" has been reinforced even by many Korean salespeople belonging to foreign companies whose products clearly offer higher value than those of their competitors. Again, managers of several foreign pharmaceutical companies have recently banned this practice, forcing their sales forces to seek alternative ways of winning sales besides paying off clients. And to the surprise of many, these no-nonsense directives by foreign executives, along with dismissals of sales managers for noncompliance, are working.

While this remains a problem with large sales to second-tier and lower firms, the largest Korean companies have tightened up on this form of corruption and its resulting inefficiencies as the companies play greater roles in international commerce. Also, the South Korean government's constant push for transparency, as part of its plan to transform the nation into a regional economic hub, has had a bit of a chilling effect on some of these practices of the past.

So how does one outmaneuver one's competitors without entering the bribery race? One way is to help customers perform their business more efficiently. For example, one could feed customers useful information, or try to provide clients with earnest solutions that are also within their reach. Most reasonable customers will eventually recognize that being helped professionally is more advantageous to their careers than simply being paid off.

On the other hand, if one feels the only way to succeed with a customer is by bribery, one should note that it may be wise to reconsider if one wishes to enter a long-term relationship with such a customer. The total costs of sales may start with a bribe today but expand into unreasonable project creep and unprofitable support demands tomorrow. Not selling to this type of customer may have a better impact on one's long-term profit-and-loss statement.

Myth #5: "Sales Is Not a Profession"

Traditionally, Korea's Confucian social order placed the merchant class at the bottom. Even the peasants regarded making a living by selling goods as undignified. Although today's Koreans no longer think this way, some stigma remains.

Interestingly, intelligence, which is highly regarded within Korean values, has traditionally not been a requirement to become a salesperson. As one Korean company president confided to us, "Both our salesmen and their buyers are not so smart." Given this traditional Korean sales environment, managers have not required salespeople to acquire professional selling skills. In fact, many Korean sales managers at best vaguely understand what professional selling is beyond being on top of product knowledge and knowing how to effectively schmooze prospects and customers.

Many Korean firms have done little or been ineffective in constantly updating the sales and business knowledge of their sales forces to catch up with changing technology and shifting corporate environments. The sales profession has too often been reserved for employees who could not get into more competitive fields—save those for whom the company chose sales as a strategic training ground prior to placement in more "important" posts. So to most Koreans, while sales is a job that requires hard work, it receives little respect (except financially, when successful), and very few believe that sales is a profession that requires breadth and depth of business knowledge.

There is an encouraging sign, though. In some foreign tech companies, salespeople wield considerable power. This could be because it takes intelligence to understand the complexity of high-tech products, and salespeople are recognized for the contribution they make to their organization's bottom line. When Korean salespeople start viewing themselves as problem-solvers for customers and as contributors toward their organizations' profits, they will raise the status of their profession. In order to reach a similar goal, salespeople should constantly strive to obtain new knowledge and skills through continuing sales and business education and training.

Myth #6: "The Customer Orders You. You Don't Lead the Customer."

Confucian values discourage challenging someone with more authority. From the above Korean beliefs comes another myth: "Try to please the customer by providing what the customer wants—without questioning."

There is no doubt that the customer is king—and perhaps even God—in Korea. Therefore, one has to be customer-driven to succeed. Unfortunately, many Korean executives have come to expect their salespeople to simply take orders and then work with others, such as fulfillment staff and engineers, on how to somehow meet the terms and conditions of the sales orders.

It is hard—if not impossible—for the Korean salesperson who has not gone through the proper training on the discipline of consulting and educating customers to have the self-confidence to take the necessary initiative. Consequently, most salespeople end up placing control of the transaction entirely into the customers' hands. When that happens there is very little management—only monitoring of the sales cycles.

But while this is not common, it is possible to train a salesperson to educate, lead, and manage the customer—and not simply to take orders. The solution requires the entire organization to provide more than lip service to the business unit's commitment to selling. Senior management must openly and routinely recognize that dedicated, professional salespeople are at least as critical and honored as anyone else in the organization. Beyond incentive remuneration, it is equally important to invest in their professional as well as product skills as a way to demonstrate how important these key individuals are to the organization's overall well-being.

Myth #7: "Koreans Buy Only From Koreans"

While it is true that Koreans prefer to buy from Koreans, one may also say that Americans prefer to buy from Americans. Normally, the biggest problem for non-Korean salespeople is the language barrier and the presumed accompanying ignorance about how to do business in Korea.

While foreigners who can converse competently enough to sell in Korean are rare, there is an increasing number of young Koreans with English language skills who are willing to consider leading-edge foreign products from foreign sales professionals. To be sure, selling in English via foreign sales staff is not the easiest path to take. Yet it should not be discounted at all times, as English-speaking foreign salespeople have scored several significant wins by selling into this market.

Koreans are practical people, and as much as they would naturally prefer to stay within their comfort zones, it is possible to sell into this market if a foreign salesperson has an exceptional product or service, especially when other options such as partnering with a Korean firm or hiring a Korean salesperson are not possible.

24. SELLING THROUGH KOREAN DISTRIBUTORS

ESTABLISHING INDIRECT SALES IN KOREA

Indirect selling can be one of the least expensive and lowest-risk strategies in sales. Among foreign corporations selling into Korea are a number of companies that use local distributors. Often, foreign companies organically grow their operations throughout Asia by contracting local companies before setting up a representative office and hiring their own local staff.

While this approach offers obvious advantages, it also contains many hidden pitfalls. While the go or no-go decision criteria for selling through offshore channels may be less demanding than calculating the return on investment through a direct presence, several factors should still be carefully considered. Before entering into any kind of international distribution agreement with a Korean distributor, it may be wise to ask oneself just why one is entering the Korean market, rather than using the same resources to expand in existing markets. If the rationale is purely opportunistic, chances are one's firm will not get much further than securing the few customers who happen to be well-known to one's distributor.

ENTHUSIASM FOR FOREIGN PRODUCTS

Koreans are enthusiastically curious about foreign goods and services. While price is generally an overriding consideration, there are foreign products that compete in Korea on their unique values—even if they cost more than local competing products or solutions. In any event, it is critical to concretely identify one's competitive advantage from the Korean perspective rather than that of one's marketing department.

As may be expected, the more enhancing and least disruptive goods and services will fare best. Other products may be intrinsically disruptive and will therefore require much more selling and after-sales support. In this case, Koreans will naturally consider if there are cheaper, local alternatives with sufficient Korean-speaking after-sales support.

THE RIGHT FIT

Finding a distributor in Korea is easy, but finding an effective one can be difficult.

The good news is that many individuals and firms can assist in this task. Since this is a compact business society, one can say that almost everyone knows everyone else, one or two people removed. It is not wise, therefore, to select an English-speaking distributor or market entry specialist primarily because he "knows all the key players." Most folks who have ten years or more experience and have been reasonably successful can qualify by that criterion alone.

What actually makes a good distributor may vary from industry to industry. A safe bet, however, is to find one that is already selling profitably to market leaders. The ideal distributor should be well-known and respected, but not so large as to consider one's product as simply another arrow in its sales quiver.

There are several war stories of foreign firms coming to Korea and being attracted to some of the biggest names in their field. The stories vary, but they share a common theme. In the beginning, everything looks extremely positive. The distributor's staff members are very bright, many speak decent or even very good English, and they are already working with, or at least very familiar with, one's target companies. Then, one day, the foreign company receives communication introducing them to a new product manager or even a new product team within their distributor. What the foreign partner did not realize or take into adequate account was that very large distributors often rotate their staff every couple of years— and sometimes even more frequently. Consequently, prior investment in training the distributor's sales and after-sales staff can suddenly disappear with one of these frequent organizational reshuffles.

On the other hand, it can be equally disastrous to collaborate with too small of a distributor, one that is financially over-dependent on the success of one's product. While such a distributor may offer the fullest measure of dedication to one's product line, it may not have the financial or human resource capacity to expand once it starts selling. Sometimes, a distributor that is too small is forced to partner with a larger, more credible Korean company; however, this results in the price of one's products becoming unmarketable, since the third party needs its additional margin. In the end, customers often delay payments to the distributor for large capital asset sales until the customer is fully satisfied with the purchase. This, in turn, has often resulted in near-fatal cash flow problems for these small firms.

While there is no magic criterion that applies to all industries, one should evaluate multiple candidates and consider finding an appropriate-sized partner that has a strong reputation and appropriate customer base, one that is already profitably selling complementary—or at least not competing—products. The goal is to find a distributor that has enough skin and flexibility to survive both types of challenges—and yet is not so big that it will take one's products and services lightly.

THE DEAL

It is not uncommon for a Korean distributor to ask its foreign partner for so-called "one-time, special" pricing discounts on the first deal and demand that the foreigner partner send its support staff for the duration of the project, given the lack of product understanding by the local after-sales staff. This can happen if the Korean distributor has decided not to make a serious investment in training its staff; such distributors may also refrain from sending employees abroad until after they are sure that the foreign product will be successful in Korea. While this may seem to be a prudent strategy from the Korean distributor's viewpoint, it is frequently the quick start to a potentially unsuccessful relationship. This can easily happen even when there has been a clear prior agreement as to the level of support to be provided by the foreign partner. If a prospective Korean partner is not willing to seriously invest in product and possibly sales training up front, one may wish to consider walking away. Also, one should keep in mind that if the foreign firm makes a pricing concession for a market entry deal, it may have set the benchmark by which all other deals will be closed in this tight-knit business community.

When it comes to sending support personnel to Korea, the foreign partner draws the line and agrees only to send support staff for limited amounts of time during the course of the project. Usually, the ensuing confusion from the lack of on-site spot support, regardless of the amount of off-shore phone support, leads both parties to agree in retrospect that it would have been cheaper to have kept a foreign partner's support staff on site the entire time.

How Korean firms look at written agreements can be at odds with their foreign partners' perspective. Korean firms look at such agreements as generally acceptable guidelines on how to approach an uncertain future.

In the Korean businessperson's mind, one must be flexible in dealing with discovered realities—even if such accommodation may go against the core of the foreigner's agreement.

If the foreign firm is unfamiliar with doing business in Korea, it becomes exasperatingly difficult to know when to concede in deference to local market requirements and when to say "no." Usually, the vendor-distributor relationship is still green. The matter of trust becomes a serious issue with both sides, where the foreigners start wondering if they are being taken for a ride, while their Korean counterparts start fuming that the foreigners are reneging on prior assurances of being competent and worthy partners.

Normally, one can hide from the customers the temporary disruption or suffering of vendor-distributor relations. If one does not quickly and sufficiently address the matter, however, word will leak out into the market. And in Korea, where personal relationships dictate that friends share almost everything, businesses may find that there are no secrets.

WAR STORIES

In one war story involving partnerships with local distributors, the distributor purposely price-gauged its customers while it possessed a monopoly in the market for a high-tech system. Not stopping there, the distributor disabled some of the product's functionality in order to sell multiples of the product, when a single, fully functional product could have addressed each customer's multiple needs. In the meantime, the distributor reverse-engineered the core product with the intent of introducing a competing "Made in Korea" product that would be not only cheaper, but also more fully functional.

In another war story, a local software distributor provided excessively customized services as a way to sell its services—rather than working closely with a foreign vendor's development staff. After several years, the "Koreanized" solution was so overwhelmingly localized that the core product had become barely recognizable. Consequently, while the rest of the foreign vendor's overseas markets were moving along onto next-generation products, Korean customers lagged behind and often abandoned use of the foreign products, since there was little incentive to upgrade.

In both worst-case scenarios, the common denominator was that there was no one on the ground watching out for the foreign vendors' best interests. At the same time, sending in rescue operatives late in the game can be an exercise in futility, since local practices can position the foreign product as being too expensive, thereby creating major marketing headaches in expanding customer base. Furthermore, customers may already be accustomed to using the products in inappropriate or inefficient ways. Taking corrective measures may cause a great deal of embarrassment within customer organizations. Therefore, much consideration must be given to building successful partnerships with distributors.

POSSIBLE ROLES

The single biggest cause of failure in partnerships between foreign companies and distributors must be conflicting expectations of each other. Rarely does an in-depth conversation take place. While one would assume that such divergent opinions would be resolved in the course of negotiating a sales distribution agreement, too often this turns out not to be the case. Consider the two most common roles of the distributor: those of full representative and midwife, a distributor who knows the marketplace and introduces one's sales and support staff to clientele during and following the sales cycle.

Commonly found in the case of cutting-edge products and technologies, and often expensive, midwives allow the foreign company to get close to the customer base and have greater control over how the customer base buys and implements one's product. In the end, this knowledge can be critical, as it may be very difficult—if not impossible—to move the customer base along to the next generation of products and services if the distributor improperly sells or implements the product.

A full representative, on the other hand, is a distributor who is fully trained and able to conduct the entire sales cycle; it is also capable of providing primary or level-one technical or after-sales support to local customers. Full representation is often applicable to a product or service that may be unique in terms of features and functions, but is already familiar to the market and is composed of qualities or technologies well understood by the after-sales staff.

The obvious drawback with the full representative is that it essentially "owns" its share of the market and will often keep the foreign partner away from the customer base out of fear that the foreign company may go around it in the future. Also, while end-user pricing methods undisclosed to the foreign firm may bring short-term windfalls to the distributor, it may deny the foreign firm future sales as the local market seeks less expensive alternatives.

GETTING UP TO SPEED

In any event, the end goal for foreign companies is to have their distributors be as competent as possible. Too often, foreign enterprises believe that by training the sales and after-sales staff in their product or service, they will soon be able to rely on the distributor. Yet when the first major strategic sales opportunity takes place, the distributor and the foreign company suddenly find themselves at odds, no matter how clearly the distribution agreement may have been written.

Even if there is full review between the foreign partner and distributor, both sides often underestimate the difficulty in getting the local staff properly trained. Local employees tend to be a bit overconfident in their knowledge attainment, and foreign firms tend to be a bit too eager to accept their Korean partners' assurances.

The biggest cause of disappointment may be the communication barrier between foreign support staff and local line staff. While local employees can read English fairly or extremely well, they usually find themselves at a total loss when it comes to phone conferences. Furthermore, they may seem to understand what is said during product training, when in fact they are getting less than half of the delivered content. All of this has a nasty way of being revealed when the pressure is on to meet what a foreign firm may consider an unrealistic or overly aggressive deadline established by, or based on, sales promises given to the prospective customer.

KEYS TO SUCCESS

Given the above, one may wonder how one can be successful in Korea without a direct presence here. One way is to limit one's expectations of success and allow a business acquaintance, someone whom one may have met at a trade show, or whomever to sell the least difficult product to a small part of the market. The danger with this strategy, of course, is that one may end up with expensive support of one-off sales in Korea while missing a potentially larger and more profitable market.

A more effective alternative is to find an agent who has a fair appreciation for doing business in Korea and abroad and who can actively keep one in touch with one's distributor and the marketplace. Working with the distributor at least on a weekly basis, the agent stays up to date on the distributor's staff, prospects, and customers in order to advise both foreign firm and local partner on small, conflicting matters before they fester into major issues.

A good example of this involves the timeliness of communication. In a culture that stresses "Just do it now!" Koreans are often exasperated by the slow response they get from their foreign partners. Time differences in global partnerships can be equally irritating for both partners, but it is often difficult for Koreans to appreciate that the foreign partner is trying to systematically service multiple concurrent market needs and that Koreans' demands are not cued to the front upon demand. At the same time, foreign partners are often slow to understand and appreciate the time and emotional demands that customers and prospects routinely place on Korean distributors.

With concise and timely communication of issues, the agent may allow for the foreign firm to make effective decisions, and in the meantime assist the local distributor in understanding the benefits behind certain management practices (such as frequent sales forecasts and adherence to business plans). Upgrading performance through experience-based consulting—including the evaluation or suggestion of alternative sales strategies, uncovering hidden conflicting agendas, and provision of results-oriented sales training—is also a possibility. Note that foreign firms and their distributors tend to spend a great deal of resources on product training and assume the sales employees already possess effective skills from their years of experience. "Relationship selling" is essential to sales strategies in both Korea (friendship-weighted) and the U.S. ("professionalism"-weighted); engaging in just one form of relationship selling may very possibly result in market areas being inadequately explored.

In the end, the decision to establish indirect sales in Korea must be made in conjunction with the question, "Who is going to keep an eye on the store?" After all, one's local partner will be selling one's product, advancing one's brand, and largely determining the success of one's company in this economy.

25. RELATING TO BUREAUCRATS

The influence of governments on economy and business seems to be becoming more pervasive in both developed and developing countries. Even nations that regard themselves as being founded on a laissez-faire, political/economic structure of free enterprise are increasingly bound to governmental regulations. In this respect, Korea is no exception. Foreign businessmen often experience frustration and express the need for assistance in the delicate matters of dealing with the various Korean government regulations and bureaucracy. Common topics include:

- the government's role in economic and social development,

- the historical background of the bureaucracy,

- the decision-making process of government officials, and

- ways of dealing successfully with officials.

THE ROLE OF GOVERNMENT

Behind Korea's near-miraculous economic development are the bureaucrats who have envisioned, designed, guided and implemented various development plans with zeal and dedication. Two generations of bright and far-sighted economic planners/technocrats have successfully managed the transformation of one of the world's most backward economies into a developed country in less than five decades. They deserve much credit for their composition and orchestration of an extraordinary economic achievement.

Among the initial factors contributing to this economic success, government bureaucrats played a major role in laying the foundations for industrialization, such as establishing social overhead capital and other infrastructure. They infused a positive mental attitude or "can do" spirit in the people, and they set priorities for the most efficient utilization of limited resources.

At the same time, the Korean government has blocked business initiatives by design or by ignorance. In worst-case scenarios, the government has taken an openly adversarial approach when political agendas dictate, as has been the case in the past with local companies like Daewoo and Kukje. In other words, the Korean government can work for one or against one, and much of that may depend on how well one's company works with the bureaucrats, as well as how politicians view one's Korean operations.

BUREAUCRATIC TRADITION

Confucian Background

Despite exposure to and adoption of such Western concepts as individualism, egalitarianism, and mass participation, Korea's traditional Confucian authoritarian structure is still very much entrenched, especially within governmental officialdom. Under this Confucian vertical hierarchy, the ruler or king, the public official, the man, the father, the elder and the scholar constitute the superior class—in contrast to the corresponding inferiors: subjects/citizens, women, children, the younger, the unlearned and private citizens.

This hierarchical system has changed drastically, however, as a result of the extensive economic transformation of society. The Korean War also disrupted much of the old traditional value system. While people still tend to submit to political authority and bureaucrats tend to impose themselves on the people as the superior ruling class, since the last generation some intellectuals have been resisting this hierarchical patronage and have become more self-assertive. Still, such deep-rooted social norms and conventions do not change overnight. The conflict between the traditional ways and modern developments is often evident.

Self-Preservation

The real power for change in the bureaucracy is at the director (*samu-gwan*) and deputy sub-director (*gwa-jang*) levels. Although the people holding these positions are relatively low in the bureaucratic hierarchy, they are the gatekeepers. Only through their direct involvement do documents move upward to the ministers who make the actual decisions. They are personally responsible for specific bodies of regulations. At the same time, like his or her counterparts in other countries, the bureaucrat's primary instinct is for self-preservation. Under the bureaucratic system, one's position is usually secure as long as one does not make any major blunders. The three things that the mid-level bureaucrats do not wish are: 1) to be discovered making the wrong decisions by internal and external government auditors, 2) to hear from their senior officials that the directors-general are saying, "The mid-level is making my life miserable," and 3) to cause their ministry to be chastised by the press or questioned by higher-level government bodies, including the Presidential or Prime Ministerial offices. Therefore, officials naturally tend to be quite prudent in handling affairs in the private business sector, lest a hasty decision cause adverse repercussions and thus jeopardize their positions.

Often, problems are caused by lower-level bureaucrats who don't understand the issues, including when change is in Korea's overall best interest. Rather, the bureaucrat is preoccupied with questions like, "Why should I take the initiative to open this market segment?" These same government people work with regulations consisting of rules that are often not very transparent and are open to conflicting interpretations, requiring an official and final decision through the appropriate individual *samu-gwan*'s interpretation, or "*yugwan heseok*."

To make things even riskier for these bureaucrats, they live in a society where the Korean media often do not understand the issues, and thus create unfair pressures on the government decision-makers. So even when a *samu-gwan* has a good grasp on the issue at hand, he or she may not be interested in taking the right initiative if the press is critical of the issue—he or she needs to be concerned about being unfairly criticized by the press. The bureaucrats are also subject to public censure by members of the National Assembly and NGO leaders—both groups notorious for making irresponsible statements and allegations.

Given the above, the best thing a bureaucrat can do is to do nothing, or to be convinced that something needs to be done as a defense against the pressures mentioned above. Consequently, whatever strategy one employs to change a regulation, it is normally essential to take the time and effort for long-term education of the middle bureaucracy. One may often get the impression that officials are "dragging their feet" or are being evasive or non-committal, and this is because officials are overly sensitive about the long-term security of their positions.

Centralized Decisions—Important but Overestimated

It is generally accepted that the top official is ultimately responsible for any adverse results from decisions made by his or her subordinates, even though he or she may not have been directly involved. One sometimes sees a top government minister resigning, taking the responsibility for an accidental blunder made by lower-level officials—which may even have transpired during his predecessor's term of office. Due to this centralized decision-making process and responsibility system, the approval process is often extended to include the top level of the bureaucratic hierarchy, even for minor issues, which makes the procedure more complicated and time-consuming.

Yet with the above in mind, it should be pointed out that one of the most common—and expensive—errors foreign firms make in trying to effect change is focusing too much time and money on the top officials, who are often rotated among bureaucracies, and even in and out of government, by the winds of politics. It is the lower-level professional bureaucrats who make careers of managing laws and regulations, and it is ultimately they who have the most power in many cases.

An all-too-common scenario runs like this: an expatriate country manager discovers a regulation that prevents his company from being as successful as it should be in the Korean market. He then reports the matter to the regional or global head office. The issue is then vetted by internal or external legal counsel, who normally have only peripheral knowledge of Korea at best. These lawyers then contact an international law firm in Seoul, which often boasts of having on its payroll former ministers who can certainly get the regulations changed by their influence. While this may sound optimal at first, there are in fact several war stories where firms have spent literally millions of dollars in reimbursed expenses and legal fees over months and even years—often, in the end, without the desired results.

PENETRATING THE BUREAUCRACY

One needs to understand why change is or is not appropriate from all sides of the issue. If the regulatory change benefits only one's company, one's chances for change are about nil—no matter whom one may be hiring to influence the powers that be. However, if one's desired change also benefits domestic companies, one may have a 90 percent chance of success. Whenever one can also help other Korean industry members, the chances are good that they will climb on to the bandwagon.

In any event, it is critical to analyze the risks of change from the bureaucrats' point of view. At the same time, one should be prepared to do all the legwork so that it is as easy as possible for the relevant ministry to act. Government relations doesn't need to be about lobbying with excessive entertaining. If one has a good reason for the government to change something, then one should make it a real issue. Don't blame the bureaucrats. If one doesn't know which bureaucrat controls the regulation one wishes to change, one should get an organization chart. From that, one can usually find the right person.

Makings of a Suitable Climate

Nothing is more powerful than public opinion in influencing officials. Public opinion is an effective prelude to facilitate official approval. Support from other parties directly or indirectly related to the respective government authority can also help to open the door for rapport and confidence. If one can discover some group or club to which the official is related, contacting someone in that organization could bring out some common ground or method of approach that might create the climate for favorable communication. The influence of peer persuasion must never be underestimated.

Taking advantage of informal, neutral contacts with government officials, even when there is no immediate need for their intervention, could pave the way for future requests. Keeping them informed of the beneficial work one is doing or intends to do is of the utmost importance. Then, when they are needed, the stage has already been set for instant communication and time-saving considerations. Good PR is an indispensable ingredient of business success, not only for building a good image among the general public but also in dealing with authorities.

Sufficient Document Justification

The better justified an application is, the higher the chances of it getting an approval—whether to secure an import license or make a major investment. The regulations governing business procedures generally provide broad guidelines, leaving a wide range of discretion and interpretation up to the responsible officials. Written rules often do not cover all the aspects of private business ventures. These rules are usually in a constant state of flux and change anyway. So related authorities often must make judgments based on the spirit and intent of general guidelines, thus allowing them some range for interpretation and flexibility.

The foreign investment venture's justification should underscore the benefits to the host country in terms of technology development, employment and exports. Hitting all these targets can more readily enlist the favorable attention of officials. An application's preparation requires a great deal of skill and tact and could be compared with writing a good résumé. Sometimes one must be creative in formulating sufficient justification in order to fulfill the requirements, but may only need to be nominally specific in meeting the letter of the law and relevant regulations. In lieu of this, it is often desirable to engage professional services for advice in formulating and presenting sensitive applications to the authorities.

Accommodate Their Disposition

Some bureaucrats tend to be more bureaucratic than necessary at times. Some authorities seem to have a certain "compensatory mentality." Most officials, especially in the economic ministries, are the "cream of the nation's crop," being products of Korea's best education. It is not uncommon to find officials with prestigious overseas university degrees. They are not, however, on par financially with their peers in the private sector. While this public sector/private sector disparity may be true in many countries, the inequality can be a reason for some bureaucratic excesses that surface from time to time.

To counteract such attitudes requires a great deal of humility and patience. These people are, in fact, respected officials of Korea, and to show deference and respect will only enhance the chances of one receiving what one wants to secure. Rather than taking the attitude of negotiating as equal partners, taking instead the position of asking a favor will be received with more cooperation from them. Outside intervention should be utilized with tact. Often, direct pressure from "the ambassador" or "the official delegation" can be risky. This tactic could cause the local official to "lose face" and disturb his or her "*gibun*." The final result could be very disappointing.

Be Patient Yet Persistent

There are occasions when the government's policies are not clear, or a certain regulation may be outdated and require amendment for the benefit of the interested parties. Occasionally, one may even experience differences of opinion or policy among concerned ministries. For a government agency or a group of officials to firm up a policy or formal opinion usually entails considerable time and "noise level" by those who seek a resolution of the situation. Time is one of the most important resources for business, and one may not be able to wait to embark on a formidable task in moving this immense bureaucracy toward the desired course. If, however, one's position is in line with the general policy direction, it may be advisable to bide one's time, while still maintaining a presence through regular communication. Past examples of success attest to the virtue and merit of being patient yet persistent in dealing with certain official rules and regulations.

DELEGATE OFFICIAL CONTACTS TO ASSOCIATES

Rather than having an expatriate deal directly with government officials, a qualified associate or an intermediary may prove far more effective. A local co-worker may be more intimidated by authoritarian officials, but at the same time, he or she can tolerate the sometimes unpleasant attitude of a government official more than an impatient expatriate. The foreigner can become quite irritated at an unkind official who is blatantly showing his or her authority, and could destroy lines of communication to the point of hopelessly losing his or her case.

To summarize the advantages of utilizing a Korean co-worker:

- he or she is more familiar with protocol and the political nuances of delicate dealings with officials, such as "face,"

- he or she is more at ease in the communication process due to using the same language, and

- he or she is more in tune with the cultural mores and conventions affecting relationships with officials.

EMPLOYING GOVERNMENT RELATIONS SPECIALISTS

If one does not have the resources to have a Korean employee be the ongoing representative to the bureaucracy, and/or if one's need is clearly beyond one's capacity to handle an issue on one's own, one may consider hiring the services of a government relations firm.

Contrary to many foreign companies' expectations, attorney firms are often not be the best places to turn for government relations. Usually they are not the most cost-effective. Law firms play critical roles in many international business matters, but cost-effective—or even simply effective—government relations is not one of their strong points. Government relations also requires much more than just very long-term relations with key people in the government and staying on top of who's who, particularly with annual administrative shuffling of government personnel. A savvy government relations firm is creative and capable of launching a multi-pronged strategy that may require going beyond what one would normally consider part of government relations.

Having stated the above, one needs to recognize that the Attorneys' Act reserves to attorneys alone the right to interface with the government on behalf of a third party when such activity is undertaken for a fee. Korean law restricts paid lobbying to attorneys only. People who offer government relations consulting must work with attorneys to avoid violating the Attorneys' Act.

However, for other more mundane, less politically sensitive activities at government offices on behalf of third parties, including foreign companies, a non-lawyer is permitted to provide services for a fee at government offices, provided the person has notarized "power of attorney (POA)" specifically authorizing him or her to perform stated tasks (on behalf of said third party) at government offices.

For example, if a foreign company wants to register a branch or local company in Korea or submit applications for foreign investment, the company is permitted to issue POA to anyone it wishes to make inquiries, interface with appropriate government offices, and prepare and submit applications on its behalf in Korea. The POA also allows the individual to take other actions on the company's behalf with government (and private) offices at the principal's instruction and as specified in the POA—even if that party is not a lawyer.

Not all law firms will agree with the above. Some law firms may try to interpret the Attorneys' Act to mean that only a licensed Korean lawyer is permitted to act on behalf of a third party (foreign company, in this case) for any and all activities that involve any and all government offices. Yet foreign companies have proceeded with non-attorneys who have received POA authorization to provide services on behalf of the foreign company, with no problems or objections whatsoever at the several concerned government offices. Nonetheless, in the course of carrying out services in Korea for foreign companies, many consultants routinely hire a law firm to review legal documentation, especially complex contracts.

To understand how a true government relations firm handles issues, please consider the following from one such firm, Saturn Communications, which has developed the "Mimas" Issue Management Model. This model uses supporting facts and information to reinforce awareness and to develop interests via an issue management model based on how messages are developed and used to create awareness, develop interest and induce action.

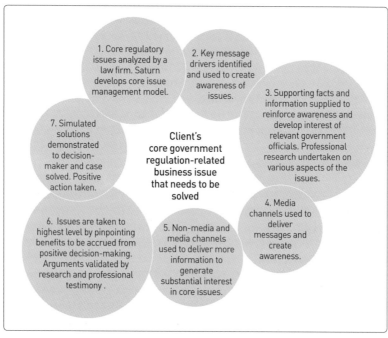

Figure 26.1

Some hypotheses used by Saturn in developing and implementing the above Mimas Management Model are as follows:

1. Bureaucrats at all levels are patriots—they genuinely love their country.

2. Bureaucrats normally do not have negative views of foreign companies as long as their goals do not harm Korea's national interests.

3. All work regarding the regulatory issue is carried out by a deputy director-level official with about 10 years of experience.

4. A director supervises the deputy director, but the director generally does not give a clear direction to the deputy director on how to handle the issue. There are exceptions. An instruction may come from the top (minister, prime minister, or the president's office), and the deputy director may not have a say.

5. The positive or negative personal view of a deputy director, although his job is a mechanical one and is the starting point of the long process of documentation, is important in writing the first argument about the issue that is dear to the foreign company.

6. A deputy director or his immediate supervisor will be the one investigated by the auditor's office if anything goes wrong, including an instance of bad media coverage regarding the issue.

7. A foreign company must understand how the issue will be processed. Sometimes cooperation between different departments of the same ministry is required, so there is no guarantee that both departments will agree on how important the issue may be.

8. The role of the director-general is important. A director reports to the director-general, who is the most senior working-level official. The director-general must be convinced of the importance of the issue. Typically, a director-general reports directly to the minister. However, this is not true in all cases. The foreign company must verify before putting the issue into motion within the bureaucracy.

9. Some issues require inter-ministerial cooperation. One ministry may believe that the issue is important to the Korean economy or industry, but another ministry may have a totally different view.

10. The National Assembly must be completely informed, and the foreign company must convince the National Assembly that the issue is important for Korea and Korean industry.

11. Never go to the government and seek a regulatory change if the beneficiary is only one's company.

12. Hire a professional PR company. Don't hire a PR company because of its name. Young, untrained, and unprofessional PR men or women do not understand how the issue must be handled. Issues management expertise normally must be found outside of one's company. It requires a high level of understanding and contacts. Saturn Communications, for example, does not do PR itself, but hires outside PR agencies. In Korea, finding a PR company among the hundreds that understand the dynamics of issue management is like finding a needle in a haystack. This is because issue management is a new area of PR with fewer practitioners.

13. Educate, educate, and educate all—including the doorman at the ministry.

14. Law firms alone cannot do the work—they are handicapped by their own limitations of being lawyers.

15. Never hire a broker (except a securities broker to buy stocks).

16. Never pay a penny to anyone during the entire process. Keep the process transparent. Don't buy expensive dinners or treat bureaucrats in a room salon.

17. Don't give gifts. If anyone is asking for one or hinting to receive one, walk out.
18. Don't talk to reporters about the issue unless advised by your issues manager in advance. They can kill the issue by misreporting.

19. When you hire an issues manager, trust the manager. If you cannot trust him or her, then don't hire him or her.

20. Don't demand too much documentation from the issues manager. Sometimes the issues manager does a lot of work on the phone without leaving a paper trail.

21. A good issues manager hires a lawyer when documentation is required.

22. Issues management is the other name of transparent and scientific lobbying.

The above is not a template on how to effect change. Each case is different and requires different tactics and strategies. The above, however, is a good list of principles and illustrates what is often needed in addition to creativity, patience, and tact; all of this is more involved than paying a lobbyist to play golf with high-level government officials.

When thinking about how to change a regulation, it's important to keep in mind the following:

- Each case needs a different approach.
- One needs to be very, very patient.
- Government employees are usually positive, but they will ask, "Why should we change?"
- Distill big reports and analyses into simple, short reports translated into Korean.
- Work with the media intelligently.
- If one is in regulatory jeopardy, it is because one has not succeeded with the right director.
- If the change is not good for Korean companies as well as one's own, one needs to find a way that the bureaucrats, too, will benefit. Otherwise, one probably needs to adjust one's Korean business model.

MAINTAIN CONTACT

Depending on the size and type of a business, there are situations where there is no need for government sanction. Many business activities of private industries, however, are under the jurisdiction of some sort of government rule or decree. It is therefore desirable to open and maintain channels of communication with the relevant authorities, even though there may be no immediate need for their consideration. The problem in trying to maintain continual contact is that career officials are often transferred from one position to another and/or promoted to higher positions; they do, however, usually remain within the same department, ministry, or agency.

So once a tie is established, especially without involving any immediate business interests, the relationship may prove to be beneficial—if not necessarily for any specific favor, then as a permanent source of advice and information that may be of invaluable help some time in the future. At the same time, it is in everyone's best interest for one to constantly educate the government official about current events and changes in one's industry.

WHY ALL THE SCANDALS?

A regular feature of Korean newspapers is the latest corruption scandal.

As already noted, regulations are often opaque—sometimes intentionally so—and very often too restrictive. This can be as big of a problem for Korean companies as for foreign ones. Unlike foreign companies, which frequently rely on lawyers, most Korean companies use "professional brokers"—famous individuals of influence (*al'eum al'eum*) who can act on their behalf with the government. These brokers are so well known in their industries that Korean companies conclude without question that they must employ them to achieve their goals.

The problem is that eventually, these power brokers trip up in their influence-peddling, and often are not able to completely cover their tracks when lobbying for other firms. So when a broker gets investigated, all of his or her past as well as current clients get exposed.

Moral of this story: One should work with one's staff or "above-board" professionals and avoid relying on special influence brokers (even if one's employees recommend them).

26. GETTING YOUR PRODUCTS TO MARKET

O f all this book's topics, product distribution is by far the most rapidly changing. The proliferation of new retail models, from corner convenience stores to mega-warehouse discounters, has created a revolution in Korea. But even that is only second to the sea change being created by television, the Internet, and wireless phone retailing.

It was not so long ago that the manufacturer was king and set most of the terms and conditions for wholesalers and retailers. The reason was simple: manufacturers were the heroes of Korea's "economic miracle," with the best exporting goods in exchange for badly needed hard currency. Logistics systems were multi-layered, strangled on an evolving transportation infrastructure, with most goods destined for final sale via tens of thousands of tiny retailers.

Since the 1970s, Korea's highways, railways, ports, and airports have all matured to world-class status. While "mom and pop" retailers are still largely responsible for most points of sale, they are under a multi-front attack that dooms most to extinction in the coming decades. Two of their three largest competitors, convenience stores and discount warehouse retailers, have been around for a quarter century. But the traditional retailer's executioner may be the third competitor, online retailing, which is now starting to achieve its full potential.

MAJOR RETAIL CHAINS

Historically, and even to this day in rural Korea, the traditional retail exchange has been the village market day (*jangnal*), which takes place about every five days. Surrounding the market square have been small retailers who have serviced the consumers on non-market days as well as on *jangnal*.

The first major advance from this retail model came during the Japanese occupation when the first department stores, such as Mitsukoshi, established Seoul branch stores. Since the Japanese managed these operations, only Seoul benefited from this kind of consolidated retailing. Unlike Western department stores, however, manufacturers and wholesalers established individual retail operations under a single roof in these high-rises rather than selling to the department store at wholesale. In other words, one may say that the village market place had been consolidated, to a large degree, into a single building.

In 1945, the Korean government took over Mitsukoshi Department Store in Seoul. The store was eventually sold to Samsung Group, which renamed the store "Shinsegae." For many years, Shinsegae continued to represent the epitome of Korean retailing, although most of the old Mitsukoshi practices continued essentially unchanged. From this model, other department stores were established.

Today, Korean department stores are sparkling merchandisers of the widest array of goods in a single location. But since they are actually comprised of competing retailers on each floor, there is often a great deal of redundancy that offers the consumer benefits of price competition even as the buyer must work to find the right item among the superfluity of vendors. While there is prestige in giving gifts or being known as a regular customer of a major department store that sells high-quality products at premium pricing, the stores are rarely located near most consumers. Consequently, except for those wealthy in time as well as money (and an interesting class of addicted department store buyers who shop at least every other day), buying at a department store has been more the exception than the rule.

In more recent years, specialized super department stores have evolved, specializing as electronics or garment mega-markets. While successful as attractive consumer magnets, these specialized markets have greatly emulated and amplified the department stores' redundancy factor. In recent years, the major mega-electronics stores have fallen behind the discount warehouse stores. Whereas these specialized super-department stores need to retain 25 percent of retail prices to survive, the new discount warehouse stores can do well with only 10 to 15 percent margins due to high volume and stronger price negotiating power with manufacturers. Nonetheless, department stores' sales remain impressive. The total sales for these stores in 2005 were 16.5 trillion won—more than US$16 billion.

CONVENIENCE STORES

The first two competitors to department stores arrived in the mid 1990s: convenience stores and large discount (warehouse) stores.

The first Korean convenience store, an investment by Japan's 7-Eleven chain, began operation in 1989 in the Jamsil part of southeastern Seoul, shortly after the 1988 Olympics. One year later, the first truly Korean convenience store, GS Retail's LG25 (forerunner of GS25), began operations. While steady progress occurred during the initial years, 2001 was a turning point when new store numbers began to skyrocket. In 2006 alone, over 10,000 new (not net additional) stores were added at a growth of more than 12 percent over the previous year's number of stores. In 2005, the turnover at a total of 9,085 convenience stores totaled 4.6 trillion won—almost US$5 billion. In November 2006, the Chosun Ilbo newspaper reported estimates that 2006's annual total would be greater than 5 trillion won, with more than 10,000 stores in operation by year's end. As of January 2006, about five million people stopped by convenience stores per day—compared to four million at discount stores and three million at traditional department stores.

The number of convenience stores, meanwhile, surged to 8,855 from 1,557, increasing 20 percent on average every year from 1999 to 2008. Retail outlets also surged explosively to 316 from a mere 25 a dozen years before, growing 28.9 percent on average each year during the 1999 to 2008 period.

Korean convenience stores are following the Japanese example in many ways. Besides providing the most common goods in an efficient manner, Korean convenience stores now offer consumers the convenience to pay utility bills, cell phone charges, Internet fees, and newspaper subscriptions. Varying on the chain, these stores are providing local outlets for banking, post, photo finishing, and even auto and accident insurance. In July 2006, Shinhan Bank installed retail banking services in Lotte Mart, Korea's third largest convenience store chain. Since then, other banks have followed suit.

While large discounters and department stores offer a larger variety of goods, often at cheaper prices, they almost invariably require a special effort to commute and find parking. And once the consumer is inside, it can be a major physical effort to track down the targeted product. Most convenience stores, on the other hand, are roughly 82.5 square meters in size and within a minute's walk from one's residence or place of work. In fact, many people pick up their prepared breakfast and lunch meals from these mini retailers.

As of this writing, the top convenience store chains were 7-Eleven, Buy The Way, FamilyMart, and Ministop. In addition, there are hybrid large-chain convenience stores such as Tesco's Homeplus Express.

LARGE DISCOUNT (WAREHOUSE) STORES

In 1994, Costco entered a JV with Shinsegae Department Store to create Korea's first major discount store in Seoul, Price Club Korea. In the period leading up to the Asian financial crisis three years later, the two partners learned from each other. Shinsegae became familiar with warehouse-like discount superstores, and Costco learned about Korean retailing. The two companies split apart, with Costco buying out most of Shinsegae's interests in the three existing stores for US$94 million. While Costco has so far failed to meet its plans to expand to a total of ten stores (as of 2010, there are seven stores in Korea), its Seoul stores have become its most profitable stores worldwide, specializing in the retail of imported goods at low prices.

Meanwhile, stodgy Shinsegae, Korea's oldest department store, took its lesson and launched E-Mart, a hybrid of a Costco operation and what the Koreans guessed (correctly) might work best in Korea. Free from partner consensus, E-Mart started aggressively buying up cheap parcels of land and opening ten new stores annually. Listening to Korean consumers, who liked the cheap prices but felt uncomfortable with bulk purchases, E-Mart offered discounted pricing in smaller quantities and in familiar environments similar to conventional department stores, rather than warehouses. Furthermore, E-Mart—and other Korean major discounters—also offer more fresh produce and feature special in-store events. Korean discounters also provide additional retail experiences such as fast food outlets, food stalls, and full restaurants.

Within a few years, E-Mart moved to the number one slot and represented as much as one-third of discount retail sales in 2009, with sales amounting to a figure roughly in excess of US$9.4 billion. That figure represented about 80 percent of Shinsegae's total retail sales of 10.4 trillion generated by seventy-one stores in 2004; by 2010, there were 127 stores (including 16 Wal-Mart outlets), plus 24 in China. In many ways, E-Mart has become the model that Lotte Mart (as of 2006, 47 outlets with US$4 billion in sales), Home Plus (as of 2010, 66 outlets, among Tesco Korea's 347 stores) and others have followed.

France's Carrefour and America's Wal-Mart took a more Western approach in line with their global strategies—and proved to be much less successful than the market leaders. Britain's Tesco PLC, which partnered with the Samsung Group to form Samsung Home Plus, had done better than other foreign investors in this market sector. In fact, in 2004 Home

Plus ranked second in the market after E-Mart, with annual revenues of US$3.5 billion generated by 31 stores. And today, Tesco's most valuable market outside of Britain is South Korea, with 111 hypermarkets and 134 Home Plus Express smaller stores generating some US$4.57 billion in sales. With some 20,000 employees in Korea, there are just four expatriate managers, even though the shareholding is 95 percent British.

Wal-Mart had only 16 stores in Korea, with just one store in the Seoul metropolitan area. As a result, it could not achieve economies of scale, and most Koreans did not become familiar with the company's name. Furthermore, the high shelving and bulk packaging, which were beyond most local consumers' imagination, put off Korean shoppers. Later, Wal-Mart moved to break down the bulk packaging, but it was too late. In May 2006, Wal-Mart sold all 16 stores to E-Mart owner Shinsegae for 825 billion won (approximately US$825 million).

In 2006, Carrefour profitably sold its Korean operations to E-Land—originally a fashion retail company, but one with superior logistics and distribution outlets capable of handling a wider variety of goods. Some industry observers have suggested the French company was too bureaucratic and slow to discoveries to adapt to new Korean market conditions. Others, on the other hand, believe the Carrefour business managers felt overly constrained by Korean regulations when their know-how could be better placed in other key markets, such as Eastern Europe and China. In any event, in 2008 the 36 E-Land Homever stores were absorbed by Tesco Samsung's Home Plus department store chain.

Nationwide, sales for all large discount stores came to 21.4 trillion won, or more than US$20 billion

ONLINE RETAILERS

As one foreign consumer products company country manager put it, "Technology is changing Korea!" Korea is one of the most advanced countries in the world when it comes to high-speed Internet and cell phone penetration. According to the International Telecommunication Union in November 2009, nine out of ten Koreans use a cell phone. That is, Koreans maintain 43.5 million mobile phone subscriptions—or 90.2 for every 100 residents. Back in 1960, South Korea had only one telephone for every 300 people—barely one-tenth of the world average at the time. By 2005, more than 90% of households had a fixed-line phone, three times the world average. Moreover, five years ago, three-quarters of the population carried mobile phones, which meant that almost everyone had one, other than very young children and very elderly people. With government encouragement and the benefit of a densely populated, mainly urban environment, South Korea has been relatively easy to wire up. Today, apartment blocks display government notices by the front door certifying the speed of their internet connection.

There has been incredible growth behind home shopping channels and Internet channels, all of which provides great access to Korean consumers. It is now possible for a company to get its own shopping mall on the Internet and to explore new sales and marketing innovations.

TV Home Shopping

In 1996, Korea's TV home shopping industry came into existence. TV home shopping sharply expanded during the first two years of the new millennium, averaging over 60 percent growth annually. In 2003, due to an economic downturn and a drop in number of new cable subscribers, the industry's growth slowed to 10 percent, with total market sales of about US$3.5 billion.

The first two TV home shopping operators were LG and CJ, later joined by Hyundai, Woori and Nongsusan in 2001. Since then, Hyundai has made the most aggressive advances in terms of sales, market share and customer satisfaction. All five of these original operators provide Internet and catalog shopping services reaching an estimated 12 million cable-connected television receivers.

2006 and 2007 were also difficult years for Korea's TV home shopping industry. The latest hope for the industry is T-Commerce, where viewers use a special remote control device rather than phoning in a purchase request. Since this is supposed to be easier than making a purchase over the Internet and web sites, there are some very sanguine forecasts. Only time will tell if this will jumpstart the electronic commerce channel.

While TV home shopping remains a strong and competitive retail channel, the fastest-growing channel has been and continues to be the Internet.

Cybermalls

As of October 2005, according to the Korea National Statistical Office, there were 2,229 Korean cybermalls, mainly dealing in retail e-commerce transactions between business and consumer—an increase of 22.2 percent year-on-year. In October 2005, clothing/fashion and related goods made up 17.2 percent of all cybermall purchases, followed by home electric appliances/electronics/telecommunications equipment (16.7 percent), travel arrangement and reservation services (13.2 percent), household goods/motor vehicle parts and accessories (10.5 percent), and computers and computer-related appliances (9.4 percent).

Not content with conventional Internet shopping malls, Korean Internet retailers are constantly trying to upgrade the shopper's experience. For example, in 2006 GSeshop installed on its web site a 3-D depiction of a department store, where visitors can click on displayed products on the shelves. Not to be outdone, GSeshop's competitor CJ Mall began screening live broadcasts on its shopping site. Similarly to television home shopping, a "shopping jockey" introduces various goods and chats in real time with potential customers, answering their questions on the spot.

Today, online retailing has been a boon for delivery companies and a bane for Korean drivers, who find the roads even more congested thanks to delivery motorcycles and trucks. And it is no wonder, considering that in 2006, total sales for all Korean online retailers were as much as US$14 billion. However, that includes online retailing from brick-and-mortar establishments such as major discount stores and department stores. In fact, online sales by these two major retail sectors have been larger than for the pure online Internet shopping malls.

There are specific problems, however, with Korean online retailing. Consumers have often complained about ending up with different products than were displayed. And not surprisingly, there can be serious customer dissatisfaction caused by product size and specification disputes. Finally, some online retailers may find themselves in legal jeopardy by unwittingly acting as jobbers for potentially dangerous products, such as high-pressure air guns.

27. SELECTING YOUR DISTRIBUTION SYSTEM

*T*here are several distribution systems operating in Korea. An observant marketing manager can find advantages and disadvantages in each system and must choose the one(s) most appropriate for his or her product line.

MAJOR CHANNELS

General Trading Companies & Importers

Imported products, such as high-priced consumer products and household durables, can be distributed through the large general trading companies or by the importers themselves. Their distribution channels have been in existence for quite some time and are therefore relatively well developed.

Manufacturers, however, maintain very little control over this distribution system. There is also limited potential for growth with many of these products, as their high prices push them into the upper end of the market. A few notable exceptions to this rule do exit, however.

Distributors

The importance of independent distributors to the growth of Korean industry has been recognized, and their development is proceeding at a rapid pace. Department stores and supermarket and convenience store chains, as well as major discount stores, have proven popular. But they now have gigantic purchasing power and routinely demand—and get— exceptional pricing, as well as supplier-financed promotions.

Manufacturers

Often, goods can be distributed through channels established by other manufacturers. Such a mutually beneficial move serves to expand and diversify one's product line. It also allows one to utilize one's distribution system to its full capacity by accepting products from other manufacturers. Here, it is important that the products of the two manufacturers in question be compatible in nature—i.e., related but not directly competitive. Consumer and food and beverage companies are particularly well suited to use Korean manufacturers' logistics and distribution systems. Some companies, such as Nongshim, a manufacturer of instant noodles, have excellent distribution and inventory control systems down to the neighborhood mom and pop store level. Partnering with such a company may maximize possible market penetration.

Partner/Parent JV Company

In a JV relationship, the local partner/parent company usually distributes the products of its subsidiary. In this situation as in all business encounters, good, cordial working relationships are absolutely necessary for success. One should also provide proper motivation to the Korean partner's sales force for their "stepbrother products," since one cannot simply assume they will push one's products as aggressively as their parent's goods.

In-House Distribution

Distribution is one of the most important factors affecting the success or failure of a consumer product. This basic fact reveals the critical nature of the control of distribution channels. Although costly in terms of time and money, the establishment of one's own distribution system can be greatly beneficial in the long run. Such a plan should be executed gradually over a period of time: product by product, segment by segment, and region by region. As long as one maintains a sustainable comparative advantage, developing one's own distribution is desirable.

EFFECTIVE DISTRIBUTION PROCEDURES

Select Distributors Carefully

Since the role of distributors is so important, one has to pay careful attention to their capabilities before making a commitment to any one of them. Consider in depth their strengths and weaknesses, and in channels such as supermarkets vs. convenience stores; also, weigh qualities such as regional strength and merchandising capabilities. One must also compare the compatibility of their existing products with one's own and investigate the financial stability and reputation of the owner. Try to be open-minded about retail venues such as television home shopping, the Internet and cell-phone purchasing. Korea is more advanced in these areas than most countries, including those of the West.

Build Relationships

Whether one distributes directly to the consumer or to wholesalers or JV partners, personal relationships play a major role in business transactions. Business must be regarded as the building of a network of relationships. Without such a network, it is extremely difficult for a business to be prosperous. Although time-consuming and costly to build, relationships, once established, are both durable and profitable.

Expand Gradually

The concentration of population in urban areas makes expansion relatively easy, especially in physical distribution. Companies with limited resources may take a step-by-step approach by region, such as starting with Seoul and its metropolitan area, which usually represent half of the market, and perhaps later the three major cities of Busan, Daegu and Gwangju and the rest of the country. If a wide range of products is involved, a product-by-product approach may be taken. Innovative online distribution can make one's products available nationwide immediately.

Maintain a "Feel for the Market"

Closeness to the market is one of the major traits common among large and successful Korean corporations. The local market is quite dynamic, and the pace of change—often at Internet speed—is so rapid that lucrative opportunities may pass one by or competitors may take over one's share of the market if one is not attentive to the changes.

Develop Independence

Dependence upon the good will of the distributor is not always desirable. Since one of the most important elements for successful marketing is distribution capability, one has to strive to develop expertise and capability in this area, as well as in working with such intangibles as a network of personal relationships through local employees. Here, stability and the loyalty of local executives and staff are of paramount importance.

At the same time, Korea is a world leader when it comes to development of leading-edge distribution channels. It may be critical to the success of one's Korean operation to closely monitor what the newest online shopping and distribution developments are.

THE WAY TO GO

Product suppliers have found some distribution systems rather precarious, but crucially imperative. An effective and economical distribution channel is absolutely indispensable to significant business expansion and growth. The prudent business executive must probe the alternatives and devise an efficient system that expedites his or her product to the consumer as quickly and reasonably as possible. In some cases, just getting one's products into a single national discount or convenience store chain may be enough to get one's products launched in Korea. At the same time, the next truly big distribution opportunity for one's products may take place on the Internet or among cell phone users.

Imagination and ingenuity, along with the help of local counterparts, can devise such a system. New and collaborative ideas may give one insight into knowing which way to go. One thing is certain: the Korean market will not stay static, and neither should one's distribution strategy.

28. HOW DOES KOREA STACK UP?

*T*oday, South Korea's retail turnover is roughly one-eighteenth of the U.S. level and one-seventh of the Japanese market's. But the two most striking characteristics, as with much of the Korean economy, are the market share domination by the largest players and rapid growth in the underdeveloped sectors.

Lotte stores have a whopping 6.3 percent of total retail sales, and Shinsegae outlets have an even larger 6.5 percent. The biggest consolidated retailers in the U.S. (Federated Stores) and in Japan (Takeshimaya) can only boast about half that percentage in their respective markets. Meanwhile, the two giants Lotte and Shinsegae are in a fierce competition to open up new premium and television home shopping channels while increasing the number of large retail stores, raising sales even more.

On the other hand, Korean large store chains (department stores and large discounters) cover as much as 48 percent of retail sales. But that is much smaller than analogous enterprises in the U.S., with 78 percent market share, and Japan, with 75 percent market share.

The real growth, however, lies elsewhere. According to a late 2006 analysis by Hannuri Investment & Securities, the underdeveloped retail distribution market has potential growth of as much as 48 percent by modernization and consolidation. Today, professional distribution companies are achieving this at a much faster rate than in the U.S. and Japan.

So while Korea's top two distribution giants' market shares are expected to increase, much greater opportunities still remain in Korea's relatively backward retail distribution supply chains. Today, the Koreans are aggressively moving to upgrade this important part of their economy.

29. KOREA'S DEFENSE INDUSTRY

Considering that Korea has technically been in a state of war since the beginning of the Korean War, with a half-century armistice substituting for a genuine peace, it is no surprise that the Korean defense industry is large. What can be surprising is how large it has grown over the years. For example, the approved Calendar Year (CY) 2008 South Korean defense budget was US$28.97 billion—an increase of over US$2.3 billion, or more than 8.8 percent, over CY 2007. As recently as 2005, Korea was the eighth largest defense spender, with outlays of some US$21 billion. According to a report made by the Stockholm International Peace Research Institute (SIPRI) in 2007, South Korea was the world's ninth largest importer of military goods, worth some US$2.56 billion. Considering the fact that South Korea exported US$337 million worth of military wares during the same period, along with its overall defense spending, the Republic of Korea has a large and robust defense industry, which can, in turn, be any foreign seller's strongest competitor.

How the South Korean military spends its money is often controversial, given that there is a natural, nationalist desire to foster development of Korean companies and thereby assist the domestic economy and develop greater independence from foreign military technology. At the same time, there is a very strong desire to have the latest and greatest defense systems to provide a greater technological edge over North Korea's forces, which have greater numerical (and nuclear) superiority. This means that there is a need for importing and licensing from foreign countries, particularly from the U.S., all while refraining from over-dependency on just one country for state-of-the art weaponry. For good or evil, when it comes to defense systems integration, the total can be greater than the sum of the parts when one takes into account the huge role played by the U.S. Armed Forces in Korea. American contractors often have an overwhelming advantage.

This doesn't mean non-U.S. defense companies do not have a chance to compete for Korean military procurement contracts, but they can be at a significant disadvantage—particularly if the U.S., for example, has integrated those same products in other theaters like NATO. At the same time, however, the Korean government is trying to diversify. As a result, western European and Israeli companies in particular have been successful in this market.

Though much smaller in scale, there has been a significant rise in the Korean defense industry, which is increasingly finding new markets outside of Korea. For example, the Iraqi War has made it necessary for American armed forces to look for alternative sourcing of supplies, including ammunition. Some Korean companies are now acting as defense contractors for the American military's requirements abroad as well as within Korea.

AGENTS

Before going any further, it is worth noting that most if not all foreign defense manufacturers and suppliers use Korean agents, who are typically retired officers from the ROK military. Most of these agents work for small companies or agencies of retired officers. A small number of agents work alone, but most agents work for one of these small companies, since it is much easier for them to qualify to represent American companies as employees rather than independent agents.

When selecting an agent, one should consider how well he may know key members of the various branches of the ROK armed forces and the Agency of Defense Development (ADD) and Defense Acquisition Program Administration (DAPA). The agent should be registered and certified by DAPA to supply products to the Ministry of National Defense (MND).

Practical considerations when selecting an agent include considering the last military rank the candidate held and how long that person has been outside of the military. One long-term expatriate defense contractor noted that those from the general ranks have often been too long removed from the more journeyman-type tasks relevant to the seller's concerns. Better candidates are normally found among those who come from the Korean equivalent of the "working" ranks of Lieutenant Colonel and Colonel and who have been out of the military no longer than two or three years. This particular group of people generally possesses the strongest and most current networks of key people who can make it easier to market within the Korean defense establishment.

By law or regulation, military agents can charge no more than 5 percent contingency of the value of the contract, though many pad their income with unspecified expense reimbursements. Obviously, all major expenses need to be preauthorized, and all reimbursements must be documented with receipts. Keep in mind that most agents end up with just one percent of this amount, with the other four percent covering out-of-pocket expenses.

Some foreign executives suggest that until one has seen a demonstrated track record proving it is unnecessary, it is best to regularly follow up on one's agent to ensure that he or she is taking the initiative rather than waiting for directions on what to do next, and that all matters are being promptly addressed.

AGENCY FOR DEFENSE DEVELOPMENT (ADD)

As demonstrated, there is a lot of money involved in defense contracts. As such, these transactions often generate strong political winds in favor or against current military spending trends or in reaction to past practices.

Perhaps Korea's "Rock of Gibraltar" among these political winds is the ADD. Established in 1970, its mission is for the "Research, Development, Test and Evaluation of weapons, equipments and related technologies to reinforce defense capability for self-reliant national defense." (Please note their web site at www.add.re.kr.)

At a minimum, ADD is the technology gatekeeper for all armament and military-related goods and services provided to the MND. ADD's mission is to ensure quality and integration capacity with legacy systems and/or compliance with future systems. For a foreign vendor, it is imperative to understand that one must get ADD's benediction as a preliminary to eventually compete as a potential vender. In other words, there are no shortcuts around this agency.

At the same time, keeping in mind that ADD's core mission includes fostering the development of a self-reliant national defense; foreign intellectual property may be at risk without prudent safeguards in place when one's proposal or products are being vetted by ADD. This may be fair game given the big picture, so the wise proceed with caution, since there is no other, appropriate course if a foreign company wishes to be a supplier to the MND.

DEFENSE ACQUISITION PROGRAM ADMINISTRATION (DAPA)

On January 1, 2006, the MND established the military acquisition agency DAPA. Unlike its predecessor, the Defense Procurement Agency (DPA), DAPA is technically a civilian agency that is run with military support, but that also reports to the MND. The new agency is designed to ensure more transparency in the defense procurement processes. Not surprisingly, many of DAPA's senior managers are retired military officers. Ideally, DAPA is supposed to be above the infighting that can take place among the various branches of the ROK military. In any case, though, it never hurts to learn from which service one's counterpart retired or may have served in his or her earlier years.

As one may well imagine, the overall procurement process is quite involved. A good starting point can be meeting with one's embassy officials responsible for defense contracts and getting their inside updates on how defense sales are progressing between one's country and South Korea. One's Korean staff and/or agent should also have a subscription to the MND newspaper, "The Korea Defense Daily." It is also a good idea to bookmark the DAPA homepage (www.dapa.go.kr/eng/index.jsp) on one's Internet browser, since weapon systems acquisition announcements appear there. Someone should regularly monitor the website on one's behalf for the most recent announcements. Should anything appear that looks like a sales opportunity, one needs to register with DAPA to be invited to a project briefing and to obtain a Request for Proposal (RFP). Recipients of the RFPs, which require additional, detailed technical data to support the test and evaluation (T&E) process, normally have 90 days to respond. For more information, one should check with one's embassy and ask about the request procedures for weapon system introductory briefings, as well as the detailed steps now required of all military vendors.

One final point: one should become familiar with the DAPA Electronic Commerce System (www.d2b.go.kr), which is an evolving part of the procurement and bidding processes for purchasing parts for systems and equipment currently used by the Korean military. DAPA designed this e-commerce system to facilitate the existing bidding process and to improve the entire foreign procurement process. By allowing suppliers or agents to submit bids on the website, DAPA hopes to offer a more transparent, accurate, and time-efficient bidding process to potential foreign suppliers. Public announcement of bidding information on the website allows DAPA to promote a reliable and expedited foreign procurement process.

As noted in the online retail section of this book, e-commerce is a rapidly expanding feature in the Korean business scene. DAPA, too, is increasing efficiency and reducing costs through the use of e-commerce. Foreign defense manufacturers should become well acquainted with this new and convenient online bidding process by visiting the DAPA website.

DAPA should have this full-scale electronic bidding system up and running by the time of this book's printing. At present, foreign entities without local agents can register with DAPA. One of the problems DAPA continues to face is how to authenticate foreign entities in the e-bidding system. Therefore, it is again critical for foreign companies to coordinate with their embassy personnel, and in most cases it may be necessary to hire local agents in order to do business in the Korean defense industry.

30. WORKING WITHIN
THE KOREAN LEGAL SYSTEM

As a business professional, it may not be essential for one to have a detailed knowledge of how the South Korean government operates to conduct one's operations, but a simple understanding of the legal framework, where to go for information, and whom to employ when necessary can be essential.

THE BASICS

The Korean legal system is based on civil law. It was essentially modeled on the Japanese legal system during the Japanese colonial period. The Japanese system, in turn, was based on the German model. In 1948, the Republic of Korea was inaugurated with these Japanese-created laws in place, while also incorporating laws influenced by the American legal system during the three-year U.S. military occupation.

For both practical and nationalist motives, a good deal of this Japanese-originated body of law was amended during the 1950s and 1960s with laws similar to those found in the American legal system. The populist democratic movement of the 1980s also brought significant changes, as manifested in the revised Constitution of 1987.

Of particular significance to business managers, many new policies required revision of several statutes and laws to accommodate Korea's opening to the global market as it readied itself to join the OECD and WTO. More recently, the IMF crisis at the end of the last century resulted in dramatic deregulation and legislation focused on making the government and economy much more transparent, efficient and foreign capital-friendly.

The Constitution defines the government as being a democratic republic consisting of three branches—the executive, the legislative, and the judiciary. All laws must comply with, or at least not contradict, the Constitution. The legislative branch enacts all laws, but regulations can be revised either with the review of the executive branch or entirely within the executive branch. The President also has the authority to submit bills to the National Assembly. The President may issue presidential decrees concerning issues delegated through law, as well as do what is necessary within Constitutional boundaries to enforce the law. Furthermore, the President is granted emergency powers in times of internal turmoil, external menace, natural calamity, or grave financial or economic crisis.

The Prime Minister and the head of each executive ministry (Minister) may issue ordinances on behalf of the Prime Minister, and each Minister can issue regulations concerning matters that are within his or her jurisdiction. The National Assembly, the Constitutional Court and the Supreme Court have the authority to enact regulations relating to proceedings, internal rules and the conduct of business.

The Constitution guarantees those treaties that are duly concluded and promulgated and the generally recognized rules of international law. Additionally, the Constitution protects the status of aliens as prescribed by international laws and treaties. As a result, treaties have the same effect as domestic law. Korea is not, however, signed to any convention or treaty that recognizes the judgments of any foreign court. In order for a foreign judgment to be recognized and enforced, a judgment must be first obtained from a Korean court.

Administrative agencies may issue administrative rules for conducting their assigned duties. Local governments can enact ordinances regarding the welfare of local residents as prescribed by international laws and treaties, plus the management of property.

While there is no common law such as in the U.K. or the U.S., sound reasoning can be the basis for determining civil cases. Interpretative techniques used in common law, however, are sometimes employed. Some legal professionals have noted that in recent years the differences between civil and common law have lessened because of the influence of U.S. and international law.

The Supreme Court is called on to interpret acts and subordinate statutes. However, unlike in the Anglo-American legal system, there are no American-style judicial precedents, so a decision by the Supreme Court does not have the precedential value on future cases' persuasive effect. The Supreme Court's rulings do have a binding effect on the lower courts when a case is sent back. The separate Constitutional Court only has the power to make decisions on the constitutionality of laws, and their decisions on the unconstitutionality of the law are binding for all courts and government agencies.

THE CONSTITUTION

The Korean Constitution was first promulgated in 1948 and has been amended nine times; the last time was in 1987. The current Constitution, a result of the successful struggle for genuine democracy, provided for direct election of the President for the first time in Korea and abolished presidential long-term emergency powers, including the authority to dissolve the National Assembly. It also extended fundamental human rights.

THE GOVERNMENT

Korea is a democratic republic based on the separation of powers and a system of checks and balances. There are three branches of the government: the executive branch, the legislative branch and the judicial branch.

1. Executive Branch

The executive is comprised of the President, the Prime Minister, and the State Council. The President appoints the Prime Minister, with the consent of the National Assembly, and members of the State Council, on the recommendation of the Prime Minister. The State Council is composed of the President, the Prime Minister, and other members whose number shall be no more than 30 and no fewer than 15. There are 18 ministries that handle national administrative affairs.

The Constitution grants some autonomy to local governments. Local governments are divided into two types: one for the Special Metropolitan City and six Metropolitan Cities, and one for the *do* (pronounced "dough"), which applies to the provinces. The nine provinces are subdivided into 89 counties (*gun*). Within them are communities ranging from the hundreds of hamlets (*myeon*) and towns (*eup*) to the 74 cities (*shi*). Within the largest cities of whatever type, there are autonomous wards, inconsistently spelled as *gu* or *ku*.

2. Legislative Branch

The National Assembly is a unicameral legislature consisting of 253 members representing five political parties, with each member elected for four-year terms by direct, secret ballot. Another 46 members are selected in a proportional representation among political parties winning five or more seats in the direct election.

The National Assembly is charged with deliberating over and passing legislation, auditing the budget and administrative procedures, ratifying treaties, and approving state appointments. Furthermore, it has the power to impeach or recommend the removal of high officials.

Most of the National Assembly's 17 standing committees coincide with the executive branch's ministries to deliberate on policy matters. Unless introduced by the President, bills must be backed by at least 20 members before they can be reviewed and approved by relevant committees before they reach the floor. To secure final passage, a bill must receive at least a simple majority of those present. After passage, bills are sent to the President for approval within the mandated 15-day period.

Each year, the President submits the budget bill to the National Assembly. The budget must be submitted at least 90 days before the start of the fiscal year, and the final version of the budget must be approved at least 30 days prior to the fiscal year.

Regular National Assembly sessions are held once a year, for no more than 100 days, but extraordinary sessions, by request of the President or a caucus, may be held, though for no more than 30 days. Sessions are normally open-door, but they can be closed to the public by majority vote or by decree of the Speaker of the National Assembly.

3. Judicial Branch

The judicial branch is headed by the Constitutional Court. This system was established in 1987 to help guard against the excesses seen with past regimes. Nine justices make up the Constitutional Court, three of whom are recommended by the Chief Justice of the Supreme Court, three by the National Assembly, and three by the President. All justices, however, must be appointed by the national President. The President of the Constitutional Court is appointed by the national President, but must be approved by the National Assembly. The members of the court serve for renewable six-year terms, but cannot be older than 65, with the exception of the President of the Constitutional Court, who may serve until age 70.

The Constitutional Court is only responsible for constitutional review and for deciding impeachment cases. All other judicial matters are overseen by the Supreme Court. This is the final court of appeal for all ordinary cases. Like the Constitutional Court, the Supreme Court is located in Seoul. There are fourteen Supreme Court Justices, including a Chief Justice. A Supreme Court Justice must be at least 40 years old and have at least 15 years of experience practicing law. With the exception of the Chief Justice, the Justices serve for six-year terms with possible reappointment. The Chief Justice alone cannot be reappointed.

Below the Supreme Court are the five High Courts (appellate courts) and the thirteen regional District Courts of original jurisdiction—plus the Family Court, the Patent Court, and the Administrative Court.

SOME PRACTICAL PECULIARITIES IN DEALING WITH KOREAN LAW

As elsewhere, there are some common considerations as to when to use a law firm in Korea. But there can be some alternative methods that reduce legal costs. At the same time, there can be other situations where legal services are more expensive than in most countries.

In the area of negative surprises, the costs of Notary Public services can appear range from the pricy to the extraordinarily expensive. Unlike in the U.S. and elsewhere, where the costs of notarizing a document can be nominal or even free in some cases, the minimum one may expect to pay in Korea is 20,000 won—and the cost may often be much, much more. The reason for this is that a Korean Notary Public's role is much more involved than in the West. Besides validating the identification of the signatory, the Notary Public must validate the document and keep in permanent escrow a proper, legal copy of the original document to serve as evidence should there be a future dispute as to the contents and date of the original document. Often, the pricing of such notary services is done on a tiered basis, premised on the value of the transaction that the notarized document manages.

On the other hand, one way to reduce one's legal fees is to learn how to use the paralegal services of the many *beop-mu-sa* firms. For substantially less in fees than those charged by full-fledged law firms, these firms can handle many aspects of mortgages and land ownership registration, as well as properly draw up applications and petitions to appropriate government bodies. While many of the forms that need to be completed can be found on the Internet, a good *beop-mu-sa* will competently fill out these forms in such a way to increase one's chances of being successful with bureaucrats. A *beop-mu-sa*, however, is not a substitute for a lawyer for any legal matters beyond filling out forms and applications. Should one need assistance with a JV, litigation, small claims greater than 20 million won or company registrations—particularly if more than a single stockholder is involved—one really should employ a genuine attorney.

One missing paralegal service that often needs to be handled by a law firm is legal transcription. So far, the need for proper legal transcription performed outside of law firms has, for some reason, not been recognized. Consequently, should one need to have professional transcripts recorded for depositions, in various stages of discovery, one will probably have to employ someone within a law firm.

How to Select an Attorney

There are excellent and ethical attorneys in every country; this is certainly also the case in Korea. At the same time, one may conclude that as many as 70 percent of attorneys in Korea—both the local ones and some foreign ones— are commercially incompetent. While all are no doubt intelligent and highly educated, the manner in which many approach their clients' needs harks back more to the early 20th century than the cusp of the 21st century. Unfortunately, most Korean attorneys fail to appreciate or do not care to consider the commercial context of their counsel.

Based on what one reads in the press, doing business here is tough. But generally, the difficulties are greatly overstated. One often hears such exaggerated nonsense over beers with "old Korea hands." The views garnered from attending various chambers of commerce meetings can be similarly misleading.

For example, two of the biggest gripes one hears among foreign business managers are labor's inflexibility and the lack of transparency within government. At the core of these criticisms, there are indeed some hard facts. At the same time, the perception of the actual complexity and difficulty may be far removed from reality—at least relative to the true circumstances when such issues are first encountered.

In any case, when such matters get out of hand, where does one turn? To attorneys, of course. And what do attorneys commonly advise? That Korean labor is very inflexible and government regulators are very opaque. Why? Because "This is Korea."

The tragicomedy is that cynical self-interest cultivates much of Korea's allegedly thorny business environment. Furthermore, the conventional wisdom regarding how difficult it is to do business in Korea goes largely unchallenged. As a result, both experienced and inexperienced foreign executives frequently hesitate too long, turn to legal counsel too late, and then meekly accept huge legal bills. In this scenario, it is often hard to see who is at greater fault—the foreign managers or their attorneys. But one can say that the actual Korean business environment is frequently and unfairly blamed.

At chambers of commerce meetings, a good 15 to 20 percent of all attendees are lawyers, representing themselves as saviors for management issues in Korea's "very difficult" commercial environment. In other words, whether directly or indirectly, attorneys are there, ready to step between the foreign business managers and the rest of Korea, while reminding the foreigners that business in Korea can be very expensive in legal fees.

To be fair, if there is fault, it doesn't simply lie at the attorneys' feet. Like any other aspect of running a successful business, good management demands defining need and controlling costs. A successful business manager knows when to bring in an attorney, how to keep him or her on a leash, and how to address problems early while they are still small, manageable and inexpensive. That is, if the manager is diligent and competent, doing business in Korea is neither inherently difficult nor necessarily expensive.

One should remember that using legal services is similar to employing medical services. If one takes prudent, preventive measures, such as health check-ups or legal reviews, ultimate costs can be kept reasonable. But if one waits until disaster strikes and a life-saving surgery or major legal defenses are absolutely imperative, pricing can end up being incredibly expensive.

But just how expensive are Korean legal services? On an hourly basis, Korea can in fact be considered reasonable compared to developed Western countries. Typical rates range from 150,000 to 400,000 won an hour, depending on the attorney's reputation and experience. However, the hourly rates are not the pitfall.

At some of the best-known Korean law offices, the author has witnessed and heard numerous accounts of foreign business clients meeting three, four or more attorneys at once. There is always at least one fully competent attorney who dominates that side of the conversation; the others usually sit like the proverbial bumps on a log, saying nothing. Often, the reason they do not participate is readily apparent—their lack of conversational English skills prevents them from adequately following along with the conversational trail. So it is fair and proper for a business executive to challenge the number of attorneys in a hearing. There is often good reason for additional attorneys. But one should not blame the law firm after the fact without questioning beforehand the need for multiple attorneys to attend.

Recently, the author heard the account of one Korea resident American attorney working alongside his foreign client in conjunction with another, very large Korean law firm. That lawyer saw the Korean attorney entourage phenomenon happening yet again. Fed up with how his client company was being taken to the cleaners in a veritable tsunami of law firm billable hours, the lawyer directed a simple, relevant question to the bumps on the log present. When these attorneys were unable to respond appropriately, the lawyer snapped, "What the heck are you doing here?" Although the lawyer's directness is commendable, it should actually have been the client—not the attorney—who raised the issue.

If the savvy business manager doesn't control the legal expenses, managerial neglect can contribute to needless billable hours. The truth is, no business manager, foreign or domestic, need tolerate such real or accidental abuses from the Korean legal community. But cost-effective legal services only come with proper management of one's legal counsel.

That includes knowing what one is buying. Established firms with blue-chip credentials are well known to introduce prospective clients to their best-known attorneys, including previous government ministers, former senior prosecutors, and prominent retired judges. Foreigners new to Korea are immediately and justifiably impressed with the law firm's star partners, who indeed have stellar careers and credentials. Having such luminaries on the payroll, he or she is told, will justify the large bill the manager at the client business can expect to receive, since such political muscle is, purportedly, absolutely necessary to open doors and win special favors.

In truth, the situation is normally remarkably different. Law firm luminaries almost always emanate from the Korean establishment. They want to keep their membership in good standing in the "old boy network." For that reason, they are often very hesitant to rock the boat or aggressively assert their potential leverage for a single client's needs—particularly if the client is viewed as "small fish." In Korea, "small fish" usually means anything less than one of the large Korean conglomerates, the *chaebol*s. Instead, the really necessary work is assigned to squadrons of junior attorneys, who often generate copious memoranda or participate in endless meetings. "Picking up the phone" and solving everything with "one phone call" may be possible, but that is the exception—and even then it usually happens only when the issue is relatively small, manageable and non-controversial.

On the other hand, Korean billing rates are reliably fair, though legal matters are almost always solved with lesser-known attorneys, not with the political clout as advertised. The large bill is not the result of star attorneys' political pull; that big invoice is actually based on legions of behind-the-scenes "billable hours." To make matters worse, the written product is often so ambiguous as to be commercially worthless, yet surely painfully expensive.

So how can the savvy business professional in Korea successfully navigate these troubled waters? First and foremost, always keep in mind one vital point: the client ultimately does not hire a law firm—the client hires an attorney.

Should one need to hire an attorney beyond administrative tasks, such as in the case of litigation or defense from a government probe, it is worth keeping in mind how the Korean legal system actually works. A good way to begin is to consider the relevant education system.

As a Korean senior research fellow once suggested over dinner, the three most antiquated sectors of modern Korea are education, law, and media. What he meant was that those three professional niches are the most rigid and hierarchical, with less regard for properly serving their clientele than most other parts of society. Furthermore, Koreans have largely accepted the status and relative prestige of these three communities with surprisingly little protest, even if complaints are fairly common.

Aspiring legal professionals take their judicial exam upon graduation from university, normally with a law major. Those few people who pass this three-day test are put into a two-year government program where they are further trained. At this point, few if any can even write a simple legal brief. Upon graduating from the government program, the new legal professional has, depending on his or her overall ranking within his or her class, as few as one option or as many as three options for a vocation. The best graduates may become judges, prosecutors, or lawyers—but most become judges. (It should be noted that according to Joongi Kim's 2007 paper "The Judiciary's Role in Good Governance in Korea," until recently, 90 percent of the judiciary came from just five universities, and 64 percent came from Seoul National University. This naturally fosters an in-group elitism.) Attorneys who do not place within the top tier but still do very well may become prosecutors or lawyers. New legal professionals in the bottom tier of educational background simply become lawyers.

In contrast, in Western countries, most attorneys, barristers, and solicitors undergo rigorous study in post-graduate law schools before preparing for bar examinations, frequently after obtaining a four-year degree, which is often in business or political science. During these two to three years of post-graduate law study, future legal professionals learn how to conduct legal research and write legal documents, analyze a legal situation, determine effective legal recourses within commercial and government environments, and advocate their client's case beyond a simplistic legalistic perspective. As a result, foreign-trained attorneys are much more likely to deliver concise, logical, and meaningful legal counsel that resonates with the commercial issues at hand.

Furthermore, it is critical to keep in mind that very few Korean legal professionals retire at the end of their careers as judges or prosecutors. The vast majority of judges and prosecutors eventually rotate out of government service and enter private practice. As a result, most judges and prosecutors understand that their years in government service are limited. As such, it is wise for these professionals to maintain a good rapport with potential future employers—i.e., the major law firms.

Adding to this dynamic is Confucianism and the premium placed on seniority in terms of age and rank. Consequently, should one hire an attorney, it can be critical to hire one who retired out of the government system at a grade higher than the current position held by the prosecutor or presiding judge. This is not necessarily a requirement; that said, however, if one's legal representative was once the government's "senior" within the legal establishment, it can be amazing how much leniency the government legal official may display toward one's attorney, and thus one's case. If an attorney with high prior government service rank is going to play his cards on one's behalf, it is crucial to confirm that the attorney actually picks up the phone and does not simply relegate the task to a junior subordinate. The key is to secure an attorney who will personally go to the bat for one's sake.

Sure, the effective attorney may need political pull in certain cases. But it is far more important for a lawyer to be effective and efficient than for him or her to be famous. The trick is to hire the right person for the job, rather than the name value of a certain individual or the firm with which he or she is affiliated. With some searching and reference checking, one can find attorneys who will handle one's case in 21st century fashion.

Once a manager settles on a law firm, the business client should identify the lead attorney being assigned to the case. The business professional should not be shy about asking the hard, qualifying questions, such as what kind of relevant prior experience the lead and supporting attorneys possess, what positions the attorneys held in other law firms, and what ranks the attorneys achieved in prior government service. The smart business professional learns the identities and backgrounds of every lawyer involved in the case. He or she demands efficiency and effectiveness, and discourages the addition of lawyers if the numbers are not needed. Above all, a competent business manager insists at the outset on a detailed bill, with dates and services adequately notated and the billing lawyer identified.

One other suggestion, before picking up the phone to call an attorney, is to first review the need to do so with other managers. Once there is a clear consensus on the need for an attorney and an agreement on defining the issue that an attorney is to handle, the managers should write down relevant questions before asking for legal counsel. This is a good practice anywhere, but especially in Korea—particularly when talking with a Korean attorney. Given the possibility of miscommunication with one's Korean legal counsel, this seemingly menial method of preparation can prevent major, needless costs resulting from the attorney and the client thrashing about before eventually coming to a clear and mutual understanding of the issues.

On the other hand, with the influx of Western-trained foreign lawyers in Korean firms, foreign and Korean business managers can take advantage of a legal community better prepared for and geared toward international issues. While foreign lawyers are not yet permitted to practice law in Korea, the capable foreign lawyer can still be effective in many ways. For example, he or she can serve as a contact point, making communication more comfortable and productive. In addition, the foreign lawyer can serve that vital role as the attorney the company hires, as opposed to the firm that the business client retains. The foreign lawyer can manage the company's case and work with the law firm's Korean attorneys in getting the job done efficiently. Finally, foreign-trained attorneys generally have a better grasp of business than most Korean attorneys, who often have little or no understanding of concepts outside the Korean legal profession. A foreign or foreign-trained attorney normally can do a better job of balancing commercial concerns with legal requirements.

At the same time, several foreign lawyers have impressive Korean language skills. The astute manager, on the other hand, makes sure that the Korean-speaking foreign lawyer is not just a salesperson adept at bringing in foreign clients, and that he or she will take an active role in one's company's case.

Ultimately, the best way to select an attorney is through references. Ask around the Korean business community, both domestic and foreign. Good attorneys, Korean and foreign, are around—they just take some old-fashioned legwork to find.

So doing business in Korea can be difficult but need not incur outrageously expensive legal fees. Like most Korean services, many Korean law firms have been slow to embrace the 21st century when it comes to client services. The good news is that there are excellent attorneys found in large- and middle-sized Korean law firms. But it is up to the competent business professional to select and properly manage his or her attorneys, just as he or she would be expected to do anywhere else in the world.

How to Avoid—or Handle—Credit Fraud

In Korea, there is often less recourse beyond what is specifically detailed in the civil law code books than in the common law nations.

For example, the title of goods can be viewed as transferred upon delivery to the second party—regardless of actual payment. The seller can still cancel property transfer for non-payment. But if there is a lack of cooperation by the buyer in returning the property, there is little legal recourse other than tort action. Furthermore, if the second party sells the same property to a third party who innocently believes the second party has full ownership of the property, the third party may retain ownership of the property due to his or her innocence. This means that under Korean law, there is no easy repossession recourse in cases of non-payment.

In 2000, a noteworthy example of this difference between Korean civil and Western common law took place. Daewoo Motors, which was then desperately trying to avoid bankruptcy, had a sales campaign called "The Big Zero," whereby new car buyers could take possession of cars and register vehicle ownership with the local government with no money down and zero interest payments. Daewoo contracted a foreign insurance company to cover the campaign's risk. The insurance company's Seoul office did incomplete legal due diligence and assumed the full risk of unpaid-for vehicles, thinking they could repossess when necessary. That was a US$200 million mistake. Many of the "buyers" falsified their personal and contact information—and simply disappeared with the cars. Even those cars that could be found could not be repossessed under Korean law in a way similar to the U.S., where private repossession companies exist. Technically, it was possible for the automobile company to reclaim the vehicles, but there was no cost-effective way to go about it. The foreign insurance company was left holding the bag. The loss was large enough to force closure of the Korea branch and to ruin a number of careers.

Due diligence is always a prerequisite for being successful in business—and even more so when it comes to avoiding Korean credit fraud.

In Korea, reliable security—or collateral—is generally limited to real property and government guarantees. It is important to keep in mind that when property is auctioned in times of distress, it rarely goes for more than 70 percent of market value even in the best cases. Since a bank has usually already lent up to 50 to 60 percent of a property's value, that makes second and third property liens essentially worthless.

Factory machinery can be considered secured assets, but only if the equipment is bolted down to the building as fixtures. If it is in any way mobile, however, it is not considered to be a securable asset—nor is the facility's inventory.

So what options are available to protect one's business?

First of all, don't expect much protection from promissory notes. They have no executory effect—one can only sue in civil court if the promissory note issuer defaults. Often, however, the values of the notes are too small to justify taking on the expense of legal action. Again, rather than promissory notes, one is better off with security against land and buildings.

That brings us back to real estate. One should not trust a debtor's appraisal, since appraisers often conspire with debtors. Essentially, all appraisers are honest—unless asked to be dishonest. And no one accepts government appraisals, since they are normally significantly less than actual market value. So it is best to hire one's own appraiser. The extra hassle and expense can be a very important investment.

One may be offered post-dated checks (*yaksudo*), but they are essentially IOUs and, as such, are non-negotiable. Bank checks (*supyo*) are valid for only six months upon issuance—assuming, of course, that there is still money in the account at encashment time.

In any event, when it comes to corporate checks, representative directors are held responsible. If one still needs to rely substantially on corporate checks, a representative director's personal guarantee may be valuable. But it is highly recommended to get the spouse's guarantee as well, since representative directors routinely transfer their wealth to their wives to reduce personal financial liability. Similarly, it is good to get a copy of the family register (*hojeok*), so that one can track down other possible hidden wealth in case of a major dispute.

And that brings us to the interesting matter of getting personal information.

Many foreign business professionals don't realize that in Korea, it is illegal to track down family information after someone has defaulted on payment. So it's critical to collect such information before business transactions begin, when relations are still cordial and upbeat.

One must remember that Korean law restricts public access to information more than in most countries. The good news, however, is that privately provided information is readily available through many informal channels.

Koreans therefore tend to hire people from their hometowns or universities as a way to protect them from fraud. This may look like cronyism, but it is in fact the best way to protect oneself. By hiring people whom one knows or with whom one has some kind of social connection, one can easily check up on their reputations and will know whom to pursue in case of theft or fraud.

Another strategy for protection against financial default is to take a pledge on a debtor's certificate of deposit (CD) account. CDs can offer strong assurances. Such a pledge may be a strong vehicle, since it represents a lien on clear value. One may be surprised to discover how commonly such CDs may be available. CD owners often don't wish to declare their full income to the tax authorities. Instead, they frequently park their hidden wealth in CDs.

When a creditor exercises his or her pledge for indemnity, the burden of proof lies with the debtor to justify denial of the pledge's execution. The bank is technically liable if it is negligent in protecting the CD holder from fraudulent pledge execution. As a result, banks often pretend they don't have any real monitoring systems as a legal defense against negligence. In fact, however, they usually do have some kind of hidden accounting system for monitoring CDs.

Given all of this, a bank guarantee and insurance might be the only practical protection. Debt insurance, in particular, may be the best long-term solution.

When negotiating a guarantee, one should remember that guarantees are a form of contract. In Korea, the face of a contract is very legally enforceable, regardless of the parties' implied or otherwise unstated wishes. So contracts are literally as good—or as bad—as they are written.

Small businesses (that is, companies with turnover of US$10 million or less per year) should do personal credit checks of their business partners—including family backgrounds—to determine whether they can go after someone should financial relations sour.

Actually, everyone should do annual credit checks on all business partners. In this turbulent economy, it is hardly uncommon for a buyer who is financially solid today to be facing serious financial problems a few months later. Personal as well as business credit references are essential. And again, it is important to get family backgrounds and references at the beginning.

When setting up shop in Korea, consulting and working closely with an attorney who is familiar with the differences between Western and Korean law can be time and money very well invested. Based on such legal consultations and one's risk assessment, securing credit insurance could be one of one's more prudent decisions. In many ways, Korea is no better or worse than other countries—but it is different, and knowing the differences can be one of the determining factors between success and failure.

Should One's Operations Run Afoul of the Law

This is not a pleasant topic, but multinational firms and/or their employees occasionally trip over the law. Actually, this is sometimes easier to do than one may imagine. To illustrate the point, a long-term foreign resident investigated why his vehicle had been issued a parking ticket, given that others had been parking along the same curb for years. He soon discovered that most parking along curbs in Seoul is technically illegal. And such is the case for many things in Korea. This foreigner, a well-respected Korean linguist—and a somewhat notorious wag—declared, "The whole country is illegal!" This is obviously an exaggeration, but the statement works surprisingly well as an ongoing model.

The problem can be traced to two major areas. First, the laws are open to interpretation by enforcement professionals and the community at large, given their vagueness and, occasionally, impracticality. And second, since society is cutting legal corners as a matter of course, many businesses would be at a significant economic disadvantage if their managers adhered to the letter of the law.

To make things interesting, occasionally the authorities decide to crack down on transgressors of a certain regulation or law by suddenly arresting, without warning, an individual as an example for the community. Too often the defense is simply "But everyone else was doing the same!"

Should one find one's employees in legal jeopardy and be willing to come to the rescue, one may wish to consider the following:

The Korean legal system offers a great deal of latitude to its prosecutors. It is helpful to keep in mind that upon passing the exam after completing two years of training at the Judicial Research and Training Institute (*Sa-beop Yeon-su-won*), young criminal laywers make a decision about whether to become judges, prosecutors, or lawyers. While the top-scoring attorneys usually opt to become judges, some choose to become prosecutors. In the not-so-distant past, most young lawyers chose to become prosecutors, given the prior overwhelming power of the Prosecutors' Office. Few become defense attorneys immediately. Rather, most criminal defense attorneys are retired prosecutors or judges.

Should a case formally make its way to court, there is at least a 95 percent probability that the prosecution will prevail. The prosecution, however, drops many cases prior to trial. The reason they do this is that most prosecutors are more concerned about social justice than the mechanical aspects of the law. It is the duty and responsibility of the prosecutor to consider all mitigating factors. Also of huge importance is the defendant's attitude in cooperating with the investigation and, if the defendant is truly guilty, the degree of expressed remorse and contrition. If the prosecutor believes the first-time offender has learned a life lesson, there is a good chance the case will be dropped if the crime is not a major one.

If the detained person is a foreigner, one may contact that person's embassy. Normally, the police will contact the appropriate embassy as a matter of course. In practice, foreign embassies have proven to be ineffective, and in some cases their intervention has made effective legal defenses more problematic by inserting a political factor into what might otherwise have been a normal proceeding.

Given all of this, any outside assistance must be rendered quickly, since time is of the essence. The farther a case moves within the legal system, the larger the number of prosecution professionals getting involved. Furthermore, one should keep in mind that the investigator can hold a suspect for up to 48 hours without habeas corpus.

Historically, confession has been the prime source of evidence. The idea that one has a right not to have to incriminate oneself is foreign to Korean prosecutors. Questioning sessions can be lengthy, repetitive and highly stressful. Under interrogation, the suspect is often alone. Customarily, defense lawyers have not been allowed to attend investigations of their clients. Recently, some aggressive law firms have insisted on this right, which is guaranteed by law. But keep in mind that in Korea, there is no attorney-client privilege. Any communication—including email messages—between lawyer and client is subject to seizure.

During this time, the suspect is simply detained. At a brief court hearing, the police must make their case, and the court determines, normally within a few hours, whether the suspect should be formally arrested. Most of the time, this step is a formality, since if the matter appears in front of a judge, it is extremely likely the prosecution will prevail. If the defendant must appear before a judge, it is important to have a defense attorney present, a right guaranteed by Korea's Constitution. Therefore, it is in everyone's best interest to try to persuade the prosecution to exercise maximum leniency during the first 48 hours. A common error is to spend too much time shopping around for legal counsel while taking no action during this critical time.

If the suspect is formally arrested and placed in jail, however, it is not too late for a pre-trial acquittal—it only becomes a bit more complicated, since the case has sunk down a layer deeper into the legal system. A prosecutor may still reduce or even drop all charges, but he or she must now have a stronger argument to do so, since prosecutors are held responsible for their decision to defer or prosecute any given case.

There are several ways to appeal to a prosecutor. First, there are face-to-face meetings. Most prosecutors are very approachable, and many regard themselves in part as social workers responsible for improving society. If they honestly believe full prosecution may create a greater injustice, they will often back off.

On the other hand, if one's company and/or employee(s) is clearly innocent, it may be wise to adopt a radically different strategy.

Should a case go to court and the defendant be found guilty, the defendant or defense team has just seven days to file for an appellate hearing. Unlike the first trial, where there is just one judge for less serious cases, the court of appeals has a three-judge panel. Most recently, a new form of court hearing has been introduced on a trial basis. That is, a jury of peers is employed at the initial trial to advise the trial judge. The judge is under no obligation to accept the jury's advice, but must acknowledge and consider the jury's opinion in his or her final ruling.

So how does the foreign business professional keep safe, and keep his or her business safe, in this kind of legal environment?

Here are some suggestions:

- As stated earlier, compliance in Korea is weak. Right or wrong, however, multinational companies have historically been held to a higher standard than local companies. That means that multinational operations must ensure compliance is stronger than is normal for local companies. It can be very dangerous to trust Korean employee advice that it is not necessary to worry about a law or regulation. This judgment may be based on experience from working within typical Korean operations.

- Be ultra-cautious and conservative when considering possibly bending the law. If a Korean lawyer suggests the foreign company need not heed a law or regulation, the lawyer could be asking for major trouble if there is a written opinion. If the lawyer demurs in writing an opinion, it can be most foolhardy to act on a verbal opinion along those lines.

- Be aware that not all Korean law firms are prepared to fight the prosecution—even when necessary. While some firms have attorneys who have always been attorneys, most of their staff will have once been prosecutors or judges. Former prosecutors, due to personal relations with current prosecutors, are more likely to compromise. Sometimes that may be the right course of action, particularly if the company has a weak defense or is indeed guilty. So if the company is innocent, it is important to check out the track record of the law firm in standing up to prosecutors and to evaluate the career backgrounds of the defense team.

- It is important to bear in mind that, for good or evil, multinational companies are not Korean companies. Most Korean companies are often too quick to compromise, even when they are clearly innocent. They do this due to overriding political liabilities and potential legal ones. Foreign companies operate with some inherent disadvantages, but one advantage an expatriate executive should leverage is the fact that foreign companies are not necessarily expected to act like Korean companies. Consequently, a wise strategy can be to mount a legal defense as the company would in its own country, even when local employees may advise otherwise.

- **Remember:** Foreign companies can push back, and have pushed back, at the prosecutors, causing the prosecution to reassess their targeting. But prosecutors, contrary to their denials, can be politically motivated. Sometimes the motivation may be of a cynical, personal nature. Often, the motivation comes from outside of the Prosecutor's Office in the form of public opinion that is often ill-informed. Should the mass media be demanding some kind of a guilty verdict for a foreign company, the prosecutors are likely to be under a great deal of public pressure. Bottom line: one should consider one's PR efforts to be much more than simply good marketing. A good public image could be one of one's best legal defenses.

- It goes without saying, since this is true in all countries, but one cannot expect government officials to follow through on a verbal promise by another department or by a predecessor. At a minimum, get promises or interpretations in writing. These documents may not be a guarantee of immunity, but they can serve as a strong defense. So when meeting government officials regarding sensitive issues, it is critical to tape the meetings as well as keep records. Be aware that written records by themselves are not highly regarded as evidence, as they may be selectively transcribed by the company's representative. For that reason, digital and tape recorders are more accepted than in many countries.

Nonetheless, it is essential to immediately hire a competent attorney when confronted with a criminal charge.

Another way is to hire an attorney who has contacts, is willing to actually use his or her connections for the client's benefit, and is well regarded by his or her former colleagues. At the same time, a good word for leniency put in by others in government can have surprisingly positive results. So it can be critical to solicit help from parties not directly related to the case as well.

Keep in mind that one hires a lawyer and not a law firm. One should select based upon the individual attorney's reputation and ability rather than the name value of the law office.

In short, if one must act, one must immediately call an attorney who is willing to actually work for one's case.

The Korean legal system is a rapidly maturing system, but it will inevitably retain its cultural foundation of being essentially concerned with overall social justice rather than simply being a nation of laws. And like all other parts of Korean society, personal relations often have a major impact on the outcome. So if there is ever a time to "go native," it is certainly when one has to work within Korean legal jeopardy. The system works, but the foreign manager needs to put many Western notions of legal strategy aside.

PRIMARY LEGAL SOURCES

Korean primary law is divided into five categories based on the level of the legal effect. Some treaties have the same legal effect as presidential decrees and ordinances from the Prime Minister. In addition to written Korean law, there is unwritten law, including customary law, case law, and legal reasoning.

There are now proper English translations of Korea's acts and statutes. The basic codified Korean "Six Codes" are available in the Statutes of the Republic of Korea multi-volume set and from the statute online database upon subscription. The Six Codes in Korea are the Constitution, Civil Act, Civil Procedure Act, Criminal Act, Criminal Procedure Act, and Commercial Act.

Statutes of the Republic of Korea. Seoul: Popchecho (Korea Legislation Research Institute), 1997-. OCLC #39090327.

This is the only compilation of Korean statutes in English. As one may expect, the collection is huge—twenty loose-leaf volumes, plus periodic supplements. The table of contents of the Statutes of the Republic of Korea is available for free from the Ministry of Legislation's Korea Legislation Research Institute at www.klri.re.kr/ENGLISH_VERSION/publication_e. html. An online subscription service is also offered.

Economic Laws on Foreign Investment in Korea. Seoul: Korea Legislation Research Institute, Ministry of Legislation, 2000. 1,360 p. OCLC #46326512.

Economic laws and thirty-four key acts are presented in English in this single volume. The acts are organized into Basic Laws, Laws Concerning Foreign Investment, Corporate Laws, Trade Laws, Financial Laws, Intellectual Property Laws, Tax Laws, Labor Laws, and Laws Concerning Dispute Settlement. The full text of individual acts is also available online at www.moleg.go.kr/mlawinfo/english/htms/list01.html.

Recently Enacted Laws by the National Assembly, in English summary form, can be found at http://korea.na.go.kr/res/tra_list.jsp?boardid=1000000024, and English translations of laws specifically pertaining to foreigners can be found at http://korea.na.go.kr/res/low_03_read.jsp?boardid=1000000037.

Finally, there is a section on *Laws and Regulations*, including a number of acts translated into English, that may be found at the KOREA.net home page at www.korea.net/government/government.html.

Other References Found on the Internet

While there is no substitute for sound legal counsel, some web sites can give some insight on the nature of Korean law, depending on one's interest or need. Here are two of the better sites:

Lex Mundi's *Guide to Doing Business in Korea* could be more accurately titled a "legal guide to doing business." The Seoul law firm of Hwang Mok & Park periodically prepares and updates this 70-page paper. It is a good guide for a wide review of the basics of Korean law. It can be found at www.lexmundi.com/images/lexmundi/PDF/guide_korea.pdf.

FINAL CONSIDERATIONS

When shopping for a law firm, one should keep in mind that there are roughly three grades of law firms.

The most common type is one that tries to keep the defense within the legal boundaries, so that at times the client may wonder if the attorney is working more for the prosecution than the client. Often, these attorneys work for small firms, and if they have former prosecutors or judges, those attorneys will have left government service at the lower ranks. Generally speaking, the author recommends avoiding this type of law firm.

The second most common, type of law firm comprises many former government officials, judges and prosecutors. These tend to be large and well established, and can be exasperatingly expensive. As pointed out above, clients often discover too late that while these large, established firms position themselves as having inside tracks in the legal process, they are largely compromised in vigorously representing the needs of their clients.

The third and rarest type of law firm is pushing the Korean legal process into a modern paradigm with genuinely vigorous defense of the client. These firms tend to be medium-sized (50 to 150 attorneys) and less than 10 years old. They, too, often have top retired judges and prosecutors, but they are more aggressive than the top handful of established firms. As a result, they try to be competitive by applying international standards of legal counsel and representation to their business. These firms can be less expensive, since they tend to have fewer underperforming attorneys. What they often lack, however, are international credentials or fame, which makes them appear to overseas corporate counsel to be riskier options than the traditional top three or four Korean law firms. Nonetheless, the bottom line is that a truly professional attorney delivers genuine client value, regardless of his or her firm's name.

In any case, common among a number of so-called "old Korea hands" are tales of foreign firms being ripped off by expensive Korean law firms. Some of these firms do indeed have attorneys who try to isolate their foreign clients from the rest of society, and thereby create billable dependencies on the law firm.

Yet most of the horror stories one may hear in Seoul can be traced back not so much to lawyer connivance but to client managerial ineptitude or naïveté. Too often, inexperienced or incapable foreign managers allow a small problem to fester into a large, perhaps insolvable matter—and only then do they call for outside legal assistance. Had the same individuals sought legal assistance early on—had the problems been handled properly at the beginning—the resulting legal costs would have been inconsequential, and unworthy of being included in the plethora of "doing business in Korea" war stories. Often, it is too easy to blame the attorneys and their fees rather than facing up to one's own mismanagement.

31. INDUSTRIAL CASE STUDY: CHARACTERISTICS OF THE KOREAN IT INDUSTRY

*T*he Korean information systems or information technology (IT) industry is unique. It mainly consists of specialists, often found within very large customer organizations, and is largely staffed by generalists. At the same time, IT departments can be examples of what is happening in other parts of Korean corporations. As is the case anywhere, there are both good and bad points that together dish up challenges. At the risk of stereotyping, the author will try to describe the lay of the land in the IT industry from the perspective of a software vendor.

CHARACTERISTICS OF MODERN KOREA

In Korea, there is a national compulsion to be Number One. Also, Koreans rightly pride themselves on their IT knowledge and skills, and in particular on having one of the highest number of information specialists per capita in the world. These IT professionals often find themselves working for companies driven in part by a desire to have the latest and best technologies, and thereby be the most competitive.

Korea remains nationalistic, and is perhaps becoming even more so than ever. Out of national pride, they feel a strong temptation to achieve success by themselves—without foreign assistance. The author has labeled this mentality "IT *juche*," after the North Korean economic-political theory of being independent from outside dependencies. Like the North's *juche*, IT *juche* has a strong emotional appeal but sometimes comes up lacking when it comes to selecting and implementing the ideal, or even appropriate, solution.

Korean organizations tend to be factional, with factions centering on strong personalities who compete within the organization for position, power and survival. This in turn creates silos of information that are often more political than technical. These personality-centered power structures create an aura of uniqueness—even when there is little substantial differentiation with the external competition.

Korea impresses foreigners daily with a society that is seemingly always in a hurry. Without question, Korea has one of the most competitive societies in the world. Koreans are among the best educated in the sciences—at the expense of liberal arts, where rote learning is less applicable. All of this leads to Koreans being early—and often the first—adopters, but frequently slipshod in implementation.

This approach of often reckless adoption can be traced to what I call the "*Bak-sa* (Ph.D) Mentality," which has been part of the Korean consciousness for many years. That is, there is a traditional reluctance to admit inadequate knowledge in this highly competitive environment. It is no wonder that South Korea has the highest number of Ph.Ds per capita in the world. In any event, Koreans are well-known to be quick studies—and quick to proclaim mastery of a particular subject matter.

Once a new *bak-sa* appears to have mastered a new subject within his or her organization, that person often becomes highly resistant to outside advice and intervention.

"It's Technical"

Organizations routinely go through formal reorganizations once a year, and often more frequently, depending on business conditions. General managers, as they approach middle age, can expect to deal with the "promote or out" paradigm.

For the survivors, the higher one climbs, the more likely it is one will get a lateral transfer. As a result, most supervising executives in IT have an inadequate understanding of their subordinates' work beyond general management considerations.

IT departments are perhaps the most extreme cases, since they are often the sole technology centers of the company and beyond the comprehension of most executives. Yet IT executives do share common major political considerations with their peers: head count, budget size, and operational impact on the overall organization. Meanwhile, the true IT professionals work with relatively isolated supervision and are content that their supervisors are largely ignorant of what they are doing.

Price, Price, Price

Operations are usually price-driven—rarely value-driven, or even managed by genuine return on investment. It is not that individual managers are unaware or unconcerned, but large organizations are often staffed by aging general managers desperate to display their importance to the overall company by demonstrating that they will tangibly and visibly lower costs—i.e., increase their value to the company.

As a result, vendors normally compete on function and price—often in the "order-taking" capacity rather than selling. This is inherent to the traditional approach of selling in Korea. So the vendors are ultimately responsible in part for the preoccupation with price over value.

The finance and purchasing departments are generally ill equipped to evaluate technology acquisitions, and consequently push for the cheapest option. As a result, there is a strong temptation to beat down the vendors' prices or to grow the scale of a project beyond vendor profitability as a way, once again, to either prove to others in the company that one is a superior manager of vendors, or cover up the fact that one defined the project too narrowly in order to reduce the price.

Often, the beginning of the end for many new vendors is their first contract with a large client. These start-up firms frequently go bankrupt due to the associated costs from project creep. In the end, their demise results in a lack of external support, thus causing IT departments to justify expansion in head count to create internal support for acquired, but now unsupported, technology.

In time, some companies conclude that it may make more sense to hire more engineers to reinvent the wheel, since vendors cannot be trusted to adequately support their needs.

Self-Made Steam Shovels

Due to a combination of "IT *juche*," "*Bak-sa* mentality," and the presumptuous assertion that they are unique, there is a strong tendency among large Korean companies to build a steam shovel rather than buy a somewhat expensive trowel. Building their own solutions often results in a strong pride in self-development, and incidentally brings along job security as well. Only the architects and builders really understand the nature of these home-grown systems, and it is often they alone who understand how these systems integrate with other systems. There are at least two reasons for this. First, having a near monopoly on knowledge can be easily leveraged for personal advantage. And second, these designers often lack detailed knowledge, save from memory, since most do not do a good job of documenting their work. The net results within many large Korean companies are very large and inefficient systems that may require extraordinary resources to maintain.

MOVING ON TO THE NEXT GENERATION

There was a trend with many large companies to have their IT departments request the overhaul of mission-critical systems every four or five years. Officially, the rationale was that the company needed the latest technology to remain competitive. But too often, IT departments created software houses of cards through internal development. Given the ongoing pressures to make changes in the software as business and other demands dictated, modifications often went undocumented, resulting in "spaghetti" code that required extensive regression testing to ensure that new changes would not bring systems down. To save the face of the company *bak-sa*, next-generation systems had to be compatible in functionality, and sometimes in design, with prior systems—no matter how illogical or inefficient this was. This practice resulted in what many regard as "Korean-style" systems that are often mistaken by employees as a reflection of "our company's unique way" of doing business.

Korean systems seem to be constantly in turmoil, and for vendors this can be good news. Furthermore, the global credit crisis of 2008-10 forced Korean companies to move away from custom coding and in-house development to more cost-effective solutions, such as using more packaged software and outsourcing more of their IT support. Also, large companies are finally starting to reduce the head counts of their bloated IT departments.

In any event, with change come frequent openings to get one's message through, especially as IT managers look for next-generation systems. Also, Koreans in general are very curious about new ideas, if often only to potentially copy them into their internal development. In any event, Korean companies are moving from being heavily domestically centered to being more internationally competitive. More competing on the global stage results in less tolerance for internal inefficiencies. Younger general managers have better technological skills and interests, not least due to their personal use of PCs and networks. As a result, the younger generation of managers is now taking a more active interest in their IT shops.

WHAT IS LIKELY TO WORK

For a foreign company hoping to sell into the Korean IT industry, some general guidelines for success are as follows:

- Work with Korean partners who have already established their own relationships with key individuals in target accounts.

- Hire competent Korean employees who have both excellent people skills and outstanding technical skills.

- Recognize tools that allow customers to "roll their own" solutions, which are much more likely to succeed than turnkey and application systems.

- Consider that applications and turnkey solutions are much tougher to sell and present more problems in keeping clients on track with the rest of the global customer base, since Korean customers often wish to modify much more than customers in most markets.

- Keep in mind that professional services are essential for long-term success in the Korean market. Korean customers often expect 24-7 support and a response time—including arrival on site—measuring no longer than two hours in the greater Seoul metropolitan area.

- Understand that "service"—though now understood to mean billable work—retains the traditional meaning of "free." Often, customers expect the costs of service to be somehow buried into the maintenance and even license pricing of the technology. Some foreign vendors have discovered the need to bundle support services into a product's packaged price. Even in that case, they detail the value of that service on the quote, even if they discount that value in the bottom-line figure.

WHAT THE IT INDUSTRY TEACHES ABOUT KOREAN BUSINESS

From an outsider's perspective, there is often a shocking lack of genuine management control or matrices. Even if management systems are in place, there is a lack of real diligence in using these management tools other than going through the motions, and the data used are often not credible. Indeed, managers often don't stick to structured programming and instead rush ahead without documenting modifications to the systems. All of this occurs because rapid growth of the Korean economy has encouraged firms to take shortcuts rather than lose out to the competition, especially in light of the breakneck pace of the Korean economic miracle. As demonstrated, the results of this mentality can be seen in the IT shops as well as other parts of many large Korean companies.

Most IT departments and businesses have historically operated with relatively large numbers of people working extraordinarily hard for extraordinarily long hours. Yet this, too, is changing. As the Korean economy opens up to world-class competition, and as the economy has its periodic business slowdowns, Korean companies have been reevaluating their hiring strategies and are keener than ever to increase efficiencies. Given this, Korean companies are looking more aggressively for new ideas, and sometimes new technologies, from abroad. The question now is how fast each company will actually move forward, particularly given each organization's traditions and culture.

PART V.
REFERENCES

BIBLIOGRAPHY

INDEX

ABOUT THE AUTHORS

BIBLIOGRAPHY

The Legacy

The Foreign Businessman in Korea, John W. Stanley and Norman D. Smith, Kyumoon Publishing Company, Seoul, 1972: If you can find it, this book's advice from its day can offer some context on how business is now conducted in Korea.

The Key to Successful Business in Korea, Song-Hyon Jang, Yong Anh Publishing Company, Seoul, 1988: One could say this somewhat out-of-date tome is the genesis of this book.

Doing Business With Korea (Global Business Series), Paul Leppert, Jain Publishing Company (reprint edition), Fremont, CA, 1997.

Troubled Tiger: Businessmen, Bureaucrats and Generals in South Korea, M.E. Sharpe, East Gate Books, Armonk, NY, 1997: This is considered a classic by many knowledgeable "old Korea hands."

Mastering Business in Korea: A Practical Guide, Tom Coyner and Song-Hyon Jang, Seoul Selection, Seoul, 2008: This is the first edition of this book.

The Koreans

Korean Patterns, Paul S. Crane, Royal Asiatic Society, Korea Branch/Seoul Press, Seoul, 1967: In spite of its age, it is regularly reprinted since it concisely describes the foundation of Korean thinking in easy-to-understand prose.

The Dawn of Modern Korea, Andrei Lankov and Sarah L. Kang, EunHaengNamu, Seoul, 2007: An entertaining primer on 20th century Korea—an excellent background read.

The Koreans: Who They Are, What They Want, Where Their Future Lies, Michael Breen, St. Martin's Griffin, New York, 1998: This book is widely regarded as a "must" for people arriving in Korea.

Korea Unmasked—In Search of the Country, the Society and the People, Won-bok Rhie, Kimyoungsa, 2002, Seoul: A somewhat disorganized but thoroughly fascinating and critical review by a Korean using comic strips as an entertaining medium.

Seoul Selection Guides: Seoul, Robert Koehler, Seoul Selection, Seoul, 2009: Much more than a beautiful and practical guidebook to Seoul, this handbook offers a good deal of insight into the lifestyles and history of Seoul as well as of greater Korea.

The Cleanest Race: How North Koreans See Themselves and Why It Matters, B.R. Myers, Melville House, New York, 2010: A somewhat controversial but thoroughly original perspective on the North Koreans, which by extension exposes many myths about the relationship of the two Koreas.

Under the Loving Care of the Fatherly Leader: North Korea and the Kim Dynasty, Bradley K. Martin, St. Martin's Griffin, New York, 2006: With its long title and similarly massive text, this tome is considered to be the Bible for understanding the history and political underpinnings of North Korea.

Korean Village: Between Farm and Sea, Vincent S. R. Brandt, Waveland Press, Long Grove, IL, 1989: Very insightful perceptions on how the small community's traditional Confucian hierarchy coexisted with a necessarily more egalitarian day-to-day existence in the real world; an invaluable microcosm of how much of Korea still functions today.

Confucian Theory of Leadership, Chabong Kim, Bakmoongak, Seoul, 1999.

Confucianism for the Modern World, Daniel A. Bell and Hahm Chaibong (editors), Cambridge University Press, Cambridge, 2003.

The Land of Scholars: Two Thousand Years of Korean Confucianism, Jae-un Kang, Suzanne Lee (translator), Homa & Sekey Books, Paramus, NJ, 2005.

Complementary Books on Doing Business in Korea

Korean Business Law: The Legal Landscape and Beyond, Jasper Kim (editor), Carolina Academic Press, Durham, NC, 2010: The only wide-ranging guide (325 pages) in English on the basics of Korean law. Not a substitute for a lawyer or a complete legal resource, but it is an excellent starting point.

Korean Business Etiquette: The Cultural Values and Attitudes That Make Up the Korean Business Personality, Boye Lafayette De Mente, Tuttle Publishing, Rutland, VT, 2004: A good complementary guide to this book that covers more than what the title suggests.

Korean Crisis: Unraveling of the Miracle in the IMF Era, by Donald Kirk, St. Martin's, NY (Macmillan, UK), 2000, Palgrave, NY and UK paperback, 2001: A highly regarded account of how the Koreans got into a major predicament that they later succeeded in overcoming.

Korean Dynasty: Hyundai and Chung Ju Yung, Donald Kirk and M.E. Sharpe, Armonk, NY (Asia 2000, Hong Kong 1994): If you wish to understand the chaebol mentality and organization, this a great starting point.

Negotiating Your Way Through Korea, Richard Saccone, Hollym, Seoul, 2001: Many of the negotiating pointers are not unique to negotiating in Korea, but the Korea-specific examples make this a good browse.

INDEX

ABOUT THE AUTHORS

Thomas L. Coyner is the president of Soft Landing Korea (www.softlandingkorea.com), a firm that specializes in assisting companies to achieve maximum sales potential in Korea and Japan. He has 25 years of experience in Japan and Korea working for American firms, as well as seven years working for Japanese companies in the United States. When employed by an American company in Korea, he was twice Salesperson of the Year for Asia-Pacific, largely due to his success in working with Korean distributors. While most of his high-tech experience has been in software sales, he was also the Japan marketing director for a US network switching hardware corporation. He is currently working with North American and European high-tech companies. He serves as a Partner with NemoPartners Strategic Consulting Group, Senior Advisor to IPG Legal, and co-chair of AmCham Korea's SME Committee. He holds a BA in Japanese language from the University of Colorado and an MBA in International Business from the University of Southern California.

Song-Hyon Jang has been a business consultant for international companies in Korea for over 25 years, and has over three decades of cross-cultural management experience with Sandoz, Johnson and Johnson, and Schering. He has published numerous business articles in both foreign and Korean publications, and authored a number of books on business in Korea.